THE ROUGH GUIDE TO
BELIZE
WITH TIKAL & FLORES

ROUGH
GUIDES

This seventh edition updated by
Todd Obolsky and AnneLise Sorensen

Contents

Introduction to
Belize

Despite its small size, Belize offers a phenomenal range of experiences, whether you snorkel the longest barrier reef in the Americas, dive the inky depths of the Blue Hole or embark on thigh-aching treks up ancient, soaring pyramids. And while geographically it may belong to Central America, and has grown out of a historically Maya foundation, at heart Belize is Caribbean – and today thrives as a unique blend of all these cultures.

Wedged into the northeastern corner of Central America, Belize features some of the most breathtaking **coastal scenery** in the Caribbean. Throw in vast archeological sites and wildlife to rival any destination in the region, and it's easy to see why the number of visitors is steadily rising year upon year.

Belizean territory comprises marginally more sea than land, and for most visitors the sea is the main attraction. An astonishing natural wonder lies just offshore – the dazzling turquoise shallows and cobalt depths of the **barrier reef**. Beneath the surface, a brilliant technicolour world of fish and corals awaits divers and snorkellers, while a chain of islands known as **cayes**, scattered along the entire reef, protects the mainland from the ocean swell and holds more than a hint of tropical paradise. Beyond the reef lie the real jewels in Belize's natural crown – three of the only four **coral atolls** in the Caribbean.

Having long cherished its natural wonders, Belize holds the highest proportion of protected land in the hemisphere. As a result, its densely forested **interior** remains relatively untouched. The rich tropical forests support a tremendous range of **wildlife**, including howler and spider monkeys, tapirs and pumas, jabiru storks and scarlet macaws. Although it's the only Central American country without a volcano, Belize does have some rugged uplands – the Maya Mountains, situated in the south-central region, rise to over 3600ft. The country's main rivers start here, flowing north and east to the Caribbean, forming some of the largest **cave** systems in the Americas on the way.

Belize also boasts a wealth of archeological remains. The ruined cities of the **ancient Maya**, who dominated the area from 2000 BC until the arrival of the Spanish, emerge

ABOVE OCEAN LODGE IN AMBERGRIS CAYE **OPPOSITE** BARTON CREEK CAVE, CAYO

EXPLORING THE UNDERWORLD

For the ancient Maya, the **caves** that riddle the porous karst limestone of Belize were sacred. Approached via by dark, yawning holes deep in the rainforest, they were considered entrances to the underworld, which was known as **Xibalba**, the "place of fright". Despite their fearsome aspect, however, they also provided privileged access to the supposed dwelling places of gods, ancestors and spirits. Almost every cave in Belize has revealed remarkable discoveries, including wall paintings, pottery shards and the remains of fires. Because the Maya gods had to be appeased with sacrifices, visitors who brave the likes of the **ATM** cave (see p.126) may see weapons, altars and skeletons, typically left as archeologists first discovered them.

The great majority of Belize's caves can only be explored on **guided tours**, available from operators all over the country. Many also serve as venues for **adventure activities** that range from abseiling (or rappelling) and floating on inner tubes to canoeing along underground rivers.

mysteriously from the forests all over the country, while the caves too, once seen as the passageways to the underworld, conceal remarkable relics. Although only a few sites have been as extensively restored as the great Maya cities of Mexico's Yucatán Peninsula, many are at least as large, and in their forest settings you'll see more wildlife and fewer tour buses.

Culturally, Belize is a cosmopolitan blend of races and cultures that includes Caribbean, Central American, Maya, mestizo, African and European. English is the official language – Belize only gained full independence from Britain in 1981 – and Spanish is equally common, but it's the rich, lilting **Kriol**, based on English but essentially Caribbean, that's spoken and understood by almost every Belizean.

Where to go

Belize is an ideal country to explore independently; even a short visit can include trips both to the cayes and to the heartland of the ancient Maya. Almost every visitor will have

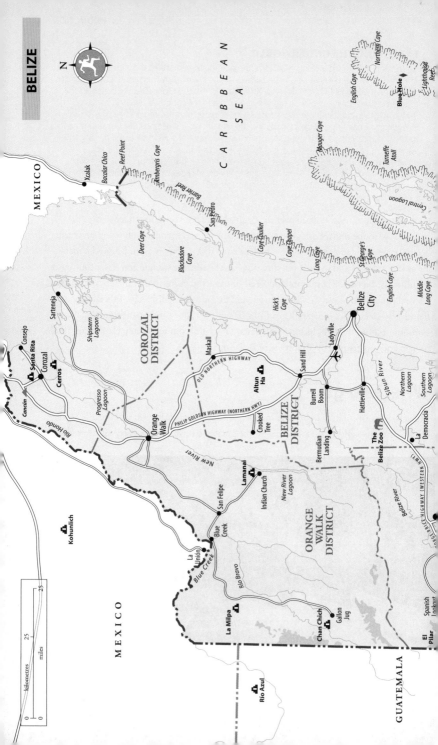

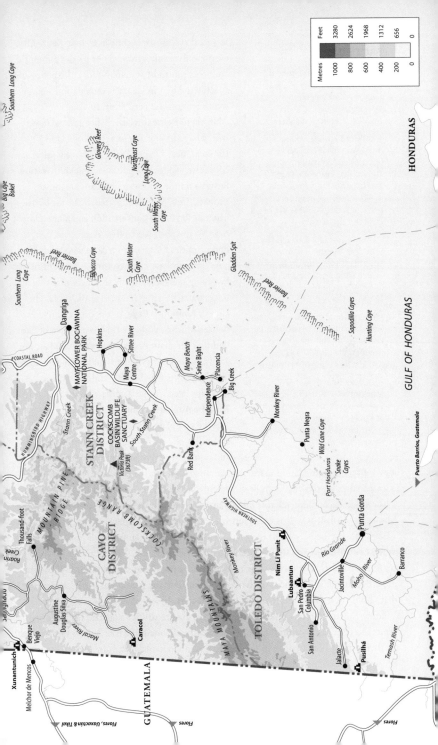

FACT FILE

- Belize has by far the **lowest population density** of any Central American country, at 42 people per square mile. The total population is around 368,000.

- **Folklore** advises Belizeans to avoid swimming on Good Friday, lest they turn into mermaids. Those living inland are taught to fear Tata Duende, a three-foot dwarf charged with protecting forest animals, who likes to bite off children's thumbs.

- The government is headed by the Prime Minister but Belize is a **constitutional monarchy** with Queen Elizabeth II as head of state. She is represented in Belize by the Governor General.

- The **national animal** is the Baird's tapir, the national **bird** is the keel-billed toucan, the national **flower** is the black orchid, and the national **tree** is the mahogany tree.

- It's been rumoured that **Madonna**'s 1987 hit *La Isla Bonita* with the line "Last night I dreamt of San Pedro" refers to Ambergris Caye, but the Material Girl has never confirmed it.

to spend at least some time in chaotic **Belize City**, even if only passing through, as it's the hub of the country's transport system. Nearby, the **Belize Zoo** is easily the best in Central America and well worth making a special effort to visit.

Northern Belize is relatively flat and swampy, with a large proportion of agricultural land. **Lamanai**, near Orange Walk, is a hugely impressive Maya site, while the lagoons, at **Shipstern Nature Reserve** on the northeast coast and inland at **Crooked Tree**, provide superb habitats for birds. The vast **Río Bravo Conservation and Management Area**, in the northwest, offers exceptional opportunities for getting up close with wildlife.

As the mainland coast consists almost entirely of low-lying marshes, anyone seeking swimming and underwater activities has to visit the cayes. The largest, **Ambergris Caye**, draws over half of all Belize's tourists, with the tiny resort town of **San Pedro** as the main destination; **Caye Caulker**, just south, is the most popular island for independent travellers. Organized diving and snorkelling day-trips head for the wonderful coral islands of **Turneffe Atoll** and **Lighthouse Reef**.

In the west, **San Ignacio** and its environs offer everything the ecotourist could want: Maya ruins and rainforest, rivers and caves and excellent, low-impact accommodation in every price range. **Caracol**, the largest Maya site in Belize, is an adventurous day-trip from here, while the magnificent ruins of **Xunantunich** lie close to the Guatemalan border. Cross into Guatemala and you can quickly reach the stunning Maya city of **Tikal**, as well as little **Flores**, a gorgeous island town.

Dangriga, the main town of the south-central region, is a jumping-off point for visitors to the **Central Cayes** and **Glover's Reef**, Belize's remotest atoll. Further south, on the coast, the laidback Garifuna village of **Hopkins** is a popular destination for backpackers in particular, while **Placencia**, at the tip of a long, curving peninsula, is a relaxed resort that's home to some of the country's finest **beaches**. Inland, the Cockscomb Basin Wildlife Sanctuary offers superb **hiking** and the chance to spot a jaguar. The majority of visitors to the coastal community of **Punta Gorda**, the main town of Toledo District, are on their way by boat to or from Puerto Barrios in Guatemala. Venture inland, however, and you'll come across the villages of the Mopan and Kekchí Maya, set in lovely countryside and surrounded by the country's only true rainforest. Here are yet more caves, rivers and Maya sites, including **Lubaantun**.

When to go

Thanks to its **subtropical** latitude, Belize's weather is always warm by European standards, and often hot and very humid. The climate in any one spot is largely determined by **altitude**: evenings in the forests of the Mountain Pine Ridge are generally pleasantly cool, while the lowland jungle is always steamy and humid. On the cayes, the sun's heat is tempered by all-but-constant ocean breezes.

Although Belize has its dry and rainy seasons, the sun shines most of the year. Rain can fall in any month, but it's rarely persistent enough to ruin a holiday. The **dry season** runs roughly from February to May, and the last couple of months before the rains can be stiflingly hot. During the **rainy season**, from June to November, mornings are generally clear while the afternoons see an hour or two of downpours. Especially heavy rains can render cave systems inaccessible and flood rural roads, particularly in the south. September and October, when the worst of the rains fall, is also the height of the **hurricane** season, though most severe storms pass well north of Belize. If you're out on the cayes or near the coast you'll need to leave, but rest assured that Belize has an efficient warning system and a network of shelters. The rain can continue into December, when cold fronts, known locally as "**northers**", can lower temperatures to 10°C for a couple of days.

The **best time** to visit Belize is thus between late December and March, which as the main tourist season is also the **priciest** time, when the vegetation is still lush and the skies are generally clear. Plenty of people come in summer, too, promoted as the "green season".

AVERAGE TEMPERATURES IN BELIZE CITY

	Jan	Feb	Mar	Apr	May	Jun	Jul	Aug	Sep	Oct	Nov	Dec
Max/min (°C)	29/19	29/20	30/21	31/24	31/24	31/23	32/23	32/22	32/22	31/22	28/20	28/20
Max/min (°F)	84/66	84/68	86/70	88/75	88/75	88/73	90/73	90/72	90/72	88/72	82/68	82/68

Author picks

Over the years, our authors have explored Belize from the depths of the ocean to the peaks of the mountains, and the beaches of the Caribbean to the jaguar lairs of the jungle. Here are some of their favourite experiences:

Lick lobster juice off your fingers There's no better spot to feast on the fresh crustaceans than on Ambergris Caye, at the beachside *Blue Water Grill* (p.104).

Cruise (safely) past lurking crocodiles On a Lamanai River tour, it's the journey and the destination: float amid wildlife and tangled trees en route to the mighty Maya complex of Lamanai (p.76).

The ultimate swim-up bar Dangle your feet in the Caribbean off a sun-warmed pier while sipping a chilled Belikin beer at the *Lazy Lizard* (p.112).

Throw on some beads and a feather headdress Shimmy down the streets of Belize City during the rollicking September celebrations (p.48).

Embrace the jungle Discover one of the several secluded, relaxing nature lodges in the forests of the Cayo District like *Hidden Valley Inn* (p.133) or *Blancaneaux Lodge* (p.132).

Spend sunrise at Tikal like the ancient Maya Greet the sun amid the stately, atmospheric temple structures at Tikal (p.160) – one of the most thrilling sites in Central America.

Imagine you could fly The hundreds of native bird species are spectacular, from the tiny emerald-throated violet crowned hummingbird to the massive grey-and-white harpy eagle (p.248).

Serene snorkelling Get kitted up and dunk your head underwater. The Turneffe Atoll (p.113) and Lighthouse Reef (p.115) are among the most beautiful snorkelling spots in the country.

> Our author recommendations don't end here. We've flagged up our favourite places – a perfectly sited hotel, an atmospheric café, a special restaurant – throughout the guide, highlighted with the ★ symbol.

ABOVE LEFT SATURDAY MARKET, SAN IGNACIO
RIGHT FROM TOP BELIKIN BEER, CAYE CAULKER; LIGHTHOUSE REEF; BLANCANEAUX LODGE

18

things not to miss

It's not possible to see everything that Belize has to offer in one trip – and we don't suggest you try. What follows is a selective and subjective taste of the country's highlights: outstanding natural attractions, underwater wonders, Maya ruins and distinctive cultural traditions. All highlights are colour-coded by chapter and have a page reference to take you straight into the Guide, where you can find out more.

1 AMBERGRIS CAYE
Page 92
Enjoy the sun and surf on Belize's largest and most popular island; come nightfall, hit the lively beach bars in San Pedro.

2 MOUNTAIN PINE RIDGE FOREST RESERVE
Page 130
Hike the hills, peaks and gorges of this vast forest reserve, taking in the tallest waterfall in Central America and perhaps staying in a luxurious riverside lodge.

3 ACTUN TUNICHIL MUKNAL
Page 126
Wade a mile along a subterranean river to reach an eerie chamber holding the calcified skeletons of Maya sacrificial victims.

4 TOUCANS
Page 192
The unmistakable keel-billed toucan is the national bird of Belize; found almost everywhere, it's best seen in the village of Sittee River.

5 TIKAL
Page 160
With its five majestic temples looming out of a magnificent protected rainforest, the Guatemalan city of Tikal may be the greatest achievement of the ancient Maya.

10

11

6 COCKSCOMB BASIN WILDLIFE SANCTUARY
Page 193
For the best jungle hiking in Belize, visit this dedicated jaguar reserve.

7 THE MUSEUM OF BELIZE
Page 49
Excellent collections of painted Maya ceramics and jade jewellery make this museum a must-see in Belize City.

8 DIVING AT GLOVER'S REEF
Page 184
Rich in marine life, Glover's Reef offers some of the best diving and snorkelling in the Caribbean.

9 PLACENCIA
Page 196
A laidback resort to suit all budgets, Placencia holds the finest beaches on the Belizean mainland.

10 CHOCOLATE FARMS
Page 219
Central America is the original home of the cacao bean, and you can now visit Maya farmers in Toledo District who make their own chocolate.

11 CARACOL
Page 134
Belize's most stupendous ancient Maya city lies deep in the rainforest at the end of a treacherous road.

12 JUNGLE LODGES
Pages 132 & 150
Remote, eco-conscious accommodation options, like Cayo's *Lodge at Chaa Creek* or *Blancaneaux*, offer a superb way to experience the rainforest.

12

Itineraries

Belize is not a very complicated place to visit. There's just one main north–south highway, parallel to the coast, while another road sets off inland, running west to Guatemala. In addition you can either fly or take a boat out to the islands. Here are three basic itineraries of between a week and ten days each, which can be combined to create a longer trip.

THE BARRIER REEF AND CAYES

The idyllic islands of the Barrier Reef are the most popular destinations in Belize. Give yourself at least four nights to enjoy Ambergris Caye and/or Caye Caulker, and a few more days to explore the sites and wildlife reserves on the mainland.

❶ **Belize City** Almost every visitor flies into and out from Belize City. Spend a night or two in this ramshackle colonial port to see the treasures in its museum and meet the local wildlife at its excellent zoo. **See p.42**

❷ **Ambergris Caye** Readily accessible by plane or boat from Belize City, the country's largest island faces the Barrier Reef, and is lined with beach resorts, outdoor adventure operations, and seaside bars and restaurants. **See p.92**

❸ **San Pedro** Still small enough to explore on foot, this lively former fishing village has superb seafood restaurants and nightlife. **See p.94**

❹ **Caye Caulker** A sunny, sleepy little island renowned for its fresh-caught lobsters, Caye Caulker abounds in well-priced hotels. **See p.106**

❺ **The Blue Hole** Dive down into this deep circular shaft to reach the labyrinth of caves beneath Lighthouse Reef, Belize's outermost atoll. **See p.114**

❻ **Crooked Tree Wildlife Sanctuary** Belize is a magnet for birdwatchers, and there's no better place to see species like the enormous jabiru stork than this diminutive sanctuary. **See p.63**

❼ **Lamanai** Canoe down the river to reach this ancient Maya site, festooned with images of crocodiles. **See p.74**

❽ **Sarteneja** An attractive colonial fishing village, perfectly poised for spotting wildlife in the nearby swamps and lagoons. See p.80

BEACHES AND WILDLIFE OF SOUTHERN BELIZE

In a ten-day trip to southern Belize, you can combine time on the beach with an island trip or two, enjoy jungle hikes with visits to ancient sites, and experience Garifuna fishing communities and Maya farming villages.

❶ **Mayflower Bocawina National Park** A delightful little reserve with great hiking and zip-lining as well as its own excellent overnight accommodation. **See p.187**

❷ **Dangriga** This appealing relic of colonial days is also the prime centre for Garifuna culture. **See p.178**

❸ **South Water Caye** Of the countless tiny islands off southern Belize, this palm-studded beauty has the best mix of upscale lodging and pristine sands. **See p.184**

❹ **Hopkins** Fishing village turned backpackers' idyll, Hopkins holds beachfront hotels to suit all budgets. **See p.187**

ABOVE CARACOL; AMBERGRIS CAYE

❺ Cockscomb Basin Wildlife Sanctuary You'd be lucky to see any of the jaguars that roam the jungles here, but the wilderness trails are exhilarating in their own right. **See p.193**

❻ Placencia This relaxed resort boasts the finest beaches on mainland Belize. **See p.196**

❼ Lubaantun The most impressive ancient site in southern Belize is the supposed home of the legendary Crystal Skull. **See p.212**

❽ Maya villages Many of the remote settlements where the Maya of rural Toledo still live now welcome overnight visitors. **See p.219**

❾ Punta Gorda This sleepy port, served by regular boats to and from Guatemala and Honduras, boasts a vibrant market. **See p.204**

THE WILD, WONDERFUL WEST

Allow a week to explore the rivers and rainforests of western Belize, and you'll have time to visit remarkable ancient sites and sample Cayo District's renowned jungle eco-lodges.

❶ Caves Branch To experience the natural splendour of the rainforest, spend a night or two at the riverside *Caves Branch Jungle Lodge*. **See p.125**

❷ ATM Take an adventurous day-trip to this subterranean Maya site. **See p.126**

❸ Mountain Ridge Pine Forest Reserve Home to luxurious eco-lodges, this vast wild area is a wonderland of rivers, mountains and waterfalls. **See p.130**

❹ Caracol Standing atop the multi-tier temple of Caana, looking out over the endless jungle, is an unforgettable experience. **See p.134**

❺ San Ignacio Bursting with hotels, restaurants and activity operators, this lively little town makes the perfect base in western Cayo. **See p.137**

❻ Macal River Along the banks of this remote river lie rainforest lodges, fascinating nature trails and botanical gardens. **See p.144**

❼ Xunantunich Reached via a hand-winched ferry across the Mopan River, this exquisite Maya site holds some amazing carved friezes. **See p.147**

❽ Tikal Don't miss the chance to cross the border into Guatemala – even if it's just for a day – to see the magnificent Maya city of Tikal. **See p.160**

❾ Flores It's well worth spending an extra night or two in Guatemala to visit this delightful little lakefront colonial town. **See p.168**

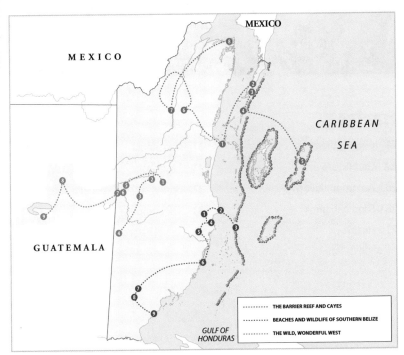

BELIZEAN BUS DRIVER

Basics

Getting there

Most visitors to Belize fly in to Philip Goldson International Airport (see p.52), about a twenty-minute drive from Belize City centre, but it's also possible to arrive by bus, boat or regional flights from neighbouring countries. Several domestic airlines facilitate transport around Belize once you arrive.

Airfare prices from the US rise during the **high season** (December to early April, especially around Christmas and Easter) and also in July and August for flights originating in Europe. For cheaper prices, try flying midweek.

Visas and red tape

Citizens of the US, Canada, the EU, Australia, New Zealand and South Africa do not need **visas** to enter Belize as tourists. Swiss, Japanese and Israeli citizens, as well as most other nationalities, do need a visa, for which they have to apply at a **Belizean embassy** or consulate in advance, as visas are not officially obtainable at the border. There is no charge to enter Belize – just fill out the immigration form on the plane or at the border. Even if you don't require a visa, keep your **passport** or a photocopy with you at all times in Belize, as you may be asked to show it at police checkpoints.

Non-US citizens passing through the US en route to Belize will possibly need a **US visa**. It's essential you confirm before you travel that your current passport will permit you to enter the US; allow at least two months if you need to obtain a US visa. For more on this, check the latest information on the US Department of Homeland Security website (**@**dhs.gov/us-visit).

All visitors to Belize are generally allowed a maximum stay of **thirty days**, but entry stamps can be renewed for up to a year. Many foreign **embassies and consulates** are still in Belize City, though the US embassy (**@**822 4011, **@**belizeusembassy.gov) is in Belmopan, which is

also the location of the UK High Commission (**@**822 2146 **@**gov.uk/government/world/belize).

Belizean embassies and consulates

These are just a few of the Belizean embassies and consulates around the world. In **New Zealand** and **South Africa**, contact the British High Commission (**@**gov.uk), which represents Belize in these countries.

Australia (Honorary Consul) 81 Highfield Rd, Lindfield, NSW **@** 02 8425 0805, **@** belizeconsul@optusnet.com.au.

Canada (Honorary Consul) Suite 3800, South Tower, Royal Bank Plaza, Toronto M5J 2JP **@** 416 865 7000, **@** mpeterson@mcbinch .com.

Mexico 215 Calle Bernado de Gálves, Col Lomas de Chapultepec, México DF 11000 **@** 555 520 1274, **@** embelize@prodigy.net.mx; there is also a consulate in Cancún **@** 988 78417, **@** nelbel @prodigy.net.mx.

UK Belize High Commission, Third Floor, 45 Crawford Place, London W1H 4LP **@** 020 7723 3603, **@** belizehighcommission.com.

US 2535 Massachusetts Ave NW, Washington DC 20008 **@** 202 332 9636, **@** embassyofbelize.org; also 5825 Sunset Blvd, Suite 206, Hollywood, CA 90028 **@** 323 469 7343.

Flights from the UK and Ireland

Flights from the UK and Ireland go via the US; round-trip fares from London, including on British Airways (**@**ba.com), cost around £500–550 in low season and £700–1000 in high season. Another option is to fly to Mexico and continue **overland**. Several European airlines fly directly to Mexico City or Cancún, often a considerably cheaper route than flying through the US; fares from London to Cancún cost around £400. From Mexico City, you can fly directly to Chetumal for around £100, and continue by bus to Belize from there. Tropic Air also offers flights between Cancún and Belize City, while there are regular buses from Cancún to Chetumal (5hr).

Fares from Belfast or Dublin to Belize (via the US) are similar to those from London. Alternatively, you can also fly direct from Ireland to Mexico and continue overland or by getting another flight to Chetumal or Belize City.

A BETTER KIND OF TRAVEL

At Rough Guides we are passionately committed to travel. We believe it helps us understand the world we live in and the people we share it with – and of course tourism is vital to many developing economies. But the scale of modern tourism has also damaged some places irreparably, and climate change is accelerated by most forms of transport, especially flying. All Rough Guides' flights are carbon-offset, and every year we donate money to a variety of environmental charities.

Flights from the US and Canada

A wide variety of US airlines fly **nonstop** and/or direct to Belize, including American Airlines (🌐aa .com), Delta (🌐delta.com), United (🌐united.com) and US Airways (🌐usairways.com). El Salvador-based Avianca (🌐avianca.com) and Southwest (🌐southwest.com) have nonstop flights from Houston. Air Canada (🌐aircanada.com) offers flights from Toronto and other main Canadian cities; WestJet (🌐westjet.com) flies direct to Belize from Toronto. Average flight times are two hours from Miami to Belize, two hours thirty minutes from Houston, and five hours from Los Angeles.

Typical **prices from the US** are around US$650 (low season)/700–900 (high season) from New York; US$650/900–1200 from Seattle; US$500/800–1000 from Houston; and US$650/800–1200 from LA. **From Canada** (Toronto, Montréal and Ottawa) expect to pay around Can$930 (low season)/1100 (high season) and from Vancouver Can$850/940–1600.

Flights from Australia, New Zealand and South Africa

From Australia and New Zealand, you'll have to fly via the US, generally and least expensively through Los Angeles. For most Australasian airlines, low season is mid-January to the end of February and October to the end of November; high season is mid-May to the end of August and December to mid-January.

From Australia, the cheapest fares (from Sydney and most of the eastern state capitals) via Los Angeles to Belize City, on Qantas (🌐qantas.com) and Delta (🌐delta.com), generally start at Aus$2900 (low season) and Aus$3700 (high season). Departing from Perth or Darwin can be Aus$400–650 higher. From New Zealand (Auckland) the cheapest flights to Belize City are via Los Angeles, on Air New Zealand (🌐airnewzealand.com) and Delta (🌐delta .com), at around NZ$2800/3500. Flying to Cancún or Mexico City from any of these cities is several hundred dollars **cheaper** than flying into Belize.

From **South Africa**, you can fly to the US or to the UK and continue your journey from there.

Overland from Mexico

Buses travel between every Mexican city and the capital, Mexico City, and from there, regular buses connect to the town of **Chetumal** (around 22hr), close to the Belizean border. From Chetumal, several Belizean and Guatemalan bus companies depart for Orange Walk and onward to Belize City.

Buses leave generally throughout the morning, with fewer in the afternoon.

Travelling **overland from the US** through Mexico is a long, two- to three-day haul, but allows you to see some of the country on the way. Greyhound buses (📞800 229 9424, 🌐greyhound.com) run regularly to all major US-Mexico border crossings, and some continue to main Mexican cities. **By car** gives you more freedom but involves a good deal of bureaucracy. Crossing the Belizean border with a car can entail **customs charges**, particularly if you plan to leave your vehicle in the country.

US, Canadian, EU, South African, Australian and New Zealand driving licences are valid in Mexico and Belize, but it's a good idea to arm yourself with an **International Driving Licence** as well; contact your local driving authority to obtain one. For details on driving in Belize, see p.25.

INTERNATIONAL AGENTS AND OPERATORS

Adventure Life US 📞 800 344 6118, 🌐 adventure-life.com. Specialists in small-group travel and customized itineraries to wilderness areas and nature reserves in Latin America and beyond.

G Adventures US & Canada 📞 888 800 4100, 🌐 gadventures .com. Canadian company offering a wide range of group trips around the world, with snorkelling, diving, kayaking and visiting Maya sites in Yucatán, Belize, Guatemala and throughout Central America.

Global Travel Club UK 📞 01268 541363, 🌐 global-travel.co.uk. Small company specializing, for over 25 years, in diving, adventure and cultural tours to Belize, Mexico and all of Central America.

International Expeditions US 📞 800 234 9620, 🌐 ietravel.com. Natural history tours and individual itineraries throughout Latin America, including Belize and Tikal.

Island Expeditions US & Canada 📞 800 667 1630, 🌐 islandexpeditions.com. Sea- and river-kayaking expeditions to Belize and other destinations in Central America.

Journeys International US 📞 800 255 8735, 🌐 journeys.travel. Long-running ecotourism company with tours to Belize and the rest of Central America.

Journey Latin America UK 📞 020 3582 8754, 🌐 journey latinamerica.co.uk. One of the industry leaders for tours and flights to Latin America, as well as hotels.

Latin American Escapes US 📞 800 510 5999, 🌐 latinamerican escapes.com. Adventure, culture, natural history and diving holidays in Belize, and the rest of Central and South America.

Naturetrek UK 📞 01962 733051, 🌐 naturetrek.co.uk. Superb birding and wildlife trips led by expert naturalists.

North South Travel UK 📞 01245 608291, 🌐 northsouthtravel .co.uk. Friendly, competitive travel agency, offering discounted fares worldwide. Profits are used to support projects in the developing world, especially the promotion of sustainable tourism.

Reef and Rainforest Tours UK 📞 01803 866965, 🌐 reefandrainforest.co.uk. Tours focusing on nature reserves, research projects and diving in Belize, Panama and Costa Rica, as well as in South America and Africa.

STA Travel US ☎ 800 781 4040, UK ☎ 0871 230 0040, Australia ☎ 134 782, New Zealand ☎ 0800 474400, South Africa ☎ 0861 78 1781; ⓦ statravel.com. Worldwide specialists in independent travel; also discount student fares.

Travel CUTS Canada ☎ 866 246 9762, US ☎ 800 592 2887; ⓦ travelcuts.com. Canadian youth and student travel firm.

USIT Ireland ☎ 01 602 1906, Northern Ireland ☎ 028 9032 4073, Australia ☎ 1800 092 499; ⓦ usit.ie. Ireland's main student and youth travel specialists, which also has a branch office in Sydney, Australia.

Getting around

Belize has a good public transport network, and buses on the three main highways – the Philip Goldson Highway (also sometimes called by its former name, Northern Highway), the George Price Highway (formerly Western Highway) and the Southern Highway – are cheap, generally frequent and fairly fast.

Belize's **boat transport** infrastructure is also strong, with frequent routes between the mainland and the cayes, and also within the cayes. River transport is popular in Belize, too – it's the most convenient way to reach some Maya ruins and isolated field stations. One of the most popular river journeys is to the Maya site of Lamanai along the New River in northern Belize, where you can spy all manner of wildlife on its banks.

Flying between Belizean destinations is the fastest way to get around, though it's not particularly cheap. **Car rental** in Belize is not inexpensive, either: it generally costs US$65–150 per day, but it does enable you to visit more places in a shorter time than you could by bus.

By plane

The main towns and tourist destinations in Belize are linked by **domestic flights** operated by the country's two chief carriers: Maya Island Air (☎ 223 1140, ⓦ mayaregional.com) and Tropic Air (☎ 226 2012, ⓦ tropicair.com). There are also several **charter airlines**. Together, Maya Island and Tropic Air provide numerous daily flights from Belize City to main destinations, including Dangriga, Placencia, Punta Gorda, San Ignacio, San Pedro and Caye Caulker. Trips are short – anywhere from 25 minutes to an hour, and rarely more than that.

One-way prices start at around Bz$70–100; note that they often offer seasonal deals and discounts.

DISTANCES FROM BELIZE CITY

Distances are based on transport routes, not as the crow flies.

Belize City to	Distance
Belmopan	52 miles (84km)
Caye Caulker	21 miles (34km)
Chetumal, Mexico	93 miles (149km)
Corozal	84 miles (135km)
Dangriga	106 miles (171km)
Guatemalan border	81 miles (130km)
Orange Walk	54 miles (87km)
Placencia	161 miles (259km)
Punta Gorda	213 miles (343km)
San Ignacio	72 miles (116km)
San Pedro	32 miles (51km)
Tikal, Guatemala	149 miles (240km)

In Belize City, airlines operate from the two airports: Philip Goldson International Airport and the smaller, domestic Belize City Municipal Airport (a few miles north of the city centre).

Flying is also the most convenient way to make **side-trips** out of Belize to neighbouring countries. Tropic Air operates flights to Guatemala City and Flores, Guatemala (for Tikal); to Roatan, San Pedro Sula and Tegucigalpa, Honduras; and to Merida, Cancún and Chetumal, Mexico. TACA also flies from Belize City to its main hub in San Salvador for connections throughout Central America.

By bus

Buses in Belize fan out to all parts of the country, with regular departures throughout the day. That said, you'll hardly be travelling in luxury. Most are of the school bus variety, brightly painted, with worn interiors. Buses are managed by an ever-changing variety of different companies, few of which have websites or printed schedules, but the good news is you're rarely far from locals who know the schedule (ask at one of the many bus stops along the road) – and in fact, they may be a more accurate source of information anyway. Most of the bus companies are headquartered in Belize City (see p.52). Service usually begins in the very early morning and finishes some time in the evening. On Sundays and holidays, some services are reduced or, in the case of smaller, local ones, often nonexistent. You'll find some bus schedules and further information at ⓦ guidetobelize.info or the blog ⓦ belizebus.wordpress.com.

The faster "**express**" buses are occasionally the comfortable coach type; they operate along all main highways, stopping only in terminals in the towns. The more common non-express or "regular" buses will stop anywhere along their route on request. Tell the driver or conductor where you're headed and they'll usually know where to let you off. You'll also often see people hailing a bus from the side of the road, even if they're not at a bus stop.

Many of the buses that ply the Philip Goldson Highway (formerly the Northern Hwy) cross the Mexican border to serve the town of Chetumal. Others terminate in Corozal town, nine miles south of the border. From Belize City, numerous bus companies also fan out to the west and south, along the George Price (formerly the Western) and Southern highways.

Once you travel beyond the main highways, you'll need to rely mostly on **local buses** operated by small agencies, which rarely have backup plans when breakdowns occur. Travelling this way is a fairly slow business, as it caters primarily to the needs of villagers – taking produce to market, and so on – but it has its rewards: you're sharing a ride with people who know the area well, and by the time your ride's over you may have made friends eager to show you around.

Fares are a true bargain compared to the cost of most things in Belize. Regular buses start at around Bz$8–10 one way; tickets for express buses are just a few dollars more. Some bus terminals don't have ticket offices; you pay the conductor directly.

By boat

Boats travel regularly between Belize City and other mainland destinations out to the cayes. Two main water taxi companies connect Belize City with Ambergris Caye and Caye Caulker (starting at Bz$24 one way, or Bz$44 round trip), each with eight to ten departures a day (see p.54). The water taxis are open speedboats that can generally hold forty to fifty passengers; some have covered areas, to protect from the rain. San Pedro Belize Express Water Taxi boats (W belizewatertaxi.com) leave from North Front Street near Tourist Village in Belize City. Ocean Ferry boats (W oceanferrybelize.com) depart from near the Swing Bridge. It's a 45-minute ride to Caulker and 75 minutes to San Pedro. Some boats also stop on request at Caye Chapel. In addition, San Pedro Belize Express boats travel at least once daily to Chetumal from San Pedro (90min). *Thunderbolt* is another ferry that travels between Corozal and San Pedro (2hr; Bz$50 one way), with a stop at Sarteneja, on request. In the south, Dangriga is the departure point for boats to the Central Cayes, as well as to Honduras (see p.181).

You can buy tickets online via the boat websites, or at the terminals and other select locations (hotels, travel agencies) either a few days before or on the day of travel. If the latter, it's wise to show up at least fifteen minutes prior to departure; at busy times, one or two extra boats will be on hand for overflow, so it's unlikely you won't find space. Note that you need to buy tickets to Chetumal at least 72 hours prior to departure to guarantee a seat.

Many **tours** include boat transport in their itineraries, often to destinations public routes don't serve,

TOUR OPERATORS IN BELIZE

If there's one thing Belize has no shortage of, it's tour companies. A huge variety of them, based in cities and towns across the country, can plan trips, from Maya sites to wildlife refuges to zip-lining and diving. We list relevant, recommended tour companies individually throughout this Guide, but to get you started, here's our pick of Belize's top established companies running trips throughout the country.

Belize Trips in the US ☎ 561 210 7015, W belize-trips.com. This longtime company can develop itineraries throughout the country, and help arrange and connect you with tours around Belize.

Dave's Eco Tours ☎ 205 5597, W davesecotours.com. Friendly, knowledgeable company, based in Belize City, that offers trips around the country, from the cayes to Cayo.

Destinations Belize ☎ 523 4018, W destinationsbelize.com. Full-service tour company based in Placencia, with customized itineraries around the country.

Discovery Expeditions ☎ 671 0748, W discoverybelize.com. From jungle tours to scuba diving, this well-run company offers tours

on land and sea.

Go Maya Belize Adventures ☎ 824 2795, W gomayabelize .com. Visit the country's top Maya sites with this top-notch company with friendly, informative guides.

S & L Travel and Tours ☎ 227 7593, W sltravelbelize.com. Long-running tour operator with excellent tours, including canoeing and birding and trips to Maya sites.

Slickrock Adventures in the US ☎ 800 390 5715, W slickrock .com. Adventure company offering sea-kayaking, windsurfing, snorkelling and river expeditions in Belize, from a base on Long Caye, Glover's Reef.

such as outlying cayes and atolls. International boat routes include Punta Gorda to Puerto Barrios, Guatemala; Punta Gorda to Lívingston, Guatemala; Dangriga and Placencia to Puerto Cortés, Honduras. It's best to book ahead for international departures by contacting the boat operator or its agents at least one day before. Also, Belize has a number of charter boat companies, including Tropic Ferry (W tropic ferry.com), which travels between the airport and your resort or hotel (Bz$170), with the bonus of rum punch served on board.

By car

Driving is a popular option with visitors, and Belize's **main roads** offer relatively easy motoring. If you plan to conduct further exploration, you'll need high clearance and probably four-wheel drive. Main roads, and even most unpaved side roads, are typically well maintained and passable except in the very worst rainstorms, though mud, dust and the occasional massive pothole can be a problem at any time. Distances in Belize are usually measured in miles. When planning your journey, bear in mind that petrol stations may be scarce outside towns.

Traffic is generally light outside Belize City, but driving standards are fairly poor and fatal accidents are high relative to traffic density. The busiest stretch of road is on the George Price Highway between Belize City and Belmopan. Road signs are becoming more noticeable along the main highways, but you'll have to watch out for **speed bumps** of variable height; these are occasionally signed, but every new driver in Belize is bound to be caught unaware at least once – with potentially disastrous consequences. Look for them on entering and leaving any settlement along the highways, as well as shortly before bus stops.

Car rental

All the main rental companies offer cars, trucks and vans, including **four-wheel drive** options, for around US$70–150 per day and another US$13–18 per day for insurance, depending on the class of vehicle. Most companies have offices at the international airport and in Belize City (see p.54).

Avis (W avis.com), Budget (W budget.com), Hertz (W hertz.com) and Thrifty (W thrifty.com) have franchises in Belize. The local firm Crystal (W crystal -belize.com) offers some of the best rental prices, can provide clients with mobile phones for use during their stay and is one of the few companies that allows you to take its vehicles to Tikal. **Reserving ahead** of time can save money and

guarantees that a car will be waiting for you on arrival. One-way rentals typically aren't available, but your rental company can provide a pick-up or drop-off at your Belize City hotel or the airport.

In most cases you'll need to be 25 to rent a vehicle (if you're aged between 21 and 25 you may be required to pay a premium), and you'll usually have to leave a credit card imprint as a damage deposit when you pick up the car. Before you belt up and drive off into the sunset, check exactly what the **insurance** covers, examine the car carefully for signs of existing damage (making sure it's marked on the rental contract) and check what spares and equipment are included. A good **spare wheel** (and the tools to put it on) is essential – if you do heavy driving on Belize's roads, a puncture is likely at least once, if not more.

By taxi

All taxis in Belize are licensed and easily identifiable by their green licence plates. Drivers operate from ranks in the centres of towns and bus stations and, particularly in Belize City, will call out to anyone they suspect is a foreigner. There are **no meters**, so you'll need to establish a rate in advance, though within towns a fare of around Bz$7–9 for one or two people usually applies. The set taxi fare from the international airport to Belize City is Bz$50.

Many taxi drivers, particularly in Belize City, offer day-trip fares to the surrounding sights (like the Belize Zoo or the Maya site of Altun Ha) that are competitive with the local tour companies. Also, some drivers (particularly those at the Marine Terminal in Belize City) are also licensed tour guides and have been through tourism training.

By bike

Touring Belize by bike is fairly straightforward, particularly in the north and west where the roads are well surfaced, and also along the Hummingbird Highway – if you can manage the hills. Some locals will be surprised to see you using this form of transport, but don't assume that you're always noticed – **stay alert** to traffic. Cycling on the highways after dark is not recommended.

Cycling is a popular sport in Belize: citizens compete internationally, and several annual races, in which visitors are welcome to take part, are heavily attended. You'll find cycle **repair shops** in many towns. Mountain or beach bikes are available for rent (from Bz$15/half day) at an increasing number of shops and resorts (sometimes free for guests). Inspect rental bikes carefully since they deteriorate quickly in coastal climes, and if you intend to cycle a lot, bring or buy your own lock, lights and a helmet, which can be difficult to find. Top places to **rent** a bike are San Ignacio, where you can ride along the forest roads in the Mountain Pine Ridge; Placencia, with a smooth, sandy resort road that makes for an enjoyable day's riding; and San Pedro, where you can leisurely pedal along the main roads, catching glimpses of beach along the way. Also, renting a mountain bike in Punta Gorda will give you the freedom to explore the Maya villages and hills of Toledo.

Bikes can only rarely be carried on top of buses; few Belizean buses have the **roof racks** so common in Guatemala. If you're lucky – and if there's room – the driver may let you put your bike in the back of the bus.

Accommodation

Accommodation in Belize ranges from world-renowned resorts to basic clapboard hotels, covering a wide range of prices and services.

Towns in Belize are so small that you can usually walk to the majority of hotels to see what's on offer. For much of the year, **occupancy rates** are fairly low, and you should have little difficulty finding a room. The exceptions are Christmas and New Year, when you'll almost certainly need to **book ahead** in resort areas.

The **cost of accommodation** in Belize is notably higher than in surrounding countries, but you'll still find plenty of budget options. Average prices range from US$30/Bz$60 at a simple budget guesthouse to US$75–125/Bz$150–250 for a decent mid-range hotel to US$200–250/Bz$400–500 and up for the swanky resorts. We give prices in US$, but you'll often see them in both currencies. The hotel tax is nine percent; it's sometimes included in the price but if not, this is usually noted in the hotel brochures/website and/or at the time of check-in. When in doubt, ask. Note that most hotels and

---

STAY WITH THE MAYA

Many of the Maya in Belize live in the south, where villages are rich in tradition and some inhabitants still speak Maya dialects, such as Mopan, Kekchí and Yucatec. A number of these villages offer **homestay** or guesthouse programmes (see p.219), where you can stay (often in rustic lodgings) with the Maya, sample traditional food and drink, listen to music, stories and myths and even learn how to make chocolate the Maya way.

---

accommodation have wi-fi, which they offer to guests for free or a small fee. If a hotel does not offer wi-fi, we note this in the review.

In our accommodation reviews in this Guide, we quote prices for the cheapest double room in high season; we also include prices, where relevant, for other types of accommodation that a hotel offers (a hostel-style room with bunk beds, etc).

Belize Explorer (W belizeexplorer.com) is a cooperative marketing group of small, affordable hotels offering rooms for around US$75/Bz$150 or less; check the website for updated listings. The Belize Hotel Association (W belizehotels.org) is a local trade organization that features vetted member accommodation throughout the country, with updated information and deals and offers.

Arriving early at your destination gives you time to look around for the best room in your budget. A good idea, especially in cheaper places, is to ask to see the room before you accept it; check that the light and fan or air conditioning work, and if you've been told there's hot water, see just what that

---

ACCOMMODATION ALTERNATIVES

Belize has jumped on the wave of accommodation alternatives, with a wide range of residential apartments and homes for rent via these popular sites:
Airbnb W airbnb.com
CouchSurfing W couchsurfing.org
Vacation Rentals by Owner W vrbo.com

CELEBRITY HOTELS

Belize has long held a great appeal for vacationing celebrities, from Jennifer Lawrence to Tiger Woods. But for some stars, one visit isn't enough. Director Francis Ford Coppola put down roots in Belize in the 1980s, opening two top-notch hotels, *Blancaneaux Lodge* in Mountain Pine Ridge (see p.132) and *Turtle Inn* in Placencia (see p.200). And, now there's another big name on the scene: actor Leonardo DiCaprio is launching a new luxurious eco-resort (see p.100) due to open in 2018 on Blackadore Caye, just west of Ambergris Caye, with this soothing name: *Blackadore Caye, a Restorative Island*.

TOP 5 BEACH RESORTS
The Phoenix See p.101
Xanadu Island Resort See p.102
Pelican's Beach Resort See p.183
Glover's Atoll Resort See p.186
Maya Beach Hotel See p.199

locations, while the inland **jungle lodges**, often in or near national parks, feature thatched *cabañas* with balconies overlooking a forest or river. Many Belizean resorts also often have an eco-friendly angle.

Another bonus is that many specialist adventure and nature tours often use the resorts and lodges as bases, so you have direct access for planning your adventures around the country. Most of the higher-end resorts have spa and massage services, perfect for unwinding after a day spent hiking or on horseback. And, a growing number of resorts employ top-notch chefs, offering excellent Belizean fare.

In low season, **rates** can sometimes start from just US$150 per night for a double room, but in high season can reach over US$300–400.

means. In towns, it's sometimes better to get a room at the back, away from the street noise, although people-watching from the front balcony can be fascinating; an upstairs room means you're more likely to benefit from a breeze.

Budget and mid-range hotels and guesthouses

Accommodation prices may overall be higher than in neighbouring Guatemala, but the good news is that nearly every town and village does have at least one budget option. Most of these are small, simple hotels and guesthouses that are family-run and informal. Amenities run the gamut. As a rule, a basic room will have a bed, light and fan and all but the most rock-bottom of places will supply a towel and soap. You'll often have the option of a private bathroom, which can be worth paying a little extra for.

Mid-range hotels take it up a notch – towels are fluffier, rooms are larger and you're generally offered the option of air conditioning (a/c).

Resorts and lodges

One of Belize's greatest accommodation draws is its resorts – and, more importantly, the resort settings. **Island resorts** usually have spectacular beach or atoll

Hostels and camping

There are few dormitory-style cheap **hostels** in Belize, although you will find some in Caye Caulker and San Ignacio. Formal **camping** facilities are few and far between – Belize is not camping country. Specialist camping supplies are scarce or unobtainable, so don't expect to find gas canisters or Coleman fuel, though kerosene is widely available; in most cases cooking will be done over a wood fire. You can only camp in forest reserves and national parks if you obtain special permission from the Forest Department in Belmopan (see p.118)

Generally, a **tent** is useful if you plan to hike off the beaten track, usually with a guide who will lead you to places where you can set up camp. A few of the rural resorts in Cayo and some villages (particularly Crooked Tree in northern Belize) have **camping areas**, but these are rare on the cayes.

BELIZEAN BLISS: WEDDINGS AND HONEYMOONS

The white-sand beaches. The tropical cocktails. The twin hammocks. It's no surprise that Belize is a popular destination for weddings and honeymoons. **Beach weddings** in the cayes top the list, but the inland also holds great appeal, with many plighting their troth atop Maya temples and under the jungle canopy at a swanky lodge. The easiest way to do the deed is at one of the many resorts that host weddings – and leave the planning to them. These range from the funky *Maruba Resort Jungle Spa* (see p.63) in the Belize District to the elegant *Victoria House* (see p.102) and *Las Terrazas* (see p.103) on Ambergris Caye. Alternatively, you can go the independent route, by working directly with local purveyors (many hotels can direct you to recommended photographers, hair stylists and so on). You'll find many Belize wedding and honeymoon experts and planners online, including ⓦromantictravelbelize.com.

The **legal requirements** are also surprisingly simple – both partners will need a valid passport or proof of citizenship, and have to reside in Belize for at least three days prior to submitting the licence application (via email or in person) at the Registrar General's Office in Belize City (Treasury Lane, at Regent St ☎ 227 7377, 🖷822 3390, ⓦbelizejudiciary.org). For more information, check with your embassy or consulate in Belize (see p.21).

Food and drink

Belizean food is a distinctive mix of Latin American and Creole-style Caribbean, with the ubiquitous rice and beans at its heart. A defining characteristic of Creole food is its blend of fresh seafood, coconut – a favourite ingredient – and lively spices. The range of international cuisines on offer increases every year, and you can find authentic delicacies from as far afield as Lebanon and Thailand.

Lunch (noon–2pm) is often the main meal of the day and, though most places also serve dinner, **dining late** is not a Belizean custom; generally, planning to get to your table by 8pm will give you a good range of options, and possibly better service. Many places will be closed by nine or earlier, even in tourist areas.

Traditional cuisine

A tasty Belizean **breakfast** treat is the dense flour biscuits known as **johnny cakes** – the name a derivation of "journey cakes", as they travel well – served with everything from eggs to beans, or topped with cheese or butter. Also delicious are **fry-jacks**, fluffy, fried dough sometimes eaten with sweet jam. Lunch, which can be very affordable at local joints (generally Bz$10–15), often comprises Creole variations on **rice and beans**. The white rice and red beans are cooked together in coconut oil and flavoured with *recado* (a mild, ground red spice) – sometimes with a chunk of salted pork thrown in for extra taste – and usually served with fried fish, stewed chicken or beef. Note that the other version you can order is rice and beans served separately – that is, the beans are stewed, sometimes with spices, and then ladled on top of boiled white rice or on the side in a bowl. If you like your flavours full on, there will always be a bottle of hot sauce on the table for extra kick; a Belizean

favourite is **Marie Sharp's pepper sauce**, bottles of which also make for popular souvenirs; you'll find it in gift shops throughout the country.

Belize's claim to culinary fame is, of course, its **seafood**, which is excellent. Grouper and red snapper are invariably fantastic, as is the lobster, conch and shrimp. Throughout the cayes, you can dine on **lobster**, when in season, served every which way – grilled or barbecued, or in pasta, scrambled eggs or omelettes and even in chow mein or curry.

At the other end of the dietary spectrum, **vegetables** are scarce in Creole food, but you can opt for larger portions of side dishes, such as potato salad and fresh coleslaw along with a green salad, fried plantain and flour tortillas.

Southern Belize is the best region for sampling traditional **Garifuna cuisine**, which includes cassava, similar to sweet potato, and used to make crispy cassava bread; and *hudut*, green and ripe plantains that are mashed into a paste, and then cooked with fresh fish.

Central American-style **streetside snack bars** are found all over the country, and provide cheap and delicious fast food. Try tasty *tamales* (savoury cornmeal, usually with chicken, wrapped in a banana leaf and steamed), tacos, empanadas (similar to tacos but the tortilla is folded in half after filling, then deep fried) and other Latin staples. In the north, particularly in and around Corozal, which is near the Mexican border, many restaurants offer a flavourful hybrid of Belizean and Mexican cuisine, including shrimp *ceviche*.

International cuisine

International restaurants have sprouted up across Belize. You'll find quality Indian places, which often have vegetarian main dishes, in Belize City and San Ignacio. Also popular is Lebanese and Middle Eastern cuisine, with good authentic restaurants throughout the country. As well, Belize has many **Chinese restaurants**, varying enormously in quality. Chinese

---

THE ROYAL RAT

Feeling adventurous? Then how about a plate of grilled rodent? **Gibnut** (elsewhere in Central and South America it's commonly called "paca") is a nocturnal rodent that's hunted in the northern and western jungles of Belize. It's then grilled, carved up and served as a local delicacy. Belizeans, particularly those who grew up in rural areas, have been dining on it for years – but gibnut first came into the international spotlight in the 1980s when it was served to Queen Elizabeth II at a state dinner in Belize and gibnut got its nickname, "Royal Rat".

So, what does it taste like? On the plate, gibnut looks like pork – slightly fatty, and often tender enough to cut with the side of a fork; in the mouth, its wild nature comes through, with a pungent, earthy gameyness. In fact, as many chefs report, when hunters haul in gibnut to the kitchen, the odour is so powerful and rank that the meat has to be dunked in a vat of lime juice for the day.

food will probably feature more in your trip than you anticipated, as it's often the only food available on Sundays, or late evenings in smaller places. And, of course, there are plenty of American-style restaurants in the tourist areas, where you can sink your teeth into juicy burgers and fries.

Drinks

Belikin, the only brewery in Belize, produces almost all the **beer** consumed here. Belikin beer comes in several varieties, including regular, a tasty, lager-type beer; a dark, rich stout; the golden, lighter Lighthouse; and the malty Premium. Belikin also features seasonal varieties, including the Sorrel Stout during the holidays, and the refreshing Verano beer for the summer. The **legal age for drinking alcohol** in Belize is 18.

Cashew nut and berry **wines**, rich and full-bodied, are bottled and sold in some villages, and you can also get hold of imported wine, though it's far from cheap. Local **rum**, in both dark and clear varieties, is the best deal in Belizean alcohol and there's plenty to choose from.

Fresh fruit juices, particularly orange, lime, watermelon and pineapple, are generally available. **Tap water** in towns, though safe, is highly chlorinated, and most villages have a potable water system. Filtered, bottled water and mineral water are sold almost everywhere, and pure rainwater is usually available in the countryside and on the cayes.

Health

Belize has a high standard of public health, and most visitors leave without suffering so much as a dose of diarrhoea. Tap water in all towns and many villages is safe to drink, though most visitors (and locals) prefer the taste of bottled water (which is widely available). Restaurants are subject to stringent hygiene regulations, so ice in drinks will almost certainly be shop-bought or made from treated water.

Still, it's essential to get the best **health advice** you can before you set off; always schedule a visit with your doctor or a travel clinic (see p.31). Many clinics also sell travel-related medical supplies, such as malaria tablets, mosquito nets and water filters. Regardless of how well prepared you are, **medical insurance** is essential (see p.35).

If you're **pregnant** or taking an oral -contraceptive, you'll need to mention this when seeking health advice on travel medicine, as some vaccines and drugs can have harmful interactions or side effects.

Vaccinations

The only obligatory inoculation for Belize is against yellow fever, and that's only if you're arriving from a "high-risk" area (northern South America and equatorial Africa); carry your **vaccination certificate** as proof. However, there are several other inoculations that you should have anyway, particularly if you intend to spend time in remote, rural areas. At least eight weeks before you leave, check that you're up to date with diphtheria, polio and tetanus jabs, and arrange for typhoid and hepatitis A inoculations. Both typhoid and hepatitis A are transmitted through **contaminated food and water**. Although the risk of contracting hepatitis B is low unless you receive unscreened blood products or have unprotected sex, travel clinics often recommend inoculation; a joint hepatitis A and B vaccine is available from GPs and travel clinics.

Rabies exists in Belize, and vaccination is recommended for anyone travelling to Latin America for over thirty days.

Malaria, dengue fever and Zika

Malaria is endemic to many parts of Central America, especially the rural lowlands. Though it poses no great threat in Belize's tourist areas – due to an effective nationwide control programme – cases do occur each year, so you should still take precautions. Ask your travel clinic about the current, recommended malaria medicine. Avoiding bites in the first place is the best prevention: sleep in screened rooms or under nets, burn mosquito coils containing permethrin, cover up arms and legs (especially around dawn and dusk when mosquitoes are most active) and use repellent containing over 35 percent DEET (15 percent for children).

Keeping mosquitoes at bay is also important in the case of **dengue fever** – a viral infection transmitted by mosquitoes. The first symptom is a fever, accompanied by severe joint and muscle pains. If you think that you've contracted malaria or dengue fever, it's imperative to get checked by a medical professional; some cases can be fatal.

In recent years there has been an outbreak of **Zika virus** across Central and South America. The disease has been linked to neurological disorders in babies; pregnant women planning a trip to Belize should check ⓦcdc.gov for the latest advice on travel.

Intestinal troubles

A bout of **diarrhoea** is the medical problem you're most likely to encounter in Belize, generally caused by the change of diet and exposure to unfamiliar bacteria. Following a few simple precautions should help keep you healthy: be sure to drink clean water (any bottled drinks, including beer and soft drinks, are already purified), steer clear of raw shellfish and don't eat anywhere that's obviously dirty. If you do go down with a dose, the best cure is also the simplest: take it easy for a day or two, eat only the blandest of foods – **papaya** is good for soothing the stomach and is also packed with vitamins – and, most importantly, ensure that you replace lost fluids and salts by drinking lots of bottled water and taking **rehydration salts**. If you can't get hold of these, half a teaspoon of salt and three of sugar in a litre of water will do the trick. If diarrhoea lasts more than three or four days or is accompanied by a fever or blood in your stools, seek immediate medical help.

Heat and dehydration

Another common cause of discomfort – and even illness – is **the sun**. The best advice is to build up exposure gradually, use a strong sunscreen and, if you're walking around during the day, wear a hat and stay in the shade. Be aware that overheating can cause **heatstroke**, which is potentially fatal. Signs are a very high body temperature without a feeling of fever, accompanied by headaches and disorientation. Lowering body temperature (with a tepid shower, cool drinks or a fan, for example) is the first step in treatment. **Avoid dehydration** by taking plenty of fluids, especially water.

Bites and stings

Aside from malaria-carrying mosquitoes, there are several other biting insects (and other animals) whose nips could leave you in varying degrees of discomfort. **Sandflies**, often present on beaches, are tiny, but their bites, usually on feet and ankles, itch like hell and last for days – antihistamine creams provide some relief.

Scorpions are common but mostly nocturnal, avoiding the daytime heat under rocks and in crevices. Species in Belize can cause a painful sting but are rarely fatal. You're unlikely to be stung, but if you camp or sleep in a rustic *cabaña*, shake out your shoes before putting them on and avoid wandering around barefoot.

Swimming and snorkelling might bring you into contact with some potentially dangerous or venomous sea creatures. Shark attacks are virtually unknown in Belize; **stingrays** are generally very gentle creatures, but if you step on one (they rest in the sand) it will give a very painful sting. Shuffling your feet in shallow water gives them warning that you are approaching. The Portuguese man-o'-war **jellyfish**, with its purple, bag-like sail, has very long tentacles with stinging cells that inflict raw, red welts; equally painful is a brush against **fire coral**. In both cases, clean the wound with vinegar or iodine and seek medical help if the pain persists or infection develops. For advice on mammal bites, read the information on rabies (see p.29).

Getting medical help

Doctors in Belize have received training abroad, usually in the US, Mexico or Cuba; your embassy keeps a list of recommended specialists. Care is split between the public and private healthcare systems, both open to travellers. A visit to a **local**

WATER PURIFICATION

Contaminated water is a major cause of illness amongst travellers in Central America, due to the presence of pathogenic organisms: bacteria, viruses and cysts. In Belize, however, water in most hotels and resorts is treated, and bottled water is available pretty much everywhere; you will only need to consider treating water if you travel to remote areas. Bottled water is also easy to find in Flores and Tikal in Guatemala. While boiling water for ten minutes kills most micro-organisms, it's not the most convenient method. Chemical sterilization with either chlorine or **iodine tablets** or a tincture of iodine liquid is effective (except in preventing amoebic dysentery or giardiasis), but the resulting liquid doesn't taste very pleasant, though it can be masked with lemon or lime juice. Iodine is unsafe for pregnant women, babies and people with thyroid complaints. Purification, involving both sterilization and filtration, gives the most complete treatment, and travel clinics and good outdoor equipment shops stock a wide range of portable water purifiers.

public clinic is usually by donation, and treatment at a public hospital (such as Belize City's Karl Heusner Memorial Hospital; see p.58) will usually incur a small charge and entail a long wait. **Private doctors** and clinics set their own (much higher) fees, but waits are minimal and facilities generally better (see p.58). Pharmacists are knowledgeable and helpful, and sometimes provide drugs only available by prescription at home; most towns have at least one pharmacy. **Herbal remedies** are also quite popular in Belize, and if you have confidence in alternative medicine, seek advice from a respected practitioner; most pharmacies can direct you.

Whether you're a frequent traveller or this is your first trip to the tropics, check the listings below to find the latest travel health advice from the most reliable providers. By far the best source for a comprehensive assessment of health risks is the website of the **Centers for Disease Control** (**CDC**) in the US; no matter where you live, check here first.

MEDICAL RESOURCES FOR TRAVELLERS

Canadian Society for International Health Canada ☎ 613 241 5785, ⓦ csih.org. Extensive list of travel health centres.

CDC US ☎ 800 232 4636, ⓦ cdc.gov/travel. Official US government travel health site.

Hospital for Tropical Diseases Travel Clinic UK ☎ 0845 155 5000, ☎ 020 7388 9600 (Travel Clinic), ⓦ thehtd.org.

International Society for Travel Medicine US ☎ 770 736 7060, ⓦ istm.org. Has a full list of travel health clinics.

MASTA (Medical Advisory Service for Travellers Abroad) UK ☎ 0870 606 2782, ⓦ masta-travel-health.com. Check the website for travel advisories, advice and nearest clinics.

The Travel Doctor – TMVC Australia ☎ 300 658 844, ⓦ tmvc .com.au. Lists travel clinics in Australia, New Zealand and South Africa.

Tropical Medical Bureau Ireland ☎ 1850 487 674, ⓦ tmb.ie.

The media

Belize, with its English-language media, can come as a welcome break in a region of Spanish-speakers. You'll find it easy to keep up with both local and international news here, with daily national newspapers and plenty of lively TV and radio shows covering current affairs.

Newspapers and magazines

Major **newspapers** include *The Amandala*, *The Belize Times*, *The Guardian* (no relation to the UK broadsheet) and *The Reporter*. *The Belize Times* is the official organ of the ruling People's United Party (PUP), while *The Guardian* is the main paper of the United Democratic Party (UDP). Several online magazines cover Belize (see p.39).

Radio

Love FM (ⓦ lovefm.com), offering easy listening, news and current affairs, has one of the most extensive networks in the country. Another major station is KREM FM (ⓦ krembz.com), with an emphasis on talk and local music. Each major district town also has its own **local station**. Mexican stations come through in the north, Honduran and Guatemalan ones in the south and west.

Television

The two main TV stations are **Channel 5** (ⓦ channel5belize.com), the country's best broadcaster, with strong news and factual programmes, and **Channel 7**, which features a mix of American and Belizean programming with local news and political discussion programmes. Cable TV is also big in the country, with a variety of channels that broadcast everything from American soaps, talk shows and CNN to sports and movies.

Festivals

Festivals are popular in Belize and often involve entire communities. They range from full-on Carnival to lobster festivals to local school fundraisers, all celebrated with flair and exuberance. The following list is just a sample of what's on when and where; check locally for exact dates and venues.

JANUARY AND FEBRUARY

Jan 1: Horse racing in Burrell Boom; Cycling Classic from Corozal to Belize City.

Feb: Sidewalk Arts Festival, Placencia.

MARCH AND APRIL

First half of March: La Ruta Maya Belize River Challenge. Lively four-day canoe race from San Ignacio to Belize City.

March 9: Baron Bliss Day. Honours this British baron, who was one of the country's most generous benefactors.

April: Easter Fair in San Ignacio. Other Easter celebrations are held throughout the country.

MAY, JUNE AND JULY

First week in May: Cashew Festival in Crooked Tree village. Celebrates the cashew nut in its many forms, including roasted over an open fire, and also cashew jam, fudge and sweet wine.

Early May: National Agriculture and Trade Show in Belmopan. One of the largest public events in Belize, with everything from crop and livestock displays to "farmer of the year" awards. Almost all the country's top artists, bands and sound systems will appear at some stage during the weekend.

Late May: Chocolate Festival of Belize. Punta Gorda hosts a full program of cacao-centric competitions, tastings and street fairs.

June: Lobster festivals in San Pedro, Caye Caulker and Placencia. Marks the official start of lobster season. Feast on this famous crustacean in all its glory, including grilled, *ceviche* and kebabs. Caye Caulker even selects a Miss Lobsterfest.

June or July: Lagoon Reef Eco-Challenge, Ambergris Caye. Annual kayak race to raise reef awareness.

Mid-July: Benque Viejo Fiesta in Cayo District. Celebration of the town's patron saint, with parades, *marimba* bands, traditional food and drink and more.

AUGUST

First week of Aug: International Costa Maya Festival in San Pedro. A celebration of Mundo Maya countries (Mexico, Belize, Guatemala, Honduras and El Salvador), with dances, parades and other cultural offerings from each.

Late Aug: Deer Dance Festival in San Antonio, Toledo District. Maya festival with costumed dance performances.

SEPTEMBER AND OCTOBER

Sept 10: National Day/St George's Caye Day in Belize City. Start of almost two weeks of festivities in the capital, known as the "September Celebrations".

Sept 21: Independence Day. Celebrations nationwide, including Carnival in Belize City, the culmination of the month's revelries.

Mid-Oct: Pan American Day. Originally known as Columbus Day, Pan-American Day celebrates Belize's ethnic diversity, with fiestas from Belize City to the cayes.

NOVEMBER AND DECEMBER

Nov 19: Garifuna Settlement Day. In Dangriga, Hopkins and other Garifuna communities, with traditional drumming, dancing, cuisine and more. The Dangriga celebrations encompass Puntafest – a long weekend of late nights, rum and rhythm – which is a must-attend event.

Dec 26: Boxing Day. Parties, dances and horse races in Burrell Boom.

Sports and outdoor activities

Belize is a boon for outdoor activities, and especially those connected to water, including diving, snorkelling, sailing and windsurfing.

The setting couldn't be better: one of the most colourful ecosystems on earth, the Belize Barrier Reef is the longest in the Americas – a complex, living wall stretching around 180 miles from just south of Cancún, Mexico down the entire coastline of Belize. **Diving courses**, for beginners or experts, are offered in Belize City, San Pedro, Caye Caulker, Placencia and many waterfront locations. A dive with PADI certification starts at Bz$300.

Belize is also tops for **fishing**. In particular, fly-fishing on a catch-and-release basis has long attracted dedicated anglers to the shallow, sandy "flats" off the cayes and atolls. Several lodges, specialist operators and local guides can arrange this as well as fishing for tarpon and other fish. All manner of kayaking, too, is very popular, including sea and cave kayaking.

Away from the coast, **canoeing**, **rafting** and **tubing** – floating along rivers in a giant inner tube – draw big crowds, particularly in Cayo District, where many companies offer these trips. Most of the same tour operators can arrange **jungle hiking**: anything from a guided walk along a medicinal plant trail to very demanding, multi-day jungle survival courses. Beneath the jungle, Belize's amazing subterranean landscape is becoming ever more accessible, with motivated, very competent **caving** guides leading tours and organizing specialist expeditions. *Caves Branch Jungle Lodge* (see p.125) in Cayo is one of the best, with everything from cave expeditions to rappelling and rock climbing to zip-lining.

Horseriding and **mountain biking** are other options in Cayo and indeed anywhere in rural Belize, with some superb routes through forested hills to Maya sites. Organizers and tour guides of these activities are listed in relevant places throughout the Guide.

Licensed guides will have a **photo ID** (often stating their main field of expertise), which must be displayed when they're conducting a tour, but it's also a good idea to research the reputations of different companies, as quality can sometimes vary. Also, the tourist offices in the main towns often have a list of recommended tour operators and can help you connect with them.

Spectator sports

The main spectator sport in Belize is **football** (soccer), which is avidly covered in the press. Belize's national team is the Football Federation of Belize (FFB; Ⓦ belizefootball.bz). Their main stadium is the FFB Stadium in Belmopan; check the website for game days and tickets, which range from free to Bz$20.

Softball, basketball and volleyball are also very popular, as is track and field, and televised American football and baseball have small followings. As elsewhere in Central America, cycling is closely followed and there are frequent races all over Belize. Finally, there are a number of horse races around Christmas and New Year.

Shopping

Compared to its neighbours, Belize has somewhat less to offer in terms of traditional crafts or local markets, the latter being primarily for food. Proper craft and gift shops are found throughout the country, but you'll often get better prices from the artisans themselves, when you can find them on the street or in villages.

The Belizean Handicraft Market Place in Belize City (see p.58) is a great place to buy **souvenirs**, with a wide range of good-quality, genuine Belizean crafts, including paintings, prints and music. For contemporary **Belizean art**, try The Image Factory Art Foundation in Belize City (see p.58). Also, procrastinators take note: the airport has a surprisingly decent array of souvenirs at competitive prices, so you can pick up last-minute gifts before boarding your plane (with the bonus of using up your leftover Belizean currency).

Wood carvings, common throughout the country, make beautiful and unusual souvenirs. Carvers often sell their wares in Belize City and at Maya sites; their exquisite renderings of dolphins, jaguars, ships and more are made from *zericote*, a two-toned wood that grows only in Belize and surrounding areas. The best wood is **kiln-dried**, though the items you see on the street may not be. **Slate carvers**, also common at Maya sites, create high-quality reproductions of gods, glyphs and stelae. In the Maya villages in southern Belize, you'll also come across beautiful **embroidery**, though the quality of both the cloth and the work is better in Guatemala. Maya, Garifuna and Creole villages produce superb drums and good basketware, including small, tightly woven "jippy jappa" baskets. Dangriga, Hopkins, Gales Point and the Toledo villages are the best places to shop for these.

One tasty souvenir is a bottle (or five) of Marie Sharp's Pepper Sauce, made from Belizean *habañero* peppers in strengths ranging from "mild" to "fiery hot". This spicy accompaniment to rice and beans graces every restaurant table in the country, and visits to the factory near Dangriga (see p.181) can be arranged.

Travel essentials

Costs

Though Belize may be one of the cheaper countries in the Caribbean, it has the fully deserved reputation of being the **most expensive** country in Central America; if you've been travelling cheaply through the region to get here, many prices are going to come as a surprise. Even on a tight budget, you'll spend at least thirty percent more than you would in, say, Guatemala. Aside from some park and reserve entry fees (and occasional taxis in Belize City), however, you'll be paying the same prices as locals.

Prices in Belize are generally lower than in North America and Europe, though not by much. What you will spend depends on when, where and how you travel. **Peak tourist seasons**, such as Christmas and around Easter, tend to push hotel prices up, and certain tourist centres – notably San Pedro – are more expensive than others.

As a general rule, a **budget traveller** who is being very frugal can get by with spending about US$45–50/Bz$90–100 per day on basics (accommodation, food and transport); trips such as snorkelling or canoeing will add to this. Travelling in a couple will reduce per-person costs slightly, but to enjoy a reasonable level of comfort and the best of Belize's natural attractions, you should allow at least US$60/Bz$120 per day per person.

Taxes

Hotel rooms in Belize are subject to a nine percent tax, usually included in the quoted price, and separate from the five to ten percent service charge that some higher-end places impose. A 12.5 percent **general sales tax (GST)** applies to most goods and services (including meals in restaurants, though not drinks). This sales tax does not currently apply to hotel rooms, though there has been talk in recent years of applying it in place of the existing nine percent hotel tax.

Land borders levy a **border tax** of around Bz$37.50, payable in either Belize or US currency. If you'll be returning to Belize within thirty days, hold onto your receipt to get a discount on the next exit tax. You used to have to pay an exit tax at the airport when leaving Belize by air, but that is now almost always incorporated into your airline ticket price.

ILLEGAL DRUGS

Belize has long been an important link in the chain of supply between producers in South and Central America and users in North America, with minor players often being paid in product, creating a stream of illegal drugs in the country. Marijuana, cocaine and crack are all readily available in Belize, and whether you like it or not you may receive offers, particularly in San Pedro, Caye Caulker and Placencia. All such substances are **illegal**, and despite the fact that dope is sometimes smoked openly on the streets, the police do arrest people for possession of marijuana; they particularly enjoy catching tourists. If you're caught you'll probably end up spending a couple of days in jail and paying a **fine** of several hundred US dollars. Practically every year foreigners are incarcerated for drug offences – the pusher may have a sideline reporting clients to the police, and catching "international drug smugglers" gives the country brownie points with the US Drug Enforcement Agency. Expect little sympathy from your embassy – they'll probably send someone to visit you, and maybe find an English-speaking lawyer, but certainly won't break you out of jail.

Crime and personal safety

While Belize has a relatively high **crime** rate, it has a great safety record for tourists, and, despite the sometimes intimidating characters of Belize City, you're very unlikely to experience any crime during your visit.

That said, it pays to be aware of the dangers. If you've got valuables, **insure** them properly, keep them close to you (preferably in a concealed moneybelt) and always store **photocopies** of your passport and insurance documents in a secure place. Trousers with zippered pockets are also good pickpocket-deterrents. Looking generally "respectable" without appearing affluent will go some way in avoiding unwanted attention. One fairly accurate overview of the possible dangers of visiting Belize and Central America is on the UK Foreign Office **Travel Advice Unit** website, ⓦ fco.gov.uk. The unit also produces a helpful leaflet for independent travellers, explaining what a consul can and cannot do for you while you're abroad. The US equivalent is the State Department's **Consular Information Service** (ⓦ travel.state.gov), which also publishes consular information sheets and lists the current dangers to US citizens.

Break-ins at hotels are one of the most common types of petty theft – something you should bear in mind when selecting a room. Make sure the lock on your door works, from the inside as well as out. In some budget hotels, the lock will be a small padlock on the outside; for extra safety, it's a good idea to supply your own so you're the only one with keys. Many hotels will have a **safe** for valuables. It's up to you whether you use it; most of the time it will be fine, but make sure whatever you put in is securely wrapped – a lockable moneybelt does the job.

Solo women travellers, in addition to exercising the usual precautions, should be especially careful when talking to new male acquaintances in restaurants and bars, particularly in the cayes and Belize City. As in many other parts of the world, drugs intended to make women susceptible to **date rape** and other violent crimes are occasionally slipped into food or drinks. Though most victims of such acts have been local women, it's still never a good idea to accept food or drinks from anyone you don't know well.

Finally, don't let anyone without the official credentials talk you into accepting them as your "guide" – all legal tour guides in Belize are licensed and will have a **photo ID**. If you have doubts about using a certain guide, trust your instinct and report the incident to the authorities.

Tourism police and reporting a crime

In addition to its regular police force, Belize has special **tourism police**, operating from local police stations. Easily identified by their shirts and caps emblazoned with "Tourism Police", they patrol Belize City, San Pedro, Caye Caulker, Placencia and many other tourist destinations around the country. Police in Belize are generally poorly paid and, despite an ongoing campaign against criminals who prey on tourists, it's often difficult to convince them to do any more than simply fill out a report. Tourism police are specially trained to assist visitors and will likely prove more helpful.

POLICE EMERGENCY NUMBERS

The police emergency number in Belize is ☎ 90 or ☎ 911; to contact the tourism police or to report a crime in Belize City, call ☎ 227 2210 or ☎ 227 2222.

If you're a victim of any crime, you should also report it to your **embassy** if you can – doing so helps the consular staff support their case for better tourist protection. This is not to say that crime against tourists is taken lightly in Belize; if criminals are caught, they're brought into court quickly, particularly compared to other countries in the region.

Culture and etiquette

On the whole, Belize is friendly and welcoming to outsiders, and, as a popular holiday destination, very accustomed to hosting visitors.

Due to the warm climate, clothing is mostly very casual; business people often dress smartly, but full suits are uncommon.

Belize shares Central America's **culture of machismo**, and local men can be boldly persistent, particularly with solo women travellers in Belize City and tourist areas. Replying to them with a short greeting and moving on quickly will usually convey your lack of interest without being insulting.

Though Belizeans rarely **tip** unless they receive exceptional service, foreigners are expected to do so in most situations. An average practice is to tip **ten percent** for food and drink, but significantly more for specialized, personal service (eg, an exceptional tour guide).

Public toilets are quite rare in Belize, though the bus station in Belize City does have them. Facilities are basic but usually very clean.

Electricity

The main supply is 110 volts AC, with American-style, two- or three-pin sockets. Any electrical equipment made for the US or Canada should function properly, but anything from Britain or South Africa will need a plug adapter and possibly a transformer. The electricity supply is generally pretty dependable, but **power cuts** do occur. In small villages where electricity is supplied by local generators, voltage will often be lower and less dependable.

Insurance

Travel insurance is important for a trip to Belize; your coverage should include emergency treatment and provision for repatriation by air ambulance. Although there is a modern, private hospital in Belize City, in emergencies you may well need treatment in a US hospital, so ensure that your policy provides you with a 24hr emergency contact number.

Consider also taking out coverage for **loss or theft** of personal possessions, as petty theft is fairly common in Belize.

Before shopping around for a policy, check first to see what coverage you already have. Bank, credit and charge cards often have certain levels of medical or other insurance included, especially if you use them to pay for your trip. While this can be quite comprehensive, it should still be considered **supplementary** to full travel insurance.

Policies vary: some are comprehensive while others cover only certain risks, such as accidents, illnesses, delayed or lost luggage, cancelled flights, etc. In particular, ask whether the policy pays medical costs up front or reimburses you later, and whether it provides for **medical evacuation** to your home country. For any policy, make sure you know the claims procedure and the **emergency helpline number**. In all cases of loss or theft of goods, you will have to visit the local police station to have a report made out (make sure you get a copy) so that your insurer can process the claim.

Internet

You'll find access to the internet (usually for free) throughout the country: most hotels and other accommodation offer **wi-fi**, usually for free, but occasionally for a fee. The same applies to restaurants and cafés – in the tourist centres especially, most places have wi-fi, and will allow you to use it for free. This means, of course, that **internet cafés** are dwindling in number, though you'll still find a couple in major towns, with prices starting at around Bz$8–10 for an hour.

LGBT travellers

Belize overall is not a gay-friendly country, and local homosexuals often keep their sexuality a secret. Few people will make their disapproval obvious to foreigners, however, and many openly welcome the gay cruises that visit the country. San Pedro is probably your best bet for a hassle-free time. Also, change is on the horizon: in August 2016, Belize's Supreme Court overturned the country's anti-gay law in a landmark ruling. Belize is the first country in the Caribbean to do so, and the hope is that other countries in the region will follow suit.

Living in Belize

Thanks to the Caribbean Sea, balmy weather, lush foliage and English as the official language, Belize has long been a popular country for **relocation**, particularly for those from the US, Canada and the UK. Additionally, Belize has a generous retired persons' incentive programme (Ⓦbelizeretirement .org), which allows expatriates to live in the country tax-free, as long as they meet certain requirements. There are downsides, of course, to living here permanently, including hefty import taxes and poor infrastructure in certain areas (advanced medical care, for example, can be lacking). And, many basic supplies are imported, which translates into a huge mark-up. As most expats will explain, the best approach Is to buy local whenever possible, and then plan one or two shopping trips a year to Mexico or the US for more sizeable purchases. But even with these challenges, the foreign community continues to grow every year. *Belize First* (see p.39) offers excellent advice to those contemplating a move to Belize, with tips on how to negotiate the country in the first few years – and beyond.

Because any company hiring a foreigner must first prove that no Belizean could do the job, most work opportunities for foreigners are in the **voluntary sector**. Work permits, available only on a yearly basis, are required for any job, paid or not. Anyone planning to stay must also apply for **permanent residency**, a lengthy and costly process that prohibits you from leaving the country for more than fourteen days in your first year. After five years of residency (or a year of marriage to a Belizean) you can apply for **citizenship**.

Voluntary work and study

There are plenty of opportunities for **volunteer work** – mainly as a fee-paying member of a conservation expedition – or study at a field study centre or archeological field school. These options generally mean raising a considerable sum for the privilege and committing yourself to weeks (or months) of hard but rewarding work, often in difficult conditions. Many of the expeditions are aimed at students taking time off between school and university, and arrange work on **rural** infrastructure projects such as schools, health centres and the like, or on trails and visitor centres in nature reserves.

Academic **archeological groups** undertake research in Belize each year, and many of them invite paying volunteers (see p.244). There is also a growing number of **field study centres** in Belize, aimed primarily at college students on a degree course, though there are opportunities for non-students to learn about the ecology and environment of Belize. If you want to learn **Spanish** relatively cheaply, you could extend a trip to Tikal by studying at one of the language schools in and around Flores, Guatemala.

If the cost of joining a volunteer expedition deters you, there are a handful of organizations that don't collect fees, as well as opportunities to volunteer independently; the **conservation organizations** in Contexts (see box, pp.250–251) all have volunteer programmes.

A helpful website is Ⓦgapyear.com (UK-based, free membership), which holds a vast amount of general information on volunteering, and a huge, invaluable database on travel and living abroad.

VOLUNTARY ORGANIZATIONS

Barzakh Falah Georgeville, Cayo District ☎ 674 4498, ✉ barzakhfalah@gmail.com. A sustainable farm community that aids orphaned, abused and abandoned children.

Cornerstone Foundation Belize ☎ 667 0210, Ⓦ cornerstonefoundationbelize.org. A Belize-based nonprofit community development organization, offering everything from literacy programmes to vocational and job skills training.

Earthwatch Institute US ☎ 800 776 0188, Europe ☎ 01865 318 838, Australia ☎ 03 9016 7590; Ⓦ earthwatch.org. Earthwatch matches volunteers from around the world with scientists dedicated to working on environmental and sustainable initiatives.

Ecologic Development Fund US ☎ 617 441 6300, Ⓦ ecologic .org. Ecologic focuses on Central America and Mexico, and aims to conserve endangered habitats by using community-based development and resource management in partnership with local organizations.

Manatee and Primate Rehabilitation Centre ☎ 650 6578, Ⓦ wildtracksbelize.org (see p.81). Centre in Sarteneja, in northern

Belize, that focuses on rehabilitation strategies, including habitat protection, raising public awareness and rehabilitating orphaned, injured or confiscated wildlife.

The Peace Corps US ☎ 855 855 1961, ⓦ peacecorps.gov. Since 1962, the Peace Corps has been sending American volunteers to Belize to teach in rural areas, work in agricultural and environmental education and assist with women's groups, youth and community outreach and health awareness programmes.

Trekforce Worldwide UK ☎ 020 7384 3028, ⓦ trekforce.org.uk. Trekforce runs projects ranging from leadership training and surveys of Maya sites to jungle treks and diving and watersports.

World Challenge Expeditions UK ☎ 01494 427600, ⓦ world-challenge.co.uk. A youth development organization, with the motto "education through exploration", that leads adventurous trips through Belize and Mexico.

Mail

Belize has a reliable internal postal system, but its **international service** can sometimes be patchy; standard cost for postcards starts at Bz$0.40, and for letters at Bz$0.75. An "express" service, considerably pricier than the cheap standard rates, has a better track record and is worthwhile when it comes to important parcels. Fedex and Global Express services are available in main towns and tourist centres.

Post offices are generally open from Monday to Friday 8am to 4pm; post offices in small villages – sometimes operated by a local out of their home – are often short on stamps and packing materials, so do any major mailing from a large town.

Money

Prices and exchange rates are stable, with the national currency, the **Belize dollar**, very conveniently fixed at the rate of two to the US dollar (**Bz$2=US$1**). US dollars (cash) is also accepted everywhere – and in some places even preferred – as currency. This apparently simple dual currency system can be problematic, however, as you'll constantly need to ask which dollar is being referred to; it's all too easy to assume the price of your hotel room or trip is in Belize dollars, only to discover on payment that the price referred to was in US dollars – a common cause of misunderstanding. In San Pedro and other high-end destinations around the country, many businesses quote prices in US dollars. Prices in the Guide are usually quoted in Belize dollars (always preceded by the symbol Bz$) and, when relevant (with accommodation and, often, for tours), in US dollars.

The Belize dollar is divided into 100 cents. Banknotes come in denominations of 2, 5, 10, 20, 50

and 100 dollars; coins come in denominations of 1, 5, 10, 25, 50 cents and 1 dollar, although 10 and 50 cent pieces are less commonly seen. All notes and coins carry the British imperial legacy in the form of a portrait of Queen Elizabeth – and quarters are sometimes called "shillings".

The **Guatemalan** unit of currency is the quetzal; note that costs in Guatemala are generally considerably cheaper than in Belize.

Currency exchange

Currency exchange is a seamless process. When you pay in US dollar (accepted everywhere), you'll receive change in Belize dollars, making this the easiest mode of exchange. Additionally, there are ATMs throughout the country, including at the airport. You can use most credit and debit cards at **ATMs** of all the major banks, including Belize Bank, Atlantic Bank, Alliance Bank and First Caribbean Bank (formerly Barclays), to get cash in Belize dollars at decent rates. Other banks will process cash advances on cards at the counter, though usually at less favourable rates than an ATM. Visa is the most useful card in Belize (and throughout Central America), but MasterCard is also accepted fairly widely. You can also, of course, exchange notes (bills) inside the bank; most don't charge for the exchange, but make sure to ask. Every town has at least one bank (generally open Mon–Fri 8am–2/3pm, some also Sat 8am–noon). It's a good idea to carry smaller bills of US currency ($20 instead of $100, for example), especially towards the end of your trip. Since change is given in Belize dollars, you don't want to be stuck with too much Belize money before you go, as it's useless outside the country.

Opening hours and public holidays

It's difficult to be specific about **opening hours** in Belize, since many family-run spots have very loose opening schedules, tied to personal holidays and the like. But in general most shops are open from 8am to noon and from 1 or 2pm to 7pm. Some shops and businesses work a half-day on Saturday, and everything is liable to close early on Friday. **Archeological sites**, though, are generally 8am to 4pm daily. On **public holidays**, virtually everything will be closed – though some public transport operates normally. Note that if the actual date of a particular holiday falls mid-week, the holiday will sometimes be observed the following Monday.

PUBLIC HOLIDAYS

January 1 New Year's Day
March 9 Baron Bliss Day
Good Friday varies
Holy Saturday varies
Easter Monday varies
May 1 Labour Day
May 24 Commonwealth Day
September 10 National Day
(St George's Caye Day)
September 21 Independence Day
October 12 Columbus Day (Pan American Day)
November 19 Garifuna Settlement Day
December 25 Christmas Day
December 26 Boxing Day

Phones

There are no area codes in Belize, so wherever you're calling within the country you'll need to dial just the seven-digit number. There is **mobile (cell) phone** coverage across most of the country and you can easily rent a mobile starting at around Bz$10–20 per day, plus an activation fee. If you rent a car, it's often possible to rent a phone along with it, while specialist companies offering mobile-phone rental include Cellular Abroad (W cellularabroad.com) and DigiCell (W digicell.bz). On the cayes, including in San Pedro, you'll also find smaller companies that offer mobile-phone rental; inquire at your hotel or guesthouse. The cheapest option of all, of course, is to take advantage of a wi-fi connection to use a service such as Skype. Until 2013 the Belizean government blocked all such systems, but they're now readily accessible throughout the country.

The country's phone system is of good quality and easy to use, and payphones continue to be fairly plentiful. **Belize Telecommunications Limited (BTL)**, the dominant telephone service, has its main office (for international calls, fax, email and internet access) at 1 Church St, Belize City (Mon–Fri 8am–5pm; W belizetelemedia.net).

Time

The international direct dialling (IDD) code (also known as the country code) for Belize is ☎ 501. To call a number in Belize from abroad, simply dial the international access code (listed in your phone book), followed by the country code (501) and the full seven-digit number within Belize.

Belize is on Central Standard Time, six hours behind GMT and the same as Guatemala and Honduras. Belize does not observe Daylight Savings Time, though Mexico does. This means that when DST is in operation (during the summer), the time in Belize is an hour earlier than in Mexico – something to bear in mind when you're crossing the border.

Tourist information

The official **Belize Tourism Board** website, W travelbelize.org, is packed with information about the country, from outdoor adventures to accommodation. At the main office in Belize City (see p.55), you can pick up city and regional maps, transport schedules, lists of recommended hotels and more. There are Belize Tourism offices in main towns around the country, including in Placencia and San Pedro. The **Belize Tourism Industry Association** (BTIA; W btia.org) represents most of the tourism businesses in the country and produces the annual

USEFUL PHONE NUMBERS

USEFUL NUMBERS WITHIN BELIZE

Directory assistance	☎ 113
International operator	☎ 114
Operator assistance	☎ 115

CALLING HOME FROM BELIZE

Note that the initial zero is omitted from the area code when dialling the UK, Ireland, Australia and New Zealand from abroad.
Australia international access code + 61
New Zealand international access code + 64
UK international access code + 44
US and Canada international access code + 1
Ireland international access code + 353
South Africa international access code + 27

Destination Belize magazine (free from tourist offices and many hotels; Ⓦdestinationbelize.com), which is filled with helpful information. The BTIA has local representatives in many resort areas. Note also that a variety of towns and regions in Belize have developed their own tourism-friendly websites (listed in the individual chapters), which are worth checking out for current news and information – good examples include Ⓦambergriscaye.com, Ⓦcorozal.com and Ⓦgocayecaulker.com.

USEFUL WEBSITES

Several excellent websites are dedicated to Belize, and these are a good place to start and refine your search for facts and practical details.

Ⓦ **belizeaudubon.org** Website of the Belize Audubon Society (BAS), useful for the latest info on the growing number of reserves and national parks and their associated visitor centres. There's more on the BAS in Contexts (see p.250).

Ⓦ **belizefirst.com** An online resource centre and magazine on Belize, featuring reviews and articles about hotels, restaurants, destinations, current events, living and working in Belize and more.

Ⓦ **belize.gov.bz** The government's own website is worth a look for an overview on current politics and tourism trends.

Ⓦ **belize.net** A good place to search for links to Belize websites.

Ⓦ **belizenet.com** A decent tourism-related site, with a range of accurate listings and links; also see Ⓦ belize.com, run by the same company.

Ⓦ **breakingbelizenews.com** Daily news on Belize, with a travel and tourism angle.

Ⓦ **channel5belize.com** Daily coverage on Belize news and headlines via TV broadcasts, articles, opinion pieces and more.

Ⓦ **lanic.utexas.edu** The homepage of the Latin American Information Center (LANIC) leads to a series of great links on Belize, which cover everything from native birds to current archeological projects.

Ⓦ **mesoweb.com** Fascinating articles and links, often written by archeologists, on the latest findings in Maya research.

Travellers with disabilities

Travelling with a disability in Belize can be challenging, but resources are increasing, and many tour companies now offer specially customized packages.

Travelling by **public bus** is very difficult, as these have no accessibility features and tend to get crowded. However, minibus **taxis** are plentiful and drivers will assist you when asked. Streets in many areas can be tricky to negotiate, as they are mostly unpaved and pavements are rare.

Most **hotels** in Belize don't have rooms on the ground floor, and even those that do often have a few steps somewhere. It's imperative to ask about a hotel's accessibility when you call to book; note that the newer and higher-end resorts, particularly in well-touristed areas like Ambergris Caye, are more likely to have disability-friendly facilities. One Belizean organization that has been at the forefront in increasing the country's awareness of people with disabilities is the nonprofit Belize Council for the Visually Impaired (BCVI; ☎ 223 2636, Ⓦbcvi.org). BCVI made international headlines in 2013, when the Belizean teen Rowan Garel became the first blind person to dive the Blue Hole, raising funds for the organization by doing so.

INTERNATIONAL RESOURCES

Disability Rights UK ☎ 020 7250 3222, Ⓦ disabilityrightsuk.org. A good source of advice on UK disability organizations and travel abroad.
Society for Accessible Travel and Hospitality (SATH) US ☎ 212 447 7284, Ⓦ sath.org. Nonprofit disability information service with links, resources, current news and more.

Travelling with children

Belize is a very child-friendly destination, and there is plenty to keep kids occupied. In particular, Belize is a wonderful country to introduce children to the richness of the animal kingdom – and the importance of protecting and sustaining it – with numerous opportunities for wildlife spotting, from howler monkeys to manatees. Top sights and activities that are often popular with the younger set include the Belize Zoo (see p.59), the Community Baboon Sanctuary (see p.61) and splashing around in the hotel pools or sparkling Caribbean waters on the cayes. Older kids and teens enjoy zip-lining and river tubing in Cayo (see p.125), snorkelling in the cayes (see p.96) and Garifuna drumming in the south (see p.180).

As for facilities and amenities, most community stores carry supplies of baby formula and nappies (diapers), and many restaurants have high chairs. The dearth of public toilets means **changing facilities** are rare. Larger resorts may have them, but for the most part babies are changed where necessary, in public or otherwise.

Few hotels and resorts prohibit children, though it's worth asking before you book. **Childcare facilities** readily exist in the larger resorts, and the concierge or hotel staff can usually help you find recommended local babysitters. Also, increasingly, condo-style hotels and resorts are opening up in the cayes and other tourist centres. These are often equipped with kitchenettes or a full kitchen, which can make all the difference in the world when travelling with snack-clamouring kids.

Belize City and District

PARROT AT THE BELIZE ZOO

1

Belize City and District

Appearances can be deceptive – and that's somewhat the case with Belize City. The narrow, congested streets can seem initially daunting and unprepossessing, even to travellers familiar with blighted urban centres. Dilapidated wooden structures stand right on road edges, offering pedestrians little refuge from cars and trucks, while almost stagnant canals are still used for some of the city's drainage. The overall impression is of a place recovering from some great calamity – an explanation at least partly true. Belize City has suffered several devastating hurricanes, most notably in October 1961, when Hurricane Hattie tore it apart with winds of 150mph and left behind a layer of thick black mud. Belize City was also hard hit by Hurricane Richard in 2010, and Hurricane Earl in 2016. But these hazards are often overstated by people who have never set foot within the city limits. For those who spend some time here, Belize City will reveal a distinguished history, several superb sights and fascinating cultural spectacles.

The city's astonishing energy comes from its sixty thousand-plus inhabitants, who represent every ethnic group in the country, with the **Creole** descendants of former slaves and British Baymen forming the dominant element and generating an easy-going Caribbean atmosphere. This relaxed attitude blends with an entrepreneurial flair, for Belize City is the country's commercial capital; banks, offices and shops line the main streets, while fruit and fast-food vendors jostle for pavement space with others selling plastic bowls, T-shirts or cheap jewellery. The jubilant **September celebrations**, which pack the already full streets with music, dancing and parades, culminate in **Carnival** (see p.48) and Independence Day.

Richard Davies, a British traveller in the mid-nineteenth century, wrote of the city: "There is much to be said for Belize, for in its way it was one of the prettiest ports at which we touched." Many of the features that elicited this praise have now gone, though some of the distinctive **wooden colonial buildings** have been preserved as heritage showpieces, or converted into hotels, restaurants and museums. Yet even in cases where the decay is too advanced for the paintwork, carved railings and fretwork to be restored, the old wooden structures remain more pleasing than the concrete blocks that are replacing them. Fires, too, have altered the old city architecture, such as the 2004 blaze that destroyed the historic Paslow Building, which stood opposite the Marine Terminal. That said, two of the very best colonial structures have been carefully restored and are open to visitors; the former city jail, built in Victorian times, is now the **Museum of Belize**, and the even earlier **Government House** is a museum and cultural centre.

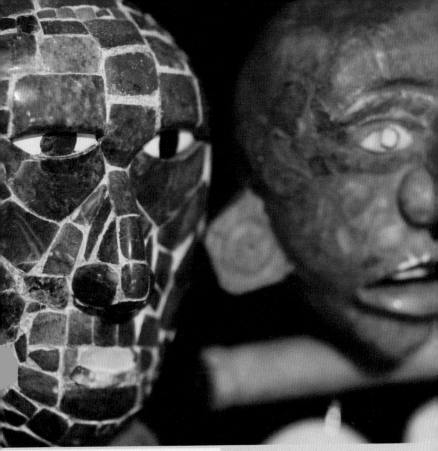

Highlights

❶ September celebrations Join the costumed throngs gyrating through the streets of Belize City during the rollicking carnival celebrations in September. **See p.48**

❷ Museum of Belize Marvel at Maya masterpieces, including painted ceramics, wooden figurines and carved flints, at this world-class museum in Belize City, housed in a beautifully restored Victorian prison. See p.49

❸ The Belize Zoo One of the best-known zoos in Central America, this beloved attraction offers a close-up view of the country's famous wildlife, from jaguars to iguanas. **See p.59**

❹ Community Baboon Sanctuary You'll hear them before you see them: follow the full-throated screeches to spy howler monkeys, scampering in the trees overhead, at this well-respected sanctuary. **See p.61**

❺ Altun Ha This superbly restored Maya site is dominated by two large plazas and has yielded numerous treasures, including a jade head, the largest carved jade piece from the Maya era. See p.62

HIGHLIGHTS ARE MARKED ON THE MAP ON P.44

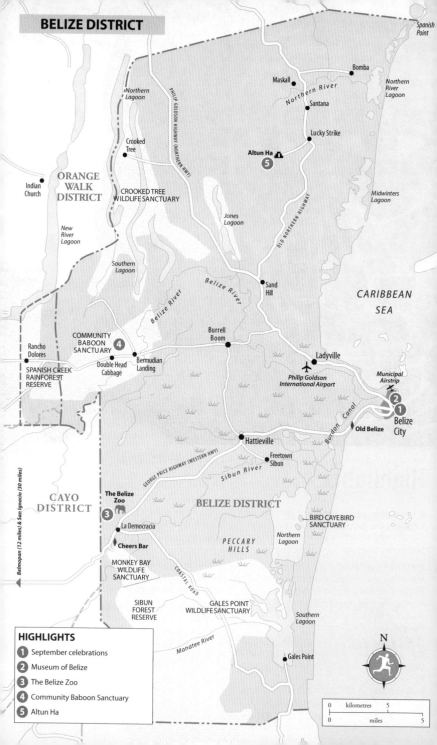

BELIZE DISTRICT

Spanish Point

Bomba

Maskall

Northern River Lagoon

Northern Lagoon

Santana

Lucky Strike

Crooked Tree

Altun Ha **5**

ORANGE WALK DISTRICT

Indian Church

CROOKED TREE WILDLIFE SANCTUARY

New River Lagoon

Jones Lagoon

Midwinters Lagoon

Southern Lagoon

Belize River

Sand Hill

CARIBBEAN SEA

COMMUNITY BABOON SANCTUARY **4**

Rancho Dolores

Double Head Cabbage

Bermudian Landing

Burrell Boom

Ladyville

SPANISH CREEK RAINFOREST RESERVE

Philip Goldson International Airport

Municipal Airstrip

2

1

Belize City

Burdon Canal

Old Belize

Hattieville

Freetown Sibun

Sibun River

GEORGE PRICE HIGHWAY (WESTERN HWY)

CAYO DISTRICT

The Belize Zoo

3

La Democracia

Cheers Bar

BELIZE DISTRICT

BIRD CAYE BIRD SANCTUARY

Northern Lagoon

PECCARY HILLS

MONKEY BAY WILDLIFE SANCTUARY

SIBUN FOREST RESERVE

COASTAL ROAD

GALES POINT WILDLIFE SANCTUARY

Southern Lagoon

Belmopan (12 miles) & San Ignacio (30 miles)

Manatee River

Gales Point

N

HIGHLIGHTS

1 September celebrations
2 Museum of Belize
3 The Belize Zoo
4 Community Baboon Sanctuary
5 Altun Ha

0   kilometres   5
0   miles   5

The city is divided neatly into north and south halves by **Haulover Creek**, a delta branch of the Belize River. The pivotal point of the city centre is the **Swing Bridge** (see box, p.50), always busy with traffic and occasionally opened up to allow larger vessels up and down. The surrounding **Belize District** (see p.59), which extends north, west and south of the city, is tailor-made for day-trips and includes some of the country's top sights, including the **Altun Ha** Maya site, the splendid **Belize Zoo** and the **Community Baboon Sanctuary**.

Brief history

In the late sixteenth century, British **buccaneers**, attracted by Spanish treasure fleets, began to take advantage of the cayes of Belize as bases for plundering raids. Ever the opportunists, they began to cut valuable logwood (a source of textile dye) in the coastal swamps, and built a settlement at the mouth of the Belize River, constructed by consolidating the mangrove swamp with wood chips, rum bottles and coral. In the 1700s, **Belize Town** gradually became a well-established centre for **Baymen** (as the settlers called themselves), their families and their slaves, though the capital of the Bay settlement remained off the coast on St George's Caye. After floating the logwood downriver to be processed, the men would return to Belize Town to drink and brawl, with Christmas celebrations lasting for weeks. The Baymen's houses stood on the seafront while slaves lived in cabins on the south side of Haulover Creek.

The rise of Belize Town

Spain was still the dominant regional power, and in 1779 a Spanish raid captured many British settlers and scared off the rest. Most returned in 1783 however, when Spain agreed to recognize their rights, and Belize Town soon grew into the main centre of the logwood and mahogany trade on the Bay of Honduras. Spanish raids continued until the Battle of St George's Caye in 1798, when the settlers achieved victory with British naval help. In the nineteenth century, colonial-style buildings began to dominate the shoreline – the "Scottish clique" cleaned up the town's image and took control of its administration – while in 1812 Anglican missionaries built the Anglican cathedral of St John to serve a diocese that stretched from Belize to Panama.

Fires in 1804, 1806 and 1856 destroyed large swathes of Belize Town, while epidemics of cholera, yellow fever and smallpox also wreaked havoc. Despite this, the town continued to grow, with immigrants from the West Indies and refugees from the Caste Wars in Yucatán. In 1862 Belize became **British Honduras**, with Belize City (as it was now known) its administrative centre; in 1871 it was upgraded to a Crown colony, with its own resident governor appointed by Britain.

The independence movement

The twentieth century was dominated by Belizean uncertainty over its relationship with the "mother country". In 1914 thousands volunteered to assist the war effort in the Middle East, but they were confronted by a wall of prejudice and racism and consigned to labour battalions. In 1919 the returned soldiers rioted in Belize City, an event that marked the onset of black consciousness and the **independence movement**. Compounding an already tense situation, on September 10, 1931, the city was celebrating the anniversary of the Battle of St George's Caye when it was hit by a massive **hurricane** that flooded the entire city and killed a thousand people – ten percent of the population. Many parts of the city were left in a state of squalid poverty, and together with the effects of the Depression, this added momentum to the campaign for independence, with numerous rallies in defiance of Britain. In 1961 Hurricane Hattie delivered her fury: 262 people died, and plans were made to relocate the capital inland. The instigators assumed that Belize City

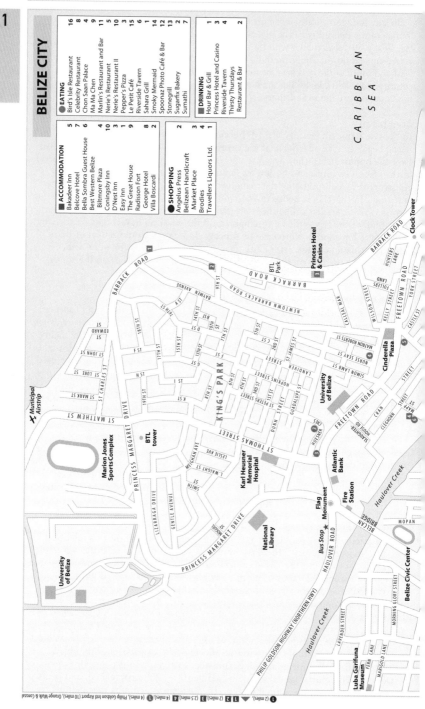

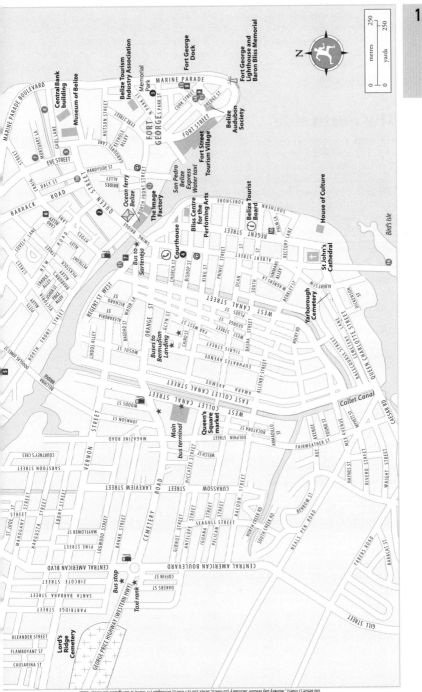

Central Bank building

Museum of Belize

Belize Tourism Industry Association

Memorial Park

Fort George Dock

Fort George Lighthouse and Baron Bliss Memorial

MARINE PARADE

FORT GEORGE

Belize Audubon Society

Fort Street Tourism Village

San Pedro Belize Express Water taxi

The Image Factory

Ocean ferry Belize

Bliss Centre for the Performing Arts

Belize Tourist Board

House of Culture

Courthouse

Bus to Sarteneja

St John's Cathedral

Yarborough Cemetery

Busus to Bermudian Landing

Queen's Square market

Collet Canal

Main bus terminal

Taxi rank

Bus stop

Lord's Ridge Cemetery

Birds Isle

MARINE PARADE BOULEVARD

BARRACK ROAD

QUEEN STREET

CENTRAL AMERICAN BOULEVARD

GEORGE PRICE HIGHWAY (WESTERN HWY)

CENTRAL AMERICAN BOULEVARD

N

0   metres   250
0   yards   250

1

would become obsolete as Belmopan grew, but in fact few people chose to leave for the sterile atmosphere of the new, nominal capital, and Belize City remains by far the most populous place in the country. Since independence in 1981, foreign investment and tourism – including a boom in cruise ships – have contributed to development, and Belize City continues to operate as the country's chief commercial and business centre.

The north side

The north side, which unfolds north of the Swing Bridge, is the city's more upmarket area, dotted with the pricier hotels and international restaurants, as well as the superb **Museum of Belize**. Here you'll also encounter the advance guard of trinket sellers, street musicians, hustlers and hair-braiders, announcing you're near the **Fort Street Tourism Village** (see below) and Belize's **cruise ship terminal**, which often handles thousands of visitors in a single day. Look out to sea – you'll almost always spy at least one or two massive cruise ships floating on the horizon.

The north side is also where you embark on boats to the cayes (see p.54).

BTL Park

Barrack Rd, on the seafront

The attractive seafront **BTL Park** was built on land that has a famous history: it was here that Charles Lindbergh landed the Spirit of St Louis, the first aeroplane to touch down in Belize, in 1927. BTL Park – named after Belize Telemedia Limited, the country's main telecommunications company – has evolved into a very popular meeting spot, and often hosts open-air concerts and other civic events. The park also features historical panels that trace Belize City history. The biggest party takes place during the Independence Day celebrations in September (see below).

Fort Street Tourism Village

Fort St • 8am–4pm, only when cruise ships are in port, which is usually during the week • ⓦ tourismvillage.com

Catering to cruise ship passengers, the **Fort Street Tourism Village** is filled with stalls and shops, many selling unauthentic items – tourist trinkets and liquor – but tucked away here and there, you can occasionally find some worthy souvenirs, like Belizean hardwoods. The adjoining cruise ship terminal is a long dock with numerous outdoor restaurants and bars, serving burgers, tacos and, most popularly, tropical cocktails. Note that just outside the Tourism Village, local vendors have also set up a makeshift flea market, where you can buy local goods for considerably less.

GET READY TO DANCE: SEPTEMBER CELEBRATIONS

Belize may be in Central America, but when it comes to carnival, it's enthusiastically and colourfully Caribbean. **Independence Day** in Belize isn't just celebrated for a day or two – but for an entire month; festivities kick off in Belize City with a series of lively concerts. This leads to ceremonies to mark the Battle of St George's Caye on September 10, which then gives way to carnival in mid-September, when the city erupts with gorgeously costumed dancers who shimmy through the city to electrifying Caribbean rhythms. The month culminates in Independence Day celebrations on September 21, when BTL Park fills with revellers, music, dance and much more.

BARON BLISS

One of Belize's most famous benefactors never actually set foot on Belizean soil. **Baron Henry Ernest Edward Victor Bliss** was an eccentric Englishman with a Portuguese title and considerable wealth, the origins of which remain a mystery. Bliss arrived off the coast of Belize in his yacht *Sea King* in 1926 after hearing about the tremendous amount of game fish in local waters. Unfortunately, he became ill soon after and died without ever having been ashore, but he must have been impressed by whatever fish he did catch, as he left most of his estate to the colony – meticulously stipulating how the money was to be spent. This became the **Bliss Trust**, which has been used to help build markets and libraries, contribute to the country's artistic and cultural programmes, improve roads and water supplies and create the Bliss School of Nursing. In gratitude, March 9 (the date of his death) was declared an official public holiday – **Baron Bliss Day** – commemorated by boat races and the La Ruta Maya canoe race (see p.137) from San Ignacio to Belize City.

Fort George Lighthouse and Baron Bliss Memorial

At tip of Fort George Peninsula • Not open to the public

At the tip of the Fort George Peninsula – an area that was once Fort George Island until the narrow strait was filled in 1924 – is the **Fort George Lighthouse**, which looms over the Belize Harbour. The lighthouse sits atop the tomb of and memorial to **Baron Bliss** (see box above), one of Belize's greatest benefactors. Though it isn't open to the public, the lighthouse rising against the Caribbean is wonderfully photogenic – bring the camera.

The Museum of Belize

Gabourel Lane, at the north end of Queen St • Mon–Thurs 8.30am–5pm, Fri 8.30am–4.30pm • Bz$10 • ☎ 223 4524, ⓦ nichbelize.org

Built in 1857 and housing prisoners until 1993, this former colonial prison was beautifully transformed and reopened as the **Museum of Belize** in 2002, the 21st anniversary of Belize's independence. Today, the elegantly proportioned, two-storey structure of sand-coloured brickwork, set in lawns and gardens, looks more like a country mansion than its former incarnation.

The lower floor, with plenty of exposed, original brick and bars on the windows, displays photographs and artefacts celebrating the history and the people of the city as it grew over the last 370 years. Here you can also peruse a complete collection of the country's stamps; the earliest one, depicting Queen Victoria, dates to 1837. The building's original role is not glossed over, either; there's an old jail door and small exhibit of before-and-after photos chronicling the structure's evolution.

The star attractions are upstairs, however, in the **Maya Masterpieces** gallery; a permanent, world-class collection of some of the best artefacts recovered from Belize's Maya sites. Well-lit glass cases display fine painted ceramics, including the striking Buenavista Vase discovered in Buenavista in Cayo, which depicts the mythical Hero Twins dancing in the costume of the young Maize Gods after having defeated the Lords of Death – the central theme of the Maya creation story, the Popol Vuh (see p.259). Other treasures include painstakingly formed **eccentric flints**, carved from a single piece of stone, and an exceptionally well-preserved wooden figurine, probably of a ruler, from a cave in Toledo District. Upstairs are the splendid **Jades of Belize**, the country's trove of jade discoveries including a replica of the famous jade head from Altun Ha, stunning mosaic masks, pendants, ear flares and necklaces. The museum also features one of the best-displayed collections of insects in Belize; bug-lovers won't want to miss it.

Temporary exhibits are also top-notch, and have covered everything from sports in Belize to "Communicating through Art: From Cave Paintings to Cartoons", which traced Belizean art history, from ancient times to the present.

1

THE SWING BRIDGE

Belize City's most recognizable landmark, the **Swing Bridge**, reflects the city's history. The first wooden bridge was built in the early 1800s, replacing a system in which cattle and other commodities were winched over the waterway that divides the city – hence the name **Haulover Creek**. Its next incarnation, the Liverpool-made Swing Bridge, opened in 1923 and is the only manually operated swing bridge left in the Americas. When in action, it's intriguing to watch: using long poles inserted into a capstan, four men lever the bridge until it's facing the harbour mouth, and then the boats sail through. Note that during the few minutes that the bridge is open, the creek traffic is busier than that on the roads, with the whole city jammed up. The bridge used to open twice daily, but these days, it does so less frequently, usually only when large boats are passing through or during special occasions when dignitaries are in town. Either way, it's worth stopping by for postcard views of Belize City from the bridge, with Haulover Creek bobbing with colourful fishing boats.

The south side

The **south side** is the older section of Belize City; in the early days, the elite lived in the seafront houses while the backstreets were home to their slaves and labourers. These days it's the city's commercial centre, with shops, banks and travel agencies. **Albert Street**, running south from the Swing Bridge, is the main retail thoroughfare, with banks, supermarkets and T-shirt and souvenir shops.

Regent Street

Parallel to Albert Street and a block closer to the sea, **Regent Street** also has multiple shops and vendors, as well as the former colonial administration and court buildings, known together as the **Courthouse**. These well-preserved examples of colonial architecture, with their columns and finely wrought iron, were completed in 1926 after an earlier building was destroyed by fire. The Courthouse overlooks a tree-lined square with an ornamental fountain in the centre, known as Central Park until it was renamed **Battlefield Park** in the early 1990s, commemorating the heated pre-independence political meetings that took place here.

Bliss Centre for the Performing Arts

Southern Foreshore, on the waterfront a block south of the Courthouse • **Visitor centre** Mon–Fri 8am–5pm; performances usually 6–9pm; check calendar for dates • ☎ 227 2110, ⓦ nichbelize.org

The handsome **Bliss Centre for the Performing Arts** is an epicentre of Belizean culture, hosting concerts and plays from around the country. Operated by the **Institute of Creative Arts** (ICA), the centre features a sleek, marble-lined entrance hall that opens onto a six-hundred-seat theatre. The ICA serves as a catalyst for the creative arts in Belize, supporting and promoting local dance, music, theatre, visual arts and creative writing while also working closely with the Ministry of Education to foster artistic training and education.

St John's Cathedral

Southern end of Albert St • Daily 6am–6pm • Free

St John's Cathedral is the oldest Anglican cathedral in Central America and one of the oldest buildings in Belize. Its construction lasted from 1812 to 1820 and used red bricks brought over as ballast in British ships. With its square, battlemented tower, it looks like a large English parish church. The main structure has survived almost two hundred years of tropical heat and hurricanes, though a fire in 2002 destroyed most of the roof, which was then fully restored. In the first half of the nineteenth century, several indigenous kings of the Mosquito Coast held their coronation ceremonies here.

Yarborough Cemetery

West of St John's Cathedral • Daily 6am–6pm • Free

Although the graves have fallen into disrepair, a browse among the stones at **Yarborough Cemetery** will turn up fascinating snippets of history. The cemetery was named after the magistrate who owned the land and permitted the burial of prominent people here from 1781; commoners were admitted only after 1870.

The House of Culture

Regent St, east of St John's Cathedral • Mon–Fri 8.30am–5pm • Bz$10 • ☎ 227 3050, ⓦ nichbelize.org

The colonial Government House, now restored and renamed the **House of Culture**, has a beautiful, breezy, seafront setting, shaded by royal palms and complete with an immaculate lawn. Built in 1814, it was the governor's residence when Belize was a British colony; at midnight on September 20, 1981, the Belize flag was hoisted here for the first time as the country celebrated independence.

The house has always been used for official receptions, particularly on Independence Day. But the present governor-general, Sir Colville Young, wanted to make this superb example of Belize's colonial heritage open to everyone, so in 1996 it was designated a

---

EMORY KING

Any sailor shipwrecked on a foreign shore would doubtless be grateful to the land that saved him, but only one who'd been unfathomably moved by the experience would want to spend the rest of his life there. That's exactly what happened to **Emory King** (1931–2007), American-born wit, raconteur, estate agent, historian, broadcaster, writer, businessman and film extra, when his schooner *Vagabond* crashed onto the coral off English Caye, British Honduras in 1953. Realizing that the colony presented unrivalled opportunities to a young man of limited means but boundless entrepreneurial spirit, he stayed on, intrigued by this colonial backwater.

Finding the **Belize City** of the early 1950s much like a nineteenth-century village, with only a handful of cars (which, to his astonishment, drove on the left), a sickly electric power system and a few telephones to represent the modern age, he set about trying to change it. Working first as Secretary of the Chamber of Commerce, then Secretary of the Tourist Committee (when tourists were counted in dozens), Emory advised foreign investors and found land for American farmers in search of the next frontier. His most enduring gift to his adopted country, however, was persuading the **Mennonites** (see box, p.71) to settle here in 1958; their back-breaking pioneer work is Belize's greatest agricultural success story.

Emory King's involvement in Belize led to cameo roles in all the Hollywood movies filmed here. In *The Mosquito Coast* (1985), based on the novel by Paul Theroux, he played a down-at-heel, drunken landowner offering to sell Harrison Ford a piece of land – a part he claimed was not typecasting. In 1998 the government appointed him **film commissioner**, and he soon secured the production of *After the Storm*, based on the Hemingway short story and filmed in Placencia and Ambergris Caye, followed by the "reality television" series *Temptation Island*, and the establishment of the **Belize Film Festival** (ⓦ belizefilmfestival.com).

King died in 2007, but his **books** about Belize live on, and are sold all over the country; a good one to start with is *Hey Dad, This is Belize*, a whimsical account of family life, followed by *I Spent it All in Belize* (which includes the highly astute line, "If you want to be a millionaire in Belize, you'd better come with two million"). His **website**, ⓦ emoryking.com, provides everything you need to know about the man – or at least everything that he was prepared to tell.

1

museum, later becoming the House of Culture. A flight of steps under a columned portico leads to the front door; inside, a plush, red carpet stretches down the hall to a great mahogany staircase, and beyond here doors open onto the back porch, overlooking the sea. On the grounds, the carefully restored *Sea King*, the tender of Baron Bliss's yacht of the same name, stands as testimony to the skill of Belizean boatbuilders. The plant-filled gardens are a haven for birds and it's worth bringing a pair of binoculars.

A wide range of Belizean arts are presented here, among them painting, dance, **Garifuna** drumming, musical performances and, in a room off the front porch, contemporary visual arts. It's also a popular venue for weddings and banquets. In the main room, a panoramic painting of Belize City in the early 1900s overlooks the collection of colonial silverware, glass and furniture, while a different room displays a fascinating compilation of vintage photographs and postcards of Belize.

Luba Garifuna

4042 Fern Lane • Mon–Fri 8am–5pm • Bz$5 • ☎ 202 4331, ⓦ nichbelize.org

Garifuna culture may have its roots in southern Belize, but the country's premiere – and first – Garifuna museum is in Belize City, founded by Garifuna expert Sebastian Cayetano. The **Luba Garifuna**'s humdrum residential exterior belies the well-curated Garifuna treasures inside, which includes traditional clothing and accessories, photographs, and colourful arts and crafts.

ARRIVAL AND DEPARTURE

BELIZE CITY

BY PLANE

Belize is served by two airports: Philip Goldson International Airport, 10.5 miles northwest of the city at Ladyville, just off the Philip Goldson Hwy; and Belize City Municipal Airport on the seafront, around 2 miles north of the city centre. Belize's domestic airlines, Tropic Air (see p.23) and Maya Island Air (see p.23) make stops at both; note that domestic flights from the Municipal Airport are usually around Bz$50–75 less than those from the International Airport. In general, no matter where you fly in the country, trips are short – usually 25min to 1hr, and rarely more than that. One-way prices start at around Bz$70–100; note that both airlines often offer seasonal deals and discounts. Many major US airlines fly into Belize, including American and Delta (see p.22).

Taxis From the International Airport, a taxi into town costs Bz$50; if you want to cut the cost, share with other travellers or walk to the Philip Goldson Hwy (25min) and flag down one of the frequent passing buses (Bz$2 to the centre). To get from the Municipal Airport into town, your only option is to take a taxi (around Bz$10).

Destinations Cancún, Mexico (1–2 daily; 1hr 30min); Flores, Guatemala (for Tikal; 2–4 daily; 45min); Honduras, including Roatan (1 daily; 1hr 45min) and San Pedro Sula (1 daily; 1hr); Punta Gorda (8–10 flights daily; 1hr), stopping on request at Dangriga (25min) and Placencia (45min); San Pedro and Caye Caulker (at least hourly, daily 7.30am–5pm; 25min).

BY BUS

Main bus terminal The city's main bus terminal is on West Collett Canal St, off Cemetery Rd, west of the city centre, in what was formerly Novelo's Bus Terminal (named after a now-defunct bus company). Nearly all inter-city buses leave from in or around here, plying the country's main highways: the George Price Hwy (Western Hwy), the Philip Goldson Hwy (Northern Hwy) and the Hummingbird and Southern highways. Note that the bus terminal is in a fairly rundown section of town; though it's only a mile from the Swing Bridge and you can easily walk, it's safest to take a taxi, particularly after dark. Transport peters out at dusk and there are no overnight buses. Within the terminal, it can all seem very disorganized – bus schedules are mostly handwritten and simply tacked to the walls. But though these can be hard to decipher, there's usually no need to do so – locals and bus drivers know the schedules well, and can fill you in. Note that there are dozens of bus companies, with names and ownership changing frequently. Note, too, that some buses, notably to Flores, Guatemala and south to Sarteneja and other cities in the north, depart from other street corners in the centre of the city (see p.54). Tickets are usually purchased on the bus; though there is no official bus terminal website, ⓦ belizebus.wordpress.com has helpful info on schedules.

Destinations Belmopan (every 15min; 1hr 15min; 5am–9pm); Benque Viejo, for the Guatemalan border (at least hourly; up to 3hr; 5am–9pm); Chetumal,

1

Mexico (10 daily; up to 3hr 30min; 5.30am– 7pm); Corozal (hourly; 2hr 30min; 5.30am–7pm); Dangriga via Belmopan (at least hourly; 3hr 30min; 6am–5pm); Hopkins via Dangriga (6 daily; 4hr; 7am–2pm); Maskall, for Altun Ha (Mon–Sat 3 daily; 1hr 30min); Orange Walk (hourly; 1hr 30min; 5am–7pm); Placencia via Dangriga (3–4 daily; 4–6hr; 7am–2pm); Punta Gorda via Dangriga and Mango Creek (8 daily; 5–7hr; 5.30am–3.30pm); San Ignacio via Belmopan (at least hourly; up to 2hr 30min; 5am–9pm).

Other bus stops From the Caye Caulker Water Terminal, buses depart to Flores, Guatemala (2 daily; 5hr) and Tikal (2–3 daily; 5hr). From Regent St, near the Swing Bridge, buses travel to Sarteneja via Orange Walk (2 daily; 3hr 30min).

BY BOAT

Water taxis Boats to Ambergris Caye are operated by the San Pedro Belize Express Water Taxi (☎ 223 2225, ⓦ belizewatertaxi.com), which departs from North Front St, near Tourism Village, and the Ocean Ferry Belize (☎ 223 0033, ⓦ oceanferrybelize.com), leaving from North Front St, near Swing Bridge. Both offer five to nine daily departures to Caye Caulker (45min) and San Pedro (1hr 30min). Boats operate 8am to 5pm; confirm schedules online or via phone. Prices range from Bz$24 to Bz$40 one way, and Bz$44 to Bz$70 return. Both will also stop at other cayes, like Long Caye and Caye Chapel, on request. For more info, see the northern cayes and atolls chapter (3). From either terminal, it's a short walk to the city centre and most hotels; otherwise, taxis are generally waiting for boats.

GETTING AROUND

On foot Although Belize City is by far the largest urban area in the country (the capital, Belmopan, is one tenth of its size), the city centre is compact enough to make walking the easiest way to get around. You can easily walk between most of the city's hotels and the city centre; after dark, though, it's best to travel by taxi (see box below).

By taxi Taxis, identified by green licence plates, cost Bz$8–10 for one or more passengers within the city; for other journeys, agree on the fare in advance. They wait for passengers at most of the main transport points, including both airports and the bus and water taxi terminals. Also, most hotels and restaurants will call a taxi for you.

By bus The city centre is easily walkable, so city buses don't cover the centre, but rather are used by locals to commute to outlying residential areas. Since there are no main sights in the residential areas, these buses are rarely if ever used by tourists.

Car rental Highly reputable Crystal (Mile 5 Philip Goldson Hwy ☎ 223 1600 or toll-free in Belize ☎ 0800 777 7777, ⓦ crystal-belize.com) has some of the best rental prices in the country, is one of the few outfits that allows you to take vehicles over the Guatemalan border and can provide mobile phones for use during your stay. Additionally, Belize City is the headquarters for most of the major global car rental agencies. Avis, Budget, Hertz and Thrifty (see p.25) all have offices at the international airport, as well as satellite offices in town; check websites for details.

SAFETY ON THE STREETS

You'll probably hear of Belize City's reputation long before you step foot in the city. Travellers and locals alike share stories of the city's abandoned, dangerous streets, crumbling buildings, prison-like grilles over windows and flourishing drug trade. Yes, this reputation may be deserved (and very evident) – but only in certain parts of the city. The northern half, in and around the upscale hotels, the cruise ship terminal and the Fort George area, is perfectly safe, both day and night, as are the busy central commercial strips of Regent and Albert streets. Note, though, that the area around Tourism Village can sometimes draw **pickpocketers** and the like, so keep an eye out. The area to avoid at night is the **south side**, which is south of Haulover Creek and around the Collett Canal. If you must pass through, it's advisable to take a taxi at all times.

All that said, no matter where you are in the city, it's always sensible to proceed with caution: most people are friendly, but quite a few may want to sell you drugs or ask for a dollar or two. The best advice is to stay cool and be civil; don't provoke trouble by arguing too forcefully and never bring out large wads of cash. The chances of being mugged increase **after dark** anywhere in the city.

The introduction of **tourism police** in the mid 1990s made an immediate impact on the level of hassle and this, coupled with the legal requirement for all tour guides to be licensed, has reduced street crime. The tourism police sport green "Tourist Unit" badges on their sleeves, and will even walk you back to your hotel if it's near their patrol route; their phone number is ☎ 227 6082.

BELIZE DISTRICT TOURS

1

One of the best ways to explore the Belize District – and further inland – is on a tour covering all the main sights, including Belize Zoo, Community Baboon Sanctuary, Crooked Tree Wildlife Sanctuary, Maya ruins at Altun Ha or Lamanai and more. Even though you can visit any of these independently, taking a tour is often just as competitively priced – and you get the bonus of expert guides with deep knowledge of Belizean culture and history. Note that many tour companies based elsewhere in Belize – such as on the cayes or in the south – will also include the Belize District on a tour on request. **Recommended tour companies** based in Belize City are the long-running S & L Travel and Tours (91 N Front St, 📞 227 7593, 🌐 sltravelbelize.com) and Dave's Eco Tours (123 Cemetery Rd, 📞 205 5597, 🌐 davesecotours.com).

INFORMATION AND TOURS

Belize Audubon Society 12 Fort St 📞 223 5004, 🌐 belizeaudubon.org. Headquarters of this premier conservation organization, with lots of information on Belize's natural wonders, plus a gift shop with books, maps and posters relating to the country's wildlife reserves. Mon–Fri 8am–5pm.

Belize Tourism Board (BTB) 64 Regent St 📞 223 1913, 🌐 travelbelize.org. The BTB office has lots of information about the city – and the rest of the country – including a hotel guide and city map, information on Maya sites and more. Mon–Thurs 8am–5pm.

Belize Tourism Industry Association (BTIA) 10 N Park St 📞 227 1144, 🌐 btia.org. This association represents most of the country's tourism businesses and publishes *Destination Belize*, a magazine filled with helpful information and hotel recommendations. Mon–Fri 8am–noon & 1–5pm.

Programme for Belize 1 Eyre St 📞 227 5616, 🌐 pfbelize.org. This long-established conservation organization manages the Río Bravo Conservation and Management Area (see p.77); stop by for information on access and volunteering at Río Bravo. Mon–Fri 8am–5pm.

ACCOMMODATION

Belize City has a wide range of **hotels**, from budget to high-end. Most of the more upmarket hotels are in and around the historic Fort George area north of the Swing Bridge, while the budget and mid-range digs are south of Haulover Creek. There's usually no need to book ahead as you'll almost always find something in the price range you're looking for. If you're looking for more intimate hotels and B&Bs – and don't mind being a couple of miles out of town – try the neighbourhood of Buttonwood Bay, off the Philip Goldson Hwy, where you'll find a few choice options.

Bakadeer Inn 74 Cleghorn St 📞 223 0659. Clean, simple rooms with a/c, ceiling fan, TV and private bath with tub. Take the usual precautions when walking this area after dark. Rates are excellent for three or four sharing. US$55

Belcove Hotel 9 Regent St W 📞 227 3054, 🌐 belcove.com. It's hard to get more central than this brightly painted hotel, right next to the creek with a view of the Swing Bridge. Basic but tidy rooms, some with a/c, private bath and TV; coffee is included. Tours are arranged, including to the hotel's private island at Gallows Point, on the reef, 9 miles from Belize City. If you are arriving at *Belcove* after dark, take a taxi, as this part of town can get slightly less salubrious at night. US$40

Bella Sombra Guest House 36 Hydes Lane 📞 223 0225, 🌐 lasbrisasdelmar.net. Outside, the neighbourhood can be a bit rough, especially after dark. Inside, this cheery spot is secure, with comfortable rooms with a/c and kitchenette. Plus, they can help arrange airport transfers, as well as tours to Altun Ha and other sights. US$49

Best Western Belize Biltmore Plaza Mile 3 Philip Goldson Hwy 📞 223 2302, 🌐 belizebiltmore.com. One of Belize City's bigger hotels is located just off the highway, but is decently insulated from the noise. Spacious a/c rooms surround a palm-filled courtyard. The *Victorian Room* restaurant serves seafood, steaks and a varied lunch menu, plus a brunch buffet on Sundays; a fine selection of Caribbean rums are poured at the *Biltmore Bar*, with live music on Thursday nights. Facilities also include a fitness centre. US$125

Coningsby Inn 76 Regent St 📞 227 1566. Decent but worn rooms with a/c and private bath in a relatively quiet part of the city centre, which can feel a bit sketchy at night. There's a balcony over the street and they also serve a hearty breakfast of scrambled eggs, sausages and fry-jacks for a fee (US$5–9). US$55

D'Nest Inn 475 Cedar St, Belama, 3 miles north of downtown 📞 223 5416, 🌐 dnestinn.com. Set in a quiet residential district, the cheery, two-storey house calls its rooms "nests". Each is individually decorated, some with four-poster beds and antique furniture; all have a/c and sparkling bathrooms. The garden flourishes with hibiscus,

1

orchids, white lilies and a splashing bird bath, and there's a mangrove-lined canal nearby. A tasty breakfast is included. Best if you have your own transport, though a taxi is only Bz$10 into town. US$95

Easy Inn Mile 2 Philip Goldson Hwy ☎ 223 0380, ⓦ easyinnbz.com. You can't overlook this squat inn that's painted in blazing orange. Inside, it's less colourful, but the minimalist rooms are well maintained, as are the clean bathrooms. US$62

★**The Great House** 13 Cork St, Fort George ☎ 223 3400, ⓦ greathousebelize.com. From the setting to the staff to the rum cocktails at the on-site *Smoky Mermaid* (see opposite), this is one of the best places to stay in Belize City. The modernized, four-storey wooden building – painted all white – dates from 1927, and lies just 100yd from the sea. The spacious a/c rooms all have private bath, TV and hardwood floors; some have a balcony. Breakfast included. US$160

Radisson Fort George Hotel 2 Marine Parade, Fort George ☎ 223 3333, ⓦ radisson.com/belizecitybz. The city's flagship hotel is well managed and enviably located on the seafront. All rooms have a big TV, fridge and minibar, and most have sea views; ask if a Club Tower room is available – these have the finest vistas of the Caribbean Sea. Pamper yourself at the spa, with everything from aromatherapy massages to mango facials. Plus, there's a business centre, several good restaurants and the cosy *Le Petit Café* (see opposite). US$175

Villa Boscardi 6043 Manatee Drive, 2 miles north of downtown off the Philip Goldson Hwy ☎ 223 1691, ⓦ villaboscardi.com. A definite cut above the average Belize accommodation. Set in a quiet residential neighbourhood, this deluxe B&B with a lush garden features uniquely decorated rooms with private bath, a/c and TV. Wake up to a hearty complimentary breakfast, with fresh fruits and homebrewed coffee. Gracious owner Françoise can help plan tour itineraries and activities for every budget. US$90

EATING

Belize City offers a wide variety of cuisine, from excellent seafood to the humble but tasty **Creole** fare of rice and beans. Like elsewhere in the country, you'll find a preponderance of Chinese restaurants, which are wildly popular with Belizeans, particularly as cheap takeaway. For a change of pace, dine out at one of the **Lebanese** and **Indian** restaurants, which offer wonderfully authentic cuisine from the home country. Amazingly – and refreshingly – no major US-based fast food chains have made major inroads into Belize (that's right – no *McDonald*'s or *Starbucks*). Popular instead are street-side stands that sell hot, filling meat pies for less than a Belizean buck and makeshift outdoor barbecues, usually on Saturdays, in and around the town centre, where you can eat chicken (Bz$7–10) along with side dishes of tortillas, rice and beans, potato salad and the like. Note that most of the established hotels have their own quality restaurants. Also, keep in mind that Belize City is generally an early-to-bed town. Most restaurants stop serving dinner by 9pm, if not earlier.

Bird's Isle Restaurant 90 Albert St ☎ 207 2179. Relax under a thatched roof by the sea and enjoy Belizean food (Bz$15–30), like grilled snapper and stewed chicken. It's a friendly, community-oriented place, with great tropical cocktails – try the piña colada – and lively karaoke on Thursday nights. Hours vary, but generally Mon–Sat 11am–2.30pm & 5–10pm.

Celebrity Restaurant Marine Parade, behind the Central Bank ☎ 223 7272, ⓦ celebritybelize.com. Feast on top-notch international cuisine (Bz$25–40) – T-bone steaks, beef quesadillas, conch *ceviche*, burgers and linguine tossed with fresh shrimp – at this bright, airy, plush restaurant. You can catch glimpses of the Caribbean Sea out of the window. Plus, they offer one of Belize City's better selections of wine. Daily 11am–11pm.

Chon Saan Palace 1 Kelly St, near Cinderella Plaza ☎ 223 3008. Indisputably Belize City's best Chinese – and beloved by locals – in a large dining room. The huge and varied menu (Bz$20–30) includes sweet and sour chicken, salmon sushi and superb Beijing duck, plus dim sum. Mon–Sat 11am–3pm & 5–11.30pm, Sun 5–11pm.

Ma Ma Chen 7 Eve St ☎ 223 4568. This no-frills but comfortable family Chinese restaurant has one of the most extensive vegetarian menus in town, including dumpling soup and tasty spring rolls stuffed with vegetables and tofu. Mains Bz$13–25. Mon–Sat 10am–5pm.

Marlin's Restaurant and Bar 11 Regent St W ☎ 227 6995. Tasty, large portions of inexpensive Belizean and Mexican-influenced dishes – *escabeche*, grilled catch of the day – served indoors or on the veranda. Filling breakfasts. Hours vary, but generally Mon–Sat 7am–9pm.

★**Nerie's Restaurant** 12 Douglas Jones St ☎ 223 4028. This inviting restaurant serves excellent Belizean cuisine in a clean, well-run dining room. This is the place to get adventurous – start off with stewed cow foot soup, and then try the *gibnut* (also called "paca" – a flavourful, meaty nocturnal rodent) with rice and beans. Also tasty are the beef fajitas, whole snapper and cassava pudding for dessert. Mains Bz$11–23. *Nerie's II* at Queen St and Daly St (daily 7.30am–10pm) has a similarly good menu and prices. Mon–Sat 7am–5.30pm.

Pepper's Pizza 4 St Thomas St ☎ 223 5000. If you're in the mood for a slice, this long-established pizzeria delivers (literally – it does takeaway). Try the cheese pizza with peppers. Bz$15–30. Mon–Thurs 10am–10pm, Fri & Sat 10am–11pm, Sun 10am–9pm.

1

Le Petit Café Near the Radisson, Cork St ☎ 223 3333. Enjoy good coffee and fresh, warm-from-the-oven baked treats, including ham-and-cheese croissants and cinnamon buns, in a pleasant café atmosphere with outdoor tables. Daily 6am–8pm.

Riverside Tavern 2 Mapp St ☎ 223 5640. A four-sided bar, with bottles lining backlit shelves, stands in the centre of this high-end tavern on the riverbank. Fill up on seafood *ceviche* and excellent juicy burgers at wooden tables or on the breezy outdoor deck. Mains Bz$20–35. This is also a great place to kick off the night (see p.58). Daily 11am–10pm.

Sahara Grill Mile 3 Philip Goldson Hwy, across from Best Western Belize Biltmore Plaza ☎ 202 3031. For a refreshing change from Belizean cuisine, stop by this well-run restaurant to feast on Lebanese and other Mediterranean dishes, including creamy hummus, falafel, grilled kebabs and stuffed grape leaves. Mains Bz$15–30. Hours vary, but usually Mon–Sat 11am–3pm & 5–10pm, Sun 5–10pm.

★ Smoky Mermaid In The Great House, 13 Cork St ☎ 223 4759, ☻ smokymermaid.com. One of the best spots in Belize City for alfresco seafood. Sit amid the gnarled roots and heavy branches of native trees – alongside a mermaid fountain – with the colonial *Great House* looming behind. Try the *ceviche* and fresh shrimp

with cashew pesto. Start off the evening at the nightly happy "hour" (3–7pm), with rum cocktails (Bz$5). Mains Bz$14–20. Daily 6.30am–10pm.

Spoonaz Photo Café & Bar 89 N Front St ☎ 223 1043. This inviting café – an easy stroll to the ferry docks – offers a top-notch changing menu, including cappuccinos and fry-jacks with refried beans, scrambled eggs and sausage links, quiche, curry lobster over white rice and dense brownies. Tropical cocktails are served on the deck. Mains Bz$10–20. Mon–Thurs 7am–6pm, Fri–Sat 7am–8pm, Sun 7am–3.30pm.

Stonegrill In the Radisson, Cork St ☎ 223 3333. Poolside restaurant where you select your dish – seafood, chicken or beef, kebab-style (Bz$40 upwards) – and cook it yourself on a slab of heated volcanic rock. Get the tasty nachos to start. Daily 11am–10pm.

Sugarfix Bakery 8 Huesner Crescent ☎ 223 7640. This is the place to get your sugar fix, with fresh goods baked daily, including butter croissants (try the gooey chocolate croissants – Bz$3.25), ham-and-cheese Johnny cakes (Bz$2) and the best cheesecakes in Belize City (Bz$7.50). Mon–Fri 6.45am–7pm, Sat 6.45am–3pm.

Sumathi 190 Barrack Rd ☎ 223 1172. Good North Indian and tandoori food (Bz$20–40) in a quiet spot. Dishes include lamb vindaloo, shrimp masala and vegetarian choices like chickpea curry. Tues–Sun 11am–11pm.

DRINKING

While Belize City's nightlife pales in comparison with the easy-living bars of the cayes, there is a decent variety, from outdoor bars with fruit cocktails to lively karaoke nights. The more sophisticated bars are in the higher-end hotels, like the *Smoky Mermaid*, in the patio beneath *The Great House*, where you can enjoy drinks amid tropical foliage. The liveliest strip in the city is the relatively safe stretch of Barrack Road around BTL Park. At weekends, the pavements fill with a youngish, local crowd traipsing from one nightspot to the next.

Hour Bar & Grill 162 Barrack Rd ☎ 223 3737. Enjoy cocktails with spot-on views of the Caribbean Sea at this breezy waterfront bar and grill. In between drinks, fill up on burgers, pulled pork and nachos. Daily 11am–11pm, though sometimes closes earlier during the week.

Princess Hotel and Casino Barrack Rd ☎ 223 2670, ☻ princessbelize.com. This massive hotel and casino looms over the waterfront, and offers one-stop-shopping entertainment – under one roof you'll find a flashy casino (daily noon–4am) where you don't have to be a high roller

YO HO HO AND A BARREL OF RUM

Rich and dark, with a hint of molasses and tropical fruit, **Travellers One Barrel** is the finest **rum** in Belize. History has a lot to do with it: Travellers Liquors is Belize's oldest rum distillery, originally launched as a bar in 1953 by Jaime Omario Perdomo Senior and given the name "Travellers" because its customers were always en route to somewhere else. Since the 1970s, it's been run by Don Omario's sons and continues to flourish; for an overview of the rum's history (and, more importantly, a tasting), head to the **distillery** (Mile 2.5 Philip Goldson Hwy; Mon–Fri 8am–5pm, or by special appointment for tours; Bz$2; ☎ 223 2855, ☻ onebarrelrum .com), where you can peruse displays of old photos, vintage rum bottles and storytelling dioramas, as well as views of the bottling factory. The tour also includes tastings of the famous One Barrel rum, along with white and flavoured rums. If the tasting's not enough, head to the adjoining raised wooden **bar** (usually Mon–Fri noon–9pm, but hours vary so check upon arrival), a lively spot where the rum flows freely, as do the Caribbean sounds.

1

THE IMAGE FACTORY

For more than two decades, contemporary Belizean art has been synonymous with an iconic institute: **The Image Factory**. Founded in 1995, the non-profit Image Factory Foundation (91 N Front St ☎610 5072, ⓦimagefactory.bz; Mon–Fri 9am–5pm, or by appointment) is dedicated to promoting and exhibiting local art, collaborating with Belizean artists and organizations. For a superb overview of the contemporary arts scene, stop in to the Image Factory headquarters, which is a hybrid gallery – exhibits range from paintings to photography – store, archive and performance space. You may even get the chance to meet the artists themselves, particularly during the opening of a show. The Image Factory Foundation also publishes a Belizean arts magazine, *BAFFU* (ⓦkprensa.com) named after the Kriol phrase "baffu ah cahn gamma", which translates as: trying to accomplish something, but not getting it done – a reflection of the continual creative evolution of artists.

to try your luck at blackjack, poker and roulette. The casino features nightly entertainment, from local bands to scantily clad dancers. For cocktails and club music, head to the *Vogue Bar and Lounge*, with a daily happy hour (6–8pm). Hours vary, but usually Mon–Wed & Sun noon–midnight, Thurs–Sat noon–2am.

★ **Riverside Tavern** 2 Mapp St ☎223 5640. The classiest nightspot in this part of town swells with a lively crowd of Belizeans and foreigners. Dark-wood-and-brass interior and a spacious outdoor deck are matched by an extensive cocktail menu. Daily 11am–10pm.

Thirsty Thursdays Restaurant & Bar 164 Barrack Rd ☎223 1677. Lively bar on the strip, with plenty of drink specials and fun events, from beer buckets to karaoke. Wed–Thurs 5pm–midnight, Fri–Sat 5pm–2am.

SHOPPING

Albert and Regent streets, south of the Swing Bridge, form the shopping centre of Belize City, with everything from discount shoe stores to the city's largest supermarket and department store, *Brodies*. Belize City also has a variety of souvenir shops, including the *Belizean Handicraft Market Place*, next to Memorial Park, and the makeshift stalls just outside the Tourism Village (see p.48), where locals sell regional crafts.

Angelus Press 10 Queen St ☎223 5777. This long-established bookshop features a wide range of books on Belize, including maps and guides, along with office supplies. Mon–Fri 7.30am–5.30pm, Sat 8am–noon.

Belizean Handicraft Market Place Memorial Park ☎223 3627. For local souvenirs, stop by this market, which is filled with Belizean hardwood crafts, including bowls, picture frames and chopping boards, as well as Maya basketry and hot sauces and spices. Hours vary, but generally Mon–Sat 9am–5pm.

Brodies Albert St & Regent St ☎227 7070, ⓦbrodiesbelize.com. This massive grocery and department store in the heart of town sells everything from clothing and outdoor equipment to canned goods and liquor. In fact, this is a good spot to pick up souvenir bottles of local rum at reasonable prices. There's also an on-site pharmacy. There's another outlet at Mile 2.5 Philip Goldson Hwy. Mon–Thurs 8.30am–7pm, Fri 8.30am–8pm, Sat 8.30am–9pm.

Travellers Liquors Ltd Mile 2.5 Philip Goldson Hwy ☎223 2855, ⓦonebarrelrum.com. Stocks a wide range of liquors, including the signature Travellers One Barrel Rum as well as cashew wines and more, all at decent prices. Mon–Fri 9am–5pm.

DIRECTORY

Banks and exchange Most banks, including First Caribbean International Bank and Scotiabank, are in the city centre, on and around Albert St; all have ATMs that accept foreign-issued cards and can process cash advances over the counter.

Medical care The Karl Heusner Memorial Hospital (Princess Margaret Drive, near Philip Goldson Hwy ☎223 1548, ⓦkhmh.bz) is the principal hospital of the Belizean health service. It has most medical specialities and a 24hr accident and emergency department. For quick but expensive medical care, head to the private hospital, Belize Medical Associates (5791 St Thomas St ☎223 0302, ⓦbelizemedical.com), with all the main specialities and 24hr emergency room.

Pharmacy *Brodies* (see above) has a well-stocked pharmacy.

Police The main police station is on Queen St, a block north of the Swing Bridge (☎227 2210). For emergencies, dial ☎90 or 911 nationwide. Alternatively, contact the tourism police (see box, p.54).

Post office The main post office is on N Front St, northeast of the Swing Bridge (Mon–Fri 8am–4.30pm).

Belize District

The Belize District has countless options for day-trips from the city, no matter which direction you go – west, north and south. Along the **George Price Highway** (formerly the Western Highway), you'll find the world-renowned **Belize Zoo**, the **Monkey Bay Wildlife Sanctuary** and more. A journey north on the **Philip Goldson Highway** (formerly the Northern Highway) brings you to a richly diverse array of wildlife reserves and Maya history, including the **Community Baboon Sanctuary**, home to black howler monkeys, and the organic farm, the **Spanish Creek Rainforest Reserve**; the fascinating Maya site of **Altun Ha**; and the **Crooked Tree Wildlife Sanctuary**, with some of the best birding in the country. Along the **Coastal Road**, which runs for around 35 miles from La Democracia to Dangriga, is tiny **Gales Point**, surrounded by richly diverse wetlands.

Old Belize

Mile 5 George Price Hwy • **Museum and beach** Mon & Sun 10am–4pm, Tues–Sat 8am–4pm • **Restaurant** Daily 11am–10pm • Museum Bz$10, beach Bz$30, zip line Bz$40 • ☎ 222 4129, ⓦ oldbelize.com

As you leave the city, you first pass through the Lord's Ridge cemetery, then skirt the coastline, running behind a tangle of mangrove swamps and on to **Old Belize**, a museum showcasing the history and cultures of the country. Old Belize was created as an interactive cultural overview of the country, targeted towards time-pressed cruise ship passengers with half a day or so to spend in port. The museum holds some interest, but it's the adjoining open-air **restaurant** and man-made beach with water slide and zip line that has given the place its staying power on the tourist circuit. That said, if you have anything more than a day in the Belize District, it's worth going further afield to see the real deal – like a Maya site or the Belize Zoo.

The museum features videos on the country's varied ethnic groups and natural riches and a series of rooms that each highlight a different era in the country's history. The humid **rainforest room** contains a waterfall and a cage of fluttering blue morpho butterflies, while a dimly lit **Maya village** is populated with life-sized stone carvings and a replica wood-and-thatch home. Early industry also features, with a steam-powered sugar mill, and *chicle* (the base ingredient of chewing gum) trade and logging. Old Belize is also good for one-stop **souvenir shopping**, with reasonably priced wooden products, local hot sauces and books on Belize. The restaurant's name, *TGI Crazy Gringo*, gives a good indication of its angle: it's more about tropical cocktails than authentic cuisine – burgers, nachos and chicken fingers figure prominently on the menu – but it's fun for an hour or so.

Cucumber Beach and Marina

Though fairly small and fashioned out of reclaimed land, **Cucumber Beach** is well groomed and faces the lagoon, with lots of water activities that are especially a hit with youngsters and families. A huge waterslide, rising up 50ft from the beach, elicits squeals of delight, as does the zip line that traverses the lagoon. Also here is the **Cucumber Beach Marina**, which draws both recreational and commercial boats.

Belize Zoo

Mile 29 George Price Hwy • Daily 8.30am–5pm, last admission at 4.15pm; nocturnal tours (included in entry free) daily 6pm • Bz$30 adult, Bz$10 child • ☎ 220 8004, ⓦ belizezoo.org • Most Belmopan-bound buses from Belize City can drop you off outside the zoo

One of the finest zoos in the Americas south of the US, and long recognized as a phenomenal conservation achievement, the **Belize Zoo** opened in 1983 after an ambitious wildlife film (*Path of the Rain God*) left Sharon Matola, the film's production assistant, with a collection of semi-tame animals no longer able to fend for themselves in the wild. This now means the chance to see the native animals of Belize at close quarters, housed in spacious enclosures that resemble their natural habitats. The zoo's

1

menagerie has never been supplemented by animals taken from the wild – all are either donated or confiscated pets, injured wild animals, sent from other zoos (for its internationally recognized captive breeding programmes) or residents since birth. And, unless you're a seasoned wildlife photographer, this is likely to be the best place to get close-up photographs of the animals of Belize.

Exploring the zoo

The zoo's trail is arranged as "a walk through Belize", taking you to the pine ridge, the forest edge, the rainforest, lagoons and the river forest; hand-painted signs identify what you're seeing. Along the way you'll spy a **Baird's tapir** (known locally as a "mountain cow") and all the Belizean cats – and then some – including **jaguars**. Numerous aviaries house vividly coloured **scarlet macaws**, toucans, parrots, jabiru storks, a spectacled owl and several vultures and hawks, though Panamá, a magnificent **harpy eagle** (named for his home country), is best-known for his role in an ambitious breeding programme crucial to the reintroduction of the eagle to Belize. Other inhabitants include deer, spider and howler monkeys, peccaries, agoutis, numerous snakes and the two species of **crocodile** found in Belize. For a wonderfully unique experience, take the 6pm **nocturnal tour** (included in zoo entry), when you'll often see more animals than during the day, since many are nocturnal. If you do this tour, it's recommended you stay the night at the *Belize Zoo Jungle Lodge* or the *Belize Savanna Guest House* (see below).

The **gift shop** is well worth a browse, with a huge range of souvenirs, including popular children's books with a strong conservation message written by Sharon, the zoo's founder. All proceeds go to the zoo. The zoo also operates an Adopt an Animal programme, where your funds will contribute to the maintenance and wellbeing of a particular species. Check the zoo website for information.

ACCOMMODATION   BELIZE ZOO

Belize Zoo Jungle Lodge/Tropical Education Center Across the highway from the Belize Zoo ☎822 8000, ⓦbelizezoo.org. This well-appointed facility has a variety of accommodation set on 84 acres of pine savannah, including dormitories with shared bath, geared towards student groups. The facility also encompasses a classroom, library and kitchen and dining areas, and has an elevated bird deck, for excellent birdwatching, and self-guided nature trails. Additionally, there are forest *cabañas* on raised platforms, with shared bath. All rates include breakfast and dinner. Dorms US$30, *cabañas* US$70

Savanna Guest House Mile 28.5 George Price Hwy, just before the Belize Zoo ☎822 8005 ⓦbelizesavannaguesthouse.com. Run by Richard and Carol Foster, well-known naturalists and documentary filmmakers, this comfortable guesthouse has elegantly rustic rooms with hardwood floors; rates include a continental breakfast. US$60

Monkey Bay Wildlife Sanctuary

Mile 31.5 George Price Hwy • Open daily during daylight hours • Free, though there are also tours offered (from Bz$50) • ☎822 8032, ⓦmonkeybaybelize.com • Most non-express buses travelling between Belize City and Belmopan will drop you at the sanctuary turn-off, a 5min walk to the entrance.

Explore the Belizean wilderness while learning how to preserve it at the long-running **Monkey Bay Wildlife Sanctuary**, a nature reserve and education centre that unfolds between the George Price Highway and the **Sibun River**. The "bay" part of the name comes from a beautiful swimming spot by a sandy beach on the river, overhung with trees once inhabited by howler and spider monkeys; the monkeys are slowly returning after a long absence following hurricane disturbance, while the river watershed also supports abundant birdlife, jaguars, tapirs and Morelet's crocodiles. The eighteen-square-mile sanctuary offers a superb range of outdoor activities, including hiking, canoeing, caving and birding, all of which can be arranged upon arrival at the sanctuary.

The sanctuary headquarters comprises a wooden **field research station**, serving as library, museum and classroom, as well as a screened dining room – offering great local cuisine – and bunkhouses. Although the sanctuary specializes in hosting

1

academic programmes in natural history and watershed ecology, the sanctuary is open to independent visitors and is a wonderfully relaxing **place to stay** for a day or two (see below).

Monkey Bay is also the contact point for visits to **Cox Lagoon Crocodile Sanctuary**, a 70-square-mile private wetland reserve north of the highway in the Mussel Creek watershed. Home to over one hundred Morelet's crocodiles, it also hosts numerous other reptiles, jabiru storks, howler monkeys and jaguars. Visitors can camp, canoe, hike and fish, and all trips can be arranged with the Monkey Bay staff.

ACCOMMODATION AND EATING — MONKEY BAY WILDLIFE SANCTUARY

Cheers Mile 31.25 George Price Hwy ☎ 822 8014, ⓦ cheersrestaurantbelize.com. This breezy restaurant serves a varied menu, from hearty breakfasts to quesadillas to grilled chicken with rice and beans (mains Bz$10–20). It's a perfect spot to refuel while trundling down the highway, and if you'd like to take a longer rest, consider staying in one of the well-kept *cabañas*. Mon–Sat 6am–8.30pm, Sun 7am–7.30pm. US$65

Monkey Bay Wildlife Sanctuary Mile 31.5 George Price Hwy ☎ 822 8032, ⓦ belizestudyabroad.net. The sanctuary offers varied accommodation, including camping on raised platforms under thatched roofs, dorms, private rooms and a spacious mountain-view cabin. The field station is also a viable exponent of sustainable living, utilizing solar and wind power and rainwater catchment. Delicious, healthy food is served on request, some of it grown in the station's organic gardens; note that they also have excellent vegetarian and vegan options. Camping US$9, dorms US$20, doubles US$30, cabin US$50

Burrell Boom and around

The tiny, historical community of **BURRELL BOOM**, on the Belize River, is about 20 miles northwest of Belize City, and is reached down the Philip Goldson turn-off to Bermudian Landing. In logging days, a huge, heavy, metal chain called a "boom" was stretched across the river to catch the logs floating down. Burrell Boom is a pleasant base for exploring the area, and the river is never far from view. The primary sight is the nearby Community Baboon Sanctuary.

The Community Baboon Sanctuary

Near Bermudian Landing, 7 miles west of Burrell Boom • Visitor centre daily 8am–5pm • Bz$10 (includes guided trail walk) • ☎ 220 2181, ⓦ belizehowlermonkeys.org

The **Community Baboon Sanctuary**, established in 1985 by primate biologist Rob Horwich and a group of local farmers (with help from the Worldwide Fund for Nature), is one of the most interesting conservation projects in Belize. A mixture of farmland and broadleaf forest, the sanctuary stretches along nineteen miles of the Belize River valley – from Flowers Bank to Big Falls – and comprises a total of eight villages and over 250 landowners. Farmers here voluntarily harmonize their own needs with those of the wildlife in a project combining conservation, education and tourism; visitors are welcome and you'll find plenty of places to rent canoes or horses. The tiny **visitor centre**, in the middle of the sanctuary, features exhibits and information on the riverside habitats and animals, and a library.

The main focus is the **black howler monkey** (locally known as a "baboon"), the largest monkey in the New World and an endangered subspecies of howler that exists only in Belize, Guatemala and southern Mexico. They generally live in troops of between four and eight, and spend the day clambering through the leafy canopy, feasting on leaves, flowers and fruits. You're pretty much guaranteed to see them up close, feeding and resting in the trees along the riverbank, and they're often as interested in you as you are in them. At dawn and dusk they let rip with their famous howl, a deep and rasping roar that carries for miles.

The sanctuary is also home to around two hundred **bird** species, plus anteaters, deer, peccaries, coatis, iguanas and the endangered Central American river turtle. Special trails are cut through the forest so that visitors can see it at its best; you can wander

1

these alone or with a guide. Plus, they offer a range of other tours, including night hikes, crocodile-spotting and birding.

Spanish Creek Rainforest Reserve and Belize Bamboo

Near Rancho Dolores village, west of Community Baboon Sanctuary • Entry by appointment only • ☎ 622 3184, ⓦ belizebamboo.com

The 2000-acre **Spanish Creek Rainforest Reserve**, which unfolds on the lush banks of Spanish Creek, is filled with tropical vegetation and native hardwoods. The farm is home to **Belize Bamboo**, a small company that grows sustainably harvested, non-invasive bamboo on the property, and produces handcrafted bamboo furniture. The reserve and Belize Bamboo offer volunteer opportunities, where you can work with local farmers to learn about sustainable farming and agroforestry. Volunteering is for a minimum of four weeks, and includes lodging in breezy *palapas*, fresh, locally sourced meals and Spanish language immersion.

ARRIVAL AND DEPARTURE	BURRELL BOOM AND AROUND
By bus Burrell Boom is served by 4–5 daily buses from Belize City (Mon–Sat; 1hr 10min).	Community Baboon Sanctuary, including S & L Tours (see p.55). Also, *Black Orchid Resort* (see below) and *Maruba Resort Jungle Spa* (see p.63) can arrange trips here.
By tour Numerous tour companies offer trips to the	

ACCOMMODATION AND EATING

★**Black Orchid Resort** 2 Dawson Lane ☎ 225 9158, ⓦ blackorchidresort.com. This lovely resort maximizes its perch on the river, with leafy grounds that gently roll down to the water. The restaurant and patio bar have riverfront views and serve a menu of Belizean specialities. A pool presides over the centre of the resort and a rooftop jacuzzi and spa invites soaking and pampering. Spacious rooms are outfitted in native hardwoods and have well-appointed bathrooms. Transfer to and from the airport is included. U̲S̲$̲1̲8̲0̲

Altun Ha

Daily 8am–5pm • Bz$10

Thirty-four miles north of Belize City, and just six miles from the sea, is the impressive Maya site of **Altun Ha**. With a peak population of about ten thousand, it was occupied for around twelve hundred years until the Classic Maya collapse between 900 and 950 AD. The site was also inhabited at various times during the Postclassic period, though no new

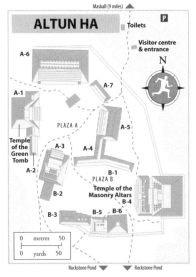

monumental building took place during this time. Its position close to the Caribbean coast suggests that it was sustained by trade as much as by agriculture – a theory upheld by the discovery of trade objects such as jade and obsidian, neither of which occurs naturally in Belize; both are very important in Maya ceremonies. The jade would have come from the Motagua valley in Guatemala, and would probably have been shipped onwards to the north.

Plaza A

Around five hundred buildings have been recorded at Altun Ha, but the core of the site is clustered around two Classic-period plazas, with the main structures extensively restored, exposing fine stonework with rounded corners. Entering from the road, you come first to **Plaza A**. Large temples enclose it on all four sides, and a

INDULGING IN THE JUNGLE

It's all in the mud. Plumbed from the earth and brimming with minerals, this is the kind of rich goop that you'll happily smear on your body parts, then submit to its rejuvenating tingle while reclining in a breezy *cabaña*, eyes closed against the warm sun. **Maruba Resort Jungle Spa** (Mile 40½ Old Northern Hwy; ☎225 5555, ⓦmaruba-spa.com; US$220) sits amid wild tropical foliage, near the tiny community of Maskall, around 13 miles north of Altun Ha. The couples-friendly resort offers pampering with a primal edge: retreat into a palm-shaded hideaway for the signature "mood mud" body scrub rooted in ancient Maya customs, and then zone out to the low thrum of piped-in drumbeats. Rooms and suites – like the "fertility suite" – are rustic-deluxe: gleaming mahogany ceilings, billowing silks, feather beds and wafting incense, along with mosaic-tiled bathrooms. The thatched restaurant and patio is surrounded by palms and bougainvillea and serves excellent Belizean and international cuisine. What sets the *Maruba* apart from the usual high-end resort are the quirky touches: a carved penis for a toilet-paper holder in a lobby bathroom; rough-hewn walls studded with glass bottles of Belikin beer and Fanta; and palm fronds as placemats. Little goes to waste at this largely self-sustaining resort, so not only will you emerge with your pores clean and glowing, but your conscience too.

magnificent tomb has been discovered beneath Temple A-1, **The Temple of the Green Tomb**. Dating from 550 AD, this yielded a total of three hundred artefacts, including jade, jewellery, stingray spines, jaguar skins, flints and the remains of a Maya book.

Plaza B

The adjacent **Plaza B** is dominated by the site's largest temple, B-4, **The Temple of the Masonry Altars**, the last in a sequence of buildings occupying this spot over the centuries. If its exterior seems familiar, it's because you might already have seen it on the Belikin beer label. Several priestly tombs have been uncovered within the main structure, but most of them had already been desecrated, possibly during the political turmoil that preceded the abandonment of the site. Only two of the tombs were found intact; in 1968 archeologists discovered a carved jade head of **Kinich Ahau**, the Maya sun god, in one of them. Standing just under six inches high, it is the largest carved jade found anywhere in the Maya world. At the moment it's hidden away in the vaults of the Belize Bank, though there is a splendid replica in the Museum of Belize in Belize City (see p.49).

ARRIVAL AND DEPARTURE **ALTUN HA**

By organized tour All travel agents and most tour companies (see p.55) in and around Belize City will arrange tours, and increasing numbers of visitors come on day-trips from San Pedro.

By bus Altun Ha is difficult to reach independently, as the track to the site is located along the Old Northern Hwy and is not well served by buses. In theory there are buses from the terminal in Belize City to the village of Maskall, passing the 1.8-mile side road to the site from Lucky Strike, but service is erratic and unreliable.

Crooked Tree Wildlife Sanctuary

Off the Philip Goldson Hwy roughly midway between Belize City and Orange Walk • Visitor centre Mon–Sat 8am–4.30pm • Bz$8

The 5-square-mile **Crooked Tree Wildlife Sanctuary** encompasses inland waterways, logwood swamps and four separate lagoons. It's an ideal nesting and resting place for the sanctuary's greatest treasure: tens of thousands of migrating and resident **birds**, including snail kites, tiger herons, snowy egrets, ospreys and black-collared hawks. Representatives of over three hundred bird species (two-thirds of Belize's total) have been recorded here.

The reserve's most famous visitor is the **jabiru stork**, the largest flying bird in the New World, with a wingspan of 8ft. Belize has the biggest nesting population of jabiru storks at one site; they arrive in November, the young hatch in April or May, and they leave just before the summer rainy season gets under way. The best time to visit is from late February to early June, when the lagoons shrink to a string of pools, forcing wildlife to congregate for food and water.

1

A TOAST TO CASHEW WINE

As a Belizean saying goes, cashew wine gives you a double buzz – once when you drink it and again the next day in the sun. The best time to test this out is at the annual Crooked Tree **Cashew Festival**, when the village celebrates the famous nut with music, dance, storytelling, crafts and tastings of cashew jams, fudges, cakes, wines and more. Crooked Tree is known for its cashew trees, some over a hundred years old, which flourish in the village's rich soil. In January and February the air is heavy with the scent of cashew blossoms, and in the spring the cashew fruits are harvested. The cashew nut is actually the seed of the cashew fruit, and the wine is made by crushing the fruits to extract the juice, and then distilling and fermenting it, often in copper pots, for three days. The result is a nutty and sweet wine, which tastes almost like a light sherry, with an alcohol content of between six and twelve percent. Cashew wine is served throughout Belize, at bars and restaurants, and you can also pick up a bottle (or five) to take home at liquor stores, supermarkets and at the Travellers distillery just outside Belize City (see p.58).

In the middle of the sanctuary is the tiny village of **Crooked Tree** itself, which straggles over a low island in the wetlands. Dating back to the early 18th century, it's the oldest inland community in Belize, with an economy based on fishing, farming and, more recently, tourism. The village serves as the main entry and information point for the sanctuary. The visitor centre here has a range of information, including diorama displays with lifelike models of the birds, mammals and insects found at the sanctuary. Here you can also ask about guided **boat tours** (see below), easily one of the best ways to tour the sanctuary, which travel on the lagoons and along sluggish, forest-lined creeks. Some boat tours make a stop at **Chau Hiix** ("small cat"), a Maya site on the western shore of the lagoon. You can also explore the sanctuary on your own; stroll down the sandy, tree-lined lanes and along the lakeshore trails, and you'll spot plenty of birds and turtles, and hear frogs croaking languidly from the shallows.

ARRIVAL, INFORMATION AND TOURS

By bus A couple of daily buses travel to Crooked Tree from Belize City (1hr); note that buses returning to Belize City usually leave in the early morning.

Tourist information The Crooked Tree Visitor Centre (Mon–Sat 8am–4.30pm), where you pay the entry fee, is near the entrance to the village, and has a variety of displays and other information on the local flora and fauna.

CROOKED TREE WILDLIFE SANCTUARY

Tours The best way to tour the sanctuary is on guided boat trips (starting at around US$75/person, with discounts for groups). All the hotels offer these tours, including *Bird's Eye View Lodge* (see below) and *Tillett's Village Lodge* (see below), as well as nature treks (US$15) and horseriding (US$40). Numerous tour companies elsewhere in the country, like S & L Travel & Tours in Belize City (see p.55), offer trips to Crooked Tree. You can also inquire about tours at the visitor centre.

ACCOMMODATION AND EATING

Bird's Eye View Lodge Near Crooked Tree Village ☎ 225 7027, ⊛ birdseyeviewbelize.com. At this longtime favourite, you can spy birds from the outdoor patio, and on the surrounding nature trails. The rooms are comfortable, with ceiling fan, while the restaurant, with views over the lagoon, serves a top-notch Belizean menu, including fresh fish and stewed chicken. The lodge offers birding packages, which take in the sanctuary, as well as Maya sites and the Baboon Sanctuary (from US$800). __US$100__

Crooked Tree Lodge Crooked Tree Village ☎ 626 3820, ⊛ crookedtreelodgebelize.com. Gaze out at the lagoon from your comfortable *cabaña* at this wonderfully relaxed lodge run by the friendly Mick and Angie. They also offer camping, and can arrange top-notch birding tours. Ease

into the night by feasting on home-cooked meals – grilled fish, fresh fruit for dessert – on the breezy deck. Camping per person __US$10__, *cabañas* __US$75__

Tillett's Village Lodge Crooked Tree Village ☎ 607 3871, ⊛ tillettvillage.com. Formerly *Sam Tillett's Hotel* (named after one of Crooked Tree's first guides, the supremely knowledgeable Sam), the local Creole Tillett family continues in the same tradition with this simple lodge. Basic but well-kept rooms and *cabañas* are surrounded by the sanctuary wetlands, and the Tilletts offer excellent boat tours (US$100/person) that traverse the lagoons, as well as nature walks (US$15) and guided horseback treks (US$40). Feast on local cuisine that's often cooked over the wood fire. __US$45__

The Coastal Road

1

The Coastal Road – also called the Coastal Highway or Manatee Highway – is somewhat misnamed: it's not a highway and also not on the coast. Yes, it is a road, but a gravel one, which can get washed out during the rainy season. But, this will be changing: in 2016, the government announced that the Coastal Highway will be vastly improved in the coming years, with new paving, alignment and bridges. The opening of new bridges is underway, with the paving projected for completion by 2020. The Coastal Road, which runs for around 35 miles from the little settlement of La Democracia on the George Price Highway to Dangriga, cuts through untrammelled wilderness, but one of the unique stops along the way is tiny **Gales Point**, surrounded by richly diverse wetlands.

Gales Point

The tranquil Creole village of **GALES POINT** straggles a narrow peninsula that extends into the Southern Lagoon, which forms a series of linked waterways between Belize City and Dangriga. Gales Point lies roughly one mile off the Coastal Road; you can also reach Gales Point via boat from Belize City (see below). It was originally settled over two hundred years ago by runaway slaves – "maroons" (from the Spanish *cimarron*, meaning wild or untamed) – from Belize City, who found solace among the mangrove-cloaked creeks and shallow lagoons. A teeming wetland area comprising the **Northern and Southern lagoons**, the area is protected as part of the Burdon Canal Nature Reserve, the largest manatee breeding ground in the Caribbean basin, and Belize's main nesting beaches of the endangered **hawksbill** and **loggerhead turtles**, which lie on either side of the mouth of the Manatee River. Wildlife is certainly the main attraction here, with other rare animals including jabiru storks and crocodiles, and numerous bird species. The faded but fairly helpful *Manatee Lodge* (see below) can set up boat tours of the area, which include everything from manatee-watching, birding, caving and more.

ARRIVAL AND TOURS

GALES POINT

By boat You can travel from Belize City to Gales Point by boat (from Bz$400, 1–4 people) along mangrove-lined inland waterways – Haulover Creek, Burdon Canal and Sibun River. Call ahead to *Manatee Lodge* (see below)

about arranging boat transport from Belize City.
Tours *Manatee Lodge* (see below) can arrange for tours with local guides, for manatee-watching (US$80–100 for up to four people), birding (US$70) and caving (US$75).

ACCOMMODATION AND EATING

Manatee Lodge Tip of Gales Point Peninsula ☎ 532 2400, ⓦ manateelodge.com. Surrounded by the Southern Lagoon, this colonial-style building roosts at the peninsula's tip. Some of the rooms have seen better days, but overall, the place is decently maintained – and they

can set up a wide range of tours in the area. They can also arrange for boat trips from Belize City, and they occasionally have canoes and small boats for rent to explore the lagoon. Call ahead, as the lodge sometimes closes for part of the year. US$80

The north

RÍO BRAVO FOREST

The north

Cruise ships regularly pull into Belize City's harbour, and sun-seekers flock to the cayes, but much of northern Belize still remains largely off the tourist trail. And for many, that's the great appeal. In the off-season, you may be one of just a few guests at the local hotels. This is a land with closer historic ties to Mexico than with the rest of Belize, where the countryside is comprised of swamps, savannahs and lagoons mixed with rainforest and farmland.

The largest town in the north is relaxed, dusty **Orange Walk**, the main centre for sugar production. Further north, **Corozal** is a small and peaceful Caribbean settlement with a strong Mexican element – not surprising, as it lies just nine miles from the border. Throughout the north, Spanish is as common as Kriol and there's a distinctive Latin flavour to life – and to the cuisine, which is a tasty mix of Mexican and Belizean. Most visitors to northern Belize are here to see the **Maya ruins** and wildlife reserves. The largest archeological site, **Lamanai**, features some of the most impressive pyramids in the country; it's served by regular boat tours along the New River. Lamanai is also popular as a day-trip among visitors based in San Pedro or from the cruise ships. Other sites in the region include Cuello and Nohmul, respectively southwest and north of Orange Walk, and Santa Rita and Cerros, both near Corozal.

The north is also a haven for wildlife, and is home to the ambitious **Río Bravo Conservation and Management Area**, which comprises 378 square miles of tropical forest and river systems in the west of Orange Walk District. This vast, practically untouched area, containing several Maya sites, adjoins the borders of Guatemala and Mexico. The most northerly protected area is **Shipstern Nature Reserve**, where a large tract of tropical hardwood forest, mangroves and wetland is preserved.

Brief history

For a long time, northern Belize was largely inaccessible and had closer ties with Mexico than Belize City. Most of the first settlers were refugees from the Caste Wars in Yucatán, who brought with them the sugar cane that formed the basis of the Belizean economy for much of the twentieth century. Indian and mestizo farming communities were connected by a skeletal network of dirt tracks, while boats plied the route between Belize City and Corozal. In 1930, however, the Philip Goldson Highway (also called by its former name, Northern Highway) brought the region into contact with the rest of the country, opening up the area to further waves of settlers.

GETTING AROUND   THE NORTH

By bus A variety of bus services regularly ply the Philip Goldson Hwy and serve most towns in the north, including Orange Walk and Corozal, with many continuing on to Chetumal, Mexico.

By car The well-paved, two-lane highway is the main route to the north; it's also called the Belize–Corozal Rd in

this part of Belize and towns and villages are all well signed from it.

By guided tour One of the most popular ways to visit the north is on a tour; several companies (see p.76) operate group excursions throughout the region, heading to Maya sites, nature reserves and rivers.

Highlights

❶ Maracas Bar & Grill, Orange Walk Watch
the riverboats glide lazily by while feasting on
local Maya-Mestizo dishes, from shrimp *ceviche*
to fresh fish with a rum glaze. **See p.73**

❷ Lamanai Journey by boat along the tranquil
New River to reach this astonishing Maya city,
with beautifully restored temples; keep an eye
out for lurking crocodiles and iguanas along the
way. **See p.74**

**❸ Río Bravo Conservation and
Management Area** This massive swath
encompasses some of the best-protected forest

in Belize and is teeming with wildlife, from tapirs
and monkeys to pumas and jaguars. **See p.77**

❹ Chan Chich Lodge Few lodges balance
conservation and comfort like this esteemed
eco-resort, with handsome thatched *cabañas*, a
sparkling pool and superb outdoor activities,
such as horseriding through the jungle.
See p.78

❺ Corozal Enjoy the best of coastal northern
Belize at this breezy town, with a palm-shaded
shoreline and inviting waterfront guesthouses
and resorts. **See p.81**

HIGHLIGHTS ARE MARKED ON THE MAP ON P.70

Orange Walk

ORANGE WALK may be the centre of a busy agricultural region and the largest town in the north of Belize – but even so, it moves at the lazy pace of a small town. The tranquil **New River**, a few blocks east of the centre, is equally slow moving. A heavily used commercial waterway during the logging days, today New River provides a lovely starting point for a visit to the ruins of Lamanai, to which several local operators offer tours (see p.76).

Orange Walk is built around Central Park, a distinctly Mexican-style formal plaza shaded by large trees. The town hall across the main road is called the Palacio Municipal, reinforcing the strong historic links to Mexico.

The land in and around the satellite villages of Blue Creek, Shipyard and Little Belize has been developed by **Mennonite** settlers (see box opposite), members of a Protestant religious group who choose to farm without the assistance of modern technology. You'll often see them, the men in wide-brimmed hats and the women in ankle-length dresses, shopping for supplies in town.

Brief history

Like Corozal to the north, Orange Walk was founded by mestizo refugees fleeing from the Caste Wars in Yucatán in 1849, who chose as their site an area that had long been used for logging camps and was already occupied by the local Icaiché (Chichanha) Maya.

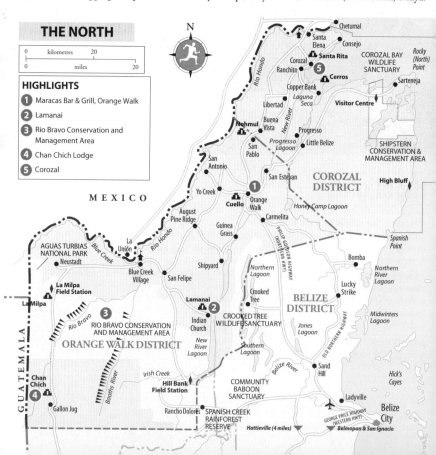

THE NORTH

| 0 | kilometres | 20 |
| 0 | miles | 20 |

HIGHLIGHTS

1. Maracas Bar & Grill, Orange Walk
2. Lamanai
3. Rio Bravo Conservation and Management Area
4. Chan Chich Lodge
5. Corozal

MEXICO

GUATEMALA

AGUAS TURBIAS NATIONAL PARK
Neustadt
La Milpa Field Station
La Milpa
Chan Chich
Gallon Jug

Chetumal
Santa Elena
Consejo
Corozal
Santa Rita
Ranchito
Cerros
Copper Bank
COROZAL BAY WILDLIFE SANCTUARY
Rocky (North) Point
Sarteneja
Libertad
Laguna Seca
Visitor Centre
Buena Vista
Nohmul
Progresso
San Pablo
Progresso Lagoon
Little Belize
SHIPSTERN CONSERVATION & MANAGEMENT AREA
San Antonio
San Estevan
COROZAL DISTRICT
High Bluff
Yo Creek
Cuello
Orange Walk
Honey Camp Lagoon
August Pine Ridge
Carmelita
Guinea Grass
La Unión
Rio Hondo
Blue Creek
Shipyard
San Felipe
Blue Creek Village
Northern Lagoon
Spanish Point
Bomba
Northern River Lagoon
Lamanai
Indian Church
Crooked Tree
CROOKED TREE WILDLIFE SANCTUARY
Lucky Strike
BELIZE DISTRICT
Midwinters Lagoon
RIO BRAVO CONSERVATION AND MANAGEMENT AREA
ORANGE WALK DISTRICT
Rio Bravo
New River Lagoon
Jones Lagoon
Southern Lagoon
Irish Creek
Booths River
Hill Bank Field Station
COMMUNITY BABOON SANCTUARY
Belize River
Sand Hill
Hick's Cayes
Ladyville
Rancho Dolores
SPANISH CREEK RAINFOREST RESERVE
Hattieville (4 miles)
Belmopan & San Ignacio
Belize City
PHILIP GOLDSON HIGHWAY (NORTHERN HWY)
OLD NORTHERN HIGHWAY
GEORGE PRICE HIGHWAY (WESTERN HWY)

2

MENNONITES IN BELIZE

The **Mennonites** arose from the radical Anabaptist movement of the sixteenth century and are named after the Dutch priest Menno Simons, leader of the community in its formative years. Recurring government restrictions on their lifestyle, especially regarding their pacifist objection to military service, forced them to move repeatedly. Having relocated to Switzerland, they travelled on to Prussia, then in 1663 to Russia, until the government revoked their exemption from military service, whereupon some groups emigrated to North America, settling in the prairies of Saskatchewan. World War I brought more government restrictions, this time on the teaching of German (the Mennonites' language). This, together with the prospect of conscription and more widespread anti-German sentiments in the Dominion of Canada, drove them from Canada to Mexico, where they settled in the arid northern state of Chihuahua. When the Mexican government required them to be included in its social security programme, it was time to move on again. An investigation into the possibility of settling on their own land in British Honduras brought them to the British colony of Belize in 1958.

They were welcomed enthusiastically by the colonial authorities, who were eager to have willing workers to clear the jungle for agriculture. Perseverance and hard work made them successful farmers, and in recent years prosperity has caused drastic changes in their lives. The Mennonite Church in Belize is increasingly split between the Kleine Gemeinde – a modernist section that uses electricity and power tools, and drives trucks, tractors and even cars – and the Altkolonier – traditionalists who prefer a stricter expression of their beliefs. Members of the community, easily recognizable in their denim dungarees and straw hats, can be seen trading their produce and buying supplies every day in Orange Walk and Belize City.

VISITING THE MENNONITES

Several Mennonite communities are open to visits, including the progressive **Blue Creek**, roughly 33 miles southwest of Orange Walk. Here you can stay in simple *cabañas* at *Hillside Bed and Breakfast* (☎ 323 0155; US$60), which is run by John and Judy Klassen. They can arrange for you to participate in Mennonite community activities, including working on the farm and riding horses. To visit other Mennonite communities, such as the conservative **Little Belize** (around 15 miles southwest of Sarteneja), where all transport is via horsedrawn carriages, ask at Shipstern Nature Reserve (see p.80) or *Lamanai Outpost Lodge* (see p.76).

From the 1850s to the 1870s, the Icaiché Maya were in conflict with both the Cruzob Maya, who were themselves rebelling against mestizo rule in Yucatán (and supplied with arms by British traders in Belize), and with the British settlers and colonial authorities in Belize. The leader of the Icaiché, **Marcos Canul**, organized successful raids against British mahogany camps, forcing the logging firms to pay "rent" for lands they used, and Canul even briefly occupied Corozal in 1870. In 1872 Canul launched an attack on the barracks in Orange Walk. The West India Regiment, which had earlier retreated in disarray after a skirmish with Canul's troops, this time forced the Icaiché to flee across the Río Hondo, taking the fatally wounded Canul with them. This defeat didn't end the raids, but the Maya ceased to be a threat to British rule in northern Belize.

Orange Walk has traditionally thrived on its **crops**, first with the growth of the sugar (and the consequent rum distillation) and citrus industries, and after the fall in sugar prices, with profits made from marijuana. In the 1990s, however, pressure from the US government forced Belizean authorities to destroy many of the marijuana fields, and today the town has much less of a Wild West atmosphere than it once did.

Banquitas House of Culture

Main St, at Bautista • Mon–Fri 8.30am–5.30pm • Free • ☎ 822 3302, ⓦ nichbelize.org

For an overview of Orange Walk history, visit the **Banquitas House of Culture**, a small museum and cultural centre on the riverbank just north of the heart of town. The *banquitas* in the name refer to the little benches in a riverbank park, used for generations by courting couples and for simply relaxing on warm evenings. There's

2

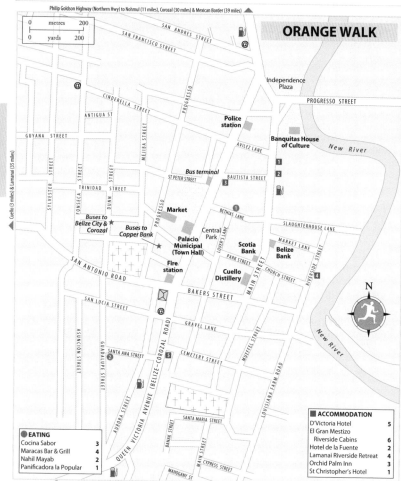

ORANGE WALK

Philip Goldson Highway (Northern Hwy) to Nohmul (11 miles), Corozal (30 miles) & Mexican Border (39 miles)

San Andres Street
San Francisco Street

Independence Plaza

PROGRESSO STREET

CINDERELLA STREET

ANTIGUA ST

GUYANA STREET

Police station

Banquitas House of Culture

New River

AVILEZ LANE

Bus terminal
ST PETER STREET

BAUTISTA STREET

Market

BETHIAS LANE

Buses to Belize City & Corozal

Buses to Copper Bank

Central Park

SLAUGHTERHOUSE LANE

Palacio Municipal (Town Hall)

Scotia Bank

MARKET LANE

Belize Bank

SAN ANTONIO ROAD

Fire station

PARK STREET

Cuello Distillery

CHURCH STREET

BAKERS STREET

SAN LUCIA STREET

GRAVEL LANE

SANTA ANA STREET

CEMETERY STREET

N

New River

SANTA MARIA STREET

■ **ACCOMMODATION**
D'Victoria Hotel   5
El Gran Mestizo
  Riverside Cabins   6
Hotel de la Fuente   2
Lamanai Riverside Retreat   4
Orchid Palm Inn   3
St Christopher's Hotel   1

● **EATING**
Cocina Sabor   3
Maracas Bar & Grill   4
Nahil Mayab   2
Panificadora la Popular   1

Tower Hill airstrip (1.5 miles), Philip Goldson Hwy (Northern Hwy) to Belize City (55 miles)

still a leafy park here, as well as an amphitheatre for outdoor performances, but the highlights are in the main building, a renovated former market. The permanent exhibit charts the history of Orange Walk District from Maya times to the present. Glass cases contain artefacts from local Maya sites, along with maps and drawings of the sites themselves. Other panels display archival materials documenting the stories of logwood, mahogany and *chicle*, which tell of the boom-and-bust cycles of extracting natural resources.

ARRIVAL AND DEPARTURE
ORANGE WALK

By plane Tropic Air (see p.23) flies twice daily (8am & 1.30pm; 20min) from San Pedro to Orange Walk, but it's important to call ahead as there may be fewer services in low season. The Tower Hill airstrip lies about 1.5 miles south of town; there are no buses, so you'll have to walk or catch a taxi.
By bus Most buses drop off and pick up just west of Central Park.

Destinations Belize City (8 daily; 1hr 30 min); Benque Viejo (1–2 daily; 4hr); Chetumal (8 daily; 30min); Corozal (daily, hourly from 5.30am–7.30pm; 1hr 30min); Indian Church near Lamanai (3 weekly Mon, Wed & Fri at 3.30pm; 2hr); Sarteneja (4 daily; 2hr).

ACCOMMODATION

Orange Walk has a range of accommodation options, including several smart, well-appointed hotels that are considerably more affordable than other parts of the country, as the town is still well off the visitor trail. As elsewhere in Belize, hotels are often the best source for up-to-date information on area tours, and can arrange trips.

D'Victoria Hotel 40 Queen Victoria ☎322 2518, ⓦdvictoriabelize.com. This concrete, brightly painted hotel just south of the town centre has sparsely furnished but clean rooms with a/c, along with a decently maintained pool. US$75

★**El Gran Mestizo Riverside Cabins** Naranjal St ☎322 2290, ⓦelgranmestizo.com. The New River has long been one of Orange Walk's natural highlights – but there were few quality spots to stay on its banks. That has changed with the arrival of these riverside cabins, which are run by the same team behind *Hotel de la Fuente*. The airy cabins include a/c, well-maintained bathrooms, a porch and views of the river. Lamanai river tours depart from the hotel dock. Per bed US$15, cabins US$80

★**Hotel de la Fuente** 14 Main St ☎322 2290, ⓦhoteldelafuente.com. One of the best hotels in town, with clean rooms, from basic doubles to larger suites, all with a/c and fridge. Thoughtful extras include bicycles for guest use, and complementary beer and wine in the lobby. The hotel also runs *El Gran Mestizo Riverside Cabins*. Suites US$30 extra. Doubles US$40

Lamanai Riverside Retreat Lamanai Alley ☎302 3955. The rooms may be no-frills, but the riverfront location makes up for it. Wake up to birds chirping and the gentle rush of the river. The open-air restaurant serves decent local cuisine including grilled fish with rice and beans. US$80

Orchid Palm Inn Belize–Corozal Rd ☎322 0719, ⓦorchidpalminn.com. This family-run, central hotel has well-kept rooms with a/c, refrigerator and coffeemaker. Complimentary seasonal fruit and coffee is offered in the lobby. US$70

St Christopher's Hotel 10 Main St ☎322 2420, ⓦstchristophershotelbze.com. This colourfully painted hotel has basic but well-maintained a/c rooms with wooden furnishings, most with access to a balcony. Explore the leafy grounds that slope down to the river. US$45

EATING

Orange Walk menus reflect the town's proximity to Mexico, with a blend of Belizean and Mexican cuisine, from seafood enchiladas to fragrant conch soup. Though most restaurants are casual – with basic furnishings and simple menus – the highlight is the freshness of the dishes, including catch-of-the-day seafood and newly picked fruits and vegetables. Orange Walk is also home to a variety of **food stands**, dotted on the main streets, which sell everything from baked goods to tropical fruits.

Cocina Sabor Philip Goldson Hwy, south of Orange Walk ☎322 3482. Northern Belize's unique culinary mix is revealed through the menu at this lively restaurant. Dishes are a blend of Mexican, Mayan and international, including Fisherman's soup, with shrimp, squid and fish in coconut milk; seafood fajitas rolled in warm, home-made flour tortillas; and crispy chicken with plantain. Mains Bz$13–25. Wed–Mon 11am–10pm.

★**Maracas Bar & Grill** Naranjal St ☎322 2290, ⓦelgranmestizo.com. Feast on Maya-Mestizo dishes – warm empanadas, shrimp *ceviche*, lobster in a garlic sauce, tropical cocktails – at this breezy restaurant and bar on the New River, where you can watch the riverboats lazily gliding by. Mains Bz$12–22. Thurs-Sun 11.30am–10pm.

Nahil Mayab Santa Ana St, at Guadalupe ☎322 0831, ⓦnahilmayab.com. Relax on the leafy outdoor patio or the handsome dining room and enjoy Yucatán- and Maya-inspired dishes like *pibil* ($20), pulled pork with pickled onions; and grilled chicken with a creamy pumpkin seed sauce (Bz$20). Mon 10am–3pm, Tues–Thurs 10am–10pm, Fri & Sat 10am–11.30pm.

Panificadora la Popular 1 Bethias Lane ☎322 3472. For a cheap and filling breakfast, try the *pan dulces* (sweet bread and pastries; Bz$2–7) and fresh bread at this long-established bakery. Mon–Sat 6.30am–8pm; Sun hours vary, but generally 8am–noon & 3–6pm.

Maya sites around Orange Walk

The Maya sites in northern Belize (with the notable exception of **Lamanai**) may not be as monumentally spectacular as those in Yucatán, but they've been the source of very important archeological finds. The area around Orange Walk has among the most productive farmland in Belize, and this was also the case in Maya times; aerial surveys in the late 1970s revealed evidence of raised fields and a network of **irrigation canals**, indicating that the Maya practised skilful, intensive agriculture. In the Postclassic era, this region became part of the powerful Maya state of Chactemal (or Chetumal), controlling the trade in cacao beans, which were used as currency and grown in the valleys of the Hondo and New rivers. For a while the Maya here were even able to resist the conquistadors, and long after nominal Spanish rule had been established in 1544, there were frequent Maya rebellions: in 1638, for example, they drove the Spanish out and burnt the church at Lamanai.

2 Lamanai

On the banks of New River Lagoon, in the village of Indian Church, 24 miles south of Orange Walk via the river • Daily 8am–5pm • Bz$10, includes museum entry • Ⓦ nichebelize.com

Lamanai is undoubtedly the most impressive Maya site in northern Belize, thanks to extensive restoration of the ancient structures, plus a well-curated museum. It's one of only a few sites whose original Maya name – *Lama'an ayin* – is known; it translates to "submerged crocodile", which explains the numerous representations of crocodiles among the ruins. "Lamanai", however, is a seventeenth-century mistransliteration that actually means "drowned insect". The site was continuously occupied from around 1500 BC until the sixteenth century, when Spanish missionaries built a church next door to lure the Indians from their "heathen" ways. By far the most memorable way to journey to Lamanai is along the New River; a number of Orange Walk operators organize day-trips (see box, p.76).

The site

Lamanai's setting on the shore of the New River Lagoon, in an isolated swath of jungle protected as an archeological reserve, gives it a special serenity long gone from sites served by the torrent of tourist buses. Over a dozen troops of black howler monkeys make Lamanai their home, and you'll certainly see them peering down through the branches as you wander the trails; mosquitoes too, are ever-present, so you'll need to be armed with a good repellent.

The most impressive feature at Lamanai, prosaically named N10-43 (informally called the "High Temple", or "El Castillo", the castle), is a massive, Late Preclassic **temple**, towering 115ft above the forest floor. When it was first built around 100 BC, it was the largest structure in the entire Maya world, though one which was extensively modified later. The view over the surrounding forest and along the lagoon from the top of the temple is magnificent and well worth the daunting climb. On the way to the High Temple you pass N10-27, a much smaller pyramid, at the base of which stands a fibreglass replica of **Stela 9**, which bears some of the best-preserved carvings at Lamanai. Dated to 625 AD, it shows the magnificently attired Lord Smoking Shell participating in a ceremony – probably his accession. This glyph has become emblematic of Lamanai and features on many of the T-shirts on sale here. North of the High Temple, structure N9-56 is a sixth-century pyramid with two stucco masks of a glorified ruler, represented as a deity (probably Kinich Ahau, the sun god), carved on different levels. The lower mask, 13ft high, has survived especially well, and shows a clearly humanized face wearing a crocodile headdress and bordered by decorative columns. The temple overlies several smaller buildings, the oldest of which is a superbly preserved temple from around 100 BC, and there are a number of other clearly defined glyphs throughout.

The archeological museum

Same hours as site • Entry included in site fee

The **archeological museum** at the site houses an excellent collection of artefacts, arranged in chronological order; the majority of these are figurines depicting gods and animals, particularly crocodiles. The most beautiful exhibits are the delicate eccentric flints – star- and sceptre-shaped symbols – skilfully chipped from a single piece of stone. Traces of later settlers can also be seen near the museum: immediately to the south are the ruins

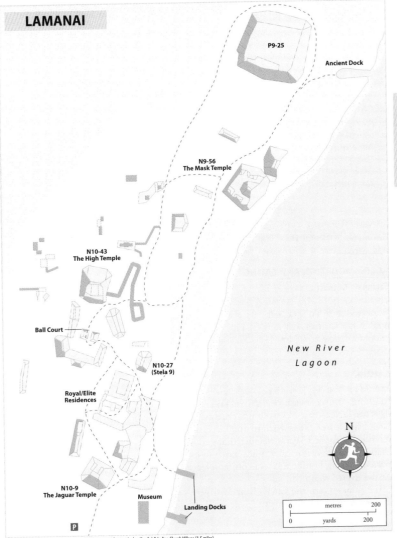

LAMANAI

P9-25

Ancient Dock

N9-56
The Mask Temple

N10-43
The High Temple

Ball Court

N10-27
(Stela 9)

Royal/Elite
Residences

*New River
Lagoon*

N

N10-9
The Jaguar Temple

Museum

Landing Docks

| 0 | metres | 200 |
| 0 | yards | 200 |

P

▼ Lamanai Outpost Lodge (1 mile) & Indian Church Village (1.5 miles)

of two churches built by Spanish missionaries, while a short trail behind the building leads west to the remains of a nineteenth-century sugar mill, built by Confederate refugees from the American Civil War. These refugees settled in several places in Belize, in an attempt to recreate the antebellum South using indentured labourers in place of slaves – but their effort failed, and within a decade most had returned to the States.

ARRIVAL AND DEPARTURE
LAMANAI

By bus It's a challenge to visit Lamanai by bus. Services travel from Orange Walk to Indian Church (1.2 miles from the site) generally twice a week (Mon & Fri) but the schedule can vary, so confirm with locals. Note that the bus

departs from Indian Church for Orange Walk early in the morning, so, unless you have your own transport, you'll have to stay at least one night (see p.76).

By boat Numerous companies offer riverboat tours to

2

LAMANAI RIVER TOURS

The Maya site of Lamanai is unquestionably the highlight of the north – but it's the boat trip there that helps make it so. Riverboats push off from around Orange Walk, and glide down the New River, with memorable wildlife-spotting along the way; you may see lurking crocodiles, iguanas, bats and dozens of species of birds. The boats also float past the only operating sugar mill in the country. Numerous operators in Orange Walk organize day-trips starting from Bz$150 per person, departing around 9am; the price will usually include a picnic lunch at the site. Note that nearly all Orange Walk hotels have an arrangement with various tour companies, so you can book trips directly at the hotel. *Hotel de la Fuente* (see p.73) and *El Gran Mestizo Riverside Cabins* (see p.73), especially, offer an excellent array of tours, so you can check with them even if you're not staying there. Among the tour companies are **Lamanai Eco Adventures** (☎610 2020, ⓦlamanaiecoadventures.com) and **Lamanai River Tours** (☎608 4044, ⓦlamanairivertours.wordpress.com). Numerous tour companies offer Lamanai trips from elsewhere in Belize, among them **Seaduced by Belize** (see p.100) in San Pedro and **Dave's Eco Tours** (☎205 5597, ⓦdavesecotours.com) in Belize City.

Lamanai (see box above).

By car Head to the south end of Orange Walk and turn right (west), where a signpost gives the distance to Lamanai as 35 miles. Continue along the Yo Creek road as far as San Felipe, where you should bear left for the village of Indian Church, 1.2 miles from the ruins.

ACCOMMODATION AND EATING

Lamanai Outpost Lodge Just south of the Lamanai site ☎235 2441, ⓦlamanai.com. The finest accommodation in the area, with very comfortable thatched *cabañas*, each with a private deck, set in extensive gardens sweeping down to the New River. The restaurant overlooking the lagoon serves excellent Belizean and international food. The lodge offers a wide range of tours, including sunrise canoe expeditions, treks along Maya medicinal trails, sunset cocktail cruises and nature hikes under the light of the moon. <u>US$175</u>

Cuello

3 miles west of Orange Walk • Mon–Fri 8am–4.30pm • Free • Permission from the distillery office at 65 Main St, Orange Walk (☎322 2183) • A taxi to the site costs around Bz$15 each way

This small Maya site of **Cuello** was excavated in 1973 by Norman Hammond, who found structures dating back to 1000 BC, making it one of the earliest sites from the Middle Preclassic Maya lowlands. That said, the site is more interesting to archeologists than the casual visitor; there's not much to look at except for a single small, stepped pyramid rising in nine tiers – a common feature of Maya temples – and several earth-covered mounds.

The ruins sit near the Cuello Rum Distillery, on the Cuello family's land, so you'll need to ask permission before visiting; ask at the distillery's small office in Orange Walk.

Nohmul

Just off Philip Goldson Hwy, 1 mile west of San Pablo village, which is 10 miles north of Orange Walk • Hours vary, but generally daily 8am–5pm • Free • Buses between Corozal and Orange Walk stop at San Pablo; a taxi from Orange Walk is around Bz$30 each way

The Maya site of **Nohmul** ("great mound") rises up on the boundary with Corozal District. It was a major ceremonial centre with origins in the Middle Preclassic period, but was abandoned before the end of the Classic and subsequently reoccupied by newcomers from Yucatán during the Early Postclassic (known here as the Tecep phase, around 800–1000 AD). The ruins cover a large area, comprising the East and West groups connected by a *sacbe* (causeway), with several plazas around them. Note that in 2013, parts of the site were terribly damaged by a construction company bulldozer excavating rock for road-building. The site is sometimes undergoing renovations; check at your Orange Walk hotel or with one of the local tour companies (see p.76) about visiting.

The Río Bravo Conservation and Management Area

In the far northwest of Orange Walk District is the **Río Bravo Conservation and Management Area**, an enormous tract of land – just under 400 square miles – designated for tropical forest conservation, research and sustainable-yield forest harvests. This conservation success story actually began with a disastrous plan in the mid-1980s to clear the forest, initially to fuel a wood-fired power station and later to provide Coca-Cola with frost-free land to grow citrus crops. Environmentalists were alarmed, and their strenuous objections forced Coca-Cola to drop the plan, though the forest remained threatened by agriculture.

Following this, a project to save the forest by purchasing it – known as the **Programme for Belize (PFB)** – was initiated by the Massachusetts Audubon Society and launched in 1988. Funds were raised from corporate donors, conservation organizations and an ambitious "adopt-an-acre" scheme, enthusiastically taken up by schools and individuals in the UK and North America. Today, the PFB continues to manage the Río Bravo area as a protected nature preserve, which also encompasses dozens of Maya sites, many of them unexcavated.

The **landscape** ranges from forest-covered, limestone escarpments in the northwest, near the Guatemalan border, to palmetto savannah, pine ridge and swamp in the southeast, around the New River Lagoon. Crossing through the middle of the region are several river valleys. The Río Bravo area has over 240 endemic tree species, and the forest teems with **wildlife**, including tapirs, monkeys and all five of Belize's large cats, as well as four hundred bird species – almost ninety percent of the country's total. The strict ban on hunting makes this one of the better places in Belize to see these beasts; even pumas and jaguars, extremely reclusive creatures, can be spotted. Wildlife-viewing is also excellent in the protected territory around **Gallon Jug**, a private estate to the south of the Río Bravo area that's home to the fabulous *Chan Chich Lodge* (see box, p.78), regarded as one of the finest ecolodges in the Americas.

One of the aims of the PFB is environmental education; as such, **field stations** have been built at **La Milpa** and **Hill Bank** to accommodate both visitors and students. Both have thatched cabins and dorms, and also offer a range of activities, from early-morning birding to rainforest treks.

La Milpa

Set in a former *milpa* clearing in the higher, northwestern forest, **La Milpa Field Station** has a tranquil, studious atmosphere; deer feed contentedly around the cabins, grey foxes slip silently through the long grass and vultures circle lazily overhead. There are also binoculars and telescopes for spotting birds. A day-visit to the field station includes a guided tour of La Milpa ruins or one of the trails (tours from Bz$50).

Three miles west of the field station is the huge, Classic-period **Maya city of La Milpa**, the third largest archeological site in Belize. After centuries of expansion, La Milpa was abandoned in the ninth century, though Postclassic groups subsequently occupied the site and the Maya here resisted both the Spanish conquest in the sixteenth century and British mahogany cutters in the nineteenth. Recent finds include major elite burials with many jade grave goods. The **ceremonial centre**, built on top of a limestone ridge, is one of the most impressive anywhere, with at least 24 courtyards and two ball-courts. The site also contains one of the largest public spaces in the Maya world: the **Great Plaza**, flanked by four temple-pyramids. The tallest structure in the group, the **Great Temple**, rises 77ft above the plaza floor, and you can climb its steep, rocky face using roots for handholds and a rope for support. Beyond here are some of the site's *chultunes* – cave-like, underground chambers carved out of stone.

2

CHAN CHICH LODGE AND GALLON JUG ESTATE

Few lodges in Belize have graced the pages of glossy travel magazines as much as **Chan Chich Lodge** (☎ 223 4419, in US ☎ 1800 343 8009, ⓦ chanchich.com; US$375). The well-known lodge offers a luxury stay in the jungle while remaining true to its conservationist roots. It sits on Gallon Jug Estate (25 miles south of La Milpa Field Station), a 130,000-acre private nature reserve created by the late Belize-born billionaire Barry Bowen. The spacious lodge features airy, handsome thatched *cabañas* and suites, each with lovely verandas and hammocks, set in the grassy plaza of the Classic Maya site of Chan Chich ("little bird"). The construction of the lodge on this spot in the 1980s was controversial at the time (all Maya sites are technically under government control), but it received Archeology Department approval once its intent to cause minimal disturbance became clear. Additionally, the year-round presence of visitors and staff prevents looting, which had previously been a real problem. Staying here offers a remarkable chance to get fully immersed in Maya history: grass-covered temple walls, crowned with jungle, tower up from the lodge, while the forest explodes with birdcalls at dawn. The grounds also feature nine miles of guided trails, and wildlife sightings are consistently high, including jaguars. On top of this is an abundance of deluxe amenities, including a pool surrounded by lush greenery, a jacuzzi and a fine restaurant that serves Belizean and international cuisine. Outdoor activities include horseriding through the jungle, canoeing and some of the best birdwatching in Belize – a range of tours, by car and walking, offers the most varied and extensive birding in the country.

Most guests fly in to the airstrip at Gallon Jug; the lodge can arrange charter flights (which generally take 30min–1hr) from most locations in Belize. It can also arrange ground transfers; if you drive yourself, note that the lodge is only accessible via Orange Walk. Call for detailed directions, as some roads may be blocked off.

Hill Bank Field Station

At the southern end of the New River Lagoon, **Hill Bank Field Station** is a former logging camp that has been adapted to undertake scientific forestry research and development. The emphasis here is more on extractive forest use, with the aim of revenue generation on a sustainable basis. Selective logging is allowed on carefully monitored plots, *chicle* is harvested from sapodilla trees and there's a tree nursery. These and other projects are at the cutting edge of tropical forest management, and there are often students and scientists working here. Five trails wind through the area, offering the chance to spy myriad wildlife, including deer and howler monkeys, as well as colourful birds and butterflies. Trails also pass natural springs, limestone caverns, mangroves and creeks, where you can go tubing and snorkelling.

ARRIVAL AND INFORMATION   RÍO BRAVO CONSERVATION AND MANAGEMENT AREA

On a tour There's no regular public transport to the Río Bravo Conservation and Management Area, but you can arrange transport there via PFB, the tour companies in Orange Walk (see p.76) or by enquiring at your hotel in Orange Walk.

Information Before visiting, or if you want to stay at either of the field stations (see above), you need to contact the PFB office in Belize City (1 Eyre St; ☎ 227 5616, ⓦ pfbelize.org). There's more in-depth information on PFB in Contexts (see p.251).

ACCOMMODATION

La Milpa and Hill Bank ☎ 227 5616, ⓦ pfbelize.org. These two field station sites feature comfortable *cabañas* (with private bath) that are thatched with botan leaves, as well as dorm facilities. All utilize the latest green technology, including solar power and composting toilets. They also offer a range of activities, including birding walks, night hikes and crocodile-spotting. Dorms US$81, *cabañas* US$87

Sarteneja peninsula

Jutting out towards Yucatán in the northeast of Belize, the **Sarteneja peninsula** is covered with dense forests, swamps and lagoons that support an amazing array of wildlife. Though the area is largely unpopulated and could once be reached only by boat, the fishing village of **Sarteneja**, the peninsula's main settlement, has been attracting tourism over the last decade. Sarteneja and the shoreline are pretty enough, but the region's main attraction is **Shipstern Nature Reserve**, three miles south of Sarteneja.

Sarteneja

The epitome of small-town coastal Belize, **SARTENEJA** offers the chance to chill out for a few days, with leisurely walks along the water followed by cheap seafood dinners at the backpacker-style lodgings. Named after the Yucatec Maya word Tzaten-a-ha (meaning "water among the rocks"), Sarteneja was largely settled in 1854 by refugees from the Caste Wars of Yucatán. Due to its historic isolation from the rest of Belize, it still retains close ties to **Mexico**, and its inhabitants are primarily Spanish-speaking mestizos.

ARRIVAL AND DEPARTURE   SARTENEJA

By bus Buses from Belize City travel regularly to Sarteneja via Orange Walk, dropping off in the centre of town.
Destinations Belize City (usually 2–3 daily Mon–Sat; 3hr 30min); Chetumal (2–3 weekly; days vary; 3hr).
By boat The *Thunderbolt* (📧 thunderbolttravels@yahoo .com, ☎ 610 4475), a daily skiff running between Corozal and San Pedro on Ambergris Caye, stops at Sarteneja (1hr 30min, Bz$50) upon request.

By car You can access Sarteneja from Belize City via the Philip Goldson Hwy, through Orange Walk. You can also get here from Corozal; this trip has the added bonus of crossing the New River and Laguna Seca at Copper Bank via hand-cranked ferry (daily 6am–9pm; free).
By plane Daily Tropic Air flights between Corozal and San Pedro will stop on request in Sarteneja. The airstrip lies about half a mile east of town.

ACCOMMODATION AND EATING

Backpackers Paradise Bandera Rd ☎ 423 2016, 🌐 cabanasbelize.wordpress. This rustic spot has simple but comfortable *cabañas*, camping and a communal kitchen. Organic seasonal fruits are grown on the premises. Camping US$6, *cabañas* US$16
Candelie's Sunset Cabanas North Front St ☎ 660 0561, 📧 candeliescabanas@yahoo.com. Take in the breeze off the water from the front porch of these well-

maintained seaside *cabañas*. US$50
Fernando's Seaside Guesthouse North Front St ☎ 423 2085, 🌐 fernandosseaside.com. This small waterfront house has basic but clean rooms with ceiling fan and private balcony, most with views out to sea. Knowledgeable Fernando can help set up a range of local tours, including snorkelling and fishing. US$50

Shipstern Conservation & Management Area

3 miles south of Sarteneja • Daily 8am–5pm, but hours vary depending on tours offered; call ahead • Entrance Bz$10; 90min tour Bz$10, early morning tour Bz$50; night tour (minimum two people) Bz$150 for two; prices vary, but generally from Bz$75 for each additional person • ☎ 632 7467, 🌐 csfi.bz

The **Shipstern Conservation & Management Area**, named for an unexcavated Maya centre in its forested depths, covers approximately 27,000 acres, dotted with small mangrove islands, saline swamps and wetlands. Roughly a third of the reserve is tropical moist forest, which includes over a hundred plant species, though the effects of Hurricane Janet, which whipped through in 1955, still show in the absence of mature growth. Elsewhere are wide belts of savannah, covered in coarse grasses, palms and broadleaf trees. The reserve is run by the Corozal Sustainable Future Initiative, and was officially designated in 2012 as part of the National Protected Areas System Plan of Belize, which further ensures its protection under the law.

Shipstern is a nature-lover's paradise. The lagoon system supports blue-winged teal, American coot, thirteen species of egret and huge flocks of American wood stork, while

MANATEES AND MONKEYS

Belize's remarkable legacy of conservation and wildlife rehabilitation is evident throughout the country, including at the fascinating **Manatee and Primate Rehabilitation Centre** in Sarteneja, on the edge of the Shipstern Lagoon. Run by the nonprofit Wildtracks (Ⓦ wildtracksbelize.org), in partnership with the Forest Department of the Government of Belize, the centre focuses on three types of species in Belize – the West Indian manatee, the Yucatan black howler monkey and Geoffrey's spider monkey –and follows a broad range of rehabilitation strategies, including habitat protection, raising public awareness and rehabilitating orphaned, injured or confiscated wildlife. The centre accepts donations and volunteers; you don't need previous experience, but are asked to commit to a minimum of a month. You can also arrange a day-visit to the centre; make contact in advance via the website.

2

the forest is home to flycatchers, warblers, keel-billed toucans, collared aracaris and at least five species of parrot. In addition to birds, there are crocodiles, manatees, coatis, jaguars, peccaries, deer, raccoons, pumas (though the tracks of larger animals are more commonly seen than the animals themselves) and an abundance of insects, particularly butterflies, which you can view at the **butterfly farm**. Camouflaged **treehouses** throughout the reserve enable you to get good views of wildlife without disturbing the animals, though you'll need a guide to find them, and the **Xo-Pol Ponds** offer an unparalleled chance to see Morelet's crocodiles and waterfowl throughout much of the year. Before trekking into the bush, make sure to cover exposed skin with clothing and a slathering of repellent – the bugs can be nasty.

Various **tours** are offered, including a ninety-minute tour that takes in the visitor centre, butterfly farm and botanical trail, an early morning birding tour (5.30–9.30am) and a night tour (4–8pm or 6–10pm) for spotting crocodiles and nocturnal creatures.

Corozal and around

COROZAL, thirty miles north of Orange Walk along the Philip Goldson Highway, is Belize's most northerly town, just twenty minutes from the Mexican border. Its location near the mouth of the New River enabled the ancient Maya to prosper here by controlling river and sea trade, and two archeological sites – Santa Rita and Cerros – are within easy reach. The town was founded in 1849 by refugees hounded south by the Caste Wars of Yucatán, and underwent substantial reconstruction after Hurricane Janet in 1955; today it's an interesting mix of Mexican and Caribbean culture, with mestizos in the majority. This is a fertile area – the town's name derives from the cohune palm, which the Maya recognized as an indicator of fecundity – and much of the surrounding land is planted with sugar cane.

Corozal is a relaxed town to spend a few days in and perhaps use as a base for day-trips throughout northern Belize. For its relatively small size, it has a wide range of accommodation, from waterfront resorts to family-run budget hotels. Palm trees shade Corozal's breezy, shoreline park, while the colourful Central Park is presided over by a clock tower. The block north of the park, where you'll now find the post office and police station, was previously the site of **Fort Barlee**, built in the 1870s to ward off Indian attacks.

Corozal celebrates Pan American Day (October 12; also known as Columbus Day) with much fanfare, merging Mexican fiesta with Caribbean carnival. Art in the Park (Ⓦ corozal.com/culture/artinpark), which generally takes place one Saturday a month, features local arts and crafts, from photography to wood carvings, in the Central Park and surrounding area.

2

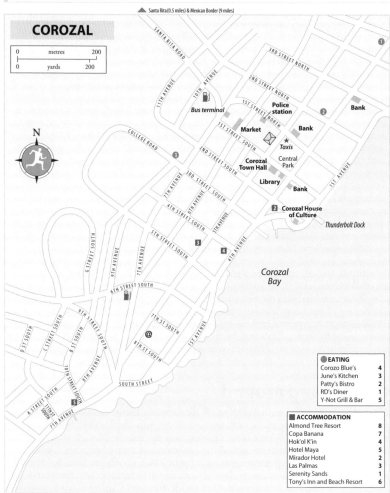

Santa Rita (0.5 miles) & Mexican Border (9 miles)

COROZAL

| 0 | metres | 200 |
| 0 | yards | 200 |

Bus terminal
Police station
Bank
Bank
Market
Taxis
Corozal Town Hall
Central Park
Library
Bank
Corozal House of Culture
Thunderbolt Dock
Corozal Bay

▼ ④, ⑤, ⑥, ⑦ (0.5 miles), ⑧ (1 mile), Airstrip (1.5 miles), Copper Bank (5 miles), Cerros (10 miles), Sarteneja (25 miles), Orange Walk (30 miles) & Belize City (84 miles)

●EATING	
Corozo Blue's	4
June's Kitchen	3
Patty's Bistro	2
RD's Diner	1
Y-Not Grill & Bar	5

■ ACCOMMODATION	
Almond Tree Resort	8
Copa Banana	7
Hok'ol K'in	4
Hotel Maya	5
Mirador Hotel	2
Las Palmas	3
Serenity Sands	1
Tony's Inn and Beach Resort	6

Corozal House of Culture

1st Ave • Mon–Fri 9am–5pm • Bz$10 • ☎ 422 0071, ⊕ nichbelize.org

The **Corozal House of Culture** opened in 2012 in a refurbished market that dates back to 1886. The well-laid-out museum features a broad array of exhibits, including local art, from wooden carvings to paintings, and an overview of Corozal history, with Maya artefacts and old photos. It also hosts special events throughout the year, such as Garifuna drumming performances, as well as occasional art classes.

Corozal Town Hall

1st St South • Mon–Fri 9am–noon & 1–5pm • Free • ☎ 422 2072

Painted a bright aqua-green, the **Corozal Town Hall** rises over the centre of town. Head inside to view an eye-catching mural by Belizean artist Manuel Villamor Reyes, which vividly depicts local history, from the Caste Wars to the devastating 1955 Hurricane Janet.

ARRIVAL, INFORMATION AND TOURS

By bus Buses from Belize City run roughly hourly (daily 5.30am–7.30pm) to Corozal (2hr 30min). The main bus stop is about two blocks west of the centre.

Destinations Belize City (hourly; 2hr 30min), via Orange Walk (1hr); Chetumal (hourly; under 1hr).

By boat The *Thunderbolt* travels to San Pedro, Ambergris Caye (1hr 30min), leaving from the dock daily at 7am and 3pm. It's important to call ahead, because in low season the schedule is sometimes limited.

COROZAL

By plane Both Tropic Air and Maya Island Air operate daily flights between Corozal and San Pedro (25min). El Ranchito Airport is a few miles south of town, and taxis generally meet all flights.

Tourist information ⓦ corozal.com.

Tours All hotels have information on local tours or offer trips themselves. The reliable Belize Transfers & Tours (☎ 422 2725, ⓦ belizetransfers.com) has a variety of tours to Maya sites in the area, watersports and more.

ACCOMMODATION

Almond Tree Resort 425 Bayshore Drive, 1 mile south of centre ☎ 628 9224, ⓦ almondtreeresort.com. Waterfront resort with bright, elegant rooms and leafy, landscaped grounds with a pool. The restaurant serves fresh, home-made seafood meals. US$60

Copa Banana 409 Bayshore Drive, 1 mile south of centre ☎ 422 0284, ⓦ copabanana.bz. Relax poolside by day and then retire to simple but well-maintained rooms with ceiling fan. Also complimentary bicycles and coffee. US$35

Hok'ol K'in 4th Ave ☎ 422 3329, ⓦ corozal.net. Enjoy lovely views of the sea at this comfortable hotel with clean, airy rooms, as well as hammocks and an inviting restaurant that serves local cuisine, including fry-jacks and tacos. US$45

Hotel Maya South End, 0.5 miles south of the centre ☎ 422 2082, ⓦ hotelmaya.net. Clean rooms with private bath, some with a/c and cable TV. The upstairs balcony has sea views, and there are also several long-stay apartments. US$45

Mirador Hotel 4th Ave, at 2nd St South, near the seafront ☎ 422 0189, ⓦ mirador.bz. Large, well-maintained hotel with rooftop views both across the bay

and over Corozal, best enjoyed from the hammocks. Rooms (of varying sizes) come equipped with cable TV, and some have a/c and bay views. US$35

Las Palmas 123 5th Ave South, between 4th & 5th streets ☎ 422 0196, ⓦ laspalmashotelbelize.com. Spacious hotel with a variety of room styles, all with a/c and refrigerators and microwave. It also has very secure parking, and can arrange meals (grilled chicken, rice and beans) for groups. US$65

Serenity Sands 3 miles north of Corozal, off Consejo Rd ☎ 669 2394, ⓦ serenitysands.com. This relaxed, eco-friendly resort lives up to its name, with quiet rooms hung with local artwork, each with balcony and waterfront views. Buffet breakfast included. US$80

★**Tony's Inn and Beach Resort** South End, 1.8 miles south of the centre ☎ 422 2055, ⓦ tonysinn.com. The large rooms with a/c and king-sized (or two double) beds overlook landscaped gardens and an inviting beach bar, and the hotel's *Y-Not Grill & Bar* is excellent, and a prime spot to meet locals and expats over grilled seafood and meats. US$85

EATING

Corozo Blue's Philip Goldson Hwy, 1 mile south of Corozal ☎ 422 0090. Dine outdoors or in at this friendly waterfront restaurant, which serves a varied menu of burgers, wood-fired pizza, fresh *ceviche* and more. Mains Bz$14–24. Sun–Thurs 10am–1am, Fri–Sat 10am–2am.

June's Kitchen 3rd St South ☎ 422 2559. Feast on a range of local dishes, from conch soup to curried chicken, served by Miss June herself. Breakfast is also excellent, with fat omelettes, hash browns and fresh orange juice. Mains Bz$10–20. Hours vary, but generally Mon–Sat 7–11am & noon–3pm.

Patty's Bistro 4th Ave, at 2nd St ☎ 402 0174. Stop by this family restaurant for excellent, well-priced Belizean, Mexican

and American dishes, from fresh snapper to burritos (mains from Bz$15); don't miss the superb Belizean *escabeche* soup, made with chicken, onion and spices. Mon–Sat 11am–9pm.

RD's Diner 25 4th Ave ☎ 422 3796. This inviting restaurant features diverse offerings at mid-range prices (mains from Bz$10), including curry shrimp, fish burgers and fajitas. It also serves hearty breakfasts – with good brewed coffee. Mon–Sat 7am–11pm, Sun 7am–3pm.

Y-Not Grill & Bar In Tony's Inn and Beach Resort, 1.8 miles south of the centre ☎ 422 2055, ⓦ tonysinn.com. Enjoy waterfront sunset views along with grilled meats and seafood, fajitas, roast chicken and burgers. Mains Bz$15–40. Daily 11am–11pm.

Santa Rita

Northwest of Corozal; follow the main road towards the Mexican border and bear left at the fork, bringing you to the raised archeological site • No set opening hours, but best to visit only during daylight hours • Free

The Maya site of **Santa Rita**, which lies about a fifteen-minute walk northwest of Corozal town, was founded as a small settlement around 1800 BC. It appears to have been continuously occupied until the arrival of the Spanish, by which time it was in all probability the powerful Maya city known as Chactemal (Chetumal), which dominated regional trade. It was certainly still thriving in 1531 AD, when the conquistador **Alonso Dávila** entered the town, which had been tactically abandoned by its inhabitants; he was driven out almost immediately by Na Chan Kan, the Maya chief, and his Spanish adviser Gonzalo Guerrero (see p.226).

Being so close to modern-day Mexico, it's not surprising that the site shares many attributes with ruins found to the north. **Pottery** discovered here connects the site with others in Yucatán, and, before it was bulldozed in the late 1970s, Structure 1 contained superb, Mixtec-style Postclassic murals similar to those found at Tulum in Quintana Roo. Due to this destruction, and the strong possibility that much of the ancient city lies beneath present-day Corozal, the only visible remains of Santa Rita are a few mounds and Structure 7, a fairly small but attractive **pyramid**. Burials excavated here include that of an elaborately jewelled elderly woman, dated to the Early Classic period, and the tomb of a Classic-period warlord, interred with the symbols of his elite status.

Cerros

On southern shore of Corozal Bay, 2.5 miles north of Copper Bank • Daily 8am–5pm • Bz$20

On a peninsula jutting from the southern shore of Corozal Bay (roughly 10 miles south of Corozal, and 2.5 miles north of Copper Bank) is the Preclassic Maya centre of **Cerros**, also called Cerro Maya. The site benefited from its position at the mouth of the New River, which enabled it to dominate regional water-borne trade. Beginning around 50 BC, it grew in only two generations from a small fishing village to a major city, one of the first to be ruled by a king. A canal bordered the central area, providing drainage for the town and the raised field system that sustained it. Despite initial success, however, Cerros was abandoned by the Classic period, made obsolete by shifting trade routes. The site today contains three large acropolis structures, ball-courts and plazas flanked by pyramids. The largest structure is a 72ft temple with superb views of Corozal from its summit. Keep an eye out for the temple's intricate **stucco masks**, representing the rising and setting sun and Venus as morning star and evening star; note that they are periodically covered to prevent erosion.

THE MEXICAN BORDER

The Mexican border is only nine miles north of Corozal; the journey by bus or car takes about an hour, including the **Santa Elena border crossing** in Belize, on the south side of the Río Hondo. Most northbound buses heading into Mexico will take you to the **bus terminal** in Chetumal (with plenty of onward express services up the coast to Cancún, or inland to Mexico City). After you've cleared Belizean immigration, the bus carries you to the Mexican immigration and customs posts on the northern bank.

Border formalities for entering Mexico are straightforward, and few Western nationalities need a visa; simply pick up and fill out a **Mexican tourist card**. If you want visa advice, check with the Mexican embassy in Belmopan. Note that when you depart Belize via a land border, you need to pay an exit fee of Bz$37.50, payable in Belize or US dollars. **Entering Belize** from Mexico is also simple: there's no fee, and you'll get a maximum of thirty days by filling out the Belize immigration form.

In between the two border posts lies the **Corozal Free Zone/Zona Libre Belice** (☎423 7010, ⓦbelizecorozalfreezone.com), a fairly chaotic area of duty-free shops which all sell pretty much the same range of cut-rate electronic and household goods, clothes, shoes and canned food. Note that the Free Zone caters mainly to shoppers on the Mexican side of the border, because visitors from Belize will have to pay the exit fee before entering the Free Zone, which is a major deterrent to any savings; also, note that there are restrictions and duties on goods brought into Belize.

ARRIVAL AND INFORMATION

By boat The easiest way to visit is by chartering a boat in Corozal (enquire at your hotel) to Cerros (from Bz$80–100 for up to four people) for the 20min ride across the bay.

By car If you have your own wheels, you can drive from Corozal to Copper Bank, which includes crossing the New River via a free, hand-cranked, 24hr ferry.

ACCOMMODATION

For a real taste of the slow life of northern Belize, spend a night in tiny, dusty Copper Bank, though make sure to call ahead to confirm that these places are open. The bonus is, of course, that Copper Bank is within walking distance of Cerros, so you can take in the site at your leisure.

Cerros Beach Resort Copper Bank ☎ 623 9766, ⓦ cerrosbeachresort.com. Rustic but well-maintained, solar-powered, thatched-roof *cabañas* are surrounded by jungle and greenery, which you can explore via nature trails. They offer complimentary kayaks and bicycles, and have a pleasant restaurant and bar. US$35

Copper Bank Inn Copper Bank ☎ 662 5281, ⓦ copperbankinn.com. Comfortable rooms in a spacious home. Also, uniquely for these parts, the inn has a swimming pool. Home-cooked meals include excellent seafood and hearty breakfast dishes like huevos rancheros. US$30

2

The northern cayes and atolls

THE TURNEFFE ATOLL

The northern cayes and atolls

Belize's spectacular Barrier Reef, which begins just south of Cancún and runs the entire length of the Belize coastline, is the longest in the western hemisphere. Its dazzling variety of underwater life and string of exquisite islands – known as cayes (pronounced "keys") – is the main attraction for most first-time visitors to the country. One of the planet's richest marine ecosystems, it's a paradise for scuba divers and snorkellers, who come for the incredible coral formations teeming with hundreds of species of brilliantly coloured fish. Such is the importance of this astonishing marine life that virtually the entire reef, including the portions surrounding the outlying atolls, and all of Belize's marine reserves – known jointly as the Belize Barrier Reef Reserve System – were declared a World Heritage Site in December 1996.

3

Most of the cayes lie in shallow water behind the shelter of the reef, with a limestone ridge forming larger, low-lying islands to the north and smaller, less frequently visited outcrops – often merely a stand of palms and a strip of sand – clustered towards the southern end of the chain. Though the four hundred cayes themselves are only a tiny portion of the country's total land area, Belize has more territorial water than land, and the islands' lobster-fishing and tourism earnings account for a substantial proportion of the country's income.

More than anywhere in the cayes, the town of **San Pedro**, on **Ambergris Caye**, has experienced a major transition from a predominantly fishing-based economy to one dominated by tourism. There are still some peaceful spots on Ambergris, however, notably the protected areas of the island, including **Bacalar Chico National Park** in the north and **Hol Chan Marine Reserve** in the south. **Caye Caulker**, south of Ambergris Caye and home to another marine reserve, is smaller and more Belizean in feel. The budget-friendly caye has long been dubbed the "backpacker isle", but it has also expanded into a more high-end market. Further south still, the original Belizean capital of **St George's Caye** holds a celebrated place in the nation's history and has some fine colonial houses along with an exclusive diving resort. **Swallow Caye**, near the tip of Belize City, is protected as a manatee sanctuary. Many of the other cayes are inhabited only by tiny fishing communities whose populations fluctuate with the season; a few have just a single luxury lodge offering diving and sportfishing to big-spending visitors.

Beyond the chain of islands and the coral reef are the **atolls**: the **Turneffe Atoll** and **Lighthouse Reef**. In these breathtakingly beautiful formations, a ring of coral just below the surface encloses a shallow lagoon, often with a caye sitting right on its edge; here you'll find some of the most spectacular diving and snorkelling sites in the country, if not the world. Lighthouse Reef is the site of beautiful **Half Moon Caye**, where you can

MAIN STREET, CAYE CAULKER

Highlights

❶ San Pedro Enjoy Caribbean breezes – and rum cocktails – at this laidback resort village, made famous by Madonna in her song *La Isla Bonita*. **See p.94**

❷ Lobster festivals Feast on the cayes' most famous crustacean at not one but two lobster festivals, on Caye Caulker and Ambergris Caye. **See p.94**

❸ Sail the Caribbean Set off across the water on a sailing boat to take in the glorious sunset; bring the camera. **See p.101**

❹ Caye Caulker Go barefoot on the sandy streets and snorkel the Barrier Reef just offshore from this relaxed little island. **See p.106**

❺ The Turneffe Atoll Spend the day diving at Belize's largest atoll and marvel at the colourful marine life in this biologically diverse environment. **See p.113**

❻ The Blue Hole View the unique splendour of the famous Blue Hole from the air or underwater – it's one of Belize's grand aquatic treasures. **See p.114**

HIGHLIGHTS ARE MARKED ON THE MAP ON P.90

view nesting red-footed boobies, and the unique **Blue Hole Natural Monument** – an enormous, collapsed cave that attracts divers from all over the world. All of these destinations are regularly visited by day-trips or live-aboard dive boats from San Pedro and Caye Caulker.

Beyond the outdoor sports, though, the tempo of life on the cayes is slow – and languidly so. If you adopt the "no shirt, no shoes, no problem" philosophy of locals

THE NORTHERN CAYES AND ATOLLS

MEXICO

Chetumal

Corozal Town

Sarteneja

Xcalak

SHIPSTERN NATURE RESERVE

Shipstern Lagoon

San Juan Ranger Station & Visitor Centre

Boca Bacalar Chico Channel

COROZAL DISTRICT

COROZAL BAY WILDLIFE SANCTUARY

Reef Point

Deer Caye

Ambergris Caye

Blackadore Caye

San Pedro

OLD NORTHERN HIGHWAY

Maskall

Bomba

BELIZE DISTRICT

Altun Ha

Northern River Lagoon

HOL CHAN MARINE RESERVE

Barrier Reef

CARIBBEAN SEA

Midwinters Lagoon

Caye Caulker

CAYE CAULKER FOREST AND MARINE RESERVE

PHILIP GOLDSON HIGHWAY (NORTHERN HWY)

Hick's Caye

Caye Chapel

Sand Hill

St George's Caye

SWALLOW CAYE WILDLIFE SANCTUARY

Dog Flea Caye

Belize River

Burrell Boom

Drowned Cayes

RENDEZVOUS POINT MARINE RESERVE

Turneffe Atoll

Hattieville

Belize City

Gallows Point Swallow Caye

Sandbore Caye

Northern Caye

Sargeant's Caye

Water Caye

Blackbird Caye

Lighthouse Reef

Northern Lagoon

Burdon Canal

Goff's Caye

English Caye

Calabash Caye

BLUE HOLE NATURAL MONUMENT

Southern Lagoon

Gales Point

Bluefield Range

Ropewalk Caye

Long Caye

BELIZE COASTAL ROAD

Alligator Caye

Caye Bokel

HALF MOON CAYE NATURAL MONUMENT

Southern Long Caye

HIGHLIGHTS

1 San Pedro
2 Lobster festivals
3 Sail the Caribbean
4 Caye Caulker
5 Turneffe Atoll
6 The Blue Hole

0   kilometres   20
0   miles   20

N

HURRICANES

Like much of the Caribbean, the cayes and other coastal areas of Belize can suffer severe hits by hurricanes. The official **hurricane season** lasts from June to the end of November, though the worst storms usually occur during September and October – tourist low season. There are excellent warning systems in place, and most of the major weather websites, including Ⓦ weather.com and Ⓦ wunderground.com, adequately cover Belize's weather systems and hurricane forecasts. If there is a hurricane developing *anywhere* in the Caribbean, prepare to leave as quickly as possible or postpone plans for a visit to the cayes.

and expats alike, you'll fit right in. A typical day might include swinging lazily on a hammock, lunching on freshly caught lobster and then sipping rum punch as the sun sets. It's no wonder that the cayes are crawling with expats – a few days in this sun-soaked corner of the world and you, too, will be considering permanent relocation.

On August 4, 2016, **Hurricane Earl** – a Category 1 hurricane – made landfall in Belize and pummelled the entire country, particularly the coastal areas, leaving a massive path of destruction in its wake. Ambergris Caye and Caye Caulker were especially pounded – collapsed buildings, uprooted trees, debris strewn across beaches and roads – and both islands continue to go through rebuilding efforts.

3

Brief history

The earliest inhabitants of the cayes were **Maya** peoples or their ancestors. By the Classic period (300–900 AD), the Maya had developed an extensive trade network stretching from Yucatán to Honduras, with settlements and shipment centres on several of the islands. At least some cities in Belize survived the Maya "collapse", and the trade network lasted throughout the Postclassic era until the arrival of the conquistadors. **Christopher Columbus** may have sighted the coast of Belize on his last voyage to the "Indies" in 1502; his journal mentions an encounter with a Maya trading party in an immense dugout canoe off Guanaja, one of the Bay Islands of Honduras. Traces of Maya civilization remain on some of the cayes today, especially Ambergris Caye, which has the site of **Marco Gonzalez** near its southern tip.

Pirates and buccaneers

Probably the most infamous residents of the cayes were the **buccaneers**, usually British, who lived here in the sixteenth and seventeenth centuries, taking refuge in the shallow waters after plundering Spanish treasure ships. In time, the pirates settled more or less permanently on some of the northern and central cayes. But life under the Jolly Roger grew too risky for them in the late 1600s, after Britain agreed to stamp out privateering under the terms of the Madrid Treaties, and a number of pirates turned instead to logwood cutting. The woodcutters, known as **Baymen**, kept their dwellings on the cayes – specifically **St George's Caye** – whose cool breezes and fresh water offered a welcome break from the steaming swamps where the logwood grew. The population of the cayes stayed low during the seventeenth and eighteenth centuries, but the St George's Caye settlement remained the Baymen's capital until 1779, when a Spanish force destroyed it and imprisoned 140 Baymen and 250 of their slaves. The Baymen returned to their capital in 1783, but waited until 1798 to take revenge on the Spanish fleet in the celebrated **Battle of St George's Caye** (see p.230). After, although the elite of the Baymen still kept homes on St George's Caye, the population of the islands began to decline as Belize Town (later Belize City) grew.

Hunting and fishing

During this period, fishermen and turtle hunters continued to use the cayes as a base for their operations, and refugees fleeing the Caste Wars in Yucatán towards the end of the nineteenth century also settled on the islands in small numbers. Descendants of these groups have steadily increased the islands' population since the mid-twentieth century, assisted by the establishment of **fishing cooperatives** in the 1960s, which brought improved traps, ice manufacturing (for shipping seafood) and access to the export market.

The hippie trail

Also during the 1960s, the cayes of Belize, particularly Caye Caulker, became a hangout on the **hippie trail**, and then began to attract more lucrative trade. The islanders generally welcomed these new visitors: rooms were rented and hotels built, and a burgeoning prosperity began to transform island life. Luxuries not usually associated with small fishing communities in the developing world – such as colour televisions and skiffs with large outboard motors – were early evidence of the effects of tourism. These days, so profound are these changes that fishing has now become a secondary activity; many of the inhabitants of the two largest northern cayes, Ambergris Caye and Caye Caulker, now depend almost solely on tourism.

3

GETTING AROUND	**THE NORTHERN CAYES AND ATOLLS**
By boat Boats operated by the San Pedro Belize Express Water Taxi (see p.97) and Ocean Ferry Belize (p.98) travel regularly between the cayes and atolls, as well as to and from Belize City and other coastal hubs on the mainland.	**By organized tour** Numerous companies (see p.100) offer organized tours throughout the cayes, from snorkelling the reef to diving Blue Hole to exploring Turneffe Atoll.

Ambergris Caye

After your first glimpse of lush **AMBERGRIS CAYE** and its beachfront main town of **San Pedro**, it's easy to see why Madonna namechecked the island in her famous song *La Isla Bonita* ("Last night I dreamt of San Pedro…"). Ambergris Caye is the Caribbean in all its sun-drenched glory: white-sand beaches, turquoise waters, verdant mangroves – and plenty of breezy outdoor bars from which to take it all in, tropical cocktail in hand.

Ambergris Caye is separated from Mexico by the narrow **Boca Bacalar Chico channel**, created partly by the ancient Maya. It's the most northerly and, at 25 miles long, by far the largest of the cayes, though the vast majority of its population is concentrated near the southern end. If you fly into San Pedro, as most visitors do, the views are breathtaking. The most memorable sight is the white line of the reef crest, dramatically separating the vivid blue of the open sea from the turquoise water on its leeward side.

SAFEGUARDING THE CORAL REEF

Coral reefs are among the most complex and **fragile** ecosystems in the world. Once damaged, coral is far more susceptible to bacterial infection, which can quickly lead to large-scale, irreversible decline. Unfortunately, a great deal of damage has already been caused on the Barrier Reef by snorkellers and divers standing on the coral or holding onto outcrops for a better look. All tour guides in Belize are trained in reef ecology before earning a licence (which must be displayed as they guide), and if you go on an organized trip, as most people do, the guide should brief you on the following **precautions** to avoid damage to the reef.
Don't anchor boats on the reef – use the permanently secured buoys.
Don't touch or stand on coral – protective cells are easily stripped away from the living polyps on their surface, destroying them and thereby allowing algae to enter. Coral also stings and can cause **burns**, and even brushing against it causes cuts that are slow to heal.
Don't remove shells, sponges or other creatures from the reef or buy reef products from souvenir shops.
Avoid disturbing the seabed around coral – aside from spoiling visibility, clouds of sand settle over corals and smother them.
Don't feed or interfere with fish or marine life; this can harm not only sea creatures and the food chain, but snorkellers too – large fish may attack, trying to get their share.

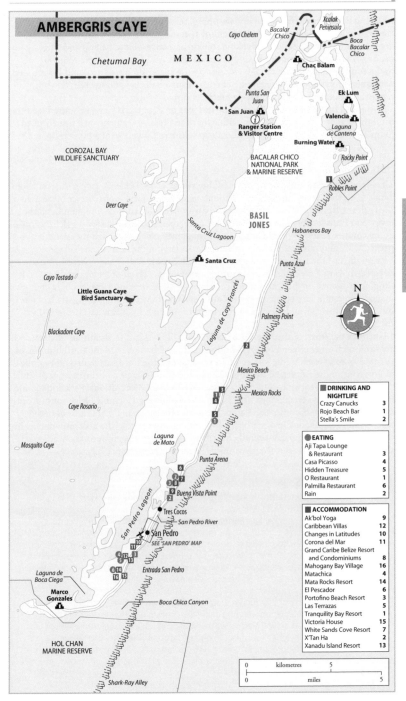

AMBERGRIS CAYE

Cayo Chelem

Bacalar Chico

Xcalak Peninsula

Boca Bacalar Chico

Chetumal Bay **MEXICO**

Chac Balam

Punta San Juan

Ek Lum

San Juan

Valencia

Ranger Station & Visitor Centre

Laguna de Cantena

Burning Water

COROZAL BAY WILDLIFE SANCTUARY

BACALAR CHICO NATIONAL PARK & MARINE RESERVE

Rocky Point

Robles Point **1**

Deer Caye

BASIL JONES

Habaneros Bay

Santa Cruz Lagoon

3

Santa Cruz

Punta Azul

Cayo Tostado

Little Guana Caye Bird Sanctuary

Palmero Point

Blackadore Caye

N

Laguna de Cayo Frances

Caye Rosario

Mexico Beach

Mexico Rocks

Mosquito Caye

3 1 4

5 1

Laguna de Mato

Punta Arena

2

6

2 7

3 8

9

2

Buena Vista Point

Tres Cocos

San Pedro River

San Pedro

SEE 'SAN PEDRO' MAP

San Pedro Lagoon

10
11
17 1 3
12 13

6 14 15

16

Laguna de Boca Ciega

Entrada San Pedro

Marco Gonzales

Boca Chica Canyon

HOL CHAN MARINE RESERVE

Shark-Ray Alley

■ **DRINKING AND NIGHTLIFE**	
Crazy Canucks	3
Rojo Beach Bar	1
Stella's Smile	2

● **EATING**	
Aji Tapa Lounge & Restaurant	3
Casa Picasso	4
Hidden Treasure	5
O Restaurant	1
Palmilla Restaurant	6
Rain	2

■ **ACCOMMODATION**	
Ak'bol Yoga	9
Caribbean Villas	12
Changes in Latitudes	10
Corona del Mar	11
Grand Caribe Belize Resort and Condominiums	8
Mahogany Bay Village	16
Matachica	4
Mata Rocks Resort	14
El Pescador	6
Portofino Beach Resort	3
Las Terrazas	5
Tranquility Bay Resort	1
Victoria House	15
White Sands Cove Resort	7
X'Tan Ha	2
Xanadu Island Resort	13

0	kilometres	5
0	miles	5

During the daytime, for those not shopping, relaxing or enjoying some other land-based activity, the **water** is the focus of entertainment, from sunbathing on the docks to **windsurfing**, **sailing**, **kayaking**, **diving** and **snorkelling**, **fishing** and even peering through the floor of a glass-bottomed boat. And you don't have to go far to find a tour company eager to take you out on the sparkling sea – the island is saturated with operators offering a huge range of trips, from a half-day sailing excursion with reggae and rum onboard to multi-day reef diving.

If you plan on **swimming**, note that the **beaches** on Ambergris Caye are narrow and the sea immediately offshore is shallow, with a lot of seagrass – meaning you'll usually need to jump off the end of a dock or take a boat trip to the reef if you want a proper dip.

San Pedro and around

The island's thriving hub is the former fishing village of **SAN PEDRO**, facing the reef about a mile from the caye's southern end. Though not a large town – you're never more than a shell's throw from the sea – its population of over five thousand is the highest in all the cayes. San Pedro is the main destination for more than half of all visitors to Belize. Some of the country's most exclusive **hotels** and **restaurants** are here, though the island is also packed with mid-range and budget places, particularly in the heart of the village.

Every inch of the half-dozen blocks that comprise San Pedro's main streets is leisurely devoted to tourist pleasure, so you're always within easy reach of a bar, restaurant, gift shop, tour agency or the Caribbean Sea. Through all its development, though, the town manages to retain lazy elements of its **Caribbean charm** with a smattering of clapboard buildings in the centre. However, lofty concrete structures continue to rise – as does the traffic.

North of the town centre, the **Boca del Rio** (usually referred to simply as "the river") is an erosion channel crossed by a toll bridge (golf carts Bz$10). On the northern side of the river, a road leads to the village of Tres Cocos and the northern resorts along miles of gorgeous, mostly deserted **beaches**. The northernmost region of the caye, accessible via organized day-trips, features the spectacular **Bacalar Chico National Park and Marine Reserve**, as well as several **Maya sites** (see p.96). Following Coconut Drive **south** from the city, San Pedro becomes **San Pablo**, the semi-official name for this area of beach resorts (and houses for the often Spanish-speaking workforce). The accommodation in the south ranges from party-friendly beachfront lodges to elegant resorts on quiet stretches of beach, like the award-winning *Victoria House* (see p.102).

ISLAND FIESTAS

San Pedro often exudes a festive atmosphere, from the free-flowing tropical cocktails to the informal jam sessions at beachfront bars, but there are certain times of year when the partying spikes. Top among them is the **San Pedro Lobster Fest** (ⓦ sanpedrolobsterfest.com) in mid-June, which celebrates the island's most famous crustacean. Marking the official start of lobster season, the San Pedro event is the first in a trio of lobster festivals – the other two are on Caye Caulker (see p.106) and in Placencia (see p.196). Feast on lobster served every which way – grilled, barbecued, in tangy *ceviche*, skewered on a stick and stuffed into omelettes. Rounding out the festival are boisterous block parties (steel drums and all) and, yes, many renditions of the B-52s' *Rock Lobster*.

Another great time to visit is during August's **Costa Maya Festival** (ⓦ costamayafestival .com), a week-long celebration featuring cultural and musical presentations from the five Mundo Maya countries (Belize, Mexico, Guatemala, Honduras and El Salvador). And, in the summer (generally June or July), check out the **Lagoon Reef Eco-Challenge** (ⓦ ecochallengebelize.com). This sixty-mile kayak race, which draws entrants from around the world, is held to raise awareness of the coral reef, and is topped off with a blow-out beach party.

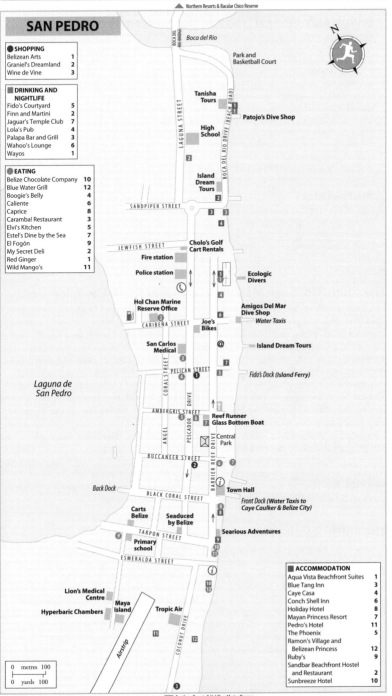

Northern Resorts & Bacalar Chico Reserve

SAN PEDRO

● SHOPPING

Belizean Arts	1
Graniel's Dreamland	2
Wine de Vine	3

■ DRINKING AND NIGHTLIFE

Fido's Courtyard	5
Finn and Martini	2
Jaguar's Temple Club	7
Lola's Pub	4
Palapa Bar and Grill	3
Wahoo's Lounge	6
Wayos	1

● EATING

Belize Chocolate Company	10
Blue Water Grill	12
Boogie's Belly	4
Caliente	6
Caprice	8
Caramba! Restaurant	3
Elvi's Kitchen	5
Estel's Dine by the Sea	7
El Fogón	9
My Secret Deli	2
Red Ginger	1
Wild Mango's	11

3

Boca del Rio

Park and Basketball Court

Tanisha Tours

Patojo's Dive Shop

High School

Island Dream Tours

SANDPIPER STREET

LAGUNA STREET

BOCA DEL RIO DRIVE (BEACH ROAD)

JEWFISH STREET

Cholo's Golf Cart Rentals

Fire station

Police station

Ecologic Divers

Hol Chan Marine Reserve Office

Amigos Del Mar Dive Shop

Water Taxis

Joe's Bikes

CARIBEÑA STREET

San Carlos Medical

Island Dream Tours

CORAL STREET

PELICAN STREET

Fido's Dock (Island Ferry)

Laguna de San Pedro

AMBERGRIS STREET

ANGEL

PESCADOR DRIVE

Reef Runner Glass Bottom Boat

Central Park

BUCCANEER STREET

BARRIER REEF DRIVE

Town Hall

Back Dock

BLACK CORAL STREET

Front Dock (Water Taxis to Caye Caulker & Belize City)

Carts Belize

Seaduced by Belize

Searious Adventures

TARPON STREET

Primary school

ESMERALDA STREET

Lion's Medical Centre

Maya Island

Tropic Air

Hyperbaric Chambers

Airstrip

COCONUT DRIVE

| 0 | metres | 100 |
| 0 | yards | 100 |

■ ACCOMMODATION

Aqua Vista Beachfront Suites	1
Blue Tang Inn	3
Caye Casa	4
Conch Shell Inn	6
Holiday Hotel	8
Mayan Princess Resort	7
Pedro's Hotel	11
The Phoenix	5
Ramon's Village and Belizean Princess	12
Ruby's	9
Sandbar Beachfront Hostel and Restaurant	2
Sunbreeze Hotel	10

Southern Resorts & Hol Chan Marine Reserve

DIVING AND SNORKELLING AROUND AMBERGRIS CAYE

Belize's **Barrier Reef** features one of the most colourful ecosystems on earth and the best way to explore it is by snorkelling and diving its crystal waters. Ambergris Caye is dotted with dive and snorkel **operators** (see p.100), all of which offer trips of varying lengths, price points and locations. **Night diving** and **snorkelling** are also offered. The reef directly in front of San Pedro is a heavily used area, and you'll generally find it in better condition to the north, towards **Mexico Rocks**, or south, towards **Hol Chan**. Large marine life found here can include **sharks** (hammerhead, bull and tiger, as well as the common and harmless nurse shark), turtles, spotted eagle rays and, if you're really lucky, manta rays and whale sharks. For the best diving in Belize and high-voltage excitement in a relatively pristine environment, take a trip to one of the **atolls**, such as the **Turneffe Atoll** (see p.113). Snorkel trips to Caye Caulker are also popular, but travelling there on your own by water taxi and taking a local tour is generally cheaper. There are also several independent sailing boat owners who will charter their craft for the day, so you can snorkel on your own; ask at your hotel.

PRICES AND FEES

PADI diving certification starts at around US$300. A more basic course (which doesn't lead to PADI certification) begins at US$150. Otherwise, two-hour, single-tank dives in the reef near San Pedro start at US$50–65; double-tank dives at US$75–100. For diving trips to the Blue Hole, expect to pay around US$300; for the Turneffe Atoll, around US$250. Snorkel tours cost around US$30–50 (for 2–4hr), depending on where you go and whether a beach barbecue is included.

The south: Hol Chan Marine Reserve and Shark-Ray Alley

Five miles south of San Pedro at the southern tip of the caye, **Hol Chan Marine Reserve** (wholchanbelize.org) takes its name from the Maya word for "little channel", and it is indeed a break in the reef that forms the focus of the reserve. Established in 1987 and the first of Belize's marine reserves, its three zones preserve a comprehensive cross-section of the marine environment, including **coral reef**, **seagrass beds** and **mangroves**. Approaching with a boat tour, you'll be met by a warden who explains the rules and collects the entry fee (Bz$20), which is sometimes included in the cost of your tour. You can also pick up more information at the Hol Chan Marine Reserve Visitor Center (see p.100) in the centre of San Pedro. You'll see plenty of **marine life**, including some very large snappers, groupers and barracuda.

Included in most of the tours is another part of the reserve, **Shark-Ray Alley**, where you can swim in shallow water with **nurse sharks** and enormous **stingrays**. Watching these creatures glide effortlessly beneath you is an exhilarating experience and swimming here poses almost no danger to snorkellers, as humans are not part of the fishes' normal diet. However, note that the area can get quite crowded and there's also the possibility that a shark could accidentally bite a hand – as has occasionally happened.

The north: Bacalar Chico and the Maya sites

A visit to the remote and virtually pristine northern section of Ambergris Caye is a highlight, both for the obvious attractions of the **Bacalar Chico National Park and Marine Reserve** and for the chance to see a number of **Maya sites** along the coast. On a day-trip from San Pedro you can visit several areas of the reserve and take in a few Maya sites.

On standard trips with local companies, you'll travel by boat through the Boca del Rio and up the west coast, stopping briefly to observe colonies of wading birds roosting on small, uninhabited cayes, such as the bird sanctuary of **Little Guana Caye**. Several species of heron and egret live in the area, and you might even spot the beautiful and much rarer **roseate spoonbill**, though landing on the islands or disturbing the birds is prohibited. To return to town you'll pass through **Bacalar Chico**, the channel partly dug by the Maya about 1500 years ago to create a shorter trading route between their cities in Chetumal Bay and the coast of Yucatán.

The **Maya sites** in the north are sometimes undergoing archeological investigation, and therefore may not be accessible. About two thirds of the way up the west coast of the caye, **Santa Cruz** is a large site with stone mounds, and was once used for the shipment of trade goods in the Postclassic era. Further on is **Chac Balam**, which was an ancient ceremonial and administrative centre, and has burial chamber remains.

Bacalar Chico National Park and Marine Reserve
Visitor centre generally open daily 8am–5pm, but also depends on visiting tours • Bz$10

Covering the entire northern tip of Ambergris Caye, **Bacalar Chico National Park and Marine Reserve** is the largest protected area in the northern cayes. Its 42 square miles extend from the reef, across the seagrass beds to the coastal mangroves and the endangered **caye littoral forest**, and over to the salt marsh and lagoon behind. The park and reserve are patrolled by rangers based at the headquarters and **visitor centre** at **San Juan**, on the island's northwest coast, where you register and pay the park fee. Near the ranger station, a 23ft-high **observation tower** allows views over undisturbed lagoon and forest. Despite all the development to the south, there's a surprising amount of **wildlife** here, including crocodiles, deer and, prowling around the thick forests, several of the wild cats of Belize, including **jaguars**.

ARRIVAL AND DEPARTURE
AMBERGRIS CAYE

BY PLANE
Flights to/from San Pedro Flying to San Pedro is the easiest and most popular approach. Tropic Air (see p.23) and Maya Island Air (see p.23) both operate flights (at least hourly, daily 7.30am–5pm; 25min) from and to Philip Goldson International Airport (from Bz$178 one way) and Belize Municipal Airport (from Bz$108 one way). Flights from both airports to San Pedro call in at Caye Caulker on request. Tropic Air also flies from San Pedro to Orange Walk (usually twice daily; 20min; Bz$106), Corozal (5 times daily; 20min; Bz$144) and Dangriga via Belize Municipal Airport (usually 5 times daily; 30min; Bz$230). Maya Island

Air offers three daily flights from San Pedro to Corozal (around 5 flights daily; 20min; Bz$104).

Transport into town Arriving at San Pedro's airport, you're at the north end of Coconut Drive and about 500yd south of the centre. It's within easy walking distance of any of the hotels in town, though golf carts and taxis will be waiting too. A ride to the centre (or anywhere else in town) starts at around Bz$8 (agree a price before setting off).

BY BOAT
Services to/from San Pedro From Belize City, boats to San Pedro are operated by the San Pedro Belize Express

---

STEP BACK IN TIME AT MARCO GONZALEZ

Accessible via a rutted wooden boardwalk through tangled, mosquito-infested mangroves and palms, the **Marco Gonzalez** Maya site (open daily during daylight hours; Bz$20; Ⓦ marcogonzalezmayasite.com) is a (very) far cry from your typical Maya tourist site – but it offers the rare chance to see an archeological excavation in progress, and to really feel like you're going off the beaten track in increasingly modernized Ambergris Caye. Situated near Laguna de Boca Ciega, on the southern tip of the island, the site dates back two thousand years to the Preclassic period, and studies have shown that it was once an important trade centre with close links to Lamanai (see p.74). **Excavations** began in 1984, by Canadian archeologists David Pendergast and Elizabeth Graham, who named the site after their young guide. In 2011, Marco Gonzalez became the first **Maya Site National Park** on Ambergris Caye, and is now partly managed by the National Institute of Culture and History (NICH). The site itself is still fairly primitive, as this is a working dig – but that's the great appeal. You're discovering it as the archeologists are, and a visit here involves skirting dirt mounds and walking gingerly through the jet-black dirt, which is dotted with the occasional Maya pottery shard and even bits of obsidian or flint that were used by the Maya as cutting tools. Undoubtedly, the best way to fully appreciate the site is by going on a **guided tour** (usually included as part of the entry fee), which is regularly offered by longtime expert guide (and chairman of the Marco Gonzalez board) Jan Brown (☎ 226 2059, ✉ janbrownbz@hotmail.com), who gives a fascinating overview of the site.

Water Taxi (T 223 2225, W belizewatertaxi.com; Bz$40 one way, Bz$70 return), departing from North Front St, near Tourist Village, and Ocean Ferry Belize (T 223 0033, W oceanferrybelize.com; Bz$34 one way, Bz$64 return), departing from North Front St, near Swing Bridge; the same companies also connect San Pedro with Caye Caulker (from Bz$24). In addition, San Pedro Belize Express Water Taxi also runs several trips per week to Chetumal, Mexico from San Pedro (Bz$100). There's also the *Thunderbolt* (T 610 4475, E thunderbolttravels@yahoo.com), which runs between San Pedro and Corozal (Bz$50 one way, Bz$90 return), stopping at Sarteneja on request; note that this sometimes offers only limited service in the off season, so call ahead.

Boat docks in San Pedro San Pedro Belize Express Water Taxi and Ocean Ferry Belize boats pull into (and depart from) their respective water taxi docks, both near the centre of town, on the front (reef) side of the island. The *Thunderbolt* docks at the Back Dock, at the back of the island. All docks are within a few blocks of the centre, marked by the tiny Central Park, on the seafront along Barrier Reef Drive. The lagoon side has been undergoing a renovation, with the construction of a new ferry terminal. Once fully open, the goal is for all boats and water taxis to dock here, instead of on the reef side of the island.

Destinations from San Pedro Belize City (14 daily; 1hr 30min); Caye Caulker (9 daily; 1hr); Chetumal, Mexico (several weekly; 1hr 40min); Corozal (2 daily at 7am & 3pm; 1hr 30min).

3

GETTING AROUND

On foot San Pedro is eminently walkable – you can easily get around on foot throughout town. This includes from the airport (about a 10min walk into town) and the main boat docks, which are on the main beach, a short stroll from the centre. It's only when you go beyond the town centre – to the south and north – that you'll need a golf cart or bike.

By bike A number of outlying hotels have courtesy bikes for guests, something you might want to consider when choosing a place to stay. You can also rent bikes from Joe's Bike Rental, on Pescador Drive (Bz$15/half day, Bz$80/full day; T 226 4371).

By golf cart Golf carts are readily available for rent throughout San Pedro. Generally prices are from Bz$30 for 1hr, Bz$86 for 8hr, Bz$130 for 24hr and Bz$530 for seven days. Most companies will deliver the cart to your hotel or pick you up from the airstrip. Rental companies include Carts Belize (T 226 4084, W cartsbelize.com), with a couple of locations, including one a block north of the airstrip and at *Xanadu Island Resort* (see p.102); Cholo's Golf Cart Rentals (T 226 2627, W choloscartrentals.com), on Jewfish St in the town centre; and Moncho's Cart Rentals (T 226 3262, W sanpedrogolfcartrental.com), at the airstrip.

By ferry and water taxi To head north, to visit the more remote resorts and restaurants (and in rainy season, when roads may be washed out), hop on Coastal Xpress (9–11 trips daily, 5.30am–11pm; T 226 2007, W coastalxpress.com), which departs from the Amigos del Mar dock near the centre. Tickets start at Bz$10; also on offer are day (Bz$50) and weekly passes (Bz$250).

INLAND TOURS AND TRIPS

For a full picture of Belize, it's well worth complementing your time in the sun and sand with an adventure to the **Belizean interior**. And, since so many visitors make Ambergris Caye their base, San Pedro has become a prime jumping-off point for trips to the mainland, with a huge range of deals. Most of the high-end resorts and hotels will either offer their own **tours** or can arrange one with an independent company. Even the budget hotels can at the very least point you in the direction of quality tour companies. If you plan on staying in San Pedro for your entire trip, it's best to focus on day-trips to Northern Belize and the Belize District – the area in and around Belize City. Tours to Cayo and the west can certainly be arranged, but if you'd like a more relaxed itinerary, you'd be better off spending a few nights on the mainland. Top **day-trips** include the Maya site of **Altun Ha** (around US$75–150, depending on additional stops; see p.62); **Lamanai** (US$125–250; see p.74); and the **Belize District** (US$75–150), which may include the Belize Zoo (see p.59), Community Baboon Sanctuary (see p.61) and Crooked Tree (see p.63). Also extremely popular is **cave tubing** (starting at US$150) and jungle **zip-lining** (starting at US$175) in Cayo – both are offered as day-trips, but keep in mind that it's a long day, leaving very early and returning just in time to catch the last boat from Belize City. All trip prices usually include lunch, soft drinks and beer and entrance fee.

In addition to the tours run by the hotels and resorts, local **tour companies** in San Pedro that cover the interior include Tanisha Ecological Tours (see p.101) and Seaduced by Belize (see p.100). On Caye Caulker, Anwar Snorkel Tours (see p.109) is a good bet for inland tours.

LEONARDO DICAPRIO'S RESTORATIVE ISLAND

Belize has long been a magnet for celebrities, from those drawn here for a vacation of sun and sand (Prince Harry, Jennifer Lawrence, Tiger Woods, to name a few) to others who decide to lay down roots, such as Francis Ford Coppola, with his string of properties (see p.200). And now there's another star who's setting up shop in Belize: **Leonardo DiCaprio**. The actor and environmental activist bought wild, untamed **Blackadore Caye**, which lies just west of Ambergris Caye, on his first visit to Belize, in 2005. And now, a decade later, he is realizing his vision: a new **eco-resort** called Blackadore Caye, a Restorative Island is set to open in 2018.

DiCaprio's resort will be the ultimate in **sustainability**, all of it powered by renewable energy from solar panels. Rainwater will be collected, mangroves are being planted to bolster the shoreline and up to half of the island will be a wildlife reserve. As for catering, the resort will partner with local farmers, fishermen and chefs to develop the menu – but, leave the bottled water at home: guests will not be allowed to bring plastic bottles onto the island. Of course, sustainable living doesn't mean scanty living – Blackadore will also be the ultimate in luxury, with beautiful, tricked-out bungalows and homes surrounded by stunning views of the bright-blue Caribbean sparkling under the sun. As DiCaprio said to the *New York Times* about his first visit to Belize: "It was like heaven on earth." With the opening of his new resort, it will be even more so.

INFORMATION

Tourist information The Belize Tourism Board office is on Barrier Reef Drive (Mon–Fri 8am–5pm; ☎ 226 4532). Be careful with other "information booths" dotted around town, as they're usually fronts for timeshares or resorts. Ambergris Caye's official website (⊛ ambergriscaye.com) is a reliable source of information, with good maps and links to most of the island's businesses. The Hol Chan Marine Reserve Visitor Center, on Caribeña St (daily 9am–5pm; ☎ 226 2247, ⊛ holchanbelize.org), has photographs and informative maps and models.

Newspapers Tap into island news via the island's newspapers, *Ambergris Today* (⊛ ambergristoday.com) and *The San Pedro Sun* (⊛ sanpedrosun.com), which cover everything from new boat routes to restaurants.

TOURS AND ACTIVITIES

DIVING AND SNORKELLING

San Pedro is packed with dive and snorkel tour operators, most of which are dotted along the beach and the main streets in the centre of town. Additionally, many hotels and resorts have their own dive shops that can arrange trips for guests. Diving trips start at US$250, while snorkel tours cost around US$30–60 (2–4hr).

Amigos del Mar Dive Shop San Pedro beachfront, next to Caye Caulker Water Taxi terminal ☎ 226 2706, ⊛ amigosdive.com. Well-run, long-established outfit offering a wide variety of dives, from the nearby reef to the Turneffe Atoll, as well as snorkelling and fishing trips, and night dives on request.

Belize Diving Adventures San Pedro beachfront, next to Changes in Latitude ☎ 226 3082, ⊛ belize divingadventures.net. Family-run business organizing dive trips to the Turneffe Atoll, Blue Hole and other popular dive sites, as well as fishing and inland tours.

★**Ecologic Divers** San Pedro beachfront, just south of The Phoenix ☎ 226 4118, ⊛ ecologicdivers.com. Excellent dive shop that combines top-notch expertise with a relaxed, fun approach for an all-round perfect day out on the reef – or further afield at the Blue Hole and other big dive sites.

Reef Runner Glass Bottom Boat San Pedro beachfront ☎ 226 2172, ⊛ ambergriscaye.com/reefrunner. Ideal for groups where some want to get wet, and others don't. Reef Runner offers snorkel trips on its well-maintained glass-bottomed boat, so if you'd prefer, you can get a colourful overview of the reef and view underwater critters without leaving the boat.

Scuba School Belize Sea Grape Drive ☎ 226 2886, ⊛ scubaschoolbelize.com. This well-run company offers personalized diving courses, including several great options for kids, like the Bubble Maker (US$135), which offers children the chance to try out scuba diving in either a pool or a controlled setting in the Caribbean. They also have dive trips to Turneffe and the Blue Hole on their convertible yacht Scuba Dreamin'.

Seaduced by Belize Vilma Linda Plaza, near the town centre ☎ 226 2254, ⊛ seaducedbybelize.com. This long-established family company runs a variety of tours, including half- and full-day snorkelling trips and sailing, as well as day and sunset trips aboard their 58ft houseboat, Sea's D Day. It also has trips to the mainland, including to Altun Ha and Lamanai, and cave tubing on the Old Belize River combined with a visit to the Belize Zoo.

Searious Adventures Tarpon St, near the town centre ☎ 226 4202, ⊛ seariousadventures.com. Top-quality company which features a wide range of tours, including snorkelling, sailing and inland trips to Altun Ha, Xunantunich and cave tubing.

Tanisha Tours Boca del Rio, near town centre ☎226 2314, ⓦtanishatours.com. Guide Daniel Nuñez is a superb naturalist, and the extensive array of trips include snorkelling, manatee-watching, Maya sites, cave tubing and zip-lining.

SAILING AND CRUISES

After exploring the Caribbean's underwater riches, enjoy time above the water. Numerous companies offer sunset sails and cruises, as well as kitesurfing and windsurfing. An evening sail is US$50–100, while beginner sailing courses start at US$5/hr. In addition to the outfits listed below, see also Seaduced by Belize and Searious Adventures under "Diving and snorkelling", above.

Belize Sailing School Caribbean Villas Hotel ☎635 4101, ⓦbelizesailingschool.com. Take sailing lessons (around US$50/hr), or learn to kitesurf and windsurf (classes start at US$100–200).

Island Dream Tours Fido's Pier ☎615 9656, ⓦislanddreamtours.com. Ease into the evening on a Sunset Dinner Cruise (US$90), or arrange for a private charter (prices vary, depending on number of people).

ACCOMMODATION

Ambergris Caye has the highest concentration of **hotels and resorts** in the country, ranging from budget to rustic-chic to five-star luxury, scattered throughout San Pedro itself, and for miles north and south of town. Note that most of the hotels outside of San Pedro will arrange for transport when you arrive, either from the airport or boat docks. In general, accommodation **prices** are higher than in the rest of Belize, but discounts, packages and deals are readily available, especially in the low season, so it's well worth asking. During Christmas, New Year and Easter you should definitely **book ahead**. All hotels listed below have air conditioning and **private bath** on offer, unless otherwise stated.

SAN PEDRO

Aqua Vista Beachfront Suites Boca del Rio, on the beach just north of the centre ☎601 4836, ⓦaquavistabelize.com; map p.95. You'd be hard-pressed to find a better beachfront location: as the name implies, the suites are right on the beach, and include flatscreen TV and full kitchen. Another bonus is the neighbouring bar, *Wayos* (see p.105). U̲S̲$̲1̲6̲5̲

Blue Tang Inn Sandpiper St ☎226 2326, ⓦbluetanginn.com; map p.95. This charming inn has a variety of rooms and suites, many with private balcony and ocean views. It also offers good diving (from Bz$1200) and fishing (from Bz$1600) packages. U̲S̲$̲1̲6̲5̲

Caye Casa Boca del Rio, just north of town ☎226 2880, ⓦcayecasa.com; map p.95. The epitome of "barefoot elegance", with welcoming boutique thatched *casitas* – complete with wooden furnishings and sparkling kitchenettes – on the beach. Or splash out on a villa (US$250); these have two bedrooms and two bathrooms, a living room, dining room and full kitchen – ideal for a family or group. U̲S̲$̲1̲9̲0̲

Conch Shell Inn 11 Foreshore St, on the beach ☎226 2062, ⓦambergriscaye.com/conchshell; map p.95. You can't miss it: emblazoned in bright pink and white, this inn sits right on the beach in the centre of town. Comfortable rooms, with simple but well-maintained furnishings, invite you to "conch out" after a day of watersports. U̲S̲$̲7̲5̲

Holiday Hotel Barrier Reef Drive, just south of the centre ☎226 2014, ⓦsanpedroholiday.com; map p.95. Originally opened in 1965, this is proudly one of San Pedro's very first hotels. It may have been around for decades, but it's kept up with the times well: the comfortable rooms, most of which face the sea, have a fridge and TV. Also on the premises are the top-notch *Caprice* restaurant (see p.104) and the casual *Celi's Deli*, with tasty sandwiches and snacks. U̲S̲$̲1̲3̲4̲

Mayan Princess Hotel Barrier Reef Drive ☎226 2778, ⓦmayanprincesshotel.com; map p.95. Staying here is like having your own apartment on the sea. The spacious beachfront suites have kitchenettes and large balconies, where you can gently swing from a hammock in the Caribbean breezes. Plus, they offer lots of extras, including free coffee and tea in the lobby, and complimentary transfers to the airport. U̲S̲$̲1̲5̲5̲

Pedro's Hotel Seagrape Drive, just south of the airport ☎226 3825, ⓦpedroshotel.com; map p.95. A cheerful, fiesta atmosphere pervades this hotel and hostel. Hotel rooms are simple but cosy and comfortable. Both the hotel and hostel have access to two pools. The on-site *Pedro's Sports Pub and Pizzeria* is a great place to connect with locals and other travellers. Dorms U̲S̲$̲2̲0̲, doubles U̲S̲$̲7̲5̲

★**The Phoenix** Barrier Reef Drive, near Caribeña St ☎226 2083, ⓦthephoenixbelize.com; map p.95. It's rare to find a hotel of this calibre so near the town centre. The great appeal is that you can lounge in the gorgeous grounds, splashing in the sun-drenched pool or unwinding at the Sol Spa – and when you're ready for some San Pedro action, you're just a few blocks away. The light-flooded condominiums are massive and sleek, and there are all sorts of personal touches, such as complimentary local mobile phones to use during your stay and fresh hibiscus flowers scattered daily atop your snow-white bed. The on-site restaurant, *Red Ginger* (see p.104), serves excellent fresh-from-the-sea cuisine. U̲S̲$̲4̲0̲0̲

Ramon's Village and Belizean Princess Coconut Drive, near the airstrip ☎226 2071, ⓦramons.com; map p.95. This friendly resort enjoys a prime position, right on the beach. At *Ramon's Village*, roomy thatched-roof *cabañas* have plenty of amenities, and the leafy grounds feature a pool – presided over by "Rey Ramon," a huge replica of a Maya mask – and a dock for sunning, swimming and napping. Across the street is the sister property, *The Belizean Princess*, with cottages set around a central courtyard. *Ramon's* US$210, *The Belizean Princess* $185

Ruby's Hotel Barrier Reef Drive, south of the centre ☎ 226 2063, ⓦ rubyshotelbelize.com; map p.95. Decent budget hotel on the seafront. The clean (though worn) rooms, some with a/c, get better views the higher up you go. US$43

Sandbar Beachfront Hostel and Restaurant Boca del Rio Drive ☎ 226 2008, ⓦ sanpedrohostel.com; map p.95. It's budget beds on the beach at one of the caye's best hostels. Friendly, well-run and secure, *Sandbar* sits just north of town, within an easy stroll of shops and bars. The freshly clean dorm rooms have comfortable beds, each equipped with privacy curtains and a locker, or go for one of the seaview private rooms. The downstairs bar is a lively hub – meet other travellers over great pizza and beer. Dorms US$20, doubles US$60

Sunbreeze Hotel South end of Barrier Reef Drive ☎ 226 2191, ⓦ sunbreeze.net; map p.95. Curving around a sandy courtyard and a pool, this well-run beachfront hotel has comfortable rooms with large bathrooms. The restaurant, *Blue Water Grill* (see p.104), is one of the best on the island. US$159

SOUTH OF SAN PEDRO

Caribbean Villas Coconut Drive, about 1 mile south of town ☎ 226 2715, ⓦ caribbeanvillashotel.com; map p.93. With ample grounds, a wildlife-viewing platform and excellent birdwatching, this is an ideal spot for nature lovers. There's a variety of large rooms and well-equipped suites, all with ocean views, on the beachfront. Snooze in a hammock, immerse yourself in the hot tub or set up a sail with the on-site Belize Sailing School (see p.101). Breakfast included. US$150

Changes in Latitudes Coconut Drive, about a half mile south of town, near the Belize Yacht Club ☎ 226 2986, ⓦ changesinlatitudesbelize.com; map p.93. Friendly hotel set in relaxing gardens half a block from the sea. Smallish but clean rooms, with use of common area that has a full kitchen. Complimentary bikes. US$105

Corona del Mar On the beach, just over half a mile south of town ☎ 226 2055, ⓦ coronadelmarhotel.com; map p.93. These spacious but faded rooms and suites come with tiled floors, kitchens and TV. Rates include a full breakfast and complimentary rum punch. Swim off the hotel's pier. US$130

Mahogany Bay Village Sea Grape Drive, near Victoria House ☎ 236 5102, ⓦ mahoganybayvillage.com; map p.93. Resorts have been sprouting across Ambergris Caye for the last couple of decades, but few have reached the scope of the new Mahogany Bay Village, which sprawls over 60-plus acres. This sun-dappled "townlet" includes *Curio – A Collection by Hilton* resort, the first *Hilton Worldwide* property in Belize. Breezy, cottage-style hotel rooms, inspired by the country's British colonial history, have gleaming hardwoods, detailed furnishings and billowing white curtains. The resort's tri-level The Great House – the largest wooden structure in Belize – is a guest hub. Amenities abound, including *Rum & Bean*, which serves potent espresso and rum cocktails; and The Farm House Deli, selling home-made breads, imported cheeses and more. Room prices had yet to be released at the time of writing.

Mata Rocks Resort Coconut Drive, around 2 miles south of town ☎ 226 2336, ⓦ matarocks.com; map p.93. Small, long-established family resort with comfortable rooms around the pool and bar, rum punch at check-in, tasty breakfasts included in the rate, free bikes for exploring and complimentary beach towels. US$165

★**Victoria House** On the beach, around 2 miles south of town ☎ 226 2067, ⓦ victoria-house.com; map p.93. Gorgeous, award-winning resort with a range of upscale accommodation in a splendid location. Luxurious, colonial-style hotel rooms, thatched *casitas* (US$345) and suites (US$385) are set in spacious grounds – not surprisingly, it's one of the most popular wedding hotels on the island. Excellent service and wonderfully relaxing; you can sun yourself near the beachfront pool, enjoy a full-body massage at the splendid spa – one of the largest on the island, with a soaring cupola – and sip cocktails in your bathing suit or feast on fresh fish at the excellent restaurant *Palmilla* (see p.104). US$205

★**Xanadu Island Resort** On the beach, about 1.5 miles south of town ☎ 226 2814, ⓦ xanaduislandresort .com; map p.93. *Xanadu* more than lives up to its name, with lovely condominium suites, all built in environmentally friendly monolithic domes that are grouped around a palm-shaded pool, with the beach just a few lazy paces away. All suites have a full kitchen and wooden decks, and the staff are delightful. They also run Carts Belize (see p.98), with a top fleet of carts to rent. US$220

NORTH ISLAND

Ak'bol Yoga On the beach, about 1 mile north of town ☎ 226 2073, ⓦ akbol.com; map p.93. One of Belize's first yoga resorts invites you to "renew your spirit" with yoga and wellness classes and retreats. Relax in breezy thatched *cabañas* amid a meditation garden. The on-site restaurant has fresh juices and excellent breakfasts. US$165

Grand Caribe Belize Resort and Condominiums 2 miles north of San Pedro ☎ 226 4726, ⓦ grandcaribe belize.com; map p.93. This may be a large resort, but each villa has an intimate feel, with comfy couches, plant-strewn bathrooms and colourful art, as well as fully equipped kitchens. The beachfront villas are about as close to the sand as you can get – step out the front door, and the sea is a few paces away. Plus, the resort features the top-notch *Rain* restaurant (see p.105). U̲S̲$̲3̲9̲0̲

Matachica Resort & Spa 5 miles north of San Pedro ☎ 223 0002, ⓦ matachica.com; map p.93. Secluded and sophisticated, *Matachica* epitomizes the Belizean penchant for blending laidback and luxury. Beachfront *casitas* are cooled off with sea breezes, and are outfitted with beds piled with high-thread-count sheets, plus there's a private patio with hammock. A bonus is the Jade Spa, where you can indulge in treatments that employ local ingredients, such as chocolate body wraps, Maya coffee scrubs and papaya facials. U̲S̲$̲2̲7̲5̲

El Pescador On the beach, about 2.5 miles north of town ☎ 226 2398, ⓦ elpescador.com; map p.93. With a choice of several rooms in a colonial-style house rich with hardwood furnishings, or one-, two- or three-bed villas (from US$425), there's plenty of choice at this family-run establishment, where fishing and diving are the most popular activities. Complimentary bikes and kayaks are available. U̲S̲$̲3̲0̲0̲

Portofino Beach Resort On the beach, 5.5 miles north of town ☎ 220 5096, ⓦ portofinobelize.com; map p.93. A mix of breezy *cabañas* and suites, from elevated Treetop Suites to Colonial Suites with French doors to Honeymoon Suites with a large balcony with hammocks. All accommodation is set amid swaying palms, with splendid ocean views. Service is wonderfully friendly and the on-site restaurant is good. U̲S̲$̲3̲1̲0̲

Las Terrazas 3.5 miles north of San Pedro ☎ 226 4249, ⓦ lasterrazasresort.com; map p.93. This lovely resort features elegant townhouses overlooking the white-sand beach, with lots of deluxe amenities and services, from the fragrant spa to the superb restaurant, *O* (see p.105), which serves international cuisine and fresh seafood. U̲S̲$̲4̲1̲5̲

★**Tranquility Bay Resort** On the beach, 12.5 miles north of San Pedro ☎ 236 5880, ⓦ tranquilitybayresort .com; map p.93. If you're looking to commune with nature head for the aptly named *Tranquility Bay Resort*, set on 12 acres of beachfront property within the Bacalar Chico National Park. The breeze-cooled *cabañas*, with Mexican-painted tiles, are just steps from the sparkling Caribbean. The *Tackle Box Sea Bar* sits right over the water, where you can watch what they call "one of Mother Nature's best shows" – tarpon, rays and other sea creatures swimming in direct view, below and around you. Breakfast and boat transfer are complimentary, as is unlimited use of kayaks. U̲S̲$̲1̲7̲0̲

White Sands Cove Resort 2.5 miles north of San Pedro ☎ 226 3528, ⓦ whitesandscove.com; map p.93. A perfect blend between relaxed and refined, this breezy resort has rustic, airy rooms, colourfully tiled bathrooms, hammocks hung under towering palms and all sorts of generous amenities, including kayak and bicycle use, free coffee and more. U̲S̲$̲2̲1̲1̲

★**X'Tan Ha** 7.2 miles north of San Pedro ☎ 226 4398, ⓦ xtanha.com; map p.93. This relaxed, self-sustaining resort – pronounced Ish-tan-ha – is ideal for those looking to check out for a few days, turn off the phone, ignore email and loll on the gorgeous beach, while refuelling on tropical cocktails at the *palapa* bar. The warmly decorated one-bedroom villas, fully equipped with kitchenette, dining room and private veranda are like having a mini home on the Caribbean Sea. U̲S̲$̲2̲8̲5̲

3

EATING

San Pedro features some of the best **restaurants** in the country, and an island highlight is, naturally, **seafood**, including excellent lobster and conch. **Prices** are generally higher than elsewhere in Belize, but you can also find plenty of **street vendors** in the town centre and local eateries, usually on the back streets, that offer excellent value, especially at lunchtime (see box below).

SAN PEDRO

Belize Chocolate Company Barrier Reef Drive ☎ 226 3015, ⓦ belizechocolatecompany.com; map p.95. This artisan, microbatch "bean to bar" chocolate company uses fair-traded cacao ("kakaw" in Maya) beans from farms in Southern Belize. Stop in for all sorts of chocolate treats,

SAN PEDRO STREET FOOD

The best of the Caribbean and Central America comes together at San Pedro's **street food vendors** which offer top-quality grub at low prices. The good news? The vendors are everywhere, from Central Park to the main streets to the beachfront. As ever, follow the locals: when you see them lining up at a stand, do the same. Many vendors are also mobile, alerting hungry customers with a distinctive chant or bell.

You'll find a wonderfully diverse array of cuisines on the menu, from Johnny Cakes to tacos to *pupusas* to fresh fruit, including pineapples that are sliced open in front of you. You can fill up for under Bz$10 – tacos and fruit go for Bz$3–4. On the weekend, as elsewhere in Belize, the outdoor barbecue grills are fired up, and you can pick up a heaping plate of barbecue and rice and beans from Bz$8–10.

including thick chocolate milkshakes, fat brownies, creamy chocolate cheesecake and bars studded with everything from local fruits and nuts to chilli peppers. Desserts and shakes Bz$3–10. Mon–Sat 9.30am–6.30pm.

★**Blue Water Grill** At the Sunbreeze Hotel ☎ 226 3347, ⓦ bluewatergrillbelize.com; map p.95. Island local Kelly and her husband Mukul run one of the best restaurants in town. The wonderfully imaginative dishes match the gorgeous setting, on a low-key stretch of beach where you can contemplate the Caribbean from your table. While rooted in Belize, the menu spans the world, and includes coconut shrimp sticks with a spicy black bean sauce (Bz$24), pan-roasted grouper with wild rice and corn (Bz$48), pork belly with wasabi mashed potatoes (Bz$38) and crisp pizzas (Bz$23–36). Or, come by for sushi night (Tues & Thurs). The wine list is well-curated, with superb vintages from Portugal to California. Daily 7–10.30am, 11.30am–2.30pm & 6–9.30pm.

Boogie's Belly Pelican St ☎ 670 8080; map p.95. Two words: meat pies. The flaky rounds, filled with chicken or beef or, when in season, lobster, are the finest on the island. Plus, this small hideaway also makes other out-of-this-world breakfast goodies, including fry-jacks and waffles, and good, strong coffee. Get there early – meat pies are often sold out by 9am. Mains Bz$1.50–7. Daily 6.30–11am.

Caliente On the beach at the Spindrift Hotel ☎ 226 2170, ⓦ calientebelize.com; map p.95. Settle into a beachfront table and feast on tasty Mexican-Belizean food, from ginger-rum shrimp (Bz$36) to Jalisco chicken (Bz$32) spiked with chilli *chipotle*. Tues–Sun 11am–9.30pm.

Caprice In the Holiday Hotel, Barrier Reef Drive, just south of the centre ☎ 226 2014, ⓦ sanpedroholiday .com; map p.95. The waterfront *Caprice* serves a creative menu, including fresh fish with mango salsa and shrimp quesadillas. Mains Bz$25–40. Top off the meal with fresh tropical cocktails, like creamy piña coladas. Daily 11am–2pm & 5.30–9pm.

Caramba! Restaurant 20 Pescador Drive ☎ 226 4321, ⓦ carambabelize.com; map p.95. The flavourful Mexican-influenced menu is matched by the potent cocktails and convivial atmosphere. Try the conch in garlic butter (Bz$16) and other seafood specialities. 11am–2pm & 5–10pm; closed Wed.

Elvi's Kitchen Pescador Drive ☎ 226 2176, ⓦ elviskitchen.com; map p.95. A San Pedro institution, *Elvi's* started out as a "humble burger stand", and now has an expanded menu that includes top-notch seafood, chicken and steaks (mains Bz$25–45). Friday is Maya Buffet night, which features live music. Mon–Sat 10am–11pm.

Estel's Dine by the Sea On the beach, at the end of Buccaneer St ☎ 226 2019, ⓦ ambergriscaye.com /estels; map p.95. One of the most popular spots on the island for breakfast – and for good reason. Fill up on fry jacks, *huevos rancheros* heaped with beans and omelettes

filled with everything from lobster to bacon and cheese. Mains Bz$12–16. Daily 6am–5pm.

El Fogón Off Tarpon St, just north of the airstrip ☎ 206 2121; map p.95. This casual, thatched-roof restaurant is one of the few on the caye where traditional Belizean cuisine is cooked over an actual "fire hearth" (in Creole, "fyah haat"). Try any number of local delicacies, including *gibnut* (a type of nocturnal rodent – much better than it sounds) and cow foot soup. Mains Bz$10–20. Mon–Sat 11.30am–3pm & 6.30–9pm.

My Secret Deli Caribeña St ☎ 226 3223; map p.95. It's not a secret any more – and once you've had a taste, you'll understand why. Join the locals who queue up at lunch for the home-made Belizean fare, from aromatic conch soup to stew chicken (mains from Bz$8). Hours vary, but usually daily 7–10am & noon–3pm.

Red Ginger In The Phoenix hotel, Barrier Reef Drive ☎ 226 4623, ⓦ redgingerbelize.com; map p.95. Sophisticated restaurant with fresh, flavourful tropical cuisine, like blackened shrimp salad with hearts of palm (Bz$28) to seafood-stuffed grouper with coconut rice (Bz$57). Cocktails (Bz$14–18) are equally tasty – try the watermelon martini. Wed–Sun 7.30–10.30am, 11.30am–2.30pm & 6–9.30pm.

★**Wild Mango's** 42 Barrier Reef Drive ☎ 226 2859; map p.95. Owned by locally renowned chef Amy Knox (who has several times been voted Belize's best chef) and featuring an innovative menu of Caribbean-Latin cuisine (mains Bz$20–45), from rum-glazed bacon shrimp to citrus-ginger snapper, as well as sinfully good desserts. Mon–Sat 11.30am–9pm.

SOUTH OF SAN PEDRO

Casa Picasso Stingray St, near the lagoon side of island ☎ 226 4443, ⓦ casapicassobelize.com; map p.93. Dine on creative tapas and mains in an arty setting (hence the name) of contemporary paintings and a courtyard strung with twinkling lights. Kick off the meal with sticky shrimp tossed in a mango jam (Bz$28) and the lobster mac and cheese (Bz$36) – which is as good as it sounds – followed by butter-poached sea bass (Bz$48). Tues–Sat 5.30–11pm (or until last diner leaves); last reservation 9pm.

Hidden Treasure Sartsoon St, south of the Banana Beach Resort ☎ 226 4111, ⓦ hiddentreasurebelize .com; map p.93. Enjoy fine Belizean cuisine, from snapper seasoned with Maya spices and wrapped in a banana leaf to marinated ribs (mains Bz$25–50). The breezy, open-sided restaurant appeals with its rustic elegance, featuring mahogany tables and wood-beamed ceilings. Occasionally closes one day a week, so call to confirm. Generally daily 5–9pm.

Palmilla Restaurant At the Victoria House ☎ 226 2067, ⓦ victoria-house.com; map p.93. Excellent fine-dining

3

menu in a romantic, candlelit setting overlooking the hotel's pool. Enjoy fresh lobster, cashew-crusted grouper and succulent chicken. Also serves breakfast and lunch. Hours may vary, but generally daily 6.30am–10pm.

NORTH ISLAND

Aji Tapa Lounge & Restaurant 2 miles north of San Pedro ☎ 226 4047; map p.93. Dine al fresco, surrounded by palms, at this breezy Mediterranean beachside nook. The seafood tapas are tops, including garlic shrimp and conch *ceviche*. Also tasty are the paella, and coconut pie. Tapas Bz$15–30. Daily 5–10pm.

O Restaurant At Las Terrazas, 3.5 miles north of San Pedro ☎ 226 4249, ⊛ lasterrazasresort.com; map p.93.

The international fusion cuisine matches the lovely Caribbean views at this elegant restaurant. Tease the palate with the fresh sweet pepper and mango salad, and then move on to seafood risotto or grilled grouper. For dessert spoon up the Caye Lime Tart. Mains Bz$32–65. Mon–Fri 10am–9pm, Sat–Sun 8am–9pm.

Rain In Grand Caribe Belize Resort, 2 miles north of San Pedro ☎ 226 4000, ⊛ rainbelize.com; map p.93. Come here for the stunning views and stay for the tasty appetizers and seafood, including *ceviche*, cashew-crusted grouper and tangy vegetarian curry. Time your visit for sunset, and start off with a cocktail on the rooftop, which affords one of the finest views on the island. Mains Bz$40–60. Daily 7am–10pm.

DRINKING AND NIGHTLIFE

3

As the tourist capital of Belize, San Pedro boasts the liveliest **nightlife** in the country. You'll find the buzziest bars and clubs near the centre of town, along the beach. Locals often gather in Central Park in the evening, which fills with food vendors, making this a good spot to grab a cheap snack after a boozy night out.

Crazy Canucks At Exotic Caye Beach Resort, south of town ☎ 670 8001, ⊛ belizeisfun.com; map p.93. This loose and lively beach bar serves tropical cocktails like the Dirty Howler Monkey, made with Kahlua, dark rum and banana. Come by on "Sunday Funday", with beach horseshoe tournaments and jam sessions starting at 3pm. Daily 11am–midnight.

Fido's Courtyard Barrier Reef Drive, on the beach, just north of the park ☎ 226 3176, ⊛ fidosbelize.com; map p.95. This *palapa*-style beach club draws a nightly crowd to the ample bar and outdoor seating. Live music most nights of the week, and a great spot to meet other travellers. Daily 11am–midnight.

Finn and Martini Laguna Drive ☎ 627 4789; map p.95. Toast the San Pedro night with a martini (or three) at this sexy cocktail lounge, run by bon-vivant, restaurateur and mixologist Findley Halliday. Don't miss the watermelon martini and the Basil Jones, named after one of the country's famous Baymen, and made with coconut vodka and fresh basil. Cocktails Bz$12–18. Hours vary, but usually 6–10pm.

Jaguar's Temple Club Near Central Park ⊛ jaguarstempleclub.com; map p.95. A hopping dance club, where locals and visitors – plus the occasional shady character – come to groove under pulsating lights. Thurs–Sat 9pm–4am.

Lola's Pub Barrier Reef Drive, across from Belize Bank ☎ 206 2120; map p.95. Mix it up with a friendly crowd of expats and locals at this sports pub. Hearty pub grub ranges from burgers to fish and chips (from Bz$10). Daily 11am–midnight.

Palapa Bar and Grill On the beach, just south of Sandbar Hostel ☎ 226 2528, ⊛ palapabarandgrill.com; map p.95. Ease into the Caribbean evening over a rum

cocktail at this hugely popular *palapa* bar on the water. Soak up the alcohol with good pub grub, like fish tacos, pulled pork sandwiches and the appropriately named juicy "Kick Ass Humongous Burger" (Bz$10–20). Daily 10am–9pm.

★ **Rojo Beach Bar** 5 miles north of town, on the beach ☎ 226 4012, ⊛ rojolounge.com; map p.93. One of the best beach bars on the island, this place hits all the right notes: open-air *palapa* seating on a gorgeous stretch of beach, awesome views, infinity pool, fresh tropical cocktails and bar snacks that far exceed the usual pub grub, like lobster pizza (from Bz$15). Plus, there are games galore, from silly beer pong to beach Jenga. Tues–Sat noon until last person leaves.

Stella's Smile 1 mile north of the bridge ☎ 602 5284; map p.93. It doesn't get much better than wine tastings on the beach at sunset. This delightful outdoor bar-restaurant pours top-notch wines, all-you-can-drink sangria and a changing menu that includes fresh fish one night, and pizza another. Weekend breakfast is crêpes and bottomless mimosas. Wine tastings from Bz$18; mains Bz$20–40. Tues–Sat 4–9pm, Sun 8am–1pm.

Wahoo's Lounge At the Spindrift Hotel ☎ 226 2002; map p.95. This fairly humdrum spot becomes the island hotspot one evening a week: on Thursdays at 6pm it hosts the caye's famous "chicken drop" – a rollicking event where a bingo-style grid of numbers is laid out on the ground. A well-fed chicken is released to walk over them, until it poops on a number. Daily noon–midnight.

Wayos On the beachfront, next to the Aqua Vista Beachfront Suites; map p.95. The perfect little beach bar – and the perfect spot to meet locals, expats and the popular owner himself, "Wayo from Cayo". Knock back a Belikin or five and enjoy the breezes off the Caribbean. Daily noon–midnight.

SHOPPING

San Pedro offers plenty of shopping, from kitschy **souvenir shops** spilling over with "Belize it or Not" T-shirts and cheap magnets to **art galleries** with unique watercolours and **handicraft centres** with beautiful Belizean hardwoods fashioned into everything from chopping boards to dolphins.

Belizean Arts Barrier Reef Drive ☎ 226 3019, ⓦ belizeanarts.com; map p.95. The island's finest shop for local art and handicrafts, including detailed woodcarvings, oil paintings depicting daily life on the cayes, watercolours of lush tropical landscapes, delicate ceramics, handcrafted jewellery and more. Mon–Sat 9am–10pm.

Graniel's Dreamland Pescador Drive ☎ 226 2632, ⓦ granielsdreamlandbelize.com; map p.95. Many tourist shops have Belizean woodcarvings, but few offer this kind of quality. Woodworker Armando Graniel has been in the business for over 25 years, and here you'll find his beautiful creations, from salad bowls and tongs to chopping boards and wall hangings. Graniel also does large-scale pieces, from cabinets to tables. Mon–Sat 9am–noon, 1–5pm & 7–9pm, Sun 10am–noon.

Wine de Vine Coconut Drive, near Island Supermarket ☎ 226 3430; map p.95. The island's best wine shop is stocked with everything from French to Italian to Spanish vintages, along with imported cheeses. Daily 9am–6pm.

DIRECTORY

Banks San Pedro has several banks, including Belize Bank and Atlantic Bank, both on the main strip of town, Barrier Reef Drive. Note that US dollars are accepted everywhere on Ambergris Caye.

Hospitals San Pedro has the only hyperbaric chamber in Belize (☎ 226 2851), located behind the airstrip; your dive operator will have all the details in case of emergency.

There are also several medical clinics, including the San Carlos Medical Clinic (☎ 226 2918) on Pescador Drive.

Police The police station (☎ 206 2022) is at the northern end of Pescador Drive.

Post office The post office is in the Alijua Building near the middle of Barrier Reef Drive.

Caye Caulker

You'll see the sign "Go slow" throughout **CAYE CAULKER**, and after a day or two on the island, that's exactly what you'll be doing. The beautiful, palm-clad island, which lies south of Ambergris Caye and 22 miles northeast of Belize City, derives its name from a local wild fruit, the *hicaco*, or coco plum. It's an island of lazy pleasures – soaking up the sun by day, and drinking rum punch to reggae music by night. But while Caye Caulker will probably always be on the Belize backpacker circuit, it now also attracts honeymooning couples, families and more upmarket travellers. Accordingly, services have sprung up to cater to them, including smart condos with sparkling pools which share the sandy lanes with clapboard budget lodgings.

Until about 25 years ago, tourism existed almost as a sideline to the island's main source of income, **lobster fishing**. Although the lobster catch increased for many years after fishing cooperatives were set up in the 1960s, the deployment of more traps over an ever-wider area led to the rapid depletion of the **spiny lobster**, once so common that it could be scooped onto the beaches with palm fronds. Their numbers remain low today, and in some years the creatures are so scarce that the fishermen call it quits by mid-January, a month before the end of the legal season. Despite this, there are always plenty of lobsters around for the annual **Lobster Fest**, held in June to celebrate the reopening of the season.

The big draw, of course, is the **Barrier Reef**, which unfolds only a mile from the shore – the white foam of the reef crest is always visible to the east. The entire length of the reef off Caye Caulker – as in Ambergris Caye – was declared a marine reserve in 1998, and visiting it is an experience not to be missed. Dozens of tour companies offer trips, from diving to sailing to snorkelling, where you can swim along coral canyons, surrounded by an astonishing range of fish, with perhaps a harmless nurse shark or two.

Caye Caulker's five-mile length is split into two unequal sections by the "**Split**", originally a small passage cut by local fishermen that's since grown into a swiftly

Caye Caulker Forest & Marine Reserve

CAYE CAULKER

● SHOPPING
Caribbean Colors	2
Celi's Gift Shop & Music Store	3
Cooper's Art Gallery	1

■ ACCOMMODATION
Anchorage Resort	12
Barefoot Beach Hotel	17
Blue Wave Guesthouse	6
Caye Caulker Condos	2
Caye Caulker Plaza Hotel	9
Caye Reef	4
Colinda Cabanas	16
De Real McCaw Guest House	7
Iguana Reef Inn	8
Lazy Iguana B&B	15
Ocean Pearl Royale Hotel	5
Sea Dreams Hotel	1
Seaside Cabañas	11
Sophie's Guest Rooms	3
Tropical Paradise	13
Tree Tops Guesthouse	14
Weezie's	18
Yuma's House Belize	10

● EATING
Amor y Café	12
Caribbean Colors	7
Crepes and Dreams	11
Errolyns House of Fry Jacks	6
Fran's Grill	3
Glenda's Restaurant	10
Habaneros	9
Happy Lobster	5
Ice 'n' Beans	4
Rainbow Restaurant	2
Rose's Grill & Bar	8
Syd's Restaurant	13
Wish Willy's	1

■ DRINKING AND NIGHTLIFE
Barrier Reef Sports Bar	2
I & I Reggae Bar	3
Lazy Lizard	1

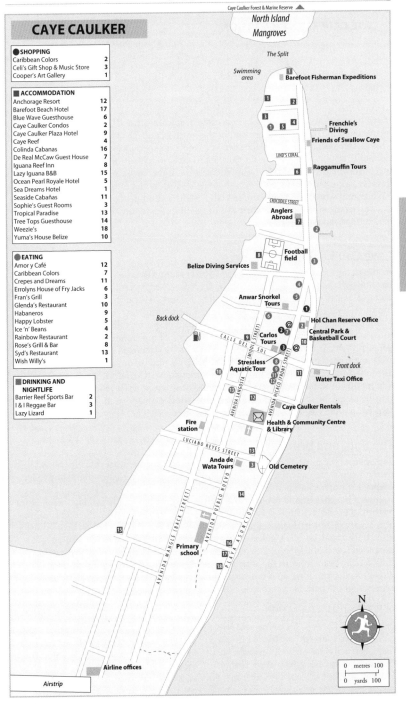

3

CAYE CAULKER ORIENTATION

Getting around the island is a breeze: you'll find three sandy **main streets** running roughly parallel to the eastern shore. Officially, these are called Avenida Hicaco, Avenida Langosta and Avenida Mangle, but the original names of "**Front**", "**Middle**" and "**Back**", respectively, are often used. Outside the village, the main streets end and only a single road leads north and south, turning into a winding path beyond the airstrip.

moving boat channel, widened by successive tropical storms. The main village, and most hotels, are on the northern end of the south island. The north island has long been largely uninhabited, but the caye as a whole is experiencing a build-up on both sides of the Split. Still, most visitors have little reason to venture to the north island, except for the occasional trip to the land section of the **Caye Caulker Forest and Marine Reserve**, whose littoral forest covers the northern tip of the caye.

No matter where you roam on the island, bring a good insect repellent: though there is a near-constant sea breeze, when this drops the air gets very sticky, and **sandflies and mosquitoes** can be unbearable.

Caye Caulker Marine Reserve

At the island's northern tip is the **Caye Caulker Marine Reserve**, which also encompasses an adjoining lagoon of the Caye Caulker Forest Reserve. This area was a coconut plantation before Hurricane Hattie hit in 1961, but has not been in active use since, so the native littoral forest has had nearly fifty years to regenerate. The mangrove shallows support fish nurseries and small species called "sardines" by fishermen, who use them as bait to catch snapper. Sponges, anemones and other colourful sea creatures grow on the mangrove roots. **American saltwater crocodiles** are sometimes seen here, but you're more likely to find them in the wild on the Turneffe Atoll (see p.113) or in the more remote coastal areas. Other native inhabitants of the littoral forest include **boa constrictors**, scaly-tailed iguanas (locally called "wish willies"), geckos and five species of land crab. Many local tour companies (see opposite) offer day-trips here.

The Split and beaches

The **Split**, at the north end of the village, is a narrow channel that splits the island into two. It has also become the caye's social and swimming hub, thanks to its sunny piers, deep, clear waters, and popular restaurant and bar, the *Lazy Lizard* (see p.112). Caye Caulker's **beaches** unfold south of the Split, and some have fairly minimal sand, as the proximity of the reef stops sand building up on the foreshore. Also, the waters off the beaches are relatively shallow. But, the good news is that the beaches are ever-growing: in 2016, through a Caye Caulker Village Council Initiative, the beach area was expanded south of the Split. What's more, Caye Caulker officials plan to develop more public beachfront in the years to come. Note that swimming out to the reef is discouraged, since it requires crossing a busy boat lane where fatal accidents have occurred in the past, as captains do not expect swimmers.

ARRIVAL AND INFORMATION

CAYE CAULKER

By plane Tropic Air (see p.23) and Maya Island Air (see p.23) operate flights between Philip Goldson International Airport (from Bz$144 one way), Belize Municipal Airport (from Bz$75 one way) and San Pedro (at least hourly, daily 7.30am–5pm; 25min), calling at Caye Caulker along the way (on request; same price). Caye Caulker's airstrip is about a mile south of the centre. From here, you can catch a golf cart taxi into the centre (from Bz$7).

By boat From Belize City, boats to Caye Caulker are operated by the San Pedro Belize Express Water Taxi (☎ 223 2225, ⊛ belizewatertaxi.com; Bz$30 one way, Bz$50 return), which departs from North Front St, near Tourist

Village, and the Ocean Ferry Belize (☎ 223 0033, ⓦ oceanferrybelize.com; Bz$24 one way, Bz$44 return), departing from North Front St, near Swing Bridge. The same companies also connect Caye Caulker with San Pedro (from $24), while the San Pedro Belize Express Water Taxi also runs several trips weekly to Chetumal in Mexico.
Destinations Belize City (14 daily; 45min); Chetumal,

Mexico (several weekly; 2hr 10min); San Pedro (14 daily; 1hr).
Tourist information There's no official tourist office in Caye Caulker, but you can find lots of info on a variety of websites, including those of the Belize Tourism Industry Association (BTIA; ⓦ gocayecaulker.com) and the Caye Caulker Village Council (ⓦ cayecaulkerbelize.net).

ACTIVITIES AND TOURS

Caye Caulker is dotted with tour companies offering everything from diving and snorkelling to sailing and fishing. General **prices** on snorkelling and diving are covered elsewhere in the chapter (see box below); for fishing, costs are around US$250–350/person for a half day, while overnight sailing tours start at around US300/person.

SNORKELLING AND DIVING

Anda De Wata Tours Luciano Reyes St ☎ 666 7374, ⓦ snorkelandadewatabelize.com. Friendly, long-established outfit that offers snorkelling and inland tours, with a personalized approach and a focus on smaller groups. Its fun slogan? "Cos it's Hotta Anda De Wata".

Anwar Snorkel Tours Front St, two blocks north of Front Dock ☎ 226 0327, ⓦ anwartours.com. Established, top-notch outfit, with snorkel trips and tours that explore underwater wildlife including manatees and seahorses. Anwar also has tours and inland trips to Altun Ha, Lamanai and river cave tubing.

★ **Belize Diving Services** Back side of the island, near the football field ☎ 226 0143, ⓦ belizedivingservices .com. One of the best dive services on the island – if not in

the entire cayes – with an unwavering commitment to safety, along with knowledgeable and patient guides.

Carlos Tours Front St ☎ 600 1654, ⓔ carlosayala @gmail.com. Snorkeling tours to Hol Chan Marine Reserve and Shark-Ray Alley, led by the conscientious guide Carlos Ayala, place an emphasis on conservation and education.

Frenchie's Towards the north end of the village ☎ 226 0234, ⓦ frenchiesdivingbelize.com. This popular company runs a wide range of dive tours, including to Turneffe and overnight trips to the Blue Hole.

Stressless Aquatic Tour Calle del Sol ☎ 624 6064, ⓦ stresslesstours.com. This well-run company offers snorkel tours throughout the area, from Hol Chan Marine Reserve to Caye Caulker Marine Reserve. They also have

DIVING AND SNORKELLING AROUND CAYE CAULKER

Caye Caulker is filled with **snorkel and dive operators** (see above) offering a wide range of trips, from half-day snorkel jaunts to serious dives that result in PADI certification.

All dive shops on the caye offer reef diving and visits to coral gardens, and many have **night dives**. A diving trip to the **Lighthouse Reef** and the **Blue Hole** is an unforgettable experience (although some people are disappointed by the lack of marine life in the depths). After the unique, slightly spooky splendour of diving over 115ft into the hole, many groups visit the fantastic 260ft wall off **Half Moon Caye**. A brief stop on the island itself lets you observe red-footed boobies and huge hermit crabs before climbing back in the boat for the Long Caye wall. The **Turneffe Atoll** has world-class dive sites, too – some believe the best diving in Belize. North Turneffe and Turneffe Elbow are the most popular trips from Caye Caulker.

You can snorkel on your own, but the most rewarding **snorkelling** experiences are likely to be on an organized tour, which can educate you on what you're seeing. Some trips visit **Hol Chan Marine Reserve** and **Shark-Ray Alley**, but these tend to be busier and more expensive, and you'll be just as happy in either Caye Caulker's own marine reserve or the outer atolls, Turneffe in particular (see p.113) – keep an eye out for the **dolphins** that often accompany boats on the way.

Other popular snorkelling destinations include Goff's Caye, English Caye and Sergeant's Caye, tiny specks of sand and coral with a few palm trees. A trip to any of these may be combined with a stop at Swallow Caye Wildlife Sanctuary (see p.112), a mangrove caye with seagrass beds near Belize City, where you can view (but not swim with) **manatees**.

Prices are similar to those in San Pedro, with two-hour, single-tank dives in the nearby reef starting at US$50–75; double-tank dives at US$75–100; and PADI certification at US$300. Diving trips to the Turneffe Atoll and Blue Hole begin at around US$250. Snorkel tours cost around US$30–60 for two to four hours, depending on destination and other extras.

half-day fishing trips, which cater to all levels, from novice to experienced.

SAILING
Raggamuffin Tours North end of Front St ☎ 226 0348, ⓦ sailingadventuresbelize.com. This established, lively company runs lovely sunset cruises and overnight sailing trips that include Tobacco Caye.

FISHING
Anglers Abroad Hattie St, near the Split ☎ 226 0602, ⓦ anglersabroad.com. Fishing trips (including overnight), from fly-fishing to deep-sea fishing to night fishing.
Barefoot Fisherman Expeditions Front St, near the Split ☎ 226 0405, ⓦ barefootfishermanexpeditions .com. This experienced group of tour guides and captains run half-day, full-day and night fishing trips.

ACCOMMODATION

Caye Caulker has a range of **accommodation**, from simply furnished, inexpensive rooms in brightly painted clapboard guesthouses to mid-range B&Bs and sleek resorts with swimming pools. The caye is easily walkable: even the furthest hotels are no more than a half-hour walk from the Front Dock. The sandy streets and paths are far less busy in the **southern** part of the caye, and most of the accommodation in this area is in the mid- to upper-range. Consult the map (see p.107) to confirm, and if you're staying at one of the further places, enquire about the availability of bicycles, which are helpful for zipping into town. For a well-curated selection of **rental properties**, check Caye Caulker Accommodations (☎ 610 0240, ⓦ cayecaulkeraccommodations.com).

IN AND AROUND THE CENTRE
Blue Wave Guesthouse North end of Front St ☎ 206 0114, ⓦ bluewaveguesthouse.com. Pleasant family-run place just paces from the shoreline, offering well-maintained a/c rooms with showers and cable TV, with both shared and private bath. Shared-bath rooms US$32, en suites US$60

Caye Caulker Condos One block from the Split ☎ 226 0072, ⓦ cayecaulkercondos.com. Excellent-quality apartments with full kitchens, a safe for valuables, a/c and large showers decorated with river stones. Take a dip in the swimming pool, borrow one of the complimentary bicycles or drink in the lovely sea views from the large rooftop *palapa*. US$100

★ **Caye Caulker Plaza Hotel** Middle St ☎ 226 0780, ⓦ cayecaulkerplazahotel.com. Overall, this is one of the best-run hotels in the town centre. Painted a cheery yellow, the hotel has clean, sizeable a/c rooms, well-maintained bathrooms with rain shower and a rooftop terrace. US$85

★ **Caye Reef** Front St ☎ 226 0382, ⓦ cayereef.com. The well-groomed *Caye Reef* features a range of inviting light-filled apartments – perfect for a family, romancing couples or a small group of friends – with a/c, two bedrooms, fully equipped kitchen and a private balcony with hammock. There's also a spacious roof terrace, where you can soak in the jacuzzi while taking in the breathtaking views. US$155

★ **Colinda Cabanas** On the beachfront, south of the cemetery ☎ 226 0383, ⓦ colindacabanas.com. Bright, spick-and-span *cabañas* with a/c, kitchens, in-room safe and other extras, including purified water in the rooms and free bikes Also, each *cabaña* has a porch with hammock, where you can gently swing to the sounds of the nearby sea. US$69

De Real Macaw Guest House Front St, south of the Split ☎ 226 0459, ⓦ derealmacaw.biz. Simple but

good-value rooms and thatched *cabañas* facing the sea. For solo budget travellers, there's the Little Budget Room in the back of the hotel – it's basic, with no a/c, but the price is right at US$20. US$55

Iguana Reef Inn At the back side of the caye, across the football field ☎ 226 0213, ⓦ iguanareefinn.com. Beautiful, airy hotel with well-furnished suites with tiled floors, local artwork, a/c and ceiling fans, queen-sized beds – and great sunset views. They rent kayaks, and also have a pool and complimentary continental breakfasts. US$160

Ocean Pearl Royale Hotel Towards the back of the island, two blocks from the Split ☎ 226 0074, ⓦ oceanpearlhotelbelize.com. Simple but comfy, well-tended rooms, some with a/c. The owners can offer plenty of local information and there's complimentary coffee in the lobby. US$50

★ **Sea Dreams Hotel** Hattie St, near the Split ☎ 226 0602, ⓦ seadreamsbelize.com. Inviting, breezy *cabañas*, around a banyan tree-shaded courtyard, with a/c and coffeemaker. With its nearby pier where you can watch the glorious Caribbean sunsets, this is the kind of place that inspires relocation – for longer stays, there are roomy one- and two-bedroom apartments (US$215). The co-owner runs Anglers Abroad (see above), and is one of the island's top experts in fly-fishing. US$120

Seaside Cabañas Just south of the Front Dock ☎ 226 0498, ⓦ seasidecabanas.com. Well-designed and furnished rooms and thatched *cabañas*, all with a/c, fridge and veranda with hammocks. Nicely decorated both inside and out in rich colours, and arranged around a pool. The beachfront *cabañas* have rooftop decks where you can soak up the sun. US$135

Sophie's Guest Rooms Almond St ☎ 661 2715, ⓦ sophiesguestrooms.webs.com. Simple but clean, these spacious budget rooms have fans (no a/c) and shared bathrooms. This is off the main drag, so the evenings are wonderfully quiet, with often just the sound of the sea and wind. US$15

★**Tropical Paradise** Luciano Reyes, just south of cemetery ☎226 0124, ⍵tropicalparadise-cayecaulker .com. One of the originals – and still going strong. Individual *cabañas*, each with a short flight of wooden steps straight up from the sand, are basic and faded but clean. The adjoining outdoor restaurant, with views over the leafy cemetery and sea, serves good local food – try the lobster omelette for breakfast and the chicken with rice and beans. US$84

Yuma's House Belize Front St, near Front Dock ☎206 0019, ⍵yumashousebelize.com. This relaxed hostel, visible from the water taxi dock, features a clean beach house with dorm beds as well as private rooms. You can cook in the communal kitchen, and outside is a pretty garden with hammocks and a deck for sunbathing. Dorms US$19, doubles US$45

SOUTH OF THE CENTRE

Anchorage Resort Near Playa Asunción ☎206 0304. Clean, if plain, tiled rooms with decent beds, private bath, fridge, cable TV and balconies overlooking the sea in a three-storey concrete building in palm-shaded grounds. The higher rooms have great views. US$85

Barefoot Beach Hotel On the beach, just south of the school ☎226 0205, ⍵barefootbeachbelize.com.

Comfortable, colourful rooms with private bath, a/c and small fridge in a concrete house on the beach. There are also roomy wooden cottages (US$130) and a sun-splashed dock. US$85

Lazy Iguana Bed & Breakfast At the back of the island, just north of the airstrip ☎226 0350, ⍵lazyiguana.net. Lovely B&B, with four comfortable, well-maintained a/c rooms, each with a private bathroom. The top floor has a thatched deck with hammocks to enjoy 360-degree views over the sea and the lagoon. Wake up to a complimentary breakfast of fresh fruit, baked goods and brewed coffee. US$110

Tree Tops Guesthouse On the beachfront, past the cemetery ☎226 0240, ⍵treetopsbelize.com. Bright and clean rooms with fridge and ceiling fans, and lovely rooftop a/c suites with fantastic views, all set in a small, peaceful, palm-shaded garden. Deservedly popular, so booking ahead is advised. US$115

Weezie's Playa Asuncion ☎376 2167, ⍵weeziescaye caulker.com. This impeccably maintained oceanfront boutique hotel is far enough away from the buzzy centre that you'll often feel like you have the island to yourself, but close enough that you can get to the main street in five minutes by bike. The range of rooms include oceanview and loft suites, and the penthouse, which fills the entire top floor, with splendid views of the Caribbean. US$119

EATING

Reasonable prices and local cuisine characterize many of the island's **restaurants**, many of which are sprinkled along Front St. Aim to eat in the early-to-mid-evening, as many places close by 9–10pm. **Lobster** (in season) is served in every dish imaginable, from curry to quesadillas; other **seafood** is also generally well priced. You can buy groceries at several shops and supermarkets around the village.

★**Amor y Café** Front St ☎610 2397. After a few days on the cayes, you'll probably be craving a quality cup of coffee. This is the place to get it. Greet the morning on the breezy deck with a jolt of caffeine, along with tasty breakfasts (Bz$7–15), including hefty waffles, eggs made to order, fruit smoothies and more. Tues–Sat 6am–2pm.

Caribbean Colors Café Front St ☎226 0208, ⍵caribbean-colors.com. Located in an appealing art shop (see p.112), this place serves wonderfully fresh cuisine with a vegetarian angle, like big quinoa salads, vegan potato and corn chowder and delicious breakfasts including banana pancakes. Mains Bz$15–30. Hours vary, but generally 7am–3pm.

Crepes and Dreams Front St ☎670 4870. A slice of Paris in the Caribbean, this inviting little spot serves warm, freshly prepared crêpes, filled with everything from seafood to Nutella and bananas (Bz$8–20). Generally daily 7am–1pm, with shorter hours in low season.

Errolyns House of Fry Jacks Middle St. This is the quintessential Caye Caulker eatery – the basic shack belies

the delicious fry-jacks ($2–5) being made within. The deep-fried dough is filled with everything from beans and chicken to ham and egg. Mon–Sat 6am–3pm.

Fran's Grill Just north of the Front Dock, on the beach. Look for this green-painted beach hut for communal meals of fresh seafood, grilled to order, along with unlimited rum punch. Seating is at weathered picnic tables, with your toes in the sand and the breeze in your hair. Mains Bz$15–30. Hours vary, but usually daily noon–9pm.

Glenda's Restaurant South of the Back Dock ☎226 0148. Justly famous for its delicious cinnamon rolls and fresh orange juice. You can also fill up on breakfast burritos and traditional Belizean lunch dishes like chicken with rice and beans. Baked goods Bz$2–5; mains Bz$14–25. Mon–Fri 7am–3pm.

Habaneros Just south of the Front Dock ☎226 0487. Considered one of the island's top restaurants, with creative gourmet international meals – from juicy pork chops to grilled lobster to tangy Caye Lime Pie – along with one of the finest selections of wine on the island. Mains Bz$20–50.

3

Daily 5.30–10pm; sometimes closed Thurs.

Happy Lobster Front St, just north of the centre. This big, breezy restaurant serves all the Belizean favourites at decent prices, including fresh grilled lobster with butter and snapper spiked with garlic, accompanied by rice and beans. The lobster omelette for breakfast is excellent too. Mains Bz$15–35. 6am–10pm; closed Tues.

Ice 'n' Beans Front St ☎ 662 5089. Kick off the morning with a potent espresso – and sunrise views – at this inviting café. The home-made sugar cinnamon donuts rival the brews, as do the flavoured shaved ices. Daily 6.30am–6pm.

★**Rainbow Restaurant** On the beach, near Front Dock ☎ 226 0281. Bask in sea breezes at this popular restaurant over the water. Try lobster in coconut sauce – or the nicely priced lobster quesadilla – washed down with a fresh watermelon juice or a chilled Belikin beer. Mains Bz$17–45. Tues–Sun 11am–10pm.

Rose's Grill & Bar Center St ☎ 206 0407. "If you haven't been to Rose's, then you haven't been to Belize" is their tagline, and they may be right. This friendly restaurant serves some of the freshest seafood on the island, grilled to order. Kick off the meal with the chunky *ceviche*. Also tasty is the barbecued chicken. Mains Bz$20–40. Daily 11am–10pm.

★**Syd's Restaurant** Middle St ☎ 206 0294. This long-established favourite has been serving Belizean comfort dishes at great prices for over thirty years. As well as its legendary fried chicken dinner (includes two side dishes), you can fill up on lobster burritos, chicken and rice and beans, home-made tortillas and more. Mains Bz$9–16. Hours vary, but usually Mon–Sat 10am–3pm & 6–9pm.

Wish Willy's At the north end of the island ☎ 660 7194, ⓦ wish-willy.com. A true Caye Caulker experience: chilled-out (sometimes too chilled-out – service can be slow) restaurant in a ramshackle building at the back of the island, where Belizean chef Maurice Moore creates tasty seafood dishes, like whole grilled fish with coconut lime. Mains Bz$20–40. Occasionally open for breakfast or lunch as well. Daily 5pm–midnight.

DRINKING AND NIGHTLIFE

Caye Caulker's casual vibe extends to its **bars**, which are all about drinking Belikins under the starry Caribbean sky, with the occasional impromptu jam session thrown in.

Barrier Reef Sports Bar Front St ☎ 226 0077, ⓦ belizesportsbar.com. This is the island's party bar, with an ongoing loop of sports on the TVs. Come by for the rocking Friday jam sessions (3–6pm) when local and visiting musicians make music together. The menu's good and hearty, including chilled Belikins and beefy burgers (Bz$15). Daily 9am–midnight.

I & I Reggae Bar Middle St. Head to this three-storey reggae hangout, where you can chill out on swing chairs on one floor, and dance to DJ music on another. Daily 4pm–1am.

Lazy Lizard At the Split. This outdoor waterside bar at the Split has gone through numerous management changes, but even so, few spots are more emblematic of Caye Caulker than here. It's an obligatory stop for visitors, but also attracts an equal number of locals, including plenty of characters and Rasta guys. The time to come by is in the later afternoon, to enjoy a cocktail or three as the sun sets. Daily 10am–midnight.

SHOPPING

Caye Caulker has a colourful array of shops, from tourist-trinket stores to galleries hung with watercolours of island scenery. You'll also find plenty of street vendors on Front St leading up to the Split, selling hardwood carvings and shell jewellery.

Caribbean Colors Front St ☎ 226 0208, ⓦ caribbean -colors.com. This aptly named shop is filled with colourful local art, including gorgeous hand-painted silks, as well as handmade jewellery and photography. Hours vary, but generally 7am–3pm.

Celi's Gift Shop & Music Store Front St ☎ 226 0346. One of the best spots on the island to pick up conch shell carvings, from earrings to rings to elegant dolphins with arching backs. The store also sells a varied array of local music on CD. Hours vary, but usually daily 9am–6pm.

Cooper's Art Gallery Front St ☎ 226 0330 ⓦ debbiecooper.artspan.com. Take some of the island home with you by picking up a painting of it, at this gallery featuring local paintings. Wed–Sun noon–8pm.

Swallow Caye Wildlife Sanctuary

About 4 miles east of Belize City and 19 miles southwest of Caye Caulker • Open during daylight hours • Bz$10 • ☎ 226 0151, ⓦ swallowcayemanatees.org • Local tour companies visit the sanctuary on request as part of day- or half-day trips

The Drowned Cayes (which include Swallow Caye) form the **Swallow Caye Wildlife Sanctuary**, just a ten-minute boat ride from Belize City (40min from Caye Caulker). This secure refuge is home to a healthy population of **West Indian manatees**. Belize has one of the largest surviving populations of these gentle giants, which congregate here to feed on the abundant turtle-grass beds, their primary food source, and use the deeper areas near Swallow Caye as resting places. The sanctuary, covering fourteen square miles, sustains an array of other marine life including bottlenose dolphins, American crocodiles and the upside-down jellyfish. It's co-managed by the Friends of Swallow Caye and the Ministry of Natural Resources, and most people visit on **day-trips**, departing from Caye Caulker or Ambergris Caye. On some of these ventures, the skipper will turn off the motor as you near, quietly pushing the boat towards the manatees in order not to disturb them.

St George's Caye

Tiny **St George's Caye**, around nine miles from Belize City, was the capital of the Baymen in the seventeenth and eighteenth centuries, and still manages to exude an air of colonial grandeur; its beautifully restored houses face east to catch the breeze and their lush, green lawns are enclosed by white picket fences. Eighteenth-century cannons are mounted in front of some of the finer houses, and for another glimpse into the past you could head to the small graveyard of the early settlers on the southern tip of the island.

Unless you stay at *St George's Caye Resort* (see below), though, the island isn't really set up for casual visitors; some fishing and snorkelling trips may call in for a brief look-around, but that usually has to be requested beforehand.

ACCOMMODATION   **ST GEORGE'S CAYE**

St George's Caye Resort ☎ 220 4444, ⓦ st-georges resort.com. This all-inclusive dive resort – one of the first dedicated dive resorts on the cayes – features rooms in a handsome main lodge as well as wood-and-thatch *cabañas* with private verandas. The dive packages include all meals and beverages, airport transfers, and a range of free activities from kayaking to snorkelling. US139

Turneffe Atoll

Belize's largest atoll is made up of numerous uninhabited islands, which form an oval archipelago rising from the seabed and enclosed by a beautiful coral reef. Situated 25 miles from Belize City, they are primarily low-lying mangrove islands – some quite large – and sandbanks around a shallow lagoon. Thanks to relatively minimal human development, the **Turneffe Atoll** is one of the most biologically diverse areas of the Caribbean. To the rejoicing of environmentalists, it was finally declared an official **marine reserve** in 2012, making it one of the largest in Belize.

The **diving** and **snorkelling** here is sublime, with an excellent range of diving spots. Highlights include Turneffe Elbow, at the the southern point, which features dramatic drop-offs and is more exposed to currents than other areas, therefore attracting stunning schools of fish; Rendezvous Point, at the northern end, with gorgeous wall dives; and Lefty's Ledge, with eye-catching spur-and-groove reefs. **Fishing** in the shallow flats of Turneffe is also tops, typically for bonefish. Most of the sportfishing is on a catch-and-release basis. Many of the resorts, as well as the Oceanic Society field station (see p.114), are on lush **Blackbird Caye**, which lies halfway down the eastern side of the archipelago. The resorts are generally quite pricey and all-inclusive, including transport from Belize City (and usually from the international airport), all meals and whatever diving and/or fishing package is arranged. Most guests will be fishing or diving much of the time, but there are always hammocks to relax in and the snorkelling right offshore is superb. Although staying out here has a heavenly, even dreamlike quality, **sandflies** and **mosquitoes** can bring you back to earth with a vengeance – so pack repellent.

3

SUN, SAND AND SUSTAINABILITY: THE OCEANIC SOCIETY

Rather than simply visiting the reef, you can also help preserve it. The nonprofit **Oceanic Society** (✆ oceanicsociety.org) at the Turneffe Atoll, founded in 1969 with the mission of preserving marine habitats worldwide, offers eight-day "**volunteer vacations**" where you can work side-by-side with researchers to monitor the health of the Turneffe Atoll's coral reefs. Accommodation is at *cabañas* at *Turneffe Flats* or *Blackbird Caye Dive Resort*. Daily activities include snorkelling the warm waters of the reef and gathering data on water quality and reef inhabitants, while in the evening you can listen to presentations on everything from marine ecosystems to reef history. The trips start at US$2990 and include accommodation, meals and boat transfer.

ARRIVAL AND DEPARTURE   TURNEFFE ATOLL

By boat Most people visit the Turneffe Atoll on dive or snorkel day-trips from Caye Caulker (1hr) and Ambergris Caye (1hr 30min); numerous companies (see p.100 & p.109) offer trips here year-round.

ACCOMMODATION

Blackbird Caye Resort Blackbird Caye, Turneffe Atoll ✆ 223 2767, ✆ blackbirdresort.com. Dive the gorgeous reef by day, and relax in deluxe *cabañas* by night at this top-notch resort. Four- and seven-night packages include transfers, all meals and diving/snorkelling. From US$1350

Turneffe Flats Lodge Blackbird Caye, Turneffe Atoll ✆ 232 9022, ✆ tflats.com. This well-run resort, with inviting beachfront *cabañas*, is primarily known as a fishing destination, offering some of the best saltwater fly-fishing on the cayes. It also does excellent dive packages as well as

"R&R packages", where you can just while away the days sunbathing and splashing in the Caribbean waters. Fishing packages from US$1690; dive packages from US$1090

Turneffe Island Resort Coco Tree Caye, southern tip of Turneffe Atoll ✆ 532 2990, ✆ turnefferesort.com. Get away from it all at this luxurious resort – one of the most upscale in the Turneffe Atoll – with swanky a/c cabins on the beach catering to upmarket fishing and diving groups. All-inclusive, four-night packages from US$1340

Lighthouse Reef and around

About fifty miles east of Belize City is Belize's outermost atoll, **Lighthouse Reef**, made famous by Jacques Cousteau, who visited in the 1970s. Its two main attractions are the **Blue Hole**, which drew Cousteau's attention (he cleared the passage through the reef), and **Half Moon Caye Natural Monument**. Also here is **Long Caye**, a private island on the atoll's southwestern side.

The Blue Hole

Bz$80, includes Half Moon Caye Natural Monument

The **Blue Hole** is technically a "karst-eroded sinkhole", a shaft about 984ft in diameter and 442ft deep that drops through the bottom of the lagoon and opens out into a complex network of **caves and crevices**, complete with stalactites and stalagmites. It was formed over a million years ago when Lighthouse Reef was a sizeable island – or even part of the mainland. Investigations have shown that caves underlie the entire reef, and that the sea has simply punctured the cavern roof at the site of the Blue Hole. Its great depth gives it a peculiar deep-blue colour, and even swimming across it is disorienting as there's no sense of anything beneath you. Unsurprisingly, the Blue Hole and Lighthouse Reef are major magnets for **divers**, offering incredible walls and drop-offs, bright corals and tropical fish. Most dive operators in the cayes offer trips here, from day-trips to overnights.

In summer 2013, Belizean teenager **Rowan Garel** became the first blind person to dive the Blue Hole, a feat covered across the country by the Belizean press – and picked up internationally as well.

Half Moon Caye Natural Monument

Audubon Society visitor centre daily 8am–4.30pm • Bz$20 • ☎ 223 5004, ⓦ belizeaudubon.org

The **Half Moon Caye Natural Monument**, the first marine conservation area in Belize, was declared a national park in 1982. Its lighthouse was built in 1820 and has not always been effective: several wrecks, including the *Ermlund*, which ran aground in 1971, testify to the dangers of the reef. The medium-sized caye is divided into two distinct ecosystems: in the west, guano from thousands of seabirds fertilizes the soil, allowing the growth of dense vegetation, while the eastern half has mostly coconut palms growing in the sand. A total of 98 bird species have been recorded here, including frigate birds, ospreys, mangrove warblers, white-crowned pigeons and – most important of all – a resident population of four thousand **red-footed boobies**, one of only two nesting colonies in the Caribbean. Several tour companies (see p.100 & p.109) offer trips here on request.

TOURS AND ACCOMMODATION

LIGHTHOUSE REEF AND AROUND

Tours Numerous companies (see p.100 & p.109) offer year-round diving and snorkelling trips to the Blue Hole and Half Moon Caye from Ambergris Caye and Caye Caulker. In addition, Slickrock Adventures (ⓦ slickrock.com) offers longer stays, with accommodation in lovely beachside cabins on Slickrock's privately owned island, Long Caye, and a range of activities on offer. Four-night packages start at $1395 per person.

3

Cayo and the west

MOUNTAIN PINE RIDGE

Cayo and the west

The fast George Price Highway – known until 2012 as the Western Highway – runs for eighty miles west from Belize City to the border with Guatemala. By the time you reach the incongruous little capital city of Belmopan, fifty miles along, you've swapped the heat and humidity of the coast for a riverine landscape of rich pastures and citrus groves, and entered the lush, irresistible Cayo district.

The largest and arguably the most beautiful of Belize's six districts, Cayo makes a compelling destination for visitors. Complementing an oceanfront stay on the cayes with a few days exploring the forests and valleys of inland Cayo, to create what Americans like to call a "surf 'n' turf vacation", enables you to see the very best the country has to offer. Apart from the spectacular landscape itself, the headline attractions are the astonishing caves such as **Actun Tunichil Muknal (ATM)**, where real-life Indiana-Jones-style expeditions lead you past ancient relics including the actual skeletons of sacrificial victims; the remote, long-abandoned Maya city of **Caracol**; and canoe or kayak trips along the **Macal River**, tumbling from the Maya Mountains in the far west.

Most of southern and western Cayo, including the entire Maya Mountain range, is protected within a vast network of national parks, wildlife sanctuaries and forest and archeological reserves that stretch from the Caribbean coast to the Guatemalan border. While much of it is dense jungle, some areas are surprisingly temperate: the **Mountain Pine Ridge Forest Reserve**, for example, is a pleasantly cool region of hills, pine woods and waterfalls.

Much of Cayo's accommodation is in **luxury lodges**, tucked away in the backcountry down dirt roads. While they're consistently wonderful, and often remarkably well priced, if you're hoping to explore the region in depth – and especially if you don't have your own vehicle – they can feel a little isolated. Belmopan being a humdrum sort of a place, the ideal base for independent travellers is the busy town of **San Ignacio**, on the Macal River just nine miles from the Guatemalan border. Note that the region as a whole is small enough that there's no need to change your lodgings night by night; most visitors stay in one or at most two hotels, and explore on **day-trips**.

4

GETTING AROUND   CAYO AND THE WEST

By bus Public transport is largely restricted to the buses that ply the George Price Highway from Belize City, via Belmopan and San Ignacio, all the way to Guatemala. Some of the villages around San Ignacio are also served by infrequent local buses, but to reach the mountain reserves and more remote Maya sites you'll need either to rent your own vehicle or to arrange guided tours.

Belmopan

Belize's purpose-built capital, **BELMOPAN**, was founded in 1970 in a Brasília-style bid to focus development on the interior, nearly a decade after Hurricane Hattie swept much of Belize City into the sea. Located immediately south of the point where the Hummingbird Highway branches off the George Price Highway, it was named to

XUNANTUNICH

Highlights

❶ River tubing and mountain adventures at Caves Branch Experience one-of-a-kind river adventures at this wonderful jungle lodge. **See p.125**

❷ Actun Tunichil Muknal Hike across rivers and through jungle before descending into an astonishing cave that was, for the Maya, the abode of the Lords of Death. **See p.126**

❸ Green Hills Butterfly Ranch and Botanical Collections Relax surrounded by clouds of colourful butterflies in this fascinating and informative botanical garden. **See p.129**

❹ Mountain Pine Ridge Forest Reserve Escape the humidity of the jungle to the cooler air of the pine forest and its many clear streams and waterfalls. **See p.130**

❺ Caracol At the greatest Maya city in Belize, you can ascend Caana, a 1200-year-old palace and temple complex that still holds the tallest structure in the country. **See p.134**

❻ San Ignacio Stay in a comfortable, affordable hotel and choose from dozens of adventure trips in this charming town, still full of colonial buildings. **See p.137**

❼ The Macal River Observe iguanas in the trees and watch the scenery slide by as you take a tranquil float along this gentle jungle river. **See p.144**

HIGHLIGHTS ARE MARKED ON THE MAP ON P.120

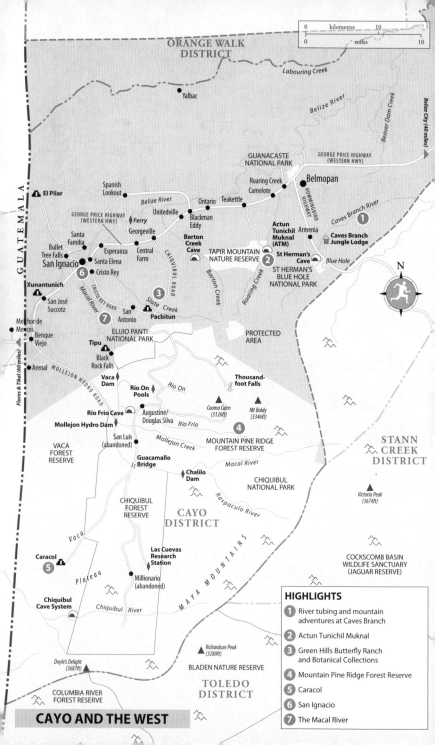

	kilometres	10
0		
	miles	10
0		

ORANGE WALK DISTRICT

Labouring Creek

Yalbac

Belize River

Beaver Dam Creek

GUANACASTE NATIONAL PARK

Belmopan

GEORGE PRICE HIGHWAY (WESTERN HWY)

Belize City (40 miles)

G U A T E M A L A

El Pilar

Spanish Lookout

Belize River

GEORGE PRICE HIGHWAY (WESTERN HWY)

Ferry

Georgeville

Unitedville

Ontario

Teakettle

Roaring Creek
Camelote

Armenia

HUMMINGBIRD HIGHWAY

Caves Branch River

1

Santa Familia

Bullet Tree Falls

San Ignacio

Esperanza

Santa Elena

Cristo Rey

Central Farm

Blackman Eddy

Barton Creek Cave

TAPIR MOUNTAIN NATURE RESERVE

Actun Tunichil Muknal (ATM)

St Herman's Cave

ST HERMAN'S BLUE HOLE NATIONAL PARK

Caves Branch Jungle Lodge

Blue Hole

2

6

Xunantunich

San José Succotz

CRISTO REY ROAD

Macal River

CHIQUIBUL ROAD

Barton Creek

Roaring Creek

3

Melchor de Mencos

Benque Viejo

Flores & Tikal (60 miles)

Arenal

MOLLEJON HYDRO ROAD

San Antonio

Slate Creek

Pacbitun

7

ELIJIO PANTI NATIONAL PARK

PROTECTED AREA

Tipu

Black Rock Falls

Vaca Dam

Río On Pools

Río On

Thousand-foot Falls

Cooma Cairn (3126ft)

Mt Baldy (3346ft)

4

Río Frío Cave

Mollejon Hydro Dam

Augustine/ Douglas Silva

Río Frío

San Luis (abandoned)

Mollejon Creek

MOUNTAIN PINE RIDGE FOREST RESERVE

Macal River

STANN CREEK DISTRICT

VACA FOREST RESERVE

Guacamallo Bridge

Chalilo Dam

Raspaculo River

CHIQUIBUL NATIONAL PARK

Victoria Peak (3674ft)

CHIQUIBUL FOREST RESERVE

CAYO DISTRICT

Vaca

Caracol

5

Plateau

Las Cuevas Research Station

Millionario (abandoned)

M A Y A   M O U N T A I N S

COCKSCOMB BASIN WILDLIFE SANCTUARY (JAGUAR RESERVE)

Chiquibul Cave System

Chiquibul River

Doyle's Delight (3687ft)

Richardson Peak (3280ft)

BLADEN NATURE RESERVE

TOLEDO DISTRICT

COLUMBIA RIVER FOREST RESERVE

CAYO AND THE WEST

N

HIGHLIGHTS

1 River tubing and mountain adventures at Caves Branch

2 Actun Tunichil Muknal

3 Green Hills Butterfly Ranch and Botanical Collections

4 Mountain Pine Ridge Forest Reserve

5 Caracol

6 San Ignacio

7 The Macal River

combine "Belize" and "Mopan", the language spoken by the Maya of Cayo. Belmopan was originally seen as symbolizing the country's new independent era, and its initial population of five thousand was expected to increase to thirty thousand. Few Belizeans other than government officials (who had no option) have moved here, however, so the population currently stands at around twelve thousand.

Other than **Guanacaste National Park**, immediately northwest, Belmopan holds no sights to speak of, so unless you need to visit an embassy or government office, there's really no reason to come here.

Laid out to house far more people than it actually holds, Belmopan spreads across a surprisingly large area; walking anywhere beyond the immediate centre is liable to take longer than you might expect. A ring road circles its administrative heart, but there's no road straight through the centre. Only if you explore on foot, therefore, will you see the **government buildings** at its core, which were modelled on the ground plan of a Maya city; the **National Assembly** even incorporates a version of the traditional roof comb, a decorative stonework and stucco crest. Now grey and ageing, when first constructed these concrete buildings won their British architect an award.

Guanacaste National Park

Intersection of George Price and Hummingbird highways, 1 mile northwest of Belmopan • Daily 8am–4.30pm • Bz$5 • ⓦ belizeaudubon .org • Buses stop at the entrance

Belize's smallest protected area, at just 52 acres, **Guanacaste National Park** is also the easiest to visit, with its entrance at the junction of the Cayo district's two main roads. It takes its name from an enormous **guanacaste** tree, which escaped the loggers because its trunk divides into three separate sections. A tall, spreading hardwood tree, it supports around 35 other plant species, including bromeliads, orchids, ferns, cacti and strangler figs, which blossom spectacularly at the end of the rainy season. Traditionally, the guanacaste's ear-shaped fruit – hence the name by which it's known in the US, the Elephant Ear Tree – ends up as cattle feed, while its partially water-resistant wood is used to make feeding troughs and dugout canoes.

After signing in at the national park's **visitor centre**, which holds a superb exhibit on the life cycle of leaf-cutter ants, and admiring the courtyard orchid display, you can follow three short **trails** through lush rainforest at the confluence of Roaring Creek and the Belize River, with the chance to plunge into a lovely swimming hole at the end of your visit. There's a large wooden deck for picnicking and sunbathing, but be sure to bring mosquito repellent.

Other botanical attractions include young mahogany trees, cohune palms, a *ceiba* (the sacred tree of the Maya, also known as a silk-cotton tree) and quamwood, while the forest floor is a mass of ferns and mosses. Although the chances of seeing four-footed **wildlife** are slim so close to the road, agoutis, jaguarundis and the like have been spotted, and howler and spider monkeys use the park as a feeding ground. Around one hundred species of **birds** are present, among them blue-crowned motmots, black-faced ant-thrushes, black-headed trogons, red-lored parrots and squirrel cuckoos.

ARRIVAL AND TOURS

BELMOPAN

By bus Belmopan's bus terminal is in the town centre, where Constitution Drive meets Bliss Parade.
Destinations Belize City (at least hourly, 6.30am–9.30pm; 1hr–1hr 30min); Benque Viejo del Carmen, for the Guatemalan border (at least hourly, 5.30am–11pm; 1hr 30min); Dangriga (hourly, 6.15am–7.30pm; 1hr 45min); Independence, for Placencia (hourly, 6.15am–5pm; 2hr 45min); Punta Gorda (hourly, 6.15am–5pm; 4hr 15min);

San Ignacio (at least hourly, 5.30am–11pm; 1hr).
Tours Belmopan's best adventure tour operator, Maya Guide Adventures (ⓣ 600 3116, ⓦ mayaguide.bz), run by father and son team Marcos and Francis Cucul, offer single- (from US$50–100) and multi-day (from US$160) tours that include jungle treks, caving, Maya ruins and kayaking expeditions on the Macal and Caves Branch rivers.

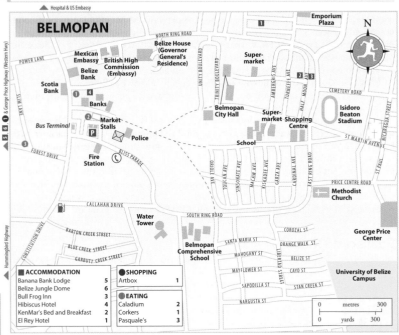

BELMOPAN

N

Hospital & US Embassy

ACCOMMODATION
■ ACCOMMODATION	
Banana Bank Lodge	5
Belize Jungle Dome	6
Bull Frog Inn	3
Hibiscus Hotel	4
KenMar's Bed and Breakfast	2
El Rey Hotel	1

● SHOPPING	
Artbox	1

● EATING	
Caladium	2
Corkers	1
Pasquale's	3

0	metres	300
0	yards	300

ACCOMMODATION

CENTRAL BELMOPAN

Bull Frog Inn 25 Half Moon Ave ☎822 2111, ⓦbullfroginn.com. This two-storey hotel/restaurant on the central ring road has 25 a/c, en-suite balconied rooms, each with one double and one single bed. Late-opening bar, and free room wi-fi. U̲S̲$̲9̲8̲

Hibiscus Hotel Melhado Parade, off Constitution Drive ☎822 0400, ⓦhibiscusbelize.com. Very central, British-owned hotel with simple a/c motel-style rooms and adjoining restaurant. Half of the hotel's profits support bird conservation. You can't check in on a Sunday or holidays, but guests already registered can stay on. U̲S̲$̲6̲0̲

KenMar's Bed and Breakfast 22–24 Half Moon Ave ☎822 0118, ⓦkenmar.bz. Family-run B&B just behind the landmark *Bull Frog*, offering ten bright a/c rooms, some with balcony and/or kitchenette, with shared living room and work space, and tropical breakfasts. The B&B has a few tour company partners. Transfers available. U̲S̲$̲8̲2̲

El Rey Hotel 23 Moho St ☎822 3438, ⓦelreyhotel.com. Unassuming residential-district home turned "budget boutique" hotel, courtesy of its exceptionally helpful English owners. All rooms are en suite; the cheapest have ceiling fans, while fancier options, spectacularly updated with vivid murals, have a/c. All meals available; be sure to try the home-made cheesecake. U̲S̲$̲4̲5̲

LODGES NEAR BELMOPAN

Banana Bank Lodge Mile 47, George Price Hwy ☎832 2020, ⓦbananabank.com. Family-run lodge on a 4000-acre cattle ranch, with a stable of over ninety horses that specializes in horseback adventures, with star-gazing and bird-spotting also possible (see the website for details of all-inclusive packages). There's a range of accommodation types available: "chalet room" dorms (sleeping up to six); impressive high-roofed *cabañas* with two bedrooms, each with fans and private bath (US$145); and nine a/c rooms and suites in the original lodge, some with private balconies and kitchenettes. All are individually decorated by top Belizean-American artist and owner Carolyn Carr. Rates include breakfast; tasty, home-cooked lunches (US$10) and dinners (US$15) are served family-style. The property is accessible with a vehicle by following signs north off the highway at Mile 49, just west of Roaring Creek, or on foot by hiking a 2-mile dirt road from opposite the airstrip at Mile 46, then crossing the river via a small ferry. Dorms U̲S̲$̲5̲0̲, doubles U̲S̲$̲1̲3̲0̲

★Belize Jungle Dome Mile 47, George Price Hwy ☎822 2124, ⓦbelizejungledome.com. Highly unusual B&B resort, centring on a geodesic-domed house beside the Belize River, specializing in adventure travel and owned by English footballer and Dutch TV presenter Andy and Simone Hunt. All five a/c rooms back onto a superb swimming pool, while a bar, romantically set in the treetops, serves coffee, smoothies, cocktails and beers. With a reputation for personalized service, the intimate family feel is also evident in the on-site restaurant, with Maya chefs cooking delicious Belizean and international meals (US$12–22) with the property's own organic fruits and veggies. All-inclusive packages available. The dome is next to *Banana Bank Lodge*; get here with a vehicle by leaving the highway at Mile 49, just west of Roaring Creek, or hike the 2-mile dirt road opposite the airstrip, a mile east of the Belmopan turn-off, and cross the river by ferry. US$95

EATING

If you're simply passing through Belmopan, or have a few minutes to spare between buses, it's easy to pick up a snack from the local **food stalls** close to the bus terminal. Note that many of the town's conventional **restaurants** are closed on Sundays.

Caladium Market Square ☎ 822 2754. The smartest restaurant in town, facing the bus terminal, serves as a rendezvous for officials and diplomats. The food isn't particularly fancy or imaginative, but it's tasty enough, and comes in substantial portions, with Belizean favourites like beans and rice with your choice of meat for around Bz$10, and shrimp or steak for more like Bz$20–30. Mon–Fri 7.30am–8pm, Sat 7.30am–7pm.

Corkers Hibiscus Plaza, Constitution Drive ☎ 822 0400, ⓦ corkersbelize.com. Lively upper-level restaurant/bar, run by the same friendly British owners as the *Hibiscus Hotel* alongside, with seating in the indoor bar area or on the large, breezy outdoor terrace. The decent pub-grub menu ranges from simple snacks and salads, through vegetarian or meaty pasta dishes at Bz$16–20, to six options of huge sharing platters of barbecued chops, ribs and sausages from Bz$52. Mon–Wed 11am–8pm, Thurs–Sat 11am–10pm.

Pasquale's Forest Drive ☎ 822 4663, ⓦ pasqualesbelize .com. Popular American-owned pizza spot with plentiful outdoor seating beside the road that connects the centre with Hummingbird Hwy. Ten-inch, six-slice pizzas start at Bz$25, and calzones at Bz$15. Mon–Thurs 11am–9pm, Fri & Sat 11am–9.30pm, Sun noon–9pm.

SHOPPING

Art Box Mile 46, George Price Hwy ☎ 822 2233, ⓦ artboxbz.com. One of the country's best and largest crafts and souvenir shops, a couple of miles east of the intersection of the George Price and Hummingbird highways, beside a minor back road that heads south into Belmopan. A popular tour-bus halt, it specializes in carved rosewood artefacts and furniture, along with colourful Belizean paintings, jewellery, pottery, music, books and T-shirts, many with Christian themes. There's also a good café, serving Gallon Jug Belize Coffee and tropical fruit ice cream, with outdoor seating. Mon–Sat 8am–6pm; café closes 30min earlier.

The Hummingbird Highway

Only paved since 1994, the scenic **Hummingbird Highway** runs for 55 miles southeast from Belmopan to meet the coast at Dangriga (see p.178). While at one time this was the main route for the transport of all the citrus fruit grown in the country down to the sea, now the road – still hosting one-lane bridges – is also used by petroleum trucks and an increasing number of ecotourists. Its initial stretch, running through lush forest with the green slopes of the **Maya Mountains** rising to the west, lies within the Cayo District, and is generally visited in conjunction with the rest of Cayo District. The second half of the highway belongs to southern Belize, covered in chapter six (see p.172).

The chief attractions here are the caves and *cenotes* (sinkholes filled with naturally clear freshwater from underground) along the **Caves Branch River**, a tributary of the Sibun that flows beneath the highway twelve miles out of Belmopan. If you're simply passing through, these can most readily be seen in **St Herman's Blue Hole National Park**. Staying at, or joining a tour with, the sole accommodation option, the veteran **Caves Branch Jungle Lodge**, enables in-depth explorations of the area's subterranean wonders, with potential activities including kayaking and rappelling.

Once past Belmopan, the only settlement en route is the verdant village of **Armenia**, which in the last couple of decades has grown to house a population of around a thousand refugees from El Salvador and Guatemala.

4

St Herman's Blue Hole National Park

Established in 1986 and managed by the Belize Audubon Society, the wildlife-rich **ST HERMAN'S BLUE HOLE NATIONAL PARK** consists, as its unwieldy name suggests, of two principal sections. Connected by an underground stream but accessed via separate entrances, **St Herman's Cave** and the **Blue Hole** stand a mile apart on the western side of the Hummingbird Highway, a dozen miles south of Belmopan. Visitors can easily reach both using public transport or their own vehicles, though to explore the **cave network** that's the park's biggest attraction you'll need the services of a guide.

Three of the five species of **cats** found in Belize – the jaguar, ocelot and jaguarundi – have been sighted within park boundaries; black howler monkeys are occasionally heard; and other mammals seen here include tapir, collared and white-lipped peccaries, tamandua (anteaters), gibnut, coatimundi, opossum, deer, kinkajou and many species of bats. It's also home to more than 175 species of **birds**, including the slaty-breasted tinamou, black hawk-eagle, crested guan, lovely cotinga, nightingale wren and red-legged honeycreeper.

St Herman's Cave

Mile 12.2, Hummingbird Hwy • Daily 8am–4.30pm • Bz$8, also includes Blue Hole • ☎ 223 5004, ⓦ belizeaudubon.org

A short way south of the point where the Hummingbird Highway crosses the Caves Branch River, **St Herman's Cave** is something rare for Belize: a cave it's possible to visit on your own. On an unaccompanied visit to St Herman's, however, you'll only get a small glimpse of what caving hereabouts has to offer. That's fine if you're also planning to take a guided tour of a cave such as ATM (see p.126) or Barton Creek (see p.128); if this is the only cave system you're likely to see, on the other hand, it's well worth hiring a guide, which is best arranged in advance through your hotel.

Beyond the **visitor centre** at the parking area – which holds good displays on local plant, bird and animal life, and bats in particular – a clearly marked ten-minute trail leads to the entrance to the cave itself. From here on in, you'll need a torch, first to descend steps cut by the Maya to reach the hole that gapes in the dripping rock face, and then to scramble over the rocks and splash along the shallow river inside. Solo visitors are only allowed to venture along the dark and eerie trail for about three hundred yards, which is enough to become thoroughly disoriented. At that point you have to retrace your steps, and if you choose can make your way back to the road via the longer "Highland" trail, which leads past unusually shaped rocks and a spectacular observation platform.

To continue any deeper into St Herman's Cave, and emerge from another opening, you need to join a **tour**. Operators such as Maya Guide Adventures (see p.121) combine the trip with an expedition through the nearby **Crystal Cave**, also known as Mountain Cow Cave, which as well as crystal formations holds calcified artefacts and even skeletons left by ancient Maya shamans. The typical cost of around US$85 per person includes the entrance fee, all equipment and lunch.

The Blue Hole

Mile 13.1, Hummingbird Hwy • Daily 8am–4.30pm • Bz$8, also includes St Herman's Cave • ☎ 223 5004, ⓦ belizeaudubon.org

Sometimes known as the "Inland Blue Hole", to distinguish it from its namesake on Lighthouse Reef, the **Blue Hole** that gave its name to St Herman's Blue Hole National Park is not so much a hole as a short, 30ft-wide stretch of underground river revealed by a collapsed karst cavern, or *cenote*. Located just a few yards off the Hummingbird Highway, it's reached by an easy hundred-yard trail from a car park that holds a grassy picnic area and entrance kiosk, but no visitor centre.

Usually cool, fresh, and coloured a spectacular turquoise – though be warned that rainy-season run-off can turn things a muddy grey – the waters of the "hole" are perfect for a refreshing dip. Surrounded by dense forest and overhung with vines, mosses and ferns, the river continues to flow on the surface for about fifty yards, before disappearing beneath another rock face. A mile-long, self-guided trail, the **Hummingbird Loop**, sets off alongside to undulate through the forest, with abundant possibilities of glimpsing wildlife en route. To enjoy it in comfort, you'll need insect repellent.

ACCOMMODATION   **THE HUMMINGBIRD HIGHWAY**

★**Caves Branch Jungle Lodge** Mile 41.5, Hummingbird Hwy ☎610 3451 in Belize, ☎866 357 2698 in US, ⓦcavesbranch.com. Just under a mile along a dirt road that leaves the highway between St Herman's Cave and the Blue Hole, this legendary lodge is set on the banks of the beautiful Caves Branch River, in a 58,000-acre estate of high canopy forest. Accommodation, all screened for insects and thanks to extra bunk beds sleeping up to four, ranges from fan-equipped *cabañas* with outdoor showers, via tiled bungalows with private verandas (US$246) to luxurious "treehouse" suites (US$426). As well as a restaurant serving family-style buffet meals, there's great on-site birding, plus a pool and massage, but most guests come for its extensive programme of adventurous tours – cave explorations, tubing and rappelling were pioneered here. Multi-day packages that include daily activities offer significant savings on room-only rates. Although passing buses stop at the entrance, without your own vehicle you're heavily dependent on the lodge's own tours and transfers. **US$169**

Between Belmopan and San Ignacio

West of Belmopan, on its 25-mile run to San Ignacio, the **George Price Highway** stays close to the valley of the Belize River, crossing numerous tributary creeks and passing through a series of villages: Roaring Creek, Camelote, Teakettle, Ontario, Unitedville, Blackman Eddy, Georgeville, Central Farm and Esperanza. Along the way, the scenery grows progressively more rugged, with thickly forested ridges always in view to the south.

Public transport here is restricted to the buses that ply the highway, which itself holds few specific attractions. If you have your own vehicle, however, or sign up for one of the many available guided tours, the unpaved roads that branch off to the south offer access to some truly extraordinary wilderness wonders. The closest to Belmopan is **Actun Tunichil Muknal**, a cave system where intrepid visitors prepared to wade a mile along an underground river are rewarded with millennia-old Maya remains. Further west, the rough **Chiquibul Road** leads south to the cool slopes of the **Mountain Pine Ridge Forest Reserve**, and the ancient city of **Caracol** beyond, and combines with the **Cristo Rey Road** to form a longer, looping route to San Ignacio that leads through some delightful Maya villages.

ATM PRACTICALITIES

Tours of **ATM** can be arranged through almost any **hotel** in the region, or with specialist **tour operators** in nearby towns such as San Ignacio (see p.140). The precise price you pay, and how long it takes, will depend on your starting point; typical tours from San Ignacio set off around 8am, get back around 4.30pm, and cost around US$110 per person. As visitors are forbidden to enter the cave without a guide, and you can't recruit one at the site, there's no point making your own way to the **trailhead**.

The only facilities of any kind at ATM – no food or drink is available – are beside the car park at the end of the road, where modern **changing rooms**, equipped with showers and toilets, enable visitors to change before and after the tour. Beyond this point, it's essential to wear something that you don't mind getting drenched and very muddy, as well as closed-toe shoes for hiking in water – reef shoes or Crocs are more suitable than hiking boots – and socks for walking and climbing on the travertine limestone deep within the cave. Your guide will provide you with a life-vest and helmet-torch.

Actun Tunichil Muknal

8 miles south of the George Price Hwy along a dirt road from Teakettle village, 8 miles west of Belmopan and 17 miles east of San Ignacio •
Guided tours only (see box, p.5)

The ancient Maya site known as **Actun Tunichil Muknal** – which means "cave of the stone sepulchre", and is usually abbreviated to **ATM** – is one of the most remarkable places you're ever likely to see. Discovered by Canadian geologist Thomas Miller in 1986, it consists of a three-mile section of underground river, only accessible by swimming and wading, and interspersed with vast subterranean chambers that contain remarkable natural formations as well as thousand-year-old Maya relics – most notably, the calcified skeletons of victims of **human sacrifice**.

ATM can only be seen on **organized tours**, which offer a wonderful combination of adrenaline-filled adventure with astonishing archeological remains. A strenuous wilderness expedition that involves hiking, prolonged immersion and clambering up precarious ledges, it's utterly unsuitable for anyone prone to claustrophobia. If you're travelling with kids, note that most tour companies have minimum age and height restrictions (usually 10 years and 40in, but check with your tour company). Note too that you can't take **photos**; as all cameras must be left in your vehicle, it makes sense not to bring one at all. And bear in mind that all tours may be cancelled for days at a time between September and November, when heavy rains can render it unsafe either to wade across the river or enter the cave itself.

Visiting ATM

Tours begin by wading waist-deep across Roaring Creek, which you cross twice more during the 45-minute rainforest hike to the **cave entrance**. After clambering down to this gaping hole in the hillside, you have to swim across a 20ft pool to reach the path within. To the Maya, such caves were entrances to **Xibalba**, "the place of fright", and the abode of the Lords of Death; as you look back towards the upper world, a mighty Maya warrior seems to be silhouetted on one wall of the cave.

Long periods of wading upstream, during which you're repeatedly obliged to squeeze between jagged outcrops, are punctuated by occasional dry sections. Fortunately the water is never cold, so there's no great hardship, though bats swooping out of the darkness can be disconcerting. A mile or so along, a short but intricate climb up from the river channel brings you to the main **ceremonial chamber**.

It's believed that the ancient Maya ventured ever deeper into this cave system during the eighth and ninth centuries, performing rituals designed to summon rain in periods of drought. At first, the only traces of their presence are large ceramic vessels that poke from the glittering, crystalline cave floor; then, further in, you start to spot human shapes, indistinct beneath the accreted coating of limestone. It's likely that only shamans and their sacrificial victims ever penetrated this far, their final frightful procession lit by flaming pine torches. And those victims are still here. Fifteen individual **skeletons** have been found, including six infants and a child as well as adults ranging from their 20s to 40s. None was actually buried: they were simply laid in shallow pools in natural travertine terraces. The tour culminates with the spectacle of the complete skeleton of a young woman, splayed out below a rock wall, alongside the stone axe that may have killed her. Nearby, another grey skull bears a stark white hole, having been shattered in 2012 when a clumsy French tourist dropped his camera while attempting the ultimate close-up – which explains the ban on cameras ever since. Given the sheer dangers of visiting the cave, and the value of its extraordinary contents, it would be no surprise if more stringent regulations were introduced in the future, or access even stopped altogether.

Spanish Lookout

Belize's wealthiest **Mennonite** settlement, **SPANISH LOOKOUT**, stands five miles north of the George Price Highway, across the Belize River. To reach it, either cross the bridge

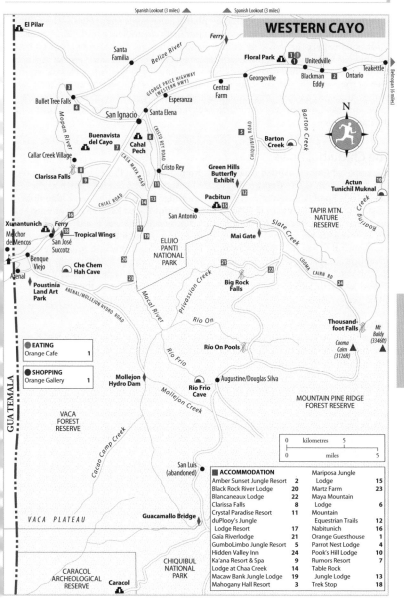

just north of the village of **Blackman Eddy**, at Mile 57, or, more excitingly, take the hand-cranked ferry (free) that operates 1.5 miles north of Central Farm, five miles further west.

While Spanish Lookout is in no sense a tourist destination – and the lack of road signs makes it pretty hard to find in the first place – it's worth seeing, an unlikely sight even in this exceptionally diverse country. Its neat farmhouses, paved roads, wide open white-fenced fields grazed by plump dairy herds and its up-to-the-minute car and tractor showrooms lend it an extraordinary resemblance to the American Midwest, an effect that has only been enhanced since the discovery of **crude oil** here in 2006 has added nodding pumps to the equation. While the Mennonites are renowned for their enthusiastic embrace of modern technology, they were far from keen at the prospect of developing the oil fields here, which were deemed to belong to the country as a whole. The anticipated boost to the social welfare of Belize has yet to materialize, however; so far, the proceeds have merely serviced a small portion of the national debt.

The Chiquibul Road

The unpaved **Chiquibul Road** heads south from the George Price Highway from the linear little community **Georgeville**, located around Mile 62. Also known as the **Georgeville Road**, and sometimes as the Pine Ridge or Mountain Pine Ridge Road, it's the main access route to the **Mountain Pine Ridge Forest Reserve** and onwards to the Maya site of **Caracol**. Entertaining diversions during its initial nine-mile section, before it reaches the reserve, include the canoe trip through **Barton Creek Cave** and the colourful **Green Hills Butterfly Ranch**. No buses pass this way, but hotels and adventure companies offer daily tours. It's also easy to explore in your own vehicle – though you'll need four-wheel-drive if you plan to venture as far as Caracol, or indeed do anything more than the simple loop to San Ignacio on the **Cristo Rey Road** (see p.129).

Barton Creek Cave

8 miles southeast of George Price Hwy, via Chiquibul Rd • Guided tours only; recommended operators include Pacz Tours (US$85, including entrance fee, food and guide; ☎ 824 0536, ⓦ pacztours.net) and the on-site Mike's Place (US$130, with pickup and return from Cayo and hotels; ☎ 670 0441, ⓦ bartoncreekcave.com)

Known to the Maya, like so many caves, as a route into the mysterious underworld, **Barton Creek Cave** can only be accessed by river, in guided canoe trips. Like ATM (see p.126), it holds stunning natural formations as well as ancient artefacts and the skeletons of sacrificial victims. Here they're only glimpsed from a distance, picked out by torchlight, but the tours offer a real sense of adventure, without being as physically demanding as visits to ATM. These can be arranged through operators and hotels throughout the region, and typically require around four hours at the cave, plus the travelling time to get here. Unlike ATM, it's also usually possible to reach the site in your own vehicle – assuming you're happy driving on *very* rough dirt roads – and hook up with a guide on the spot. Naturally it's worth checking in advance with the on-site operator, Mike's Place (see above).

The official route to Barton Creek, signposted to the left off the Chiquibul Road four miles south of Georgeville, is now impassable. Follow the track that turns east another

---

TAPIR MOUNTAIN NATURE RESERVE

Six miles south of the George Price Highway, between Roaring and Barton creeks, **Tapir Mountain Nature Reserve** protects seventeen square miles of the foothills of the Maya Mountains to such an extent that there's no access for visitors. Managed by the Belize Audubon Society, the reserve holds a rich habitat covered in high canopy and moist tropical forest, and is home to all of Belize's **national symbols**: Baird's tapir, the keel-billed toucan, the black orchid and the mahogany tree. Nature reserves are Belize's highest category of protected land and, as the designation aims to "maintain natural processes in an undisturbed state", Tapir Mountain can only be visited by accredited researchers. Unfortunately, its status does not guarantee the reserve protection from hunters, or even from encroachment by farmers.

two miles south instead, which leads through the traditional Mennonite settlement of **Upper Barton Creek**, and fords the creek before eventually reaching a jade-green pool, where you board your canoe. On the far side, the water disappears into the jungle-framed cave entrance, and visitors follow the river underground, crouching down in places where the cave roof dips low. After around a mile you emerge into a gallery blocked by a huge rockfall. If it's been raining, a subterranean waterfall cascades over the rocks – an unforgettable sight. Beyond lie many more miles of passageways, accessible only on a fully equipped expedition. The clear, slow-moving river fills most of the width of the cave, while the roof soars up to 300ft overhead. **Maya burial sites** surrounded by pottery vessels line the banks; the most awe-inspiring is marked by a skull set in a natural rock bridge used by the Maya to reach the sacred site.

Green Hills Butterfly Ranch

Mile 8, Chiquibul Rd • Daily 8am–1pm, last tour at noon • Bz$25 with guided tour • ☎ 820 4017, ⓦ green-hills.net

The fascinating **Green Hills Butterfly Ranch**, home to the largest collection of butterflies in Belize, spreads across a lush hillside eight miles south of the George Price Highway, opposite the horseriding centre Mountain Equestrian Trails (see p.133). While primarily a centre for scientific research, it's also open to visitors, for whom the main attraction is the enclosed, beautifully landscaped, 3,300 square foot **flight area**, where flocks of gorgeous tropical butterflies flutter around, settling occasionally on flowers to sip nectar. Over eighty different species have been bred here, though you'll usually see around twenty-five to thirty at any one time, depending on the time of year and the breeding cycle. Enthusiastic, well-trained local guides give excellent briefings.

Early-morning visitors may be lucky enough to watch butterflies emerging from jewelled chrysalises; many of the chrysalises are shipped for exhibit in the US. It's also possible, by appointment, to observe the flight of large owl butterflies, which takes place at dusk. To raise butterflies you also need to know about their diet; the adjoining botanical garden is home to Belize's national **passionflower** collection, as well as countless epiphytes (air plants), cycads, heliconias and orchids, and a tropical fruit orchard.

The ranch is run by Dutch biologists Jan Meerman and Tineke Boomsma, both of whom have published extensively – including a *Checklist of the Butterflies of Belize* – on insects, reptiles, amphibians and flowers. They've also discovered several new species, including a **tarantula** – *Citharacanthus meermani* – at Green Hills itself.

Cristo Rey Road

The unpaved **Cristo Rey Road** runs for just over twelve miles from Santa Elena, San Ignacio's sister community on the east bank of the Macal River, to meet the Chiquibul Road near the northern edge of the Mountain Pine Ridge Forest Reserve (see p.130). The most direct route between San Ignacio and the reserve, it also forms a convenient loop drive with the Chiquibul Road; most day-trip tours enter the area via one road and leave it by the other.

As well as offering access to various riverside lodges (see p.133) – though only those on the eastern side of the Macal, not those reached via the Chial Road to the west – it passes through a succession of pretty Maya villages, where roadside stores sell locally made crafts.

San Antonio

Surrounded by scattered *milpa* farms and overlooked by the forested Maya Mountains, the village of **SAN ANTONIO** stands nine miles south of San Ignacio along the Cristo Rey Road. Most of its inhabitants are descended from Yucatec Maya (or *Masawal*) refugees who fled the Caste Wars in Yucatán in 1847. They speak Yucatec and Spanish as well as English, and also refer to the village by the Maya name of **Tanah**.

Tanah Mayan Art Museum

Cristo Rey Rd • Daily 7am–7pm • Bz$8 • ☏ 4823 4023

North of the centre, the tiny **Tanah Mayan Art Museum**, holds displays on local history and traditions, and sells slate carvings and other artworks. It's run by Maria Garcia, the niece of a famed Maya *Curandero* (healer) Don Elijio Panti, who died in 1996 at the age of 103.

Elijio Panti National Park

Immediately south of San Antonio • ⊕ epnp.org

Maria Garcia played a prominent role in establishing the **Elijio Panti National Park**, a 31-square-mile forest enclave that hugs the perimeter of the Mountain Pine Ridge. This breathtaking reserve has no formal opening hours and few facilities for visitors; it may be possible to arrange a guided tour if you call in at the Tanah Mayan Art Museum, while **horseback expeditions** with José Tzul can be booked through Cayo Adventure Tours (☏ 824 3246, ⊕ cayoadventure.com).

Pacbitún

Just off Cristo Rey Rd, 2 miles east of San Antonio • No formal opening hours or admission fee

A short way west of the point where the Cristo Rey Road meets the Chiquibul Road, an unmarked side road leads to the minimally cleared ruins of **Pacbitún** (meaning "stones set in the earth"). One of the oldest Preclassic sites in Belize (dated to 1000 BC), it became a major Maya ceremonial centre during the Classic period, and farming terraces and mounds are still evident in the surrounding hills. Out of 24 temple pyramids and a ball-court, only the area around high Plaza A has been cleared, where you'll find the tombs of two elite women, which yielded a massive haul of Maya drums, flutes, ocarinas and maracas.

Mountain Pine Ridge Forest Reserve

A vast rugged wilderness of rolling hills, peaks and gorges that starts roughly ten miles south of the George Price Highway, the **Mountain Pine Ridge Forest Reserve** holds some of the most magnificent scenery in all Belize. Its heights are formed from some of the oldest rocks in Central America, granite intrusions that have thrust upwards from the bedrock that underlies the entire isthmus. Interspersed among them lie sections of limestone riddled with superb **caves**. Generally a mixture of grassland and **pine forest** growing in the nutrient-poor sandy soil, the vegetation grows denser in the warmth of the river valleys, while to the south of the Macal River the pines give way to rainforest.

Other than a handful of **tourist lodges** (see p.132) and the small forest reserve headquarters at **Augustine/Douglas Silva**, the Pine Ridge is virtually uninhabited. Almost all the visitors who pass this way are heading to the ancient city of **Caracol** (see p.134), but it's well worth detouring slightly off the route to see attractions like the towering **Thousand-foot Falls** on the northern flanks of the ridge, the scenic swimming pools along the **Río On** stream, and the readily accessible **Rio Frio** cave.

The only road into the reserve itself is the **Chiquibul Road**, which leaves the highway at Georgeville (see p.128), though that's joined by the **Cristo Rey Road**, a more direct route from San Ignacio, just over a mile north of the **gate** where all visitors have to sign in (there's no admission fee or opening hours, though recommended visiting hours are 8am–4pm). All the roads are unpaved, so they're liable to become dangerously muddy during the rainy season; it's best to use a 4WD vehicle and enquire locally about current driving conditions before you set off.

Thousand-foot Falls

10 miles along Cooma Cairn Rd, which branches west from the Chiquibul Rd at Mile 14

Five miles south of the intersection of Cristo Rey and Chiquibul roads, 3.6 miles beyond the entrance to the Pine Ridge reserve, **Cooma Cairn Road** heads off to the east.

THE PINE RIDGE LIVES ON

Belizeans regard the Mountain Pine Ridge Forest as a national treasure, so the severe infestation of the **southern pine bark beetle** that first affected it in 2000 has caused anguish throughout the country. As they feed, the beetle larvae kill the trees, and a new generation of larvae appears every four or five weeks. As you drive the sandy roads of the reserve, you'll see areas of bare, lifeless pines, sometimes stretching to the horizon; nearly 75 percent of the region's trees have been destroyed. Fortunately, the situation has been brought under control by a wide-ranging **reforestation programme**, and the forest is expected to recover. Even dead trees make an important contribution, providing hunting grounds for woodpeckers and other insect-eaters and thinning the forest as they fall, which makes recurrences of the infestation less likely.

A dirt road that's even rougher than the Chiquibul Road, it's usually passable nonetheless in an ordinary vehicle. After 3.3 miles, it passes the turn-off to the **Hidden Valley Inn**, a remote property with its own network of superb trails that are unfortunately open to guests only (see p.133). Continuing for another six miles brings you to a point overlooking what's said to be the tallest waterfall in Central America, **Thousand-foot Falls**.

Despite their name, the falls drop for a total of around 1600ft. From the overlook, however, roughly half a mile distant at the edge of a sheer slope, you can only see perhaps the top third of the falls. The spectacular setting, fortunately little affected by the pine beetle outbreak, makes it worth the trip; across the gorge, the long, slender plume of water disappears into the thickly forested valley below. You can't see the river itself, but this is the headwater of Roaring Creek, which flows through the ATM cave not far north (see p.126). Don't try to clamber any closer; it's an extremely dangerous climb. Dawn and dusk are the best times to view the falls as you'll likely be the only visitors. The viewpoint holds a rather rundown shelter with toilets, but no other facilities.

Big Rock Falls

1.5 miles west past Blancaneaux, off Chiquibul Rd

Only the physically fit will be able to weather the steep and strenuous (though short) trek to **Big Rock Falls**, a somewhat wide cascade on the Privassion Creek. The road up to the car park shows off views of the creek and falls, huge granite boulders, and the forest decorated in tiny orchid blossoms and green foliage. Once you climb down, via wooden steps and ropes to hang on to, the 150ft falls can be best appreciated while splayed out on the rock bed with a picnic lunch. As the pool beneath the falls is quite deep, it's almost mandatory to clamber up a little and take a dive or two. But don't relax too much, as the way back up to the car park is even more taxing than the way down.

Río On Pools

Ten miles south of the entrance to the Pine Ridge reserve, the Chiquibul Road crosses the **Río On**, one of several streams that drain west towards the Macal River. A short spur road to the west leads to the **Río On Pools**, where the river collects into pools between huge granite boulders before plunging into a gorge right beside the road. A gorgeous spot for a swim, it makes a great afternoon stop on your way back from Caracol, when the pools have had time to warm up and you'll be glad of a chance to cool down.

Augustine/Douglas Silva

The small settlement of **Augustine/Douglas Silva**, 26 miles south of the highway and five miles beyond the Río On Pools, holds the reserve's **headquarters**. Originally known as Augustine, it was later renamed Douglas Silva in honour of a local politician. Not all the signs were changed, however, and a complete transition never occurred. Most of the houses here are long abandoned, but there are normally some forestry workers around, who should be able to advise you on road conditions and safety if you're heading to Caracol.

Río Frio Cave
1 mile west of Augustine/Douglas Silva

A signposted track leads west from Augustine/Douglas Silva to the **Río Frio Cave**; most Caracol tour companies drive all the way to the site, but if you're in your own vehicle the going is rough enough to make it worth walking for twenty minutes instead. At the end, you're confronted with the largest cave entrance in Belize, a gaping 100ft hole where the Río Frio emerges from beneath a small hill. In fact it's more of a tunnel than a cave; if you enter the foliage-framed mouth, and are carrying a torch, it's possible to clamber over limestone terraces for half a mile until you're back out in the open. Sandy beaches and rocky cliffs line the river on both sides.

GETTING AROUND
BETWEEN BELMOPAN AND SAN IGNACIO

By bus Regular buses run along the George Price Hwy between Belize City and Belmopan in the east, and San Ignacio and Benque Viejo in the west. In addition, two companies run buses connecting San Ignacio with the village of San Antonio/Tanah (1hr) on the Cristo Rey Rd:

Mesh buses leave from next to Western Dairies daily at 5.15am, 7am, 1.30pm & 4pm; Tzib Brothers services leave from next to the Macal River, and also pick up at the Cayo Welcome Center; departures are daily at 6am, 8.30am, 12.30pm & 1pm.

ACCOMMODATION

ALONG THE GEORGE PRICE HIGHWAY
Amber Sunset Jungle Resort Unitedville, Mile 59, George Price Hwy ☎824 3141, ⒲ambersunsetbelize.com; map p.127. Five-room luxury resort with a friendly personal touch, perched on a high hillside a bumpy quarter-mile drive south of the highway. Guest accommodation is in canopy-level "treehouses", some sleeping up to six, with beautiful hardwood floors, king-size beds that swing from the thatched ceilings by ropes at each corner, in-room hammocks, indoor showers and sunken, screened outdoor baths. Delicious meals in the panoramic *Jungle Pot* restaurant; pool and bar, plus a wide range of tours and packages. US$175
Orange Guesthouse Mile 60, George Price Hwy ☎824 2341, ⒲belizegifts.com/guesthouse; map p.127. Simple but tasteful en-suite rooms, tucked on the north side of the highway behind the excellent Orange Gallery (see p.134), with superb polished hardwood fittings and tiled floors, plus fans and a/c. A short trail leads down to a beautiful swimming hole on pretty Barton Creek. There's a good on-site restaurant (see p.134), and the owners, helpful with area info, also offer a smart house for longer rentals, plus canoeing, caving and sightseeing tours. US$80
Pook's Hill Lodge Off mile 52.5, George Price Hwy, 5 miles south of the highway from Teakettle Village ☎832 2017, ⒲pookshilllodge.com; map p.127. This luxury lodge, set in a clearing on a terraced hillside once occupied by the ancient Maya, offers eleven comfortable

thatched *cabañas*, all with electricity and hot water, overlooking the thickly forested Roaring River valley, with breathtaking views of the Mountain Pine Ridge. Two, targeted at birders, are reached by a bridge over a creek and offer a higher vantage point and greater seclusion. Excellent meals (US$8–20) are taken in a lantern-lit dining room, above which a thatched deck with easy chairs and hammocks serves as a bar. All tours available; as the closest accommodation to Aktun Tunichil Muknal, this is the best base for tours. US$200

THE CHIQUIBUL ROAD
★**Blancaneaux Lodge** Mile 15, Chiquibul Rd ☎824 3878, in US ☎800 746 3743, ⒲blancaneauxlodge.com; map p.127. Sumptuous lodge owned by Francis Ford Coppola located 1.2 miles along a track off the main road, with comfortable and spacious hardwood and thatch *cabañas* and villas overlooking Privassion Creek, and beautifully landscaped grounds, from the palm-lined driveway to the croquet lawn and organic garden. The pricier villas (US$729), which sleep four, have two enormous rooms featuring Guatemalan textiles and screened porches with gorgeous views. Italian specialities, including pizzas from a wood-fired oven, are served with home-grown organic vegetables and Coppola's wines, and there's also a poolside Belizean restaurant. A heated pool and Indonesian massage house ensure relaxation, while service is exceptional. Prices are considerably lower off-season. US$429

Gaïa Riverlodge Mile 15, Chiquibul Rd ☎ 834 4024, ⓦ gaiariverlodge.com; map p.127. This superbly located lodge is set amid granite and pines on a hillside 2.5 miles beyond *Blancaneaux Lodge*, a total of 3.7 miles off Mountain Pine Ridge Rd. Known until recently as *Five Sisters Lodge*, it holds comfortable palmetto-and-thatch *cabañas* with hot showers and decks with hammocks, plus deluxe rooms with waterfall views. Electricity is via an unobtrusive hydro, complemented by wonderfully romantic oil lamps. Popular with honeymooners, it also holds gorgeous flowered gardens and a nature trail through broadleaf forest to waterfalls. The Five Sisters Falls, viewed from the dining-room deck, can also be explored via a tiny funicular. A rocky island in nearby Privassion Creek offers a thatched bar and small beach. Good-value meals also available to non-guests. US$200

GumboLimbo Jungle Resort Mile 2, Chiquibul Rd ☎ 650 3112, ⓦ gumbolimboresort.com; map p.127. Attractive collection of spacious, family-style stone *cabañas*, owned by a friendly British family and just 2 miles from Georgeville. Set around a pool, with a view south across forested valleys to the Mountain Pine Ridge, each offers tasteful decor, large showers and wide French windows opening onto private terraces; everything's powered by solar and wind energy, and the abundant breeze means there's no need for a/c. Lunchtime burgers, burritos and salads (for around Bz$18), also available to non-guests (booking essential), are served in a large bar/dining *palapa*. A four-course evening meal (Bz$40–45) is available by arrangement. US$105

★**Hidden Valley Inn** 4 Cooma Cairn Rd ☎ 822 3320, ⓦ hiddenvalleyinn.com; map p.127. Twelve spacious cottages at a high elevation, within a private twenty-square-mile reserve located 5 miles along the dirt road that leads east from Mountain Pine Ridge Rd towards Thousand-foot Falls. You'll forget you're in the tropics here with pines, tree ferns and your own fireplace stacked with logs to ward off the chill. Great meals (not included), and swimming pool with hot tub. Hiking, mountain bike and 4WD trails take you to secret waterfalls popular with honeymooners – guests can arrange to have one entirely to themselves – while expert guides lead tours on- and off-site. Excellent birding, with frequent sightings of the rare orange-breasted falcon. Transfers and multi-day all-inclusive packages available. US$335

Mariposa Jungle Lodge Off Chiquibul Rd toward San Antonio village ☎ 670 2113, in the US ☎ 304 224 2136, ⓦ mariposajunglelodge.com; map p.127. This well-arranged eco-resort in the rainforest is superb for privacy and as a jump-off for tours of the jungle and local ruins. The a/c cabañas, featuring ceramic tiles and furniture made on-site with Belizean hardwoods, come with high-quality pillows and mosquito netting for the canopy beds, en-suite bathrooms and private porches with hammocks, and

there's a small L-shaped pool and deck (with a cantina for snacks and a full bar) as an alternative to actively meeting nature in the jungle. The main building holds a lounge and restaurant offering lovely meals (US$15 for breakfast, US$35 for four-course dinner). US$195

★**Mountain Equestrian Trails** Mile 8, Chiquibul Rd ☎ 669 1124, in US ☎ 800 838 3918, ⓦ metbelize.com; map p.127. Belize's premier horseriding centre, set in tropical forest on the edge of the Pine Ridge, offers ten rooms in thatched, oil lamp-lit *cabañas*, with private baths and viewing decks. Electricity is only available in its social hub, the *Cantina*, which serves tasty Belizean and Mexican meals in large portions. All guests come on multi-night packages that centre on horseback or vehicle tours or on-site bird-watching. Five nights for two, with tours and meals US$2760

CRISTO REY ROAD

★**Crystal Paradise Resort** Cristo Rey Rd, Cristo Rey village ☎ 615 9361, ⓦ crystalparadise.com; map p.127. Owned by the Belizean Tut family, this is a welcoming, relaxed place with wooden rooms (US$129) and thatched *cabañas*, all with private hot-water bath, plus one larger cottage (US$125). The deck outside the dining room overlooks the Macal valley (you can't see the river but it's an easy walk), and attracts numerous hummingbirds. Victor has constructed thatched roofs for many of Cayo's resorts; sons Jeronie and Everald arrange birding and adventure tours throughout the district as well as to Tikal; and Teresa prepares delicious and filling meals, costing US$25 per person for breakfast and dinner. *Cabañas* US$95

Macaw Bank Jungle Lodge Cristo Rey Rd ☎ 665 7241, ⓦ macawbankjunglelodge.com; map p.127. Solar-powered eco-lodge, set within fifty acres of grassland savannah and fruit trees surrounded by thick jungle, a short walk from the river. Mountain biking, kayaking, tubing and yoga are all on offer, or you can walk the numerous trails spotting toucans, trogans and orange-breasted falcons or simply kick back in a hammock. Five comfortable and artistic *cabañas* (three on stilts) sleep up to four and have river-rock-lined showers, varnished floors and verandas. Tasty and filling meals available: US$35 per person per day for breakfast and dinner if reserved at booking. US$145

Maya Mountain Lodge Cristo Rey Rd ☎ 824 2164, ⓦ mayamountain.com; map p.127. Set in rich forest a mile south of Santa Elena, just a short walk from the river. Eight colourfully decorated *cabañas* and a larger wooden "Parrot's Perch" building that holds seven rooms; all have private bath and a/c plus a huge shared deck with hammocks. Delicious meals are served in an open-sided room, great for birding: motmots, aracaris and trogons fly yards from your table. The lodge sometimes hosts students and has a well-stocked library and occasional after-dinner presentations. Families are welcome; kids will enjoy the pool and illustrated trail guide. Rooms $\overline{US\$69}$, *cabañas* $\overline{US\$129}$

Table Rock Jungle Lodge Cristo Rey Rd ☎ 670 4910, ⓦ tablerockbelize.com; map p.127. Named after a landmark on the Macal River trail, this beautifully appointed hundred-acre rainforest property offers spotless tiled *cabañas* with polished hardwood floors, colourful modern decor and four-poster beds – two are raised high on cantilevered perches, with sweeping valley views – plus a series of decks and trails. Soursop, orange and mango trees are all around, and there's also space to put up your own tent by the river. Guests can relax in the thatched *palapa* restaurant/bar, where the friendly staff serve excellent food and cocktails (breakfast and dinner charged at US\$32 if reserved at booking). Camping $\overline{US\$30}$, *cabañas* $\overline{US\$145}$

EATING

Orange Cafe Mile 60, George Price Hwy ☎ 824 2341, ⓦ belizegifts.com/guesthouse; map p.127. Attractive restaurant/bar, serving good Belizean, Mexican and international food on a covered garden patio that's set well back from the road. Choices range from crêpes, omelettes and burritos for breakfast, costing up to Bz\$18, to curried shrimp (Bz\$26) or steak (Bz\$32) for dinner. Daily 6am–8pm.

Western Dairies Center Rd, Spanish Lookout ☎ 823 0112, ⓦ westerndairies.com. Attached to the HQ of a Mennonite farming company, this fast-food diner/cafeteria looks like it stepped straight from the prairies of the US Midwest. The real specialities are delicious milkshakes (Bz\$5.50) and ice cream in multiple flavours, but they also serve quesadillas, burritos, burgers and hotdogs (Bz\$3–5), plus Bz\$30 pizzas. Mon–Thurs 7am–5pm, Fri & Sat 7am–7.30pm.

SHOPPING

Orange Gallery Mile 60, George Price Hwy ☎ 824 3296, ⓦ orangegifts.com; map p.127. Prominent beside the highway, this is one of the best craft and souvenir shops in Belize, featuring superb wooden furniture, sculpture, games boards and bowls, carved mostly on site – you can tour the workshop – and properly dried in a solar kiln, plus slate reproductions of Maya artwork and a wide selection of Central American contemporary art, textiles and silver jewellery. Daily 8am–8pm.

Caracol

46 miles southeast of George Price Hwy, via Chiquibul Rd • Site hours daily 8am–4pm • Admission fee Bz\$15, usually included in tour prices

Visits to the magnificent ancient city of **Caracol**, the largest Maya site in Belize, are rendered all the more romantic and mysterious by its remote rainforest location. Although it's an absolute must-see destination, surprisingly few visitors brave the fifty-mile, two-hour expedition that's required to reach it, along rough dirt roads that lead southwest from the George Price Highway almost to the Guatemalan border, and you may even find that you have the place to yourself.

In the absence of public transport, almost everyone comes on a **guided tour**, available through any local hotel or operator. Such tours, which usually include stops at the Río Frio Cave (see p.132) on the way in and the Río On Pools (see p.131) on the way back out, take around ten hours in total from the San Ignacio area, or more like eight hours from the lodges along the Chiquibul Road; typical prices are upwards of US\$100 per person. While you are allowed to drive to the site in your own vehicle, an expert guide is useful at Caracol itself – reassuring in terms of personal safety, and all but essential in coping with driving conditions that become especially hazardous after rain.

The road to Caracol

The only approach to Caracol is via the Mountain Pine Ridge Forest Reserve (see p.130). After armed robbers, said to be from Guatemala, attacked tourists on the road in 2005 and 2006, a system was set up to ensure that all vehicles accessing the site would travel with a military escort. At the time this book was researched, there had been no tourist attacks for several years – though a Belizean law officer was killed in the park in 2014 – so although in theory a group convoy leaves the military base, at a road junction a few miles south of Augustine/Douglas Silva (see p.131), at around 9am each day, and returning at 2.30pm, it's more likely that you'll simply be required to sign in at the base before continuing on your way.

Ten miles south of the base, which is usually the roughest section of the trip, the road – by now no longer officially called the Chiquibul Road – crosses the Macal River (and a geological fault line) over the low **Guacamallo Bridge**. Beyond that, the vegetation changes from riverbank pine to the broadleaf jungle of the **Chiquibul Forest**, and the road reverts to a paved surface, at least for a narrow central strip, for the final eleven miles to Caracol.

The site

The road into Caracol ends at the site's **visitor centre**, which holds a scale model of the ruins, some excellent displays and several artefacts. A new pavilion was created to house assorted stelae, stucco carvings and other monuments, and there's also a large, thatched picnic shelter and bathrooms.

Only the core of the great city itself is open to visitors, though since that consists of 32 large structures and twelve smaller ones, gathered around five main plazas, it's actually more than most manage to see. To be all but alone in this vast abandoned site, the horizon circled by jungle-covered hills, is an incredible experience.

Caana

The dominant feature, Caracol's largest architectural complex, **Caana**, or "sky place", towers 141ft above the forest. To this day the tallest building in Belize, this immense, restored edifice is the central structure of the **B Group**. Each of its three separate tiers is so broad that, as with climbing successive peaks, you can't see the next level from the one below. At the very top a plaza holds three further sizeable

4

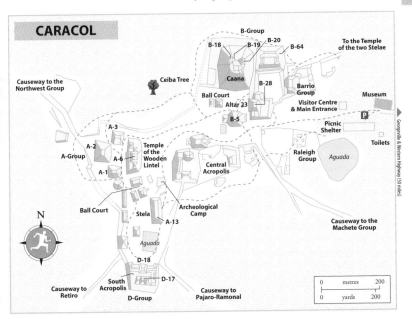

THE LOST CITY OF CARACOL

Before its rediscovery by *chiclero* (see opposite) Rosa Mai in 1937, **Caracol** was lost in the rainforest for over a thousand years. When archeologist A.H. Anderson explored here in 1938, he found large quantities of snail shells, and gave the site the Spanish name "snail". Subsequent research, however, has revealed the name by which the city was known to the ancient Maya – **Oxwitzá**, or "three hill water".

Despite decades of investigation, Caracol has still not been entirely mapped, and it's not known why the Maya built such a large city on a plateau that has no permanent water source. Occupation of the site has been traced back as far as 600 BC. By the time Caracol reached its peak, around 700 AD, the city consisted of over thirty thousand structures, covered 55 square miles, and was surrounded by agricultural terraces. The total population has been estimated at around 150,000, which gave it a far greater density than Tikal (see p.160), fifty miles northwest in what's now Guatemala. Rivalry between the two mighty city-states culminated on May 1, 562 AD, when the ruler of Caracol, **Yajaw Te K'inich II** (usually translated as "Lord Water"), conquered Tikal and established a long era of cultural domination.

Among the best preserved of the hundred-plus **tombs** to have been found is B-19, beneath the largest temple on the summit of Caana. It's almost certainly the tomb of **Lady Batz Ek**, or "black monkey", who married into the ruling K'an dynasty in 584 AD and may herself have ruled the city. Other ceremonially buried caches contain items as diverse as mercury and amputated human fingers, while epigraphers have used inscriptions to piece together a virtually complete dynastic record of the city's Classic-period rulers, from 599 to 859 AD. That's the final date recorded at Caracol, on Stela 10; evidence suggest that a great fire devastated the city around 895 AD.

pyramids. When you finally (and breathlessly) climb B-19, the tallest of the three, you'll be rewarded with views of seemingly endless ridges and mountains – a perfect environment to contemplate the Maya concept of time's enormity. Beneath Caana, a series of looted tombs still show traces of original, painted glyphs on their walls; some have lintels of iron-hard sapodilla wood supporting their entrances and are decorated with painted text.

The rest of the complex

Excavations on **Temple B5**, facing Caana across Plaza B, uncovered fantastically detailed, stucco **monumental masks** on either side of the central staircase, on which you can examine depictions of jaguars as well as the Witz ("sacred mountain") monster, wearing a headdress of water-lily pads being nibbled by small fish. In Maya cosmology, this design symbolizes the evening sun transforming into the jaguar god of the underworld and descending into the watery underworld of Xibalba to fight the Lords of Death. Legend dictates that if he's successful, he will rise again as the sun god.

To the side of Plaza B, images on **Altar 23** – the largest altar here, dated to 810 AD – show two bound captive lords from the conquered cities of Ucanal and Bital, in present-day Petén. Other glyphs and altars relate the course of the war between Caracol and **Tikal** (see p.160), with regional control alternating between

WILDLIFE AT CARACOL

As a **Natural Monument Reserve**, Caracol is also home to abundant wildlife. Bird sightings include the **orange-breasted falcon** and the very rare **harpy eagle**. You may catch sight of ocellated turkeys feeding in the plazas, while tapirs dine at night on succulent fresh shoots in the clearings. Another awe-inspiring sight is an immense, centuries-old **ceiba tree** – sacred to the Maya – with enormous buttress roots twice as tall as a human.

the two great cities. One altar celebrates the victory over Tikal in 562 AD that set the seal on Caracol's rise to power.

San Ignacio

The friendly, relaxed town of **SAN IGNACIO**, on the west bank of the Macal River 22 miles west of Belmopan, draws together much of the best of inland Belize. The heart of Cayo District and the focus of tourism in western Belize, it offers good food, inexpensive hotels and restaurants, frequent bus connections and a thriving weekly market. The evenings are relatively cool, and the days fresh – a welcome break from the heat of the coast – and there are far fewer biting insects and mosquitoes. The **population** is varied, mostly made up of Spanish-speaking mestizos but with significant Creoles, Mopan and Yucatec Maya, Mennonites, Lebanese, Chinese and even Sri Lankans.

Undoubtedly the town's best feature is its riverside location, amid beautiful countryside and surrounded by hills, streams, archeological sites, caves and forests. Major attractions in the immediate vicinity include the Maya site of **Cahal Pech** and the **Iguana Conservation Project**, but San Ignacio also makes an excellent base for day-trips and overnight expeditions further afield. Local hotels and tour operators run excursions through western Belize, as well as across the border to Tikal in Guatemala.

Among the best times to visit San Ignacio is for Baron Bliss Day on March 9, which highlights Belize's premier **canoe race**, La Ruta Maya, when teams of paddlers compete in a four-day race to Belize City (⊚larutamayabelize.com). Anyone can enter, but local guides always win.

San Ignacio is divided from its sister town to the east, **Santa Elena**, by the **Hawkesworth Bridge**, built in 1949 over the Macal River and still the only road suspension bridge in Belize. To all intents and purposes the two towns make up the same urban area, though Santa Elena itself is of little interest to tourists, with no real attractions to tempt you over the river.

Brief history

Named **El Cayo** by the Spanish, San Ignacio is still usually referred to as **Cayo** by locals (and that's often the name you'll see indicated on buses). Meaning "island", the word is an apt description of the location, on a peninsula between two converging rivers, and it indicates how isolated the European settlers felt, amid indigenous jungle inhabitants who valued their independence. **Tipú**, a Maya city at Negroman on the Macal River (5 miles south), was the capital of Dzuluinicob, where the Maya resisted attempts to Christianize them. The early wave of European conquest, in 1544, made little impact, and the area remained a centre of rebellion. Two **Spanish friars** arrived in 1618, but a year later the entire population was still practising "idolatry". Outraged, the friars smashed the idols and ordered the native priests flogged, but the Maya once again drove them out. When they returned to Tipú in 1641, Maya priests once more expressed their defiance by conducting a mock Mass using tortillas as communion wafers. Thereafter Tipú remained an outpost of Maya culture, and retained a good measure of independence until 1707, when its population was forcibly removed to Flores.

San Ignacio probably started its present life as a logging camp. A 1787 map stated that the Indians of this area were "in friendship with the Baymen". Later it became a centre for self-reliant *chicleros*, the collectors of *chicle* gum. When the black market price of Maya artefacts skyrocketed, many *chicleros* turned to looting. Until the George Price Highway was built in the 1930s (though the section beyond San Ignacio wasn't paved until the 1980s), local transport was by mule or water. Originally it could take ten days of paddling to reach San Ignacio from Belize City, though later on, small steamers made the trip in considerably less time.

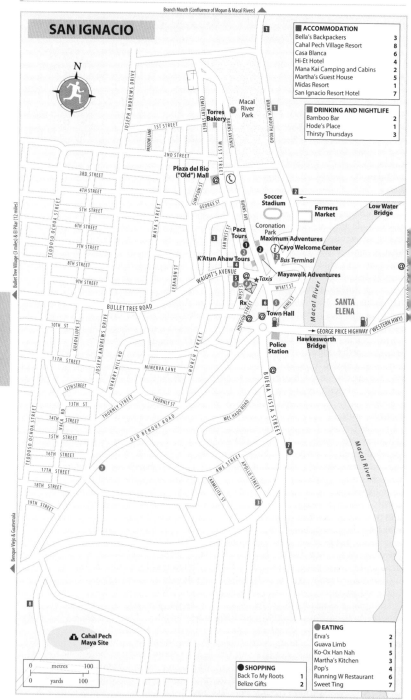

Branch Mouth (Confluence of Mopan & Macal Rivers) ▲

SAN IGNACIO

N

Bullet Tree Village (3 miles) & El Pilar (12 miles)

Benque Viejo & Guatemala

JOSEPH ANDREWS DRIVE
CEMETERY STREET
PASLOW LANE
1ST STREET
2ND STREET
3RD STREET
4TH STREET
5TH STREET
6TH STREET
7TH STREET
8TH STREET
9TH STREET
10TH ST
11TH STREET
12TH STREET
13TH ST
14TH STREET
15TH STREET
16TH STREET
17TH STREET
18TH STREET
19TH STREET

TEODOSO OCHOA STREET
MAYA STREET
SIMPSON ST
GEORGE ST
BURNS AVENUE
WEST STREET
BRANCH MOUTH ROAD
FAR WEST ST
LEBANON ST
WAIGHT'S AVENUE
BULLET TREE ROAD
GUADALUPE ST
JOSEPH ANDREWS DRIVE
QUARRY HILL RD
CHURCH STREET
MINERVA LANE
THORNLY STREET
THORNLY ST
OLD BENQUE ROAD
VACA RD
AWE STREET
CARMELITA ST
APOLLO STREET
MEL HARD ROAD
BUENA VISTA STREET
HUDSON STREET
WYATT ST
KING ST

Torres Bakery

Macal River Park

Plaza del Rio ("Old") Mall

Soccer Stadium

Farmers Market

Low Water Bridge

Coronation Park

Pacz Tours

Maximum Adventures

Cayo Welcome Center

Bus Terminal

K'Atun Ahaw Tours

Mayawalk Adventures

Taxis

Rx

Town Hall

SANTA ELENA

Macal River

GEORGE PRICE HIGHWAY (WESTERN HWY)

Hawkesworth Bridge

Police Station

Macal River

Cahal Pech Maya Site

| 0 | metres | 100 |
| 0 | yards | 100 |

Cahal Pech
1 mile southwest of San Ignacio • Daily 8am–5pm • Bz$10

The compact Maya site of **Cahal Pech**, perched atop a hill twenty minutes' walk up from town, may be smaller than the likes of Caracol and Tikal, but it's been beautifully restored and preserved, and is especially pleasant and peaceful at sunset. The **visitor centre and museum** at the site entrance holds a model and paintings that show Cahal Pech in its heyday, as well as artefacts unearthed here and elsewhere such as ocarinas, chocolate pots, arrows and carved flints, including one that looks remarkably like a modern wrench.

Brief history
Cahal Pech, whose modern Maya name means "place of ticks", is among the oldest Maya sites in Belize. Construction here dates as far back as the Early Preclassic, around 1200 BC, and the city grew to occupy much of the area now covered by San Ignacio and to dominate the central Belize River valley. Studies of the buildings and ceramics show that it remained continuously occupied until around 800 AD. Most of what's visible today dates from the Classic period, when during the eighth century AD it was the royal acropolis-palace of a Maya ruling family.

The site
Following paved cement paths through the forest, you arrive at **Plaza B**, surrounded by temple platforms and the remains of dwellings, where your gaze is drawn to Structure 1, the **Audiencia**, the site's largest building. If you're used to finely executed, exposed stonework at Maya sites, then the thick overcoat of lime-mortar here may come as a shock. The Classic Maya viewed bare, stone facings as ugly and unfinished, and covered all surfaces with a layer of plaster or stucco, which was then brightly painted. You can climb the steps at the front of the structure, but the best way to enjoy the site is to walk around the side and through **Plaza D** and its maze of ancient corridors and stairways, which gradually reveal an enchanting view of **Plaza A** – a sacred space entirely enclosed by walls and tall buildings. You're now across the plaza from Structure 1; make your way to the front, and you can then descend to your starting point.

Iguana Conservation Project
San Ignacio Resort Hotel, 18 Buena Vista St • Daily 8am–4pm; hourly tours, on the hour • US$9 • ☎ 824 2034, ⓦ sanignaciobelize.com

An enclosure in the grounds of the *San Ignacio Resort Hotel* holds the **Iguana Conservation Project**, which breeds and raises endangered **green iguanas**, and can be visited on regular tours that start from the hotel lobby. Both iguana eggs and the creatures themselves have traditionally been considered delicacies in Belize, and the main aim of the project is to educate locals and thus discourage hunting. Large groups of tourists and students are led through the facility, where they can handle the iguanas and pose for photographs. As the dragon-like reptiles are only kept here for two years before being released into the wild, none reach their full adult length of up to 6ft. They're still pretty large and fearsome-looking though, especially when the males turn bright orange during mating season (Nov–Feb).

Branch Mouth
Reached by a pretty twenty-minute stroll north of central San Ignacio – follow the track from the football field through rich farmland and thick vegetation – the point where the Macal and Mopan rivers merge to form the Belize River is known as **Branch Mouth**. At this confluence is a huge tree, with branches arching over the jade water, swallows skimming the surface, parrots flying overhead and scores of tiny fish. The forested hills that rise to the south of the confluence roll all the way south to Toledo and west across Guatemala.

ARRIVAL AND INFORMATION

By plane San Ignacio's airport, a 15min drive west of town towards Benque, is served by daily flights from Belize City on Tropic Air. Taxis may be waiting to shuttle visitors to town (from Bz$12), but it's best to arrange transport through your accommodation in advance.

By bus Services from and to Belize City stop in the centre of town just south of Coronation Park, within easy walking distance of all the recommended hotels. There's also a useful shuttle service between Philip Goldson International Airport and San Ignacio (from US$35/person; ☎ 637 9922, ⓦ belize-shuttles.trekksoft.com).

Destinations Belize City via Belmopan (every 30min, 4am–6pm; 3hr); Benque Viejo del Carmen, for the Guatemalan border (every 30min; 15min); San Antonio (Mon–Sat, 2 daily; 1hr).

By taxi Getting to or from the Guatemalan border is most comfortable by shared taxi. The Savannah Taxi Coop (☎ 824 2155) will carry up to four passengers for Bz$25. Note that taking a taxi from the Cayo Welcome Center (see below) is not recommended, as some unscrupulous drivers have been known to charge US$10 per mile.

Tourist information The modern Cayo Welcome Center, in Coronation Park on Savannah St near the bus stop (daily 9am–5pm; ☎ 824 2939, ⓦ travelbelize.org), can provide details of local attractions, and holds an exhibition on Maya finds unearthed during excavations along Burns Ave.

TOURS AND OPERATORS

Tour and activity operators based in and around San Ignacio offer a wide range of **guided tours** in Cayo District and beyond. Many only take cash (you'll find ATMs in town) and rarely is it necessary to prepay; if anyone approaches you about a tour on the street and not directly outside their office, or without a visible licence, it's likely they're trying to scam you. Almost all the local hotels and lodges also offer a very similar programme of tours, but the independent operators tend to be a little cheaper, and the fact that many have offices on San Ignacio's central Burns Ave makes it easy to shop around. Expect to pay around US$150–175 for the long day-trip to Tikal in Guatemala. Otherwise, typical **prices** range from around US$110 for full-day tours to the likes of ATM or Caracol down to US$80–90 for shorter tours, for example to Barton Creek Cave or Xunantunich. The following companies are especially recommended.

Cayo Adventure Tours Corner Bella Vista and 3rd St ☎ 824 3246, ⓦ cayoadventure.com.

Crystal Paradise Cristo Rey Rd, Cristo Rey village ☎ 615 9361, ⓦ crystalparadise.com.

Hun Chi'ik Tours San Jose Succotz ☎ 600 9192, ⓦ hunchiik.com.

K'Atun Ahaw Tours 10 Burns Ave ☎ 824 2661, ⓦ belizeculturetours.com.

Maximum Adventures 27 Burns Ave ☎ 623 4880, ⓦ sanignaciobelizetours.com.

Mayawalk Adventures 19 Burns Ave ☎ 824 3070, ⓦ mayawalk.com.

Pacz Tours 30 Burns Ave ☎ 824 0536, ⓦ pacztours.net.

River Rat Expeditions Benque del Viejo ☎ 661 4562, ⓦ riverratexpeditions.com.

ACCOMMODATION

For travellers dependent on public transport, or who'd simply prefer to be based in a town they can walk around, San Ignacio offers an ideal selection of **hotels** and **hostels** to suit all budgets. Bear in mind, though, that plenty of exciting alternatives lie hidden away in the rainforest nearby, particularly the wonderful and relatively affordable jungle lodges along the Cristo Rey Road (see p.131) and the Chial Road (see p.150).

Bella's Backpackers 4 Galves St ☎ 824 2248, ⓦ bellasinbelize.com. San Ignacio's only true hostel offers bunk beds in dorms and a few private rooms, plus an annexe apartment (US$135), a communal kitchen and several common areas in which to relax. Tours and trips can be arranged. Dorms US$13, doubles US$30

Cahal Pech Village Resort Cahal Pech Hill ☎ 824 3740, ⓦ cahalpech.com. Located across from the eponymous Maya site, enjoying spectacular views 1.2 miles up from San Ignacio, this well-designed hotel has spacious private rooms and comfortable thatched *cabañas*. Each is named after a Maya site, decorated with Guatemalan textiles and local hardwoods, and has a private bathroom; *cabañas* have wooden decks with hammocks. There's also a decent restaurant and multi-level pool. US$138

Casa Blanca 10 Burns Ave ☎ 824 2080, ⓦ casablancaguesthouse.com. Very popular central hotel with immaculate en-suite rooms, and a locked gate at the street entrance. All have private bath and cable TV, some also have a/c (US$55), and there's a comfortable sitting area with fridge, coffee and tea. Booking advisable. The *Mallorca Hotel* next door is run by the same family and is almost identical. US$35

Hi-Et Hotel 12 West St 📞824 2828, 🌐hietguesthouse
.aguallos.com. Deservedly popular budget hotel that
offers rooms with shared bath in a charming wooden
colonial-era building – those upstairs come with a tiny
balcony – and larger rooms with private bath in an
adjoining concrete annexe. Book ahead. Shared bath
US$15, en-suite US$30

Mana Kai Camping and Cabins Branch Mouth Rd
📞824 6538, 🌐manakaibelize.weebly.com. Campsite
close to the Macal River that offers tent camping with
hammocks, showers and outdoor cooking, and screened
rustic cabins sleeping up to four, each with its own
bathroom and veranda. Canoe rental available for US$20/
half day, $35/full day. Camping US$8, cabins US$25

Martha's Guest House 10 West St 📞804 3647,
🌐marthasbelize.com.   Ever-expanding   central
guesthouse, run by friendly owners Martha and John
August. Rooms are very comfortable and well furnished;
most have beautiful tiled bathrooms, cable TV and either
private or shared balcony, and there are also two guest
lounges. Luxurious family-sized suites on the top floor
(US$85) have grand views. There's also a gift shop, drop-off
laundry and good restaurant (see below). Rates include
breakfast. US$75

★**Midas Resort** Branch Mouth Rd 📞824 3845,
🌐midasbelize.com. Set among trees and pasture close to
the riverbank, within walking distance of the town centre
but with the peace and quiet of the countryside, *Midas* is
part backcountry resort, part in-town hotel. The main
building, fronting the swimming pool, has comfortable
well-equipped rooms upstairs and a bar below, while more
idiosyncratic options stretch back through the gardens,
with individual wooden or concrete *cabañas* (US$88) each
with its own porch and private bathroom, and single-
storey cottages divided into spacious en-suite quarters.
Breakfast and snacks available. Cottage rooms US$76,
hotel doubles US$118

San Ignacio Resort Hotel 18 Buena Vista St 📞824
2034, from US 📞855 488 2624, 🌐sanignaciobelize
.com. A steep walk uphill from the town centre towards
Cahal Pech, San Ignacio's premier hotel hosted Queen
Elizabeth in 1994. While not quite a match for Belize's high-
end jungle resorts, all its a/c rooms are spacious (some have
balconies), and the honeymoon suite's balcony features a
jacuzzi. The lush rainforest gardens, also home to an iguana
study project (see p.139), offer great birdwatching. The
Running W Restaurant (see below) overlooks the pool, and
there's also a bar/nightclub. US$240

EATING

As well as plenty of good, inexpensive **restaurants**, San Ignacio holds several reliable **fast-food stalls**, including a
popular taco stand in front of the post office that does spicy business until 2 or 3am. On most afternoons, small boys sell
tasty, freshly cooked *empanadas* and *tamales* on the street.

★**Erva's** 94 West St 📞824 2821. Friendly little restaurant
with outdoor seating and a huge, reasonably priced menu
of Belizean staples. Daily specials such as the delicious "black
dinner", a murky soup containing chicken, olives and hard-
boiled eggs, cost around Bz$12; burgers and burritos are
cheaper, while larger dinners such as steak, seafood and
lobster start at Bz$25. Everything is freshly prepared, so
you can expect a short wait for your food. Mon–Sat
8am–3pm & 6–11pm.

★**Guava Limb** 79 Burns Ave 📞824 4837. Bright,
relaxed café, overlooking a lush park from the upper
veranda of a blue cottage, a 5min walk north of the centre.
Under the motto "slim and trim like guava limb", it serves
healthy, largely organic salads, sandwiches and specials
like grilled snapper (Bz$18), plus espresso coffees,
smoothies made with exotic fruit like the lurid purple
dragon-fruit, and cocktails. Tues–Sat 11am–10pm, Sun
11am–5pm.

★**Ko-Ox Han Nah** 5 Burns Ave 📞824 3014. Small,
hugely popular local restaurant (its name translates to
"Let's Go Eat"), which is open to the street. It serves
excellent and unusual Belizean cuisine, including weekday
lunch specials such as cow-foot soup or "boil-up" for
Bz$10, plus more ordinary international dishes like

spaghetti and meatballs, with steak and seafood main
courses costing up to Bz$40. From 2pm onwards, you can
also get Indian-style curries for Bz$20–30. Many of the
ingredients, including fresh beef and lamb, come from the
owner's farm. Arrive early or you may well have to wait.
Mon–Sat 6am–9pm.

Martha's Kitchen 10 West St 📞804 3647,
🌐marthasbelize.com. Garden restaurant, below the
guesthouse of the same name and just as well run. Great
breakfasts with strong, locally grown coffee, for around
Bz$10, and lunches and dinners of traditional Creole food
and pizza (Bz$25–35). There's always a vegetarian choice,
like the Maya green vegetable *chaya*, with delicious cakes
for dessert, and good service too. Daily 7am–3pm.

Pop's West St 📞824 3366, 🌐pops-restaurant.com.
Small, much-loved local restaurant, serving huge,
inexpensive breakfasts from Bz$12, with bottomless cups
of coffee, plus similarly inexpensive Belizean dishes,
including a daily lunch special. Daily 6.30am–3pm.

Running W Restaurant San Ignacio Resort Hotel, 18
Buena Vista St 📞824 2034, 🌐sanignaciobelize.com.
Excellent food in tranquil resort surroundings, well away
from the centre. Full dinners incorporating organic meats
from their own ranch cost around Bz$35; fresh seafood is a

little more expensive, and local specialities such as *escabeche* (marinated fish) or black *mole* soup a little cheaper. There's a Lebanese influence in the appetizers, which include hummus and olives. Mon–Thurs 7am–9.30pm, Fri–Sun 7am–10.30pm.

Sweet Ting 96 Benque Viejo Rd ☎ 610 4174. A tiny but

brilliant little café on the western edge of town that serves espresso coffees, hot chocolate, milk shakes and a wide range of teas, but above all an extremely colourful array of fabulous cakes and pastries, which it also supplies to restaurants all over the country. A fat slab of chocolate mint cake costs Bz$5. Daily noon–9pm.

DRINKING AND NIGHTLIFE

San Ignacio attracts not only international visitors, but also plenty of weekending Belizeans, so it's home to a surprising number of **bars**, some of which can get quite rowdy later at night. It's never hard to find live music and dancing at the weekend.

Bamboo Bar Savannah Rd ☎ 629 6969. This boisterous space right by the Cayo Welcome Center is the first place many visitors down their first drink in San Ignacio. The food's strictly average, but you'll find dancing locals and live music. Every Tuesday is Ladies' Night. Mon–Fri 2pm–midnight, Sat noon–midnight, Sun 4pm–midnight.

Hode's Place Savannah Rd ☎ 804 2522, ⓦ hodesplace .com. A great spot for an evening drink, this large garden-set bar/restaurant, near the river north of the centre, has a

full international menu ranging from Bz$8 burgers upwards, plus a kids' play area and games room. Daily 10am–10pm.

★**Thirsty Thursdays** Apollo St and Buena Vista Rd ☎ 824 2727, ⓦ thirstythursdaysbelize.com. A relatively new and popular spot, *Thirsty Thursdays* is lively and fun, with events, a crew of resident DJs, weekly karaoke and happy hour 5–9pm. Wed, Thurs & Sun 5pm–midnight, Fri & Sat 5pm–2am.

SHOPPING

San Ignacio's most interesting shopping is to be had in the riverfront **market** area, between the two bridges, which ticks along quietly during the week and springs into full life on Saturdays. Otherwise, several of the small-scale stores along Burns Ave are well worth browsing.

Back To My Roots 30 Burns Ave ☎ 824 2740. Rasta drums, home-made jewellery and assorted local art and handicrafts. Mon–Wed 9am–5pm, Thurs–Sat 9am–9pm.

Belize Gifts Burns Ave ☎ 824 4159. A good selection of gifts, souvenirs and craft items, including fine carved wood, as well as a small array of books on the region. Mon–Sat 8am–9pm.

Farmer's Market Macal River Park. Every week the market square provides one of the most authentic Belizean experiences in the country – farmers bring in fresh produce and exotic tropical fruit by the pick-up truckload, dried beans in bags, meat and seafood (including barracuda), vendors hawk hot sauce, handicrafts and street food, and all manner of local characters show up. Sat 6am until mid-afternoon.

West of San Ignacio

There's plenty to see and do in the ten-mile swathe of undulating jungle that lies between San Ignacio and the Guatemalan border at **Benque Viejo**. Maya sites range from the attractively restored hilltop city of **Xunantunich**, reached by ferry from the highway village of **San José Succotz**, to the remote and only minimally excavated remains of **El Pilar**, straddling the frontier to the north, and the little-known cave of **Chechem Ha** to the south. Otherwise the big appeal for adventurous travellers is the chance to experience two different river experiences, either during relaxing **canoe trips** along the mostly gentle **Macal River**, or tubing or **kayaking** along the faster **Mopan River**. Attractive accommodation options are scattered along the highway as well as beside the rivers.

Bullet Tree Falls

Located three miles northwest of San Ignacio along Bullet Tree Road, **Bullet Tree Falls** is a predominately Spanish-speaking mestizo farming village that spreads along the forested banks of the Mopan River. A bridge crosses the river at the falls – really just a set of rapids – and there are several very pleasant and good-value **places to stay** (see p.150) on the riverbank nearby.

Immediately north of the bridge, Bullet Tree Road heads right, east, and continues northeast to the Mennonite community of Spanish Lookout (see p.126). Alternatively, a clearly signposted left turn a couple of hundred yards along leads seven miles north to the remote Maya site of **El Pilar**. If you're heading that way, call in at the **Be Pukte Cultural Centre**, south of the bridge in the heart of the village (Mon & Fri–Sun 9am–3pm; ☎093 7003, ⓦinterconnection.org/elpilar), which holds a model of El Pilar, and can provide information on local guides.

El Pilar

About 10 miles northwest of San Ignacio, via Bullet Tree Falls • Daily 8am–4pm • Bz$10 • Full details on ⓦ marc.ucsb.edu

The remote and largely undeveloped Maya site of **El Pilar** is a rough uphill seven-mile drive northwest of Bullet Tree Falls, on the Guatemalan border. Setting aside generations of mutual suspicion, Belize and Guatemala have created the **El Pilar Archaeological Reserve for Maya Flora and Fauna**, covering an area of over five square miles on both sides of the border, and offering some of the finest **birding** in Cayo; enthusiasts of avifauna and monkeys should definitely bring binoculars. Visitors willing to brave the harsh road conditions are free to make their own way here – allow about an hour for the drive from San Ignacio – but you'll get much more out of the experience if you come with an expert guide, arranged with local hotels and tour operators, via the Be Pukte Cultural Centre in Bullet Tree Falls (see p.144), or with Narciso Torres (☎634 7893), a traditional Maya forest gardener.

The ruins

Very few of El Pilar's **ruins** have been altered since their discovery. To avoid erosion, most remain covered by the forest, creating an atmosphere similar to that experienced by the first archeologists. Construction here began in the Preclassic period, around 800 BC, and continued until the Terminal Classic, around 1000 AD, when some structures were completely rebuilt. Such a long period of occupation was due to numerous springs and creeks – El Pilar is Spanish for "water basin". The city's prosperity still shows in the seventy major structures grouped around 25 plazas, appreciated along six **hiking trails** that crisscross the five-thousand-acre reserve. The four most impressive pyramids with ball-courts are between 45ft and 60ft high, grouped around the **Plaza Copal**, from whose west side a flight of steps leads down to a 90ft-wide causeway running to **Pilar Poniente** in Guatemala. Some portions of caved-in stonework have been uncovered and are on display; among them, an underground, corbelled tunnel, a standing temple and examples of elite architecture.

Shards of coloured pottery scattered all around indicate the various periods of occupation. **Chert flakes** – by-products of the manufacture of stone implements – are visible in huge quantities along the Chikin Trail. Along the Lakin Trail you'll find **Tzunu'um**, site of a traditional Maya "house" and forest garden. The more strenuous Community Creek Trail leads to the north and east, hugging the creek, and shooting off is the trail to the so-called **Citadel**. This Preclassic arrangement of concentric terraces and six structures (with some features that are not typically Maya), hidden by jungle, was recently discovered with the use of laser detection and imaging via helicopter; archeologists are still investigating its secrets.

Chial Road and the Macal River

The unpaved **Chial Road**, signposted south from the George Price Highway five miles out of San Ignacio, leads to successive isolated **rainforest lodges** (see p.150), nestling above the west bank of the **Macal River**. Almost everyone who heads this way is staying at one of the lodges, but a couple of them hold attractions that are open to non-guests, and are well worth seeing. *The Lodge at Chaa Creek* is home to the **Chaa Creek Natural**

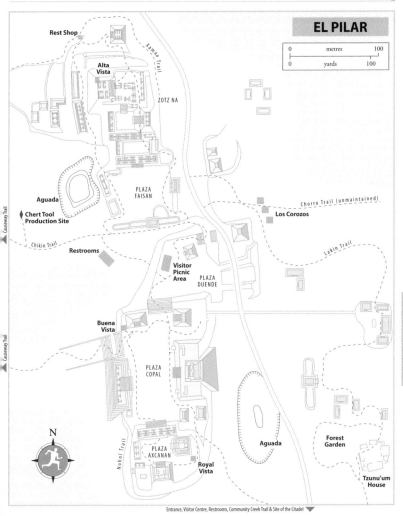

History Centre and the **Rainforest Medicine Trail**, while *duPlooy's* is the site of the impressive **Belize Botanic Gardens**.

In its upper reaches, swollen by tributary streams that flow down from the Mountain Pine Ridge and the Chiquibul Forest, the Macal River can be fast and deep enough for **whitewater kayaking**; contact activity operators in San Ignacio for details (see p.140). As it approaches San Ignacio, the Macal generally becomes much more tranquil, and makes a popular destination for **half-day canoe trips**. In theory, you could make your way to the various lodges by heading upstream along the river from San Ignacio. It's much easier to float downstream than to paddle against the current, however, so it makes sense to rent a canoe at one of the lodges, and then have it picked up in San Ignacio. It's well worth employing the services of a guide if you aim to spy on a creature or two while on the water.

Chaa Creek Natural History Centre

The Lodge at Chaa Creek, Chial Rd • Daily 8am–5pm, last tour 4pm • US$5, free to Lodge guests • ☎ 834 4010, ⓦ chaacreek.com

Perched atop a hill in the grounds of *The Lodge at Chaa Creek*, the **Chaa Creek Natural History Centre** is an interesting little museum devoted to the history, geography and wildlife of Cayo. Photographs and display panels, accompanied by preserved specimens including the extraordinary "peanut head bug", detail conservation efforts devoted to preserving the region's flora and fauna. A separate room explores Maya culture both past and present, with archeological finds complemented by a mock-up of a contemporary Maya village home.

In theory, guided tours start every hour, on the hour, but if you arrive on your own someone is normally available to show you around. Once you've seen the centre itself, you'll be led to the adjoining **Blue Morpho Butterfly Breeding Centre**, where you can walk among enormous, magnificent Blue Morpho butterflies, and even watch them emerge from chrysalises most mornings.

Maya Medicine Trail

The Lodge at Chaa Creek, Chial Rd • Daily 8am–5pm, tours at 9am and 2pm • US$5 self-guided, US$10 guided, free to Lodge guests • ☎ 834 4010, ⓦ chaacreek.com

Created in honour of Don Elijio Panti, the Maya healer who died in 1996 (see p.130), *Chaa Creek*'s **Maya Medicine Trail** sets off from the resort restaurant to wind through the forest above the riverbank. Maya medical knowledge was extensive, and signs along the trail identify about a hundred species of healing plants, many now used in modern medicine. It's a fascinating journey, pointing out vines that provide fresh water like a tap; poisonwood, with oozing black sap; its antidote, the peeling bark of the gumbo limbo tree, always growing nearby; and the bark of the negrito tree, once sold in Europe for its weight in gold as a cure for dysentery. You'll also see herbal teas and blood tonic; the **gift shop** sells all, including Traveller's Tonic, to prevent diarrhoea, and Jungle Salve, for insect bites.

Belize Botanic Gardens

duPlooy's Jungle Lodge Resort, Chial Rd, just beyond Chaa Creek • Daily 7am–4pm, last guided tour 3pm • Bz$15 self-guided, Bz$30 guided • ☎ 824 3101, ⓦ belizebotanic.org

Reached either by road or river, the **Belize Botanic Gardens** at *duPlooy's* is a remarkable project established in 1997 on fifty acres of former farmland and forest. The garden is the brainchild of *duPlooy's* owners, avid plant-lovers Ken and Judy duPlooy. Ken, who died in 2001, was held in such high esteem that a new species of orchid was named after him – *Pleurothallis duplooyii*, a tiny, purple variety, with a microscopic bloom. Daughter Heather now manages the gardens, which hold four hundred tree species, a nursery with a thousand seedlings and miles of interpretive **trails**. A first-class educational and study resource, they conserve many of Belize's native plant species within small reproductions of natural habitats. You approach the gardens through an avenue of fruit-bearing trees, which attract wild **birds**, and you can either explore on your own or follow expert naturalist guides. A fire tower offers breathtaking views of the surrounding hills, and bird hides on the two ponds allow you to spy on least grebes, bare-throated tiger herons and northern jacanas. The magnificent **orchid house**, with over one hundred species, is the best in Central America; come in April or May for the best variety of blooms.

San José Succotz

The village of **San José Succotz** lies beside the Mopan River seven miles southwest of San Ignacio, just east of Benque Viejo. A traditional town, it's inhabited largely by Mopan Maya, who throw a fiesta here on the weekend after Holy Saturday (Easter).

Under colonial administration, the Maya of Succotz cooperated with the British, a stance that angered other groups such as the Icaiché, who burned the village to the ground in 1867. People here identify strongly with their culture, and local men work as caretakers at Maya sites throughout Belize. Outside fiesta times, it's a sleepy spot; the main reason to come is to visit the Classic-period site of **Xunantunich**, up the hill across the river.

Tropical Wings Nature Center

Trek Stop, San José Succotz, Mile 70, George Price Hwy • Daily 9am–5pm • Bz$10, including guided tour • ☎ 823 2265, ⊛ thetrekstop
.com/tropical-wings

The **Tropical Wings Nature Center**, 500yd east of San José Succotz at *Trek Stop* (see p.150), is a delicate, enchanting world full of tropical colour. Native plants arch upwards, pressing against the netting on the roof, and about two dozen species of butterfly breed here, laying their eggs on the leaves. Outside you can see caterpillars in all stages of development, while inside you'll find child-friendly exhibits on biodiversity and Maya ethno-botany.

Xunantunich

7 miles southwest of San Ignacio, via San José Succotz • **Site** Daily 8am–4pm • Bz$10 • **Cable ferry** Daily 8am–5pm • Free • Buses between San Ignacio and Benque Viejo stop at the ferry

The remarkable ancient Maya site of **Xunantunich** (pronounced "Shun-an-tun-eech") towers in remote splendour above the barely inhabited west bank of the Mopan River, across from the village of San José Succotz. Visitors cross the river via a free, hand-winched **cable ferry** that sets off from alongside the highway; the ferry usually carries vehicles, but at times during the rainy season it may be restricted to pedestrians only, or service may be stopped altogether, thus precluding all access to Xunantunich. Licensed **guides** often tout for customers at the ferry, typically charging around US$30 per group for a visit of perhaps three hours. If you can find him, Alberto Panti is recommended.

4

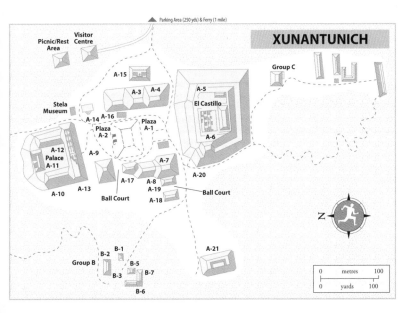

> ## THE STORY OF XUNANTUNICH
>
> Although it makes a breathtaking spectacle for modern visitors, by Maya standards **Xunantunich** was a relatively minor and short-lived city, where everything now visible dates from between 600 and 950 AD. The site's modern name means "the stone maiden" in Mopan Maya, but a chunk of stone frieze has revealed its original appellation: **Kat Witz**, or "clay mountain". It was first explored during the 1890s by Dr Thomas Gann, a British medical officer; in 1904, Teobalt Maler of Harvard's Peabody Museum took photographs and drew up a plan. Gann returned in 1924 and unearthed (looted, in modern terminology) numerous artefacts, including the carved glyphs of Altar 1, whose whereabouts are unknown.

The steep 1.5-mile hike or drive up from the ferry ends just short of the site itself, which is generally less crowded in the afternoon. There's a new **visitor centre** and museum here with some excellent displays that definitely add to the experience. The new facilities were initiated after a 2012 visit from the UK's Prince Harry.

El Castillo

Set on an artificially flattened hill, Xunantunich incorporates five plazas, although the remaining structures are grouped around just three. The entrance road leads first to Plaza A–2, while to the left, Plaza A–1 is dominated by **El Castillo** (structure A–6), the tallest building at 120ft high and a prominent symbol for Belize. Constructed in successive layers, each burying its predecessors, it was visible from sites such as Cahal Pech. It's ringed by a **stucco frieze** decorated with abstract carvings, human faces, jaguar heads and a king performing authority rituals; the original now lies concealed beneath a meticulous modern replica. The climb up El Castillo is a challenge, but the views from the top are superb, with the forest stretching out all around and the rest of the city clearly laid out.

The Palace

To your right as you enter the site, Plaza A–3 is almost completely enclosed by an acropolis-like collection of buildings, known as the **Palace**. Artefacts found here suggest that this was the place where the ruler met important officials. Human sacrificial remains found in a lower room may be linked to ceremonies conducted while the structure was being deliberately filled in during the Late Classic era, well before the entire site was finally abandoned around 1000 AD.

Benque Viejo del Carmen

The last town on the George Price Highway before the Guatemalan border is **BENQUE VIEJO DEL CARMEN**, eight miles southwest of San Ignacio. Culturally, Belize and Guatemala merge here with almost equal potency, and Spanish is the dominant language, despite English street names such as Elizabeth and Victoria. Benque, as it's usually known, is a pleasant, quiet town, home to many artists, musicians and writers, that's recently undergone a fascinating cultural revival. Several villagers produce excellent **wood and slate carvings** which are on sale at Xunantunich.

The actual **border** between Belize and Guatemala lies another 1.5 miles southwest of central Benque.

Benque House of Culture

64 St Joseph St • Mon–Fri 9am–5pm • Free • ☎ 823 2697, ⊛ nichbelize.org

For those travellers who are curious about mestizo tradition, the **Benque House of Culture** in the old police station is well worth a visit. Inside are displays of old photos and documents on the town, as well as logging and *chicle*-gathering equipment, paintings and musical instruments. Visiting exhibitions, films and local performances take place, and the managers, the Ruiz brothers, also organize the lively biennial **Festival of Mestizo and Maya Culture**, held in November. Ask here about another manifestation of local artistic spirit: the **Poustinia** sculpture park (see below).

Arenal/Mollejon Hydro Road

The unpaved **Arenal/Mollejon Hydro Road**, running south from the middle of Benque, reaches the Maya-mestizo village of **Arenal** after three miles. This community of stick-and-thatch houses is neatly bisected by the international boundary, which cuts right through the middle; there's a football pitch with a goal in each country. Although the **Mopan River** begins in the Maya Mountains to the south, it enters Arenal from Guatemala, having started its course by flowing west across the border. Arenal itself is home to the intriguing **Poustinia Land Art Park**, and also lies en route to the **Chechem Ha Cave** five miles south.

Poustinia Land Art Park

Arenal, 3 miles south of Benque Viejo • Visit by appointment only, through the Benque House of Culture • Bz$20 • ☎ 822 3532,
🌐 nichbelize.org

It's hard to imagine a more atmospheric venue for artwork than the extraordinary **Poustinia Land Art Park**. Set in thirty acres of rainforest, and the brainchild of local architect Luis Alberto Ruiz, it holds thirty **sculptures** by both Belizean and foreign artists, all exploring and portraying contemporary Belize. It seeks to build awareness of the **natural environment**, reforestation and land beautification following human abuse, and many sculptures are themselves organic, in time disappearing to be replaced by new works. *Returned Parquet*, by Tim Davies, is a fine example: reclaimed mahogany parquet flooring, laid as a path through a forest glade, which will eventually biodegrade and return to the earth. Other stimulating works include installations by David and Luis Ruiz and the schoolchildren of Benque Viejo, and a glass "apparition" door; even its hinges are glass.

   Given its thought-provoking mission, it's hard to see why Poustinia is not better known. You're likely to have the park to yourself, an opportunity for peaceful reflection a million miles from a city art gallery. Allow three hours to complete the route, and bring water. Taxis ply the route from Benque Viejo to Arenal, so transport shouldn't be a problem unless you're returning late in the day – even then, the one-hour walk back to town is enjoyable.

Chechem Ha Cave

Mile 8, Arenal/Mollejon Hydro Rd • Half-day tours take place daily at 9am & 1pm • US$25 • ☎ 660 4714

The pristine **Chechem Ha Cave**, eight miles south of Benque Viejo, is remarkable for its huge collection of intact **Maya pottery**, still lying where it was discovered by the Morales family in 1989, when they were hunting on their own land. William Morales now leads tours through the cave, and will pick groups up from Benque; be sure to bring sturdy shoes, insect repellent and water, and the will to get muddy – you can rinse off in a waterfall at the site.

   Visits begin with a dramatic half-hour hike through the jungle up to the inconspicuous mouth of the so-called "cave of poisonwood water". Once inside, you scramble through successive chambers, where ornate ceramic vessels, used for food storage as well as ritual ceremonies, poke out from up to two thousand years of accreted limestone deposits. While it's a physically demanding expedition that requires climbing agility and some use of ladders, it's not as challenging as ATM (see p.126), and because this is a "dry" cave it also remains accessible at those times during the rainy season when ATM and other Cayo caves are forced to close to visitors.

ARRIVAL AND DEPARTURE

BULLET TREE FALLS

By bus Buses connect Bullet Tree Falls with San Ignacio, though they're not particularly reliable (Mon–Sat, 7 daily; 20min).

By colectivo A shared *colectivo* taxi to Bullet Tree Falls from opposite the Belize Bank in the centre of San Ignacio costs Bz$2 per person (slightly more to each accommodation).

BENQUE VIEJO

By bus Regular buses run between Benque Viejo along the George Price Highway and Belize City via San Ignacio.
Destinations Belize City, via San Ignacio and Belmopan (regular buses every 20–30min, 4am–7pm; 3hr 15min; express buses 6–8 daily; 2hr 30min).

ACCOMMODATION

BULLET TREE FALLS

Mahogany Hall Resort Pasloe Falls Rd ☎ 622 4325, Ⓦ mahoganyhallbelize.com; map p.127. Luxury three-storey riverfront property, 1 mile along a dirt road that jerks left immediately before the bridge in Bullet Tree Falls. Superb views, very comfortable rooms and king-size suites (US$475), all with local hardwoods and artwork. Giant doors and winding staircases give the place an odd resemblance to a (not very forbidding) medieval fortress. Restaurant/bar on site. US$305

Parrot Nest Lodge Bullet Tree Falls ☎ 669 6068, Ⓦ parrot-nest.com; map p.127. Seven simple, clean riverside cabins set in beautiful gardens, four of which have their own private bathrooms, plus two treehouses perched in the branches of a *guanacaste* tree. All have verandas. Great home-cooked meals are served by owner Theo Stevens at a friendly communal table, and there's free tubing and a free daily shuttle to San Ignacio. US$67

GEORGE PRICE HIGHWAY

Clarissa Falls Mile 70, George Price Hwy ☎ 833 3116, Ⓦ clarissafallsresort.aguallos.com; map p.127. Part of a working cattle ranch, 1.5 miles north of the highway, this restful place is located beside a set of rapids on the Mopan. Offers simple thatched cottages, all wheelchair-accessible with private bath, plus space for camping. Owner Chena serves great home cooking, and there's a quiet bar overlooking the falls. Camping US$9, cottages US$75

Ka'ana Resort & Spa Mile 69, George Price Hwy ☎ 824 3350, Ⓦ kaanabelize.com; map p.127. Targeted towards American honeymooners and anyone with a taste for the latest thing in tropical luxury, this boutique resort, set in colourful gardens rather than rainforest, stands just off the highway 5 miles southwest of San Ignacio. Its stylish contemporary options include spacious suites, individual *casitas* arrayed across peaceful lawns and a couple of stand-alone villas that have their own pools; all abound in polished hardwoods and local artwork. There's also an opulent spa, an organic garden, and a high-class restaurant (with a wine cellar) that's also open to non-guests. US$315

Nabitunich San José Succotz, Mile 70, George Price Hwy ☎ 661 1536, Ⓦ hannastables.com; map p.127. About 10 miles southwest of San Ignacio, enjoying unbeatable views of the Xunantunich ruins and

surrounding countryside, the peaceful San Lorenzo farm makes a wonderful budget base for horseback trips and bird viewing. Accommodation in simple private cottages; you can opt for a package with tours that includes three family-style meals a day in the central lodge, which also houses a library and games room. The sizeable property also encompasses a long stretch of the Mopan River, which can be explored by kayak, tube, horse or foot. Per cottage (sleeps up to four) US$60

Rumors Resort Mile 68, George Price Hwy ☎ 824 2795, Ⓦ rumorsresort.com; map p.127. Perched right beside the road, 2.5 miles west of San Ignacio towards the border, this upbeat family-run hotel makes a convenient and affordable base for local tours; some of its clean, modern a/c rooms can accommodate family groups. US$120

★ **Trek Stop** San José Succotz, Mile 70, George Price Hwy ☎ 823 2265, Ⓦ thetrekstop.com; map p.127. This wonderful budget option, set in a quiet forest clearing near the highway, offers shared-bath cabins of varying sizes, with comfortable beds, nets and porches, plus a campsite, with rental tents available for US$10. Run by a local family, it uses composting toilets and solar-heated showers. As part of the Tropical Wings Nature Center (see p.147), plants here include Maya medicinal varieties, and there's a great library on Maya and natural history. The restaurant serves large portions and has good vegetarian options, and there's a shared kitchen, plus rental bikes, kayaks and tubes. Camping US$8, cabins US$26

THE MACAL RIVER

The list below only includes accommodation on the west bank of the Macal River, accessible via the Chial Rd, which heads south from the George Price Hwy 5 miles west of San Ignacio. They're presented here from north to south, and the list does not include the resorts on the river's east bank, reached via Cristo Rey Rd (see p.133). A taxi from San Ignacio to any of the lodgings listed here costs Bz$50–60. You can also choose to leave your accommodation via an easy canoe float downstream to San Ignacio; your host will take your luggage ahead while you drift along and enjoy the scenery.

★ **The Lodge at Chaa Creek** Chial Rd ☎ 824 2037, Ⓦ chaacreek.com; map p.127. Beautiful wood-and-stucco thatched roof cottages and wooden "treetop" jacuzzi suites (sleeping four) in gorgeous grounds high above the Macal, with a deserved reputation for luxury and ambience. With very comfortable beds, tiled floors, large bathrooms, screened windows and spacious wooden decks, rates include breakfast but not dinner (four courses for US$36). There's also a bar with large deck, and a stunning hilltop spa. Down by the river, the cheaper *Macal River Camp* offers comfortable wooden cabins with tarp roofs, beds and bathrooms but no electricity, for which rates include dinner and breakfast. All guests have free tours of the *Lodge's* attractions (see p.144), an early-morning bird walk and canoes. Macal River Camp US$130, cottages US$360

★ **duPlooy's Jungle Lodge Resort** Chial Rd, just beyond Chaa Creek ☎ 824 3101, ⓦ duplooys.com; map p.127. First-rate ecofriendly lodge, beautifully located on the Macal's west bank – with its own riverside beach – that's also home to the Belize Botanic Gardens (see p.146). Guests choose between spacious private bungalows with deck, king-sized and sofa beds, fridge and coffeemaker; Jungle Lodge rooms, each with queen-sized bed and porch; a treehouse on stilts; or the six-bedroom La Casona, a good-value option for groups of up to sixteen people. No a/c (fans only), and wi-fi only at the bar. Free use of bikes, canoes and tubes. Three-meal plan is US$65/day. Treehouse US$180, doubles US$205

Black Rock River Lodge Black Rock Rd, off Chial Rd ☎ 834 4038, ⓦ blackrocklodge.com; map p.127.

Rainforest eco-lodge, high above the west bank of the Macal River – 11 miles southwest of San Ignacio, the final six of them on dirt/gravel roads – with stunning views of jungle-clad limestone cliffs and the gushing rapids of the upper river. Each of its thirteen deluxe *cabañas* has a private bathroom and floor made of smooth river stones; some have a spacious deck and all are powered by hydro and solar. Trails lead to waterfalls, hilltops and caves. Horses, mountain bikes and canoes available. Excellent meals are taken in an exquisite open *cabaña* above the river; breakfast costs US$12, dinner US$22 (plus tax). Classic cabins US$120, riverfront suites US$225

ARENAL/MOLLEJON HYDRO ROAD

★ **Martz Farm** Arenal/Mollejon Hydro Rd ☎ 651 5953, ⓦ martzfarm.com; map p.127. An ideal budget river resort for anyone crossing to/from Guatemala, 8 miles southeast of Benque Viejo via a dirt road; the Martínez family will pick up from the border or San Ignacio. Accommodation is either in comfortable thatched en-suite cabins, or in shared-bath options that include a treehouse and three-bedded garden rooms. Rates include breakfast; lunch and dinner cost US$28 extra. To reach the river you climb down next to a gorgeous 90ft waterfall to a remote beach (you can also camp here); across the river, the forest beckons and there's great riding on the Martz mules. Minimum stay two nights. Treehouse US$78, rooms or cabins US$88

4

Tikal and Flores

TIKAL

5

Tikal and Flores

Guatemala's vast northern department of Petén is a treasure trove of spectacular nature reserves and hundreds of Maya ruins, many completely buried in the jungle. The jewel of the region is Tikal, arguably the most magnificent of all Maya sites. Towering over the rainforest less than two hours from the Belize border, it makes an accessible – and unmissable – side-trip, which can either be done independently or on an organized tour. Tikal's monumental temple-pyramids testify to Petén's role as the heartland of ancient Maya civilization during the Preclassic and Classic periods (around 300 BC–900 AD). It was here that Maya culture reached the height of its architectural achievement.

En route to Tikal, as you head west along the road from the bustling border town of **Melchor de Mencos**, you'll see signs for several other Maya sites. Both **Yaxhá** and the much smaller **Topoxté** occupy beautiful settings on opposite shores of Laguna Yaxhá, nineteen miles from the border, with camping and *cabaña* accommodation nearby. If you're travelling to Tikal by bus from the Belizean border, you'll need to change buses 27 miles along at the village of **Ixlú**, just a mile from the peaceful community of **El Remate**, set beside the large **Lago Petén Itzá**. Anyone with time for a more extended trip could head for the village and ruins of **Uaxactún**, north of Tikal, which also serves as a jumping-off point for expeditions to El Zotz and the remote northern sites of Río Azul and El Mirador. It's also well worth allowing enough time to spend a night or two in the departmental capital, **Flores**, a picturesque town set on an island at the western end of Lago Petén Itzá.

Archeology is not the only reason to cross the border. Petén is a huge, rolling expanse of tropical forest, swamps, lakes and dry savannahs, stretching into the Lacandón forest of southern Mexico. Tikal itself lies at the centre of a large national park, which forms part of the **Maya Biosphere Reserve**, covering six thousand square miles of northern Petén. As one of the largest forest reserves in Central America, it's extraordinarily rich in **wildlife**, particularly birds, though you're also virtually guaranteed to see **howler** or **spider monkeys**.

Laguna Yaxhá

Two beautiful lakes, **Laguna Yaxhá** and **Laguna Sacnab**, stand surrounded by dense rainforest five miles north of the main road along a spur road that branches off nineteen miles west of Melchor. Laguna Yaxhá is home to two Maya ruins that are well worth visiting: **Yaxhá**, on a hill overlooking the northern shore, and **Topoxté**, on an island near the southern shore. If you don't have your own vehicle, the easiest way to get here is on a tour from Flores or El Remate.

Yaxhá

Laguna Yaxhá • Daily 6am–5.30pm • Q80

The enormous Classic-period city of **Yaxhá**, the third-largest Maya ruin in Guatemala, stretches for a couple of miles along a ridge overlooking Laguna Yaxhá. More than five hundred structures have been mapped here, spread out over nine

FLORES

Highlights

❶ **Yaxhá** The impressive, restored ruins of Yaxhá tower above the shores of a lovely lake. **See opposite**

❷ **El Remate** Stay overnight in this relaxed little village on the eastern edge of Lago Petén Itzá and get an early start for Tikal the next day. **See p.158**

❸ **Tikal** Explore this enormous, ancient Maya metropolis, amid protected rainforest teeming with wildlife. **See p.160**

❹ **Sunrise over Tikal** One of the truly great

experiences of world travel; trek through the jungle before dawn, take your place atop Temple IV, and, if you're lucky, watch the rising sun illuminate the neighbouring temples one by one. **See p.166**

❺ **Café-Ital Espresso** A superbly prepared espresso drink made with fresh Guatemalan coffee at this little kiosk is the perfect adjunct to a visit to Tikal. **See p.168**

❻ **Flores** Stroll the cobbled streets of this tiny colonial capital set on an island, then enjoy cocktails at a lakeside bar. **See p.168**

HIGHLIGHTS ARE MARKED ON THE MAP ON P.156

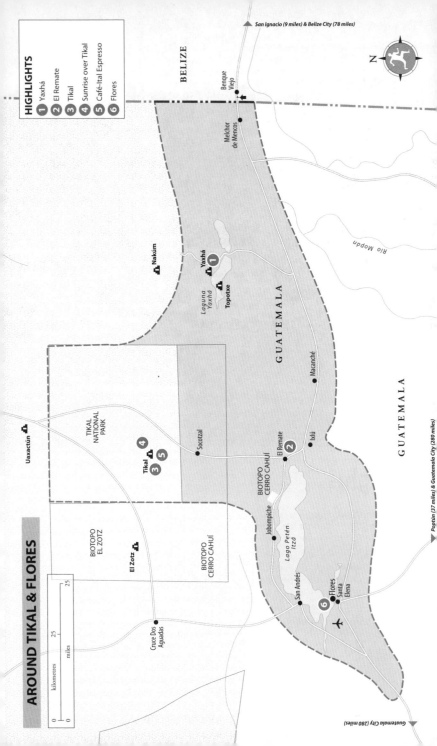

AROUND TIKAL & FLORES

San Ignacio (9 miles) & Belize City (78 miles)

N

BELIZE

Benque Viejo

Melchor de Mencos

GUATEMALA

Nakúm

Yaxhá **1**

Topotxe

Laguna Yaxhá

Macanché

Uaxactún

TIKAL NATIONAL PARK

Tikal **3** **5** **4**

Socotzal

El Remate **2**

Ixlú

BIOTOPO CERRO CAHUÍ

BIOTOPO EL ZOTZ

El Zotz

BIOTOPO CERRO CAHUÍ

Jobompiche

Lago Petén Itzá

San Andrés

Santa Elena
Flores **6**

Cruce Dos Aguadas

GUATEMALA

Río Mopán

Poptún (37 miles) & Guatemala City (280 miles)

Guatemala City (280 miles)

kilometres 0 ___ 25
miles 0 ___ 25

plazas and including several huge pyramids and large acropolis complexes. You can get a sense of its size and layout from the scale model near the site entrance. The tallest and most impressive pyramid, **Structure 216**, northeast of the entrance, rises in tiers to a height of over 98ft; the restoration enables you to climb to the top for spectacular views over the forest and lake.

Topoxté

Set on the easternmost of three small islands in Laguna Yaxhá, the Maya settlement of Topoxté is much smaller than Yaxhá itself. Although the site was occupied from the Preclassic era onwards, most of the structures now visible date from the Late Postclassic. In view of the lake's population of large crocodiles, the only way to reach Topoxté is by boat; ask at the *El Sombrero* lodge (see p.158).

CROSSING INTO GUATEMALA: TRANSPORT AND PRACTICALITIES

GETTING THERE

Hotels and tour companies throughout Belize, and especially in the Cayo district, offer day-trips and overnight tours to Tikal, but it's also straightforward to travel independently.
By shuttle bus Mayan Heart World offer a daily service between San Ignacio and Tikal (departs San Ignacio 7.30am, Tikal 2pm; US$45 one way; Belize ☏824 3328, Guatemala ☏502 2375 7072; ⓦmayanheartworld.net), and can also arrange transfers to and from Flores and El Remate.
By bus Three daily direct buses connect Belize City with Santa Elena, just outside Flores (see p.169). Otherwise, regular buses connect Belize City and San Ignacio with the town of Benque Viejo, from where *colectivo* taxis run the final mile west to the frontier (US$3).
By plane Daily flights connect Flores with Belize City and Guatemala City (see p.169).
By car If you want to drive into Guatemala from Belize, rent a car from Crystal Auto Rental in Belize City (see p.54).

BORDER PRACTICALITIES

Both the Belizean and Guatemalan border posts are on the eastern bank of the Mopan River, nine miles west of San Ignacio. Even if you're leaving Belize for just one day, the Belizean passport control will charge you Bz$37.50. Most nationalities do not need a **visa** to enter Guatemala. **Moneychangers** on either side of the border pester everyone who passes through.

PHONES

The international dialling code for Guatemala is **502**.

LANGUAGE

Guatemala is a **Spanish**-speaking country; overcharging foreigners is routine, and the better you are at getting by the less likely you are to be ripped off. Our Spanish-language guide covers the basics (see p.261).

MONEY AND COSTS

The Guatemalan unit of currency is the **quetzal** (Q); one US dollar is generally worth between 7Q and 8Q. Businesses in Tikal, Flores and El Remate often prefer to be paid in US dollars, and everyone readily accepts dollars instead of quetzales. **Costs** are generally far cheaper than in Belize; for transport, accommodation and food they can be as much as forty or fifty percent less.

CRIME AND SAFETY

In Guatemala you'll need to take even greater **safety precautions** than in Belize. While there has been little trouble in recent years, it's safest to cross the border and indeed arrive at Tikal in daylight. Violent robberies and assaults on tourists have in the past taken place in and around El Remate and within Tikal itself, but **Tourism Police** patrols in vehicles and on foot have cut the crime rate considerably.

Campamento El Sombrero Laguna Yaxhá ☎4147 6280, ⓦelsombreroecolodge.com. Solar-powered lodge on the south side of the lake, with lake-view rooms in thatched wooden *cabañas* and garden-view bungalows. The restaurant and lounge overlooking the lake, bedecked with low couches and hammocks, make a peaceful spot to stop for lunch; at the time of writing, a swimming pool was under construction too. The Italian-born owner is a great source of information about Yaxhá, and can arrange boat trips on the lake and horseback trips to other sites; she'll pick you up from the bus stop if you call in advance. Camping US$10, doubles US$125

El Remate

The small, friendly village of **EL REMATE**, a mile north of the junction where the road to Tikal branches off the main road between Belize and Flores, has become an increasingly popular base for visitors. While El Remate may not quite count as being on Tikal's doorstep – the site is another twenty miles north – it occupies a lovely spot at the northeast corner of **Lago Petén Itzá**, which allows its excellent crop of well-priced hotels and restaurants to enjoy lake views. For the moment at least, it remains pleasantly rural, so visitors can enjoy good walking and birdwatching. The best spot to swim in the lake is the little **beach** (Q5) across from the entrance to the Cerro Cahuí nature reserve.

Biotopo Cerro Cahuí

1 mile west of El Remate village centre • Daily 7am–5pm • Q35

The paved road that branches west from the centre of El Remate along the north shore of Lago Petén Itzá leads past several scattered hotels and restaurants before reaching the **Biotopo Cerro Cahuí**. This 2.5-square-mile wildlife conservation area stretches back up the hillside from the lake, and contains some of the least disturbed tropical forest in Petén. There are two potential **hiking routes**; the full three-hour trail climbs to the hilltop, passing a couple of small, unexcavated Maya sites as well as two thatched *miradores* overlooking the lake, while the shorter (1hr 30min) version doubles back a little earlier, and only offers long-range views of the Maya ruins. The best time to visit the park is in the cool of the early morning, when the wildlife is most active.

ARRIVAL AND DEPARTURE

By bus and microbus Every bus and microbus to Tikal passes through the village, and the village hotels can also arrange transfers to and from Tikal and Flores. To reach El Remate by bus from the Belize border, get off at the Ixlú junction, a mile south, and either walk or wait for a ride to

El Remate. No public transport runs along the northern lakeshore road.

Destinations Flores (around 15 daily; 45min); Tikal (around 15 daily; 40min).

ACCOMMODATION

★**La Casa de Don David** Village centre ☎ 5306 2190, ⓦ lacasadedondavid.com. Efficiently run mid-range guesthouse, owned by a welcoming Guatemalan-American family, offering spotless, comfortable en-suite wooden bungalows and rooms, most with a/c. The huge garden extends down towards the lakeshore, and holds a display of indigenous plants that centres on a mighty *ceiba* tree. The popular restaurant serves *guatemalteca* home-cooking, with meals served either in the main inn, or on an elevated lake-view deck at the foot of the garden, where drinks are served via a hilarious cable-car system. There's excellent independent travel advice, and staff can arrange trips and transport to Tikal, Flores, Belize and other sites. Rates include a meal (breakfast or dinner). US$50, with a/c US$10

Las Gardenias Village centre ☎ 5936 6984, ⓦ hotelasgardenias.com. Simple but good-value place at the main intersection, consisting of matching hotel and restaurant buildings, side by side and each having an upper deck, plus a supermarket. All rooms have decent a/c and are all en suite, with food available ranging from sandwiches (Q30) to seafood specials (Q70). Q280

Hostal Hermano Pedro Tikal Calle Camino Biblico, opposite the football pitch ☎ 2261 4181, ⓦ hhpedro .com. This large wooden house contains a multitude of rooms with private baths that open onto a communal decked balcony. Rates include breakfast and wi-fi, and there's a tour operator on site. Q208

La Lancha Aldea Jobompiche ☎ 7968 7183,

ⓦ coppolaresorts.com/lalancha. For true comfort, head nine miles west from El Remate along the north shore of the lake to reach Francis Ford Coppola's third resort in Central America. Winding paths lead through verdant grounds to plush *casitas* designed from local materials and featuring Balinese headboards, bright red-and-orange Guatemalan fabrics, marble bathrooms and ample wooden decks overlooking the lake or rainforest – but not TVs or a/c. The rustic-chic restaurant – think wooden canoes as planters – serves top-notch *guatemalteca* fare. Rates include breakfast. US$149

★**Mon Ami** Just over half a mile west of the centre, towards Cerro Cahuí ☎ 3010 0284, ⓦ hotelmonami .com. French-owned guesthouse with gorgeous, well-constructed rooms and bungalows scattered around a tranquil forested plot of land. All the accommodation has style and character, enhanced by local textiles and artistic flourishes, while the clean, inviting dorm is probably the most attractive in Guatemala. There's excellent swimming from the dock. Be sure to treat yourself to a meal here too (see below). Dorms Q50, doubles Q200

Posada del Cerro Beside entrance to Cerro Cahuí ☎ 5376 8722, ⓦ posadadelcerro.com. Perched in the forest, high above the lake a mile west of town, this stylish family-owned guesthouse offers lovely thatched cabins that combine local hardwoods with modern fittings, and have hammocks outside, plus two airy apartments (Q550) that sleep four and come with a full kitchen. Tasty meals are served to guests only. Q330

EATING

★**Mon Ami** Just over half a mile west of the centre ☎ 3010 0284, ⓦ hotelmonami.com. This charming hotel's lake-facing *palapa* serves some of the best food in town. It's not cheap, but the quality is outstanding. There's always a good set lunch for Q40 and wine available by the bottle and glass. Daily 7am–9pm.

Restaurant Cahuí Main road, near the football pitch ☎ 4918 0423. Friendly restaurant, serving meals on a breezy covered porch that's linked by two precarious swinging bridges to a lake-view platform that makes a great spot for an evening sundowner. Decent Guatemalan and international food for all meals, with burgers for Q22 or a good mixed grill for Q45. Daily 8am–9pm.

Restaurant El Muelle Main road, south of the centre ☎ 5581 8087, ⓦ hotelelmuelle.com. Smart restaurant,

separated from the lakeshore only by a very nice swimming pool that you're allowed to use if you eat here. The wide-ranging menu offers everything from sandwiches, burgers and nachos for under Q30 up to succulent *pescado blanco*, fresh from the lake, for up to Q200, and there's also a good gift shop. Mon–Thurs 7am–8pm, Fri–Sun 7am–9pm.

Restaurant Las Orquideas Half a mile west of the centre, towards Cerro Cahuí ☎ 5701 9022, ⓦ lasorquideaselremate.blogspot.co.uk. Excellent Italian-owned restaurant, a casual place where your welcoming hosts prepare food around an open kitchen. They serve fine pizza, bruschettas and pasta, with spaghetti or tagliatelle mains costing from Q65–80, plus wine by the glass and espresso. Tues–Sun 11am–9.30pm.

5 Tikal

The glorious ruined city of **TIKAL**, arguably the crowning achievement of Maya civilization, ranks among the most fascinating and beautiful ancient sites on earth. It now stands protected within the 143-square-mile **Tikal National Park**, perched atop a limestone escarpment north of El Remate.

As you get closer, the sheer scale of Tikal as it rises above the forest canopy becomes overwhelming, and the atmosphere spellbinding. Dominating the ruins are the enormous **temples**: five steep-sided pyramids that rise up nearly 200ft from the forest floor, and around which lie literally thousands of other structures, many still hidden beneath mounds of earth and covered with jungle.

While it's possible to see the big-name attractions within a couple of hours, it's worth allowing at least half a day to explore a significant amount of Tikal. Arriving in time for the **sunrise** can make for an unforgettable introduction to the site – though the dawn is not always as spectacular as tour companies like to suggest – while staying in one of the on-site **hotels** allows you to linger after the crowds have gone.

Brief history

Tikal ranks among the oldest of all Maya sites, the first village on this site having been established by 900 BC, during the **Middle Preclassic** period. Its inhabitants called it **Mutul**, or "knot of hair", an image depicted in the city's emblem glyph – a rear view of a head circled by what appears to be a knotted headband. The earliest ceremonial structures had emerged by around 200 BC, including the first version of the **North Acropolis**. Two centuries later, with the **Great Plaza** starting to take shape, Tikal was home to a large permanent population. For the next two hundred years, art and architecture became increasingly ornate and sophisticated, though Tikal remained secondary to the massive city of **El Mirador**, forty miles north.

Tikal's rise to prosperity

The closing years of the Preclassic period (250–300 AD) saw trade routes disrupted, culminating in the decline and abandonment of El Mirador. In the resulting power vacuum, the two sites of **Tikal** and **Uaxactún** emerged as substantial centres for trade, science and religion. Less than a day's walk apart, the expanding cities grappled for regional control. A winner emerged in 378 AD, when, under the inspired leadership of **Great Jaguar Paw (Toh Chac Ich'ak)**, Tikal's warriors overran Uaxactún, securing its dominance over central Petén for much of the next five hundred years.

This extended period of prosperity saw the city spread to cover eleven square miles, and hold a population of between fifty and one hundred thousand. Crucial to this success were Tikal's alliances with the powerful cities of Kaminaljuyú (in present-day Guatemala City) and Teotihuacán (north of modern Mexico City); stelae and paintings show that Tikal's elite adopted Teotihuacán styles of clothing, pottery and weaponry.

Conquest by Caracol

In the middle of the sixth century, however, Tikal suffered a huge setback. Already weakened by upheavals in central Mexico, where Teotihuacán was in decline, the city now faced major challenges from both the east, where **Caracol** (see p.134) was emerging as a significant regional power, and the north, where **Calakmul** was becoming a Maya "superstate". In an apparent pre-emptive strike against a potential rival, the ruler of Tikal, **Double Bird**, launched an "axe war" against Caracol and its ambitious leader, **Lord Water (Yajaw Te K'inich II)**, in 556 AD. Although Double Bird captured and sacrificed a noble from Caracol, his strategy was only briefly successful; Lord Water hit back in 562 AD with a devastating attack that crushed Tikal, and Double Bird was almost certainly sacrificed. The victors stamped their authority on the humiliated nobles of Tikal, smashing stelae, desecrating tombs and destroying written records.

Archeologists have long described the ensuing 130-year period of domination by Caracol and Calakmul as a "**hiatus**" in which no inscribed monuments were erected at Tikal. It has recently been shown, however, that work on Temple V started at this time.

Tikal strikes back

Towards the end of the seventh century, in any case, Caracol's stranglehold weakened, and Tikal started to recover its lost power. Under the formidable leadership of **Heavenly Standard-bearer (Hasaw Chan K'awil)**, who reigned from 682 to 723 AD, the main ceremonial areas were reclaimed. By 695 AD, Tikal was powerful enough to launch an attack against Calakmul, capturing and executing its king, **Fiery Claw/Jaguar Paw (Ich'ak K'ak)**, and severely weakening the alliance against Tikal. The next year, Heavenly Standard-bearer repeated his astonishing coup by capturing **Split Earth**, the new king of Calakmul, and Tikal regained its status among the most important of Petén cities. Heavenly Standard-bearer's leadership gave birth to a revitalized and powerful ruling dynasty: in the century after his death, all of Tikal's five main temples reached their final form, and his son, **Divine Sunset Lord (Yik'in Chan K'awil)**, who ascended the throne in 734 AD, had his father's body entombed in the magnificent **Temple I**. Temples and monuments were still under construction until at least 869 AD, the last recorded date in Tikal, inscribed on Stela 24.

Return to the jungle

While the precise reason for Tikal's **downfall** remains a mystery, it's certain that around 900 AD, almost the entire lowland Maya civilization collapsed, and that by the end of the tenth century, Tikal had been abandoned. Afterwards, the site was used from time to time by other groups, who worshipped here and repositioned many of the stelae, but it was never formally occupied again.

The site

Tikal is absolutely vast, and you can only see it on foot. Trying to walk around the entire site in a few hours is like scurrying around a major city in a single morning; it can be done, but it's likely to exhaust you before you exhaust it. However, even if you only make it to the **Great Plaza**, and spend an hour relaxing atop a temple, you won't be disappointed.

Home to the five main temples, the central area forms by far the most impressive section, and should be your priority. Around it, on all sides, lies dense jungle, crisscrossed by tracks and footpaths, and punctuated by further pyramids and ruins, some submerged beneath vegetation, others scraped clean and open to view. There's no set route that you're obliged to follow; if you have time, it's fun to circle the perimeter and only reach the prime ruins once you've grown used to the engulfing wilderness. On the lesser paths, you can easily find yourself hiking for ten or twenty minutes at a time without encountering another person, with the howler monkeys crashing through the trees alongside.

Complex Q and Complex R

Most visitors to Tikal choose to follow the least strenuous route into the site proper, which means forking slightly to the right when the main footpath reaches its first intersection, marked by a large map. A little further along, roughly ten minutes' walk from the ticket booth, the unevocatively named **Complex Q** and **Complex R** date from the reign of Hasaw Chan K'awil.

These are two of the seven sets of twin pyramids built to mark the passing of a *katun*, a period of twenty 360-day years. Only one pyramid, in Complex Q, has been restored, with the stelae and altars re-erected in front of it. The carvings on the copy of **Stela 22** (the original is in the Museo Lítico), in the small enclosure set to one side, record the ascension to the throne in 768 AD of Tikal's last known ruler, **Chitam**. He's portrayed in full regalia, complete with enormous, sweeping headdress and staff of authority.

5

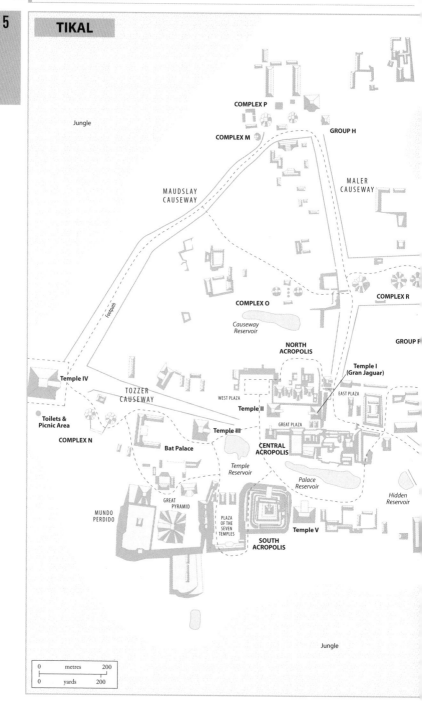

TIKAL

Jungle

COMPLEX P

GROUP H

COMPLEX M

MALER
CAUSEWAY

MAUDSLAY
CAUSEWAY

COMPLEX O

COMPLEX R

*Causeway
Reservoir*

NORTH
ACROPOLIS

GROUP F

Temple I
(Gran Jaguar)

Temple IV

TOZZER
CAUSEWAY

WEST PLAZA

EAST PLAZA

Temple II

Toilets &
Picnic Area

Temple III

GREAT PLAZA

COMPLEX N

CENTRAL
ACROPOLIS

Bat Palace

*Temple
Reservoir*

*Palace
Reservoir*

*Hidden
Reservoir*

GREAT
PYRAMID

MUNDO
PERDIDO

PLAZA
OF THE
SEVEN
TEMPLES

Temple V

SOUTH
ACROPOLIS

Jungle

| 0 | metres | 200 |
| 0 | yards | 200 |

5

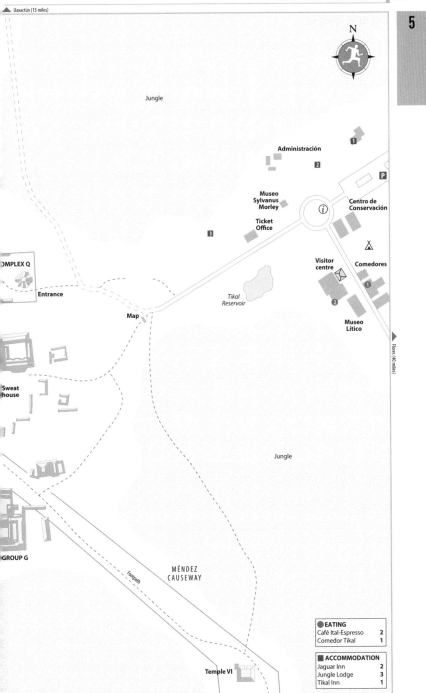

Uaxactún (15 miles)

N

Jungle

Administración

Museo Sylvanus Morley

Ticket Office

Centro de Conservación

COMPLEX Q

Entrance

Visitor centre

Comedores

Map

Tikal Reservoir

Museo Lítico

Flores (40 miles)

Sweat house

Jungle

GROUP G

MÉNDEZ CAUSEWAY

Footpath

Temple VI

● **EATING**

Café Ital-Espresso	2
Comedor Tikal	1

■ **ACCOMMODATION**

Jaguar Inn	2
Jungle Lodge	3
Tikal Inn	1

5

The Great Plaza

Surrounded by four massive structures, the **Great Plaza** at the heart of the ancient city was the focus of ceremonial activity at Tikal for around a thousand years. Indeed, the local Maya still use it; an altar for indigenous worship was established in its grassy central area in 2002, and you may see traditional ceremonies taking place.

Stand right in the middle of the plaza to appreciate its remarkable acoustic properties. Any sharp sound, such as clapping your hands, will ricochet off the staircase of Temple II to create a multiple **echo** at the exact pitch of the cry of the quetzal.

Temple I

Temple I, a steep pyramid topped by a three-room building and a hollow roof comb that was originally brightly painted, has become celebrated as the symbol of the entire site of Tikal. Also known as the **Gran Jaguar**, it was built as a burial monument to contain the magnificent **tomb of Hasaw Chan K'awil**, whose face is visible right at the top, 144ft above the ground. Within the tomb, six yards below the temple's core, the ruler's skeleton was found facing north, surrounded by more than 16lbs of jade, along with pearls, seashells and stingray spines – a traditional symbol of human sacrifice. A few pieces of magnificent pottery were also discovered, depicting a journey to the underworld made in a canoe rowed by mythical animals.

Temple II

Facing Temple I across the Great Plaza, the slightly shorter and wider **Temple II** was built to house the tomb of Hasaw's mother. It now rises 125ft, although when its roof comb was intact it would have been as tall as Temple I. Wooden staircases at the back lead to the lowest of the platforms visible from below, for fabulous views across the plaza and beyond. As a bonus, you'll almost certainly see toucans in the nearby branches.

The North Acropolis

The **North Acropolis**, which fills the whole north side of the Great Plaza, is one of the most complex structures in the entire Maya world. In conventional Maya style, it was built and rebuilt on top of itself; beneath the twelve temples visible today are the remains of about a hundred other structures, some of which have been uncovered by archeologists, as well as two giant Preclassic stone masks, which may have adorned a temple staircase. Facing the plaza and protected by small thatched roofs, the features of the masks remain quite distinct. In front of the North Acropolis are two lines of **stelae** carved with images of Tikal's ruling elite, with circular altars at their bases. These and other stelae throughout the site bear the marks of **ritual defacement**, carried out by newly enthroned rulers to erase any latent powers that the image of a predecessor may have retained.

The Central Acropolis

On the south side of the Great Plaza, Tikal's **Central Acropolis** is a maze of tiny, interconnecting rooms and stairways built around six smallish courtyards. The buildings here are usually referred to as palaces rather than temples; their precise use remains a mystery, but this was probably the main residential complex. The large, two-storey building in Court 2 is known as Maler's Palace, named after the archeologist Teobert Maler, who made it his home during expeditions in 1895 and 1904.

Temple III

The **West Plaza**, behind Temple II, is dominated by a large, Late Classic temple on its north side, and scattered with various altars and stelae. From here, the **Tozzer Causeway** – one of the raised routes that connected the main parts of the city – leads west to **Temple III**, covered in jungle vegetation. The last of Tikal's great temples to be constructed, Temple III was inaugurated by the city's thirtieth lord of Tikal on the day of a solar eclipse in 810 AD. A lightning strike in 2013 caused a 16ft crack in its fragile crest.

5

Around the back of the temple is a huge palace complex, of which only the **Bat Palace** has been restored. Further down the causeway, on the left, **Complex N** consists of another set of twin pyramids, where the superbly carved **Stela 16** depicts Hasaw Chan K'awil.

Temple IV

Looming at the end of the Tozzer Causeway, the massive **Temple IV** is, at 212ft, Tikal's tallest structure. Built in 741 AD, it is thought by some archeologists to be the resting place of the ruler **Yik'in Chan K'awil**, whose image was depicted on wooden lintels built into the top of the temple.

To reach the top, you climb a wooden staircase at the side. This is the prime vantage point used by each morning's guided **sunrise tours** (see p.166), but whatever time you come, the views from the stone terraces at the summit, which can accommodate hundreds of visitors at a time, are utterly magnificent. All around you the green carpet of forest canopy stretches to the horizon, interrupted only by the towering roof combs of other temples.

The Plaza of the Seven Temples and Mundo Perdido

South of Temple III, the **Plaza of the Seven Temples** forms part of a complex that dates back to before Christ. Its north side holds an unusual triple ball-court, while the unexcavated South Acropolis lies to the east.

Immediately west of here, the **Mundo Perdido** or Lost World – which took its modern name from the novel by Sir Arthur Conan Doyle – is a magical and very distinct section of the site, with its own atmosphere and architecture. Its main feature, the **Great Pyramid**, is a 105ft-high structure whose surface conceals four earlier versions, the first dating from 700 BC. From the top of the pyramid you'll get incredible views toward Temple IV and the Great Plaza, and makes another excellent vantage point from which to watch the sun ascending or descending.

Temple V

Located just behind the Central Acropolis, **Temple V** is best approached from the Plaza of the Seven Temples, for a superb view of the creamy limestone of its broad and freshly restored monumental staircase. An extremely steep wooden stairway to the left of the ancient stone once allowed visitors to climb to the top for stupendous views, but it's currently off-limits.

Findings from the many burials here have shown that although Temple V was previously thought to be among the last of Tikal's great temples to be built, it was in fact the earliest, dating from around 600 AD and almost certainly constructed by **Kinich Wayna**, Tikal's governor at the time. That means it was built early in the Mid-Classic "hiatus" that followed Tikal's defeat by Lord Water of Caracol in 562 AD, an era when experts had previously thought no new monuments were erected.

Museo Sylvanus Morley

Behind the main ticket booth • Mon–Fri 8am–4.30pm, Sat & Sun 8am–4pm • Q30

The one-room **Museo Sylvanus Morley**, tucked away behind the main ticket booth and also known as the **Museo Cerámico**, houses a collection of artefacts found at the site, and makes an interesting stop-off before you leave.

Highlights include the remains of **Stela 29**, Tikal's oldest carved monument (dating from 292 AD), as well as assorted tools, jewellery, polychrome pots and obsidian and jade objects. There's also a reconstruction of **Hasaw Chan K'awil's tomb**, discovered beneath Temple I and among the richest ever found in the Maya world, with beautiful polychrome ceramics and jade ornaments, including bracelets, anklets, necklaces and earplugs. One delicately incised human bone depicts deities paddling the dead to the underworld in canoes.

5

Museo Lítico

Main visitor centre • Mon–Fri 8am–4.30pm, Sat & Sun 8am–4pm • Q30

Adjoining Tikal's main visitor centre, the **Museo Lítico** or Lithic Museum is a relatively modern but nonetheless somewhat rundown gallery that holds assorted stelae and carvings from the site. With all the explanatory panels in Spanish, it's liable to disappoint English-speaking visitors.

ARRIVAL AND DEPARTURE   TIKAL

From Flores The easiest way to reach the ruins is via one of the tourist minibuses (Q80 return) that pick up passengers from every hotel in Flores, Santa Elena and El Remate. The minibuses also pick up from Flores airport starting from 3.30am for visitors flying in from Belize City.

From Belize If you're travelling from Belize on an ordinary bus and not a shuttle bus, you'll almost certainly have to change buses at Ixlú, the T-junction at the eastern end of Lago de Petén Itzá, from where plenty of minibuses head to Tikal throughout the day (Q40 one way).

INFORMATION AND TOURS

Opening hours and tickets Tikal is open daily 4am–8pm, and has three kinds of entrance ticket. The vast majority of visitors choose to buy a standard ticket (6am–6pm; Q150), which for most people allows sufficient time at the site. For the separate sunrise (4am–8am; Q100) and sunset (6–8pm; Q100) tickets, you have to be accompanied by an official guide, at additional cost. So if you want to arrive at dawn, catch the sunrise and leave at 4pm, you'll need two tickets (Q100 and Q160). Guests staying inside the national park still have to buy entrance tickets.

Website Visit ⓦ tikalnationalpark.org, but the unofficial ⓦ tikalpark.com also contains useful information about the site and activities.

Visitor centre The main visitor complex, where the road reaches the site proper, holds a café restaurant, an espresso café (see p.168), toilets and luggage storage, as well as the Museo Lítico (see above), a post office, and assorted gift shops and stalls selling souvenirs and accessories.

Guides You can book a tour with a licensed guide at the open kiosk in the roundabout at the entrance. Most are excellent and very knowledgeable, and charge around Q350 for up to five people for a 4hr tour.

Sunrise/sunset tours Hotels and tour companies in El Remate and Flores offer sunrise tours of Tikal, which offer the chance to watch the first rays of the sun illuminate the temple-tops that poke up from the jungle canopy, and hear the howler monkeys share their morning greetings. From Flores, that can involve a departure time as early as 3am. Be warned, though, that the rising sun is often obscured almost entirely by thick mist. Sunset tours are just as worthwhile.

Other tours The ⓦ tikalpark.com website contains information about birding tours (5.30am & 2.30pm, 3.5hr; US$108) as well as the Tikal Canopy Tour, which connects ten ziplines, totalling almost a mile through the jungle at heights of 75–120ft above the ground for a reasonable price (9am; US$25, plus $7.50 for hotel transfers).

ACCOMMODATION

Although you can comfortably see Tikal's main sights in one day, the three **hotels** near the site entrance, all of which have restaurants, are hugely convenient if you plan to stay longer, want to be on the spot for a sunrise tour or simply fancy waking up in the jungle. That said, they're expensive by local standards, and electricity can be sporadic. It's possible to camp in the park (Q50), but you need to bring your own equipment and supplies. The well-maintained campsite behind the main car park holds toilets and (cold) showers.

Jaguar Inn ☎ 7926 2411, ⓦ jaguartikal.com. Thirteen comfy bungalows, each sleeping two and equipped with a hot-water bathroom, fan and porch, along with a decent restaurant, and 24hr electricity. US$90
Jungle Lodge ☎ 7861 0446, ⓦ junglelodgetikal.com. Attractive lodge, with a pool and large private en-suite bungalows on well-shaded grounds, along with a few more basic rooms that share bathrooms (US$40), and a five-bed dorm. The reasonably priced restaurant and bar features international and local dishes. Dorms US$15,

en-suite doubles US$80
★**Tikal Inn** ☎ 7861 2444, ⓦ tikalinn.com. Welcoming little hotel, with helpful staff and individual thatched bungalows arranged around a pool, plus various buildings that hold more conventional rooms. The cheery restaurant serves up simple meals of grilled chicken, pastas, burgers and omelettes. Package rates are available that combine accommodations with breakfast and dinner plus a free sunrise or daytime guided tour. Doubles US$60, bungalows US$85

5

EATING

It's essential to be aware that almost **no food** is available on the site itself, other than perhaps a small packet of biscuits and a bottle of water from the little kiosks near Temples II and IV. However, a number of **comedores** at the park entrance serve limited menus of traditional Guatemalan specialities – eggs, beans, grilled meat and a few "tourist" dishes – while the hotel restaurants offer longer (and pricier) menus.

★**Café Ital-Espresso** Visitor centre. One of the greatest wonders of Tikal – genuine Italian-style coffee served by a genuine Italian, using a gas-powered espresso machine, in a tiny, simple space in the visitor centre. A limited selection of pastries is available. Daily 6.30am–4.30pm.

Comedor Tikal Opposite the visitor centre ☎ 7926 2788. This relatively secluded bar/restaurant, tucked away in a covered garden, is a popular rendezvous for guides and other locals, and sells burgers and nachos for Q30–45, and chicken or meat dishes, including fajitas, for Q50–60. Daily 6am–6pm.

Flores

Prettily poised on a tiny island in Lago Petén Itzá, very close to the mainland and connected by a causeway, **FLORES** is a sedate and easy-going place with an old-fashioned atmosphere. A delightful circular cluster of cobbled streets and ageing houses, rising on all sides to the white, twin-domed church of Nuestra Señora de Los Remedios at its pinnacle, it's a popular stopping point for independent travellers en route to or from Tikal, and well worth visiting even if you're just making a short side-trip from Belize.

Even though it's the capital of Petén, Flores itself is utterly different from the rough, bustling commercialism of the region's other towns, largely because most of its official business is conducted in its sprawling, chaotic, ugly-sister communities of **Santa Elena** and **San Benito**, on the mainland.

This spot boasts a remarkable historical role, as the final holdout of the **ancient Maya**. The water level is thought to have been as much as 50ft higher in Maya times; when Cortés, the conquistador of Mexico, passed through in 1525, the lake held five separate islands. The largest of these, **Noh Petén** or "great island", also known as Tayasal, was the capital of the Itzá, an independent Maya kingdom that the Spaniards only managed to conquer and destroy in 1697. While Flores was certainly occupied, the actual site of the Maya stronghold may well have been on what's now the **Tayasal peninsula**, just across the water, which would indeed have then been a sizeable island.

Today Flores retains the air of a genteel holiday resort, and offers pleasant surroundings for a steady stream of tourists from Guatemala and further afield to relax. If you're not going to the Guatemalan highlands but want to buy *típica* clothing and **gifts**, you'll find the shops here have better prices than at Tikal.

The Tayasal peninsula

San Miguel is served by regular boats from the northeast side of Flores

The attractive **Tayasal peninsula**, just five minutes by boat from Flores in the opposite direction to the causeway, is surprisingly overlooked by many visitors. From the lakeshore village of **San Miguel**, where the boats arrive, a twenty-minute, fairly isolated walk leads to wonderful views of the lake and its settlements. Follow the shoreline west, turn uphill after the last buildings, keep going until the track evens out to a shaded trail, and take the left branch. Eventually you'll reach a clearing from which concrete steps lead up to the wooden lookout tower or *mirador*.

Another trail starts at the clearing here, and parallels the northern side of the peninsula for ten minutes – keep the lake to your left – until it reaches a signposted left turn for **La Playita**. Immediately below, a quiet beach, equipped with picnic benches and toilets, fronts onto the turquoise water of the lake. To complete a circuit back to San Miguel village, simply turn left at the end of the beach road and follow the track for fifteen minutes.

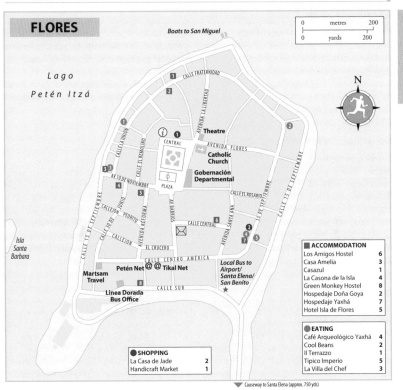

FLORES

Lago
Petén Itzá

Isla
Santa
Barbara

Boats to San Miguel

Theatre
Catholic Church
Gobernación Departamental

Local Bus to Airport/ Santa Elena/ San Benito

Petén Net Tikal Net
Martsam Travel
Linea Dorada Bus Office

ACCOMMODATION	
Los Amigos Hostel	6
Casa Amelia	3
Casazul	1
La Casona de la Isla	4
Green Monkey Hostel	8
Hospedaje Doña Goya	2
Hospedaje Yaxhá	7
Hotel Isla de Flores	5

EATING	
Café Arqueológico Yaxhá	4
Cool Beans	2
Il Terrazzo	1
Tipico Imperio	5
La Villa del Chef	3

SHOPPING	
La Casa de Jade	2
Handicraft Market	1

Causeway to Santa Elena (approx. 750 yds)

Parque Natural Ixpanpajul

8 miles southeast of Flores; turn south 5 miles east of Santa Elena • Daily, hours vary • Q170 for Skyway tour or Tarzan zipline, or Q270 for both • ☎ 4062 9812 or 2336 0576, ⓦ ixpanpajul.com • Any Poptún-bound microbus can drop visitors at the entrance

The **Parque Natural Ixpanpajul**, seven miles southeast of Santa Elena, just off the road towards Tikal, is a rainforest reserve where a network of suspension bridges and stone paths connect various forested hilltops. From the middle of the bridges you can enjoy a monkey's-eye view of the canopy, while on top of the highest hill a *mirador* offers views of virtually the entire Petén Itzá basin. All sorts of activities are available to thrill-seeking visitors, including **zip-lining**, horseback or tractor rides, and taking a night safari.

ARRIVAL AND DEPARTURE   FLORES

By air The airport is two miles east of the causeway. Tuk-tuks/taxis charge about Q20 for a ride between the airport and town. There are flights to Belize City (2 daily; 50min) with Tropic Air (ⓦ tropicair.com) and TAG (ⓦ tag .com.gt) and Guatemala City (4 daily; 50min), with Avianca (ⓦ avianca.com) and TAG.

By bus Arriving by bus from Belize or Tikal, you'll be dropped off at Santa Elena's large modern Terminal Nuevo on 6 Avenida, a mile south of the causeway. Three Guatemalan companies – Fuente del Norte, San Juan Bus and Linea Dorada – run one daily direct bus each between

Santa Elena and Belize City; all leave Santa Elena between 5am and 7am, and Belize City between 9.30am and 2pm.
Destinations Belize City (3 daily; 5hr); El Remate (every 30min; 45min); Guatemala City (15 daily; 9hr); Melchor de Menchos (*micros* every 30min; 2hr 15min); Poptún (hourly; 2hr); Tikal (6 daily; 1hr 30min).

By shuttle bus Book shuttle buses through hotels and travel agents only.
Destinations Belize City (1 daily, 5am; 5hr; Q160); Palenque (1 daily, 5am; 8hr; Q240); Tikal (several daily, 1hr; Q70 return).

5

GETTING AROUND

Car rental Budget, Hertz and Tabarini, which has the widest choice (☎ 7926 0253, ⓦ tabarini.com) operate from the airport, and there are some offices in Santa Elena. Rates (usually including insurance) start at around US$60/day for a small car.

By boat Small boats known as *lanchas* make regular crossings to the Tayasal Peninsula from the dock on Flores' northeast shore, until around 11pm daily, for a quetzal or two. You can also negotiate a rate for a day or half-day trip around the lake; the *lanchas* tend to hang out around the southwest corner of the island, close to *Hotel Petenchel* and near the dock for San Miguel.

By taxi/tuk-tuk For short hops, tuk-tuk drivers charge Q5–10 for anywhere in the Flores/Santa Elena/San Benito area.

INFORMATION AND TOURS

Tourist information Inguat has an office on Calle Centro América (Mon–Fri 8am–4pm; ☎ 5621 8835; ⓔ info -ciudadflores@inguat.gob.gt or ⓔ ciudadfloresinfocenter @gmail.com) and a desk at the airport (Mon–Sat 7.30– 11am & 3.30–7.30pm). There is no official website for Flores, but ⓦ facebook.com/VisitPeten provides useful info on the region. *Los Amigos* hostel (see below) is a good source of advice for budget travellers.

Tours Martsam Travel, Calle 30 Junio (☎ 7867 5093, ⓦ martsam.com) is a good travel agency that runs daily trips to Tikal, plus on-demand expeditions to Yaxhá, Nakum and Aguateca. Mayan Adventure, inside *Café Arqueológico Yaxhá*, Calle 15 de Septiembre (☎ 5830 2060, ⓦ the -mayan-adventure.com) also runs trips to Tikal, plus a range of superb trips to other Maya sites, including Yaxhá and La Blanca, and the little-touched ruins of Nixtun Ch'ich', a few miles west of Flores. Rates depend on the size of your party: US$90/person for one or two people, US$45/person for groups of five, plus US$11 entrance fee.

ACCOMMODATION

★**Los Amigos Hostel** Calle Central ☎ 4495 2399, ⓦ amigoshostel.com. If you find yourself wondering where all the backpackers have gone, this inconspicuous backstreet hostel is the place. Over a hundred can fit into its various brightly painted nooks and crannies, watching DVDs, swinging in hammocks, exchanging information and booking tours. Plus points include the courtyard garden, the restaurant open for all meals and serving veggie food, and the bar that stays open until 1am. The actual accommodation, though, especially in the ten-bunk dorms, tends to be cramped, while the mass 4am exodus for the Q110 Tikal sunrise tours pretty much precludes sleep. Dorms Q̲7̲0̲, doubles Q̲1̲8̲0̲

Casa Amelia Calle La Unión ☎ 7867 5430, ⓦ hotelcasamelia.com. Three-storey, pastel-painted guesthouse; all twelve of the simple but appealing rooms feature original art, there's a lake-view roof terrace as well as a ground-floor restaurant, and they offer transfers to and from the airport and bus station. Q̲4̲5̲0̲

★**Casazul** Calle La Unión ☎ 7867 5451, ⓦ hotelesdepeten.com. This colonial-style house is tastefully done up in shades of blue. All nine rooms have private bath, hot water, fridge, a/c and TV, some have balconies, and the lobby is decorated with old photographs of Flores. Relax in a blue wicker chair on the upper-level terrace that juts over the lake. U̲S̲$̲5̲2̲

La Casona de la Isla Calle 30 de Junio ☎ 7867 5200, ⓦ hotelesdepeten.com. An attractive mid-range hotel, with 26 modern rooms featuring clean, tiled baths, a/c, telephone and cable TV. There's also a swimming pool and lovely sunset views from the terrace restaurant/bar. U̲S̲$̲6̲4̲

Chaltunha Hostel 10a Avenida A, San Miguel ☎ 4219 0851, ⓦ chaltunhahostel.com. Part hotel, part backpackers' hostel, this friendly place is just across the lake from Flores in the sleepy village of San Miguel – call ahead for a free boat transfer. Private screened rooms with showers, basic four-bed dorms, and excellent travel advice, plus a small pool, a bar and restaurant. The owners have a sister hostel in San Ignacio. Dorms U̲S̲$̲1̲0̲, doubles U̲S̲$̲3̲0̲

Green Monkey Hostel Calle Sur ☎ 7867 5394, ⓦ hostelworld.com. Small, basic, friendly hostel, offering very simple but bright dorms and private rooms, some with a/c (Q250). There's not much atmosphere – except that provided by the occasional lapses in power that make it very warm – but it's clean and the beds are comfortable. Dorms Q̲8̲0̲, doubles Q̲1̲8̲0̲

Hospedaje Doña Goya Calle La Unión ☎ 7867 5513, ⓦ hospedajedonagoya.weebly.com. Spread through two adjoining buildings, this friendly, family-run budget guesthouse offers spartan but decent rooms – those with private bath and balcony cost a few dollars extra (US$16) – as well as spacious no-frills dorms. The rooftop terrace, festooned with hammocks, is a huge bonus and meals are available. Dorms U̲S̲$̲5̲, doubles (shared bath) U̲S̲$̲1̲2̲

Hospedaje Yaxhá Calle 15 Septiembre ☎ 7867 5055, ⓦ cafeyaxha.com. Budget accommodation above the recommended *Café Arqueológico Yaxhá* restaurant with well-presented clean rooms, all with private bathroom, powerful fans and free wi-fi, along with dorm rooms. Dorms U̲S̲$̲8̲, doubles U̲S̲$̲2̲6̲

Hotel Isla de Flores Avenida de la Reforma ☎ 7867 5176, ⓦ hotelisladeflores.com. A lobby with white wicker furniture gives way to clean, a/c rooms with TV, private bath and bright bedspreads; about half the rooms feature lake views, and there's a rooftop swimming pool. A skylight and hanging plants liven up each floor. US$66

Posada San Miguel San Miguel ☎7867 5312, ⓦlaposadasanmiguel.com. Delightful, great-value family *posada*, in San Miguel village and served by frequent *lanchas* across the lake. Large lakeside rooms have attractive furnishings, private bathrooms and stunning views, with a simple *comedor* downstairs and a small beach right in front. Q150

EATING

★**Café Arqueológico Yaxhá** Calle 15 Septiembre ☎7867 5055, ⓦcafeyaxha.com. An interesting café, where the menu features pre-Hispanic dishes of Maya origin, using ingredients such as yucca and squash, as well as international favourites. Typical main dishes cost Q28–60. Dieter, the German owner, runs excellent tours to the Maya sites that decorate the walls, and excellent evening slide shows. Free wi-fi. Daily 6am–10pm.

★**Cool Beans** Calle 15 Septiembre ☎7867 5400. Fine café restaurant, with tables spilling down to the lakeside garden. They go the extra mile here: quite apart from the powerful espresso coffee, the breakfasts are excellent, featuring home-made bread and jam and real butter; the sandwiches are huge (try the shredded carrot, bacon and guacamole); and the mains, at Q40–60, are delicious. Draught beer and cocktails also available. Mon–Sat 7am–9pm.

Il Terrazzo Calle La Unión ☎7867 5479. Upscale Italian restaurant, specializing in home-made pasta. The roofed deck upstairs catches the breeze and offers some pleasant views, while the cooking is terrific. Savour the beef carpaccio or delectable fettuccini prepared with grated courgette and shrimps (Q68). The decor is quirky too, with hip retro sofas and artwork. Wine by the glass is pricey at Q40, so come early for a happy-hour cocktail or two (5–7pm). Mon–Sat 11am–10pm.

Tipico Imperio Calle 15 Septiembre ☎7867 5717, ⓦrestaurantetipicoimperio.com. Friendly restaurant overlooking the lake from the east side of the island, with a spacious outdoor terrace and seating inside as well, and the best Guatemalan menu in town. The speciality is the light, succulent white lake fish known locally as simply *pescado blanco*, steamed with peppers for Q120, while burgers, tacos or tortilla soup cost Q30–45, and beef or chicken dishes more like Q60. Daily 7am–11pm.

La Villa del Chef Calle La Unión ☎7867 5667, ⓦfacebook.com/lavilladelchef. A quiet, even romantic, restaurant, with a lovely lake vista from its huge windows and terrace seating. The mixed international menu includes falafel burgers for Q49, steaks for Q89 and fresh lake fish at market prices; Q49 also buy a colossal plate of nachos and beef chilli. The tables on the lakeshore terrace are candlelit in the evenings, and profits benefit development projects in Petén. Daily 8am–10pm.

SHOPPING

La Casa de Jade Inside Café Arqueológico Yaxhá, Calle 15 Septiembre. Interesting jewellery, inspired by classic Maya designs, at fair prices. Daily 7am–9pm.

Handicraft Market Parque Central. This bustling, colourful market in the centre of town is a great place to pick up a locally made doll or other souvenirs. Daily 9am–9pm.

The south

SOUTH WATER CAYE

The south

The southern half of Belize contains the country's wildest terrain, from mangrove swamp, lagoon and savannah to sandy bays, river-hewn valleys and forested ridges. For most visitors, the immediate interest lies in the beaches, whether at Hopkins and Placencia on the mainland, or out on the cayes that perch atop the barrier reef. Time spent away from the most touristed areas, however, for example touring the Maya villages of Toledo, in the far south, or venturing into the many wildlife reserves and national parks, can be hugely rewarding.

You'll certainly find yourself with plenty of peace and quiet here. Southern Belize has a strikingly low population, and what few towns it holds are located along the coast. **Dangriga**, the headquarters of the **Garifuna** people – descended from Carib Indians and shipwrecked African slaves – allows access to idyllic **Tobacco** and **South Water** cayes. **Hopkins**, a short way south, is a beach resort in its own right, while the **Placencia peninsula** further south is lined by a continuous strip of sand, with accommodation and dining options to suit every budget.

Beyond Placencia, the **Southern Highway** is set well back from the coast, running beneath the jagged peaks and dense rainforest of the **Maya Mountains**, and passing through pine forest and citrus and banana plantations on the lower plains. With no roads penetrating the mountains themselves, the most accessible area for exploring the rainforest is the **Cockscomb Basin Wildlife Sanctuary**, known to all as the **jaguar reserve**; the hiking here is wonderful, though you're unlikely to get a glimpse of its small group of big cats.

The highway continues into the **Toledo** region, home to traditional Maya farming villages as well as ancient sites such as **Lubaantun** and **Nim Li Punit**, before coming to an end, 105 miles from Dangriga, at the sleepy, charming port of **Punta Gorda**.

GETTING AROUND

By bus and boat Buses along the Hummingbird and Southern highways connect Belize City and Belmopan with Dangriga and Punta Gorda. To reach Hopkins by bus, you'll normally need to change at Dangriga. Some buses detour off the main highway to travel all the way down the Placencia peninsula, or you can get off at Independence and catch a boat across to the peninsula from there.

Infrequent local buses from Punta Gorda serve Maya villages in the Toledo district.
By car or guided tour As ever, to reach the Maya sites and wildlife reserves, you'll need either to have your own vehicle, or to join a guided tour.
By plane Dangriga, Placencia and Punta Gorda have their own airports, served by domestic airlines.

PLACENCIA

Highlights

❶ **The Hummingbird Highway** Take the most scenic drive in the country, heading south to Dangriga. **See p.178**

❷ **Glover's Reef** Indulge your Robinson Crusoe desert-island fantasy in a beach cabin on the most stunningly beautiful coral atoll in the Caribbean. **See p.184**

❸ **The Cockscomb Basin Wildlife Sanctuary** Spend a night or two in the world's first jaguar reserve, following the tracks of the largest cat in the Americas. **See p.193**

❹ **Placencia** Stroll along the best beaches in the country, or head out to sea for snorkelling

off Laughing Bird Caye and swimming with whale sharks at Gladden Spit. **See p.196**

❺ **Monkey River** Take a river trip upstream from the coastal mangrove swamp to see howler monkeys, crocodiles and birds in abundance. **See p.201**

❻ **Punta Gorda** Enjoy the food, the friendliness and the laidback charm of Belize's southernmost town – and then take a boat on to Guatemala or Honduras. **See p.204**

❼ **Lubaantun** Admire the beautifully restored buildings of the ancient Maya "place of fallen stones", the supposed home of the famous Crystal Skull. **See p.212**

HIGHLIGHTS ARE MARKED ON THE MAP ON PP.176–177

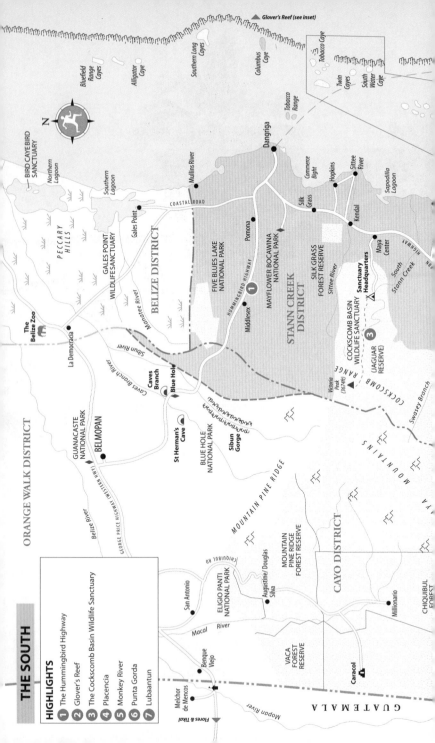

THE SOUTH

HIGHLIGHTS

1 The Hummingbird Highway
2 Glover's Reef
3 The Cockscomb Basin Wildlife Sanctuary
4 Placencia
5 Monkey River
6 Punta Gorda
7 Lubaantun

N

ORANGE WALK DISTRICT

BELIZE DISTRICT

STANN CREEK DISTRICT

CAYO DISTRICT

GUATEMALA

BELMOPAN

The Belize Zoo

La Democracia

GUANACASTE NATIONAL PARK

Caves Branch

Blue Hole

St Herman's Cave

BLUE HOLE NATIONAL PARK

Sibun Gorge

Gales Point

GALES POINT WILDLIFE SANCTUARY

BIRD CAVE BIRD SANCTUARY

Northern Lagoon

Southern Lagoon

PECCARY HILLS

COASTAL ROAD

Mullins River

Dangriga

Tobacco Range

Commerce Bight

Hopkins

Sittee River

Sapodilla Lagoon

Kendal

Maya Center

Sanctuary Headquarters

COCKSCOMB BASIN WILDLIFE SANCTUARY (JAGUAR RESERVE)

Silk Grass

Pomona

Middlesex

FIVE BLUES LAKE NATIONAL PARK

MAYFLOWER BOCAWINA NATIONAL PARK

SILK GRASS FOREST RESERVE

HUMMINGBIRD HIGHWAY

Sittee River

Victoria Peak (3674ft)

COCKSCOMB RANGE

South Stann Creek

Swasey Branch

MAYA MOUNTAINS

MOUNTAIN PINE RIDGE

San Antonio

ELIGIO PANTI NATIONAL PARK

Augustine/ Douglas Silva

MOUNTAIN PINE RIDGE FOREST RESERVE

CHIQUIBUL RD

Macal River

VACA FOREST RESERVE

Caracol

Millionario

CHIQUIBUL FOREST

Benque Viejo

Melchor de Mencos

Flores & Tikal

Mopan River

Belize River

Sibun River

Caves Branch River

Manatee River

GEORGE PRICE HIGHWAY (WESTERN HWY)

HUMMINGBIRD HIGHWAY

SOUTHERN HIGHWAY

Glover's Reef (see inset)

Bluefield Range Cayes

Alligator Caye

Southern Long Cayes

Columbus Caye

Tobacco Caye

Twin Cayes

South Water Caye

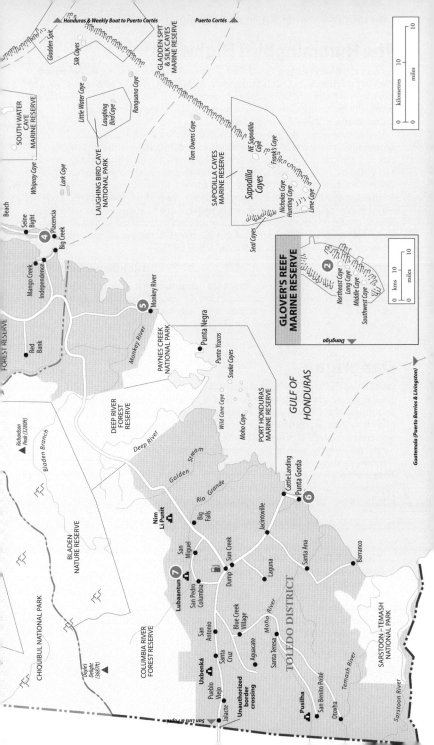

Honduras & Weekly Boat to Puerto Cortés
Puerto Cortés

Gladden Spit

Silk Cayes

GLADDEN SPIT
& SILK CAYES
MARINE RESERVE

Little Water Caye

Laughing
Bird Caye

Ranguana Caye

SOUTH WATER
CAYE
MARINE RESERVE

Whipray Caye

Lark Caye

LAUGHING BIRD CAYE
NATIONAL PARK

Tom Owens Caye

NE Sapodilla
Caye

Frank's Caye

SAPODILLA CAYES
MARINE RESERVE

Sapodilla
Cayes

Nicholas Caye

Hunting Caye

Lime Caye

Seal Cayes

Beach

Seine
Bight

Placencia ④

Big Creek

Mango Creek

Independence

GLOVER'S REEF
MARINE RESERVE ②

Northwest Caye

Long Caye

Middle Caye

Southwest Caye

Dangriga ▼

FOREST RESERVE

Red
Bank

Monkey River ⑤

Monkey River

PAYNES CREEK
NATIONAL PARK

Punta Negra

Punta Yacos

Snake Cayes

GULF OF
HONDURAS

Guatemala (Puerto Barrios & Livingston) ▼

Richardson
Peak (3280ft) ▲

Bladen Branch

DEEP RIVER
FOREST RESERVE

Deep River

Wild Cane Caye

Moho Caye

PORT HONDURAS
MARINE RESERVE

BLADEN
NATURE RESERVE

Golden Stream

Rio Grande

Big Falls

Nim
Li Punit

San Miguel

Sun Creek

Cattle Landing
Punta Gorda ⑥

Jacintoville

Santa Ana

Barranco

CHIQUIBUL NATIONAL PARK

Doyle's
Delight
(3687ft) ▲

COLUMBIA RIVER
FOREST RESERVE

Lubaantun ⑦

San Pedro
Columbia

Dump

Laguna

TOLEDO DISTRICT

San
Antonio

Blue Creek
Village

Moho River

Aguacate

Santa Teresa

Santa Cruz

Uxbenká

Pueblo
Viejo

Jalacte

Unauthorized
border crossing

San Luis & Poptún

Pusilha

San Benito Poité

Otoxha

SARSTOON–TEMASH
NATIONAL PARK

Temash River

Sarstoon River

kilometres   10   10
miles

kms   10   10
miles

The Hummingbird Highway

Beyond the Blue Hole and Caves Branch (see p.124), the stunning **Hummingbird Highway** traverses a makeshift bridge over the Sibun River (the original was washed away in heavy rains) before undulating smoothly through increasingly hilly landscape, eventually mounting a low pass. The downhill slope beyond is appropriately, if unimaginatively, called Over the Top.

As the Hummingbird Highway descends from the mountains, it enters the flat **Stann Creek valley**, the centre of the Belizean **citrus** industry. Bananas were grown here initially, with half a million stems exported annually through Stann Creek (now Dangriga) by 1891. However, the banana boom came to an abrupt end in 1906 due to disease, and to foster the growing of **citrus fruits**, a small railway was built here in 1908 – indeed, many highway bridges were originally rail bridges. Today, citrus comprises a major part of agricultural exports and is heralded as one of the nation's great success stories, though for the largely Guatemalan labour force, housed in rows of scruffy huts, conditions are poor. The presence of tropical bugs like the leaf-cutter ant has forced planters to use powerful insecticides, including DDT.

EATING   **THE HUMMINGBIRD HIGHWAY**

Café Casita de Amor Mile 16, Hummingbird Hwy. Whether you fancy an espresso coffee, a smoothie, a Bz$10 burger or a Bz$14 daily special such as spaghetti with meatballs, this cosy café, downstairs in the central octagonal tower of a quirky gabled-roof house across from the defunct Billy Barquedier National Park, makes an ideal stop-off on a long car journey. Tues–Sun 7.30am–5pm.

Dangriga

DANGRIGA, the largest town in southern Belize, is the capital of Stann Creek District. It's also the cultural centre of the **Garifuna**, a people of mixed indigenous Caribbean and African descent who are estimated to make up around four and a half percent of the country's population. Since the early 1980s Garifuna culture has undergone a tremendous revival, as evidenced by the renaming of what was previously "Stann Creek Town" to Dangriga, a Garifuna word meaning "sweet (or standing) waters".

Sprawling along roughly two miles of shoreline, and home to fewer than ten thousand people, Dangriga has the feel of a laidback Caribbean town where little ever happens. The sandy tracks that line both banks of the **North Stann Creek**, as it flows out into the ocean, lend the central area an immediate appeal. Most of Dangriga's shops, restaurants and other facilities lie either on, or just off, the long north–south thoroughfare that's known as **St Vincent Street** to the south of the river bridge, and

---

THE MYSTERY OF THE DISAPPEARING LAKE

Sadly, **Five Blues Lake National Park**, which you may well see signposted off the Hummingbird Highway near St Margaret's Village at Mile 32, is no longer worth visiting. The park used to centre on a beautiful **lake**, set amid luxuriantly forested karst scenery, and constantly fluctuating in colour between shimmering shades of blue.

Only the intriguing name now survives; the lake itself has **gone**. Abruptly, in July 2006, it simply drained away like a sink, with local fishermen reporting a noise like "the lake was crying". Baffled scientists eventually determined that the blockage responsible for creating the lake must have dissolved, allowing the water to exit through the limestone below. Since then the lake has repeatedly reappeared and disappeared, most notably in 2012, presumably as its natural "plug" re-forms only to dissolve once more. Meanwhile, with visitor numbers dwindling to nothing, the rough, six-mile dirt road to the lakebed deteriorated to become all but impassable, and there are no longer any rangers or facilities on site.

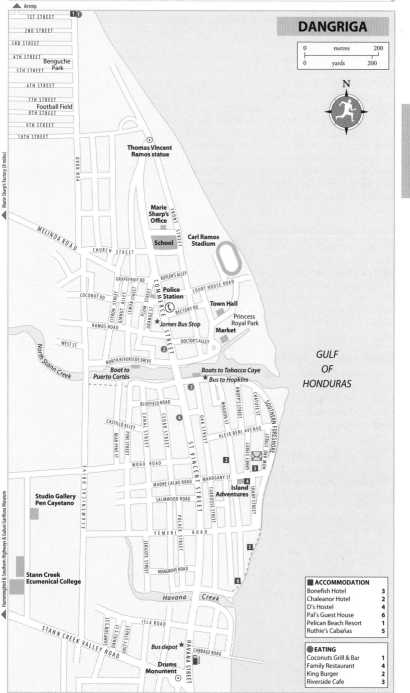

DANGRIGA

6

ACCOMMODATION

Bonefish Hotel	3
Chaleanor Hotel	2
D's Hostel	4
Pal's Guest House	6
Pelican Beach Resort	1
Ruthie's Cabañas	5

EATING

Coconuts Grill & Bar	1
Family Restaurant	4
King Burger	2
Riverside Cafe	3

Commerce Street to the north. It can seem somewhat rundown and intimidating at first glance, but it's well worth taking the time to stroll around, and soak up the relaxed, friendly atmosphere.

The one major landmark is the bronze **"Drums of Our Fathers" monument**, on the roundabout where the highway reaches the southern end of town – a tribute by Nigerian artist Stephen Okeke to the centrality of drumming in Garifuna culture. Otherwise, be on the lookout for the fine **crafts** on sale in the local shops, including distinctive basketware, woven palm-leaf hats and Garifuna dolls.

Thanks to the reef a few miles offshore, the sea is so calm at Dangriga that gentle lawns reach all the way to the waterfront. There's little **beach** to speak of, however. Only the *Pelican Beach Resort* at the north end of town comes at all close to matching the beach hotels of Hopkins and Placencia, further south, so travellers keen to sunbathe and swim seldom stick around for long. Instead Dangriga serves primarily as an overnight base for trips out to the cayes, and in particular Tobacco Caye (see p.184) and South Water Caye (see p.184).

Gulusi Garifuna Museum

Chuluhadiwa Park, Stann Creek Valley Rd • Mon–Fri 10am–5pm, Sat 8am–noon • Bz$10 • ☎ 669 0639, ⓦ ngcbelize.org

For anyone interested in the Garifuna people of Belize (see box, p.182), the **Gulusi Garifuna Museum** makes an essential port of call. Almost the first building that you see as you approach Dangriga from inland, alongside a new primary school 1.5 miles short of the sea, it's filled with fascinating exhibits on Garifuna history and culture. Maps and display panels trace the migration of the Garifuna from St Vincent to Roatán and on to Belize, while artwork, clothing, food and music help illustrate their ongoing traditions.

Pen Cayetano Studio Gallery

3 Aranda Crescent, off Ecumenical Drive• Daily 9am–5pm • Bz$5 • ☎ 628 6807, ⓦ cayetano.de

Part art gallery, part performance space, the **Pen Cayetano Studio Gallery** celebrates the work of Garifuna artist/musician Pen Cayetano, who was awarded an MBE by the British government in 2012. His striking deep-coloured oil paintings, which include numerous portraits, explore themes from Garifuna culture and Belize in general, and

---

GARIFUNA'S TRADITIONAL CELEBRATIONS

Dangriga's **musical traditions** play an important role in the most important local celebration, **Garifuna Settlement Day**, on November 19. Packed with expatriate Dangrigans returning to their roots, the town erupts into wild celebration. The party begins the evening before, with drumming, sound systems and punta dancing all night. In the morning there's a re-enactment of the original arrival of the Garifuna from Honduras, with people landing on the beach in dugout canoes decorated with palm leaves. Similar exuberance goes into Christmas and New Year, when you might see the *wanaragu* or *Jonkunu* (John Canoe) dances, with **masked and costumed performers** representing a cast of eighteenth-century naval officers and Amerindian tribal chiefs.

The tradition of **drumming** is central to Garifuna identity, and permits the Garifuna to express their unique cultural circumstances. The construction of the drums themselves is a time-consuming process that uses all natural materials. The base is a solid piece of hardwood, hollowed out with burning coals, and the drum-head of wet, scraped deerskin is held in place by jungle vines and rope and set to dry. The rhythms are an integral part of the culture, with certain ones reserved for prayer, and combined with timeworn melodies and other percussion instruments they inform all sorts of everyday activities and celebrations. Lessons, drum-making classes and performances can be taken in at the **Maroon Creole Drum School** (p.206) and at **Warasa Drum School** (p.206), while you may encounter more informal shows in various bars and restaurants in southern Belize.

he's also renowned as the originator of **punta rock**, a calypso-tinged musical genre popularized by the Turtle Shell Band from 1979 onwards. School groups flock through the compound for drumming lessons and demonstrations, and you can also admire artworks by Pen's German-born wife Ingrid and their daughter Mali.

Marie Sharp's Factory

8 miles northwest of Dangriga at 1 Melinda Rd, Melinda • Mon–Fri 7am–4pm • Free; best to call in advance for tours • ☎ 532 2087, Ⓦ mariesharps-bz.com

A delicious and much-loved dinner-table staple throughout and even beyond Belize, Marie Sharp's **hot pepper sauces** are produced on a rural 400-acre estate northwest of Dangriga. You won't learn the secret recipe if you take a free tour of **Marie Sharp's Factory**, but you'll get to see the fields and orchards where the ingredients are grown, watch the latest batches being prepared, graded from Mild, via Fiery Hot and No Wimps Allowed, up to Beware, and possibly meet the "Fiery Lady" herself. Her products, which also include fruit jams (mango and pineapple are particularly tasty) and seasonings, are also sold from a downtown office at 3 Pier Rd.

ARRIVAL AND DEPARTURE

DANGRIGA

By bus Dangriga's bus terminal, immediately north of the Drums monument at the southern end of town, is used by all local bus companies. The town centre is roughly a 10min walk from here; taxis are usually available for around Bz$6. Destinations Belize City, mostly via Belmopan (at least every 2hr, last bus 7.30pm; 1hr 30min–3hr); Hopkins (Mon–Sat 10.30am & 5.15pm; 30min); Placencia (3–4 daily, last bus 6pm; 1hr 45min); Punta Gorda (8–10 daily, last bus 6.15pm; 2hr 30min).

By plane Dangriga's airstrip, close to the shore just north of the *Pelican Beach Resort*, is served by at least eight daily flights in each direction on the Belize City–Punta Gorda run (typical one-way fares US$63 to Belize City, US$73 to Punta Gorda; Ⓦ tropicair.com and Ⓦ mayaislandair.com). A taxi into town will cost at least Bz$10.

By boat to the cayes Travellers heading out to the cayes

are advised to arrange accommodation in advance; all hotels will arrange boat transfers from and to Dangriga. Boats to Tobacco Caye (40min; from Bz$35) normally set off from alongside the *Riverside Restaurant*, just downstream from the bridge, in the early afternoon; there are no scheduled departures, but if you ask in the restaurant someone should know if one's due to leave.

By boat to Honduras A ferry making its way from San Pedro, Caye Caulker and Belize City (☎ 630 2152, Ⓦ prideofbelize.com) passes through Dangriga on its way to Puerto Cortés, Honduras, every Saturday morning at 10.30am, stopping at the north bank of the river. The Belize City-bound return departs on Monday at 3pm. Tickets from Dangriga to Puerto Cortés are Bz$110, while the total run between Puerto Cortés and Belize City costs Bz$145.

ACTIVITIES

Kayaking Island Expeditions (Ⓦ belizekayaking.com), on the Southern Foreshore, rents sea kayaks (singles Bz$70/ day, doubles Bz$110/day). They will also, for a substantial

fee, shuttle groups of kayakers out to the nearby cayes, and offer multi-day packages that include accommodation.

ACCOMMODATION

Bonefish Hotel 15 Mahogany St ☎ 522 2243, Ⓦ bluemarlinlodge.com. Welcoming little hotel in a quiet but central seafront location. Eight spacious rooms featuring TV, private bath and a/c – the nicest are upstairs – and an attractive sea-view lounge/lobby. As well as serving as the office for *Blue Marlin Lodge* on South Water Caye (see p.184), this is also a good place to arrange fishing trips. US$84

Chaleanor Hotel 35 Magoon St ☎ 522 2587, Ⓦ chaleanorhotel.com. This colonial house holds a friendly, good-value hotel with accommodation ranging from no-frills budget rooms to larger en-suite options, with private bath and TV, in which you can pay an extra US$20

per night for a/c. Free coffee, fruit and purified water available. The owner's son is a skilled guide. US$30, en suite US$90

★ **D's Hostel** 1 Sharp St ☎ 502 3324, Ⓦ valsbackpackerhostel.com. Simple concrete hostel, close to the beach, where each of the three plain, clean dorms – one male, one female, and one mixed – holds eight bunks and private wooden lockers. Rates include a free breakfast of fruit and waffles, and there's also same-day laundry service, in-room wi-fi, a book exchange, bike rental and lovely views of the sea from the rooftop. The friendly owner, Dana, prepares lunch and dinner on

6

A GARIFUNA HISTORY

The **Garifuna** (or Garinagu) trace their history back to **St Vincent** in the eastern Caribbean. Originally home to the Arawaks, the island had, at the time of the earliest Spanish explorations, recently been settled by people from South America, who called themselves Kalipuna or Kwaib. Hence, probably, the names Garifuna, meaning cassava-eating people, and Carib. Columbus's contemporaries reported encountering a mixed population, descended from Carib men and Arawak women.

When two Spanish ships carrying **slaves** from Nigeria were wrecked off St Vincent in 1635, the survivors took refuge on the island. The Caribs and Africans initially clashed, but the former had been weakened by war and disease, and the Africans gained enough of a foothold to lead to the rise of the **Black Caribs** or Garifuna. Though the British nominally controlled St Vincent for most of the seventeenth and eighteenth centuries, vying for control with France and the Netherlands, it belonged for all practical purposes to the Garifuna. In the mid-1700s, the British attempted to assert full control, but were driven off by the Caribs, with French assistance. Another attempt twenty years later was more successful, and in 1783 the British imposed a treaty on the Garifuna, granting themselves ownership of over half the island. Rejecting the treaty, the Garifuna continued to defy British rule through frequent uprisings, consistently supported by the French. From 1795, a year of bitter fighting aimed at establishing Garifuna independence inflicted horrendous casualties and led to the loss of their leader, Chief Joseph Chatoyer. The Garifuna and French finally surrendered on June 10, 1796.

Since Britain could not countenance free blacks living among slave-owning European settlers, they decided to **deport** the Garifuna, whom they hunted down, destroying their homes, uprooting culture and causing hundreds of deaths. The survivors – around 4300 Black Caribs and one hundred Yellow Caribs, as designated by the British – were transported to the nearby island of Balliceaux. Within six months, over half died, many of yellow fever. In March 1797, the remainder were shipped to **Roatán**, one of the Bay Islands off Honduras. The Spanish commandeered one of the ships and redirected it to the mainland at Trujillo; barely two thousand Garifuna lived to see Roatán. A few years later, the Spanish *comandante* of Trujillo arrived and took possession of the island, shipping survivors to his jurisdiction to augment his labour force. The Spanish hadn't succeeded in agriculture, and the proficient Garifuna benefited the colony considerably. Conscripted into the army, boys and men proved to be effective soldiers and mercenaries. As their renown spread, they were brought to other areas along the coast, and in 1802, 150 arrived in Stann Creek and Punta Gorda to be woodcutters. The understanding they gained of the coastline made them expert **smugglers**, able to evade Spanish restrictions on trade with the British.

THE GARIFUNA IN BELIZE

The incursion of the Garifuna into Belize did not please its British colonizers. Although Superintendent Barrow ordered their expulsion in 1811, the Garifuna were still streaming in when European settlers arrived in Stann Creek in 1823. Finding their mix of Catholicism, ancestor worship and polygamy outrageous, **Methodist missionaries** attempted to Christianize the Garifuna, with little success. The arrival of the largest single Garifuna migration to Belize in 1832, when several hundred fled Honduras (by then the Central American Republic) under the leadership of Alejo Benji, is still celebrated as **Garifuna Settlement Day**, each November 19.

Through the **twentieth century**, Stann Creek (later Dangriga) was a stable community, with women employed in bagging and stacking cohune nuts and men working in agriculture. The Garifuna continued to travel widely for work, however, initially confining themselves to Central America (where they can now be found all along the Caribbean coast from Belize to Nicaragua), but in World War II they joined the crews of British and US merchant ships and found their ways abroad. Since then small Garifuna communities have sprung up in New York, New Orleans, Los Angeles and London. Today, Belize has a National Garifuna Council (wngcbelize.org), which has refined a written language, publishing *The People's Garifuna Dictionary* and school textbooks, and opened a museum in Dangriga (see p.180).

demand, which you can eat outdoors, and can arrange local tours and Garífuna language and culture classes. US$20

Pal's Guest House 86 Magoon St ☎ 522 2365, ⓦ palsbelize.com. Quiet, somewhat faded hotel. All the basic tiled rooms have private baths and TVs; those with a/c cost more, although only two of them are in the nicer of the property's two buildings, a ten-room structure set right on the beach. US$40

★ **Pelican Beach Resort** First St, 1 mile north of the centre ☎ 522 2044, ⓦ pelicanbeachbelize.com. A well-managed large hotel that enjoys Dangriga's finest beachfront location; the long jetty is equipped with hammocks, and used by boats to and from its wonderful

sister property on South Water Caye (see p.184). Unusually the most attractive rooms, right by the sea in the original wooden, colonial-style lodge, are also the cheapest, as they have ceiling fans and open verandas; the more modern rooms in the annexe further back have a/c, though only some have outdoor space. Frequently used by tour and conservation groups and scientists. There's also an excellent restaurant (see below). US$135

Ruthie's Cabañas 31 Southern Foreshore ☎ 502 3184. Four bargain, thatched *cabañas* on the beach with private bath, fan, TV and porch, which can sleep one to four people. A spell here is more like a friendly homestay experience. Ruthie cooks delicious meals by arrangement. US$30

6

EATING

Disappointingly few of Dangriga's **restaurants** specialize in Garífuna food; you'll find more options in Hopkins (see p.190). For fruits and picnic supplies, try the **market** on the north bank of the creek near the seashore; other groceries are available at the supermarket just south of the bridge. There's no shortage of **bars** in Dangriga. Some, particularly those that call themselves clubs, are rather dubious; the safest spot for a Caribbean sundowner has to be the bar at the *Pelican Beach Resort*.

★ **Coconuts Grill & Bar** Pelican Beach Resort, First St, 1 mile north of the centre ☎ 522 2044, ⓦ pelican beachbelize.com. Though perhaps a little far from the centre to attract non-guests, this hotel restaurant offers the best oceanfront dining in Dangriga, with its broad, romantic terrace cooled by sea breezes. Breakfast for Bz$14 continental or Bz$25 cooked (be sure to try the delicious Bz$3 fry-jacks), burgers and burritos for lunch, at around Bz$15, and tasty dinner dishes like local shrimp cooked with mustard for Bz$30. Daily 7am–9pm.

Family Restaurant 9 St Vincent St ☎ 522 3433. An a/c oasis in baking-hot Dangriga, opposite Scotia Bank, with greasy Chinese dishes and fast food for less than Bz$15; the long menu has several vegetarian options. Daily 10am–11pm.

King Burger 135 Commerce St ☎ 522 2476. Push open

the door in its slightly forbidding facade, and this simple diner, immediately north of the creek, turns out to be a round-the-clock rendezvous for locals of all ages, serving ham-and-egg breakfasts for Bz$12, and lunch staples like a steak sandwich for Bz$6 or half a fried chicken or the Belizean delicacy conch soup for Bz$12, as well as coffee and fruit juices. Mon–Sat 7am–3pm & 6–10pm.

Riverside Cafe Riverside and Oak St ☎ 669 1473. Simple café, on the south bank of the river close to the bridge, with no outdoor space or views, which serves as the meeting place for boats to the cayes and is a useful spot to pick up information in general. Breakfast, lunch and dinner alike cost Bz$8–12, with local staples like beans and rice, beans and pigtail, stew chicken and steamed fish. The Bz$4 seaweed shake, with nutmeg and peanuts, is a must. Mon–Sat 6.30am–9pm, Sun 8am–3pm.

The Central Cayes

Some of Belize's most enticing Caribbean islands, known collectively as the **Central Cayes**, lie along and around the Barrier Reef offshore from Dangriga. Closest to the mainland are the **Tobacco Range**, a group of mangrove cayes just ten miles east of Dangriga. The largest in the range, **Man-O'-War Caye**, is a **bird sanctuary** named after the frigate (or man-o'-war) birds you'll see hanging on the breeze with outstretched wings. In the breeding season the males develop an immense, bright red balloon on their throats and the island fills with nesting birds; you can watch them for hours, but you can't land on the caye. Sunsets out here can be breathtaking, outlining the distant Maya Mountains with a purple and orange aura.

Tiny **Tobacco Caye** and the slightly larger **South Water Caye** are protected within the **South Water Caye Marine Reserve**, a World Heritage Site that offers wonderful snorkelling and diving. Rangers patrol the waters hereabouts daily, monitoring illegal fishing and other activities. In theory, they also collect an **entrance fee** of Bz$10 per day or Bz$30 per week, but it's more than likely that you'll never be asked to pay.

Both Tobacco and South Water cayes hold delightful places to stay, as does privately owned **Thatch Caye** nearby. Beyond, thirty miles from Dangriga, the coral atoll of **Glover's Reef** is one of the Caribbean's hidden treasures, with an assortment of excellent lodges and adventure outfits. It too is the centre of its own marine reserve.

Tobacco Caye

12 miles east of Dangriga

The tiny, five-acre island of **Tobacco Caye** perches right on the reef a dozen miles east of Dangriga, making it the easiest (and cheapest) to reach of the Tobacco Range cayes. Two-storey timber buildings in differing states of repair line the shore, and stand strewn across its sandy core as well, interspersed by little footpaths. Some are simple hotels and cabins, some are home to local fishing families, and some are seldom-occupied private holiday properties. Wherever you may wander in the centre you're only a minute's walk from the shore in any direction, with unbroken reef stretching north for miles.

Since the reef is within wading distance of the shore, you don't even need a boat for some superb **snorkelling and diving**, saving precious time to eat, drink or relax in a hammock.

The cayes of Columbus Reef were, incidentally, originally visited by turtle fishermen. Tobacco Caye was a trading post where passing boats could pick up supplies, including the tobacco that gave it its name.

South Water Caye

16 miles southeast of Dangriga

Five miles south of Tobacco Caye and about three times larger, **South Water Caye** is one of the most beautiful and exclusive islands in Belize. It takes its name from a well at its centre, still in existence, which provided fresh water for passing ships. While a fine selection of accommodation makes it an absolutely wonderful place to kick back and relax for a few days, it only takes ten minutes or so to explore the whole island on foot.

Like Tobacco Caye, South Water Caye sits right on the reef and offers fantastic, very accessible **snorkelling** and scuba diving in crystal-clear water. Most of the resorts have their own very good **dive shops** and can arrange trips to **Glover's Reef** (see below). Much of its eastern shoreline still consists of mangrove forest, but there's a superb and enticing **beach** at the southern end, protected by the reef as it curves around offshore. Turtles nest in the sand here, and this stretch belongs to a small nature reserve.

The tiny island visible off the caye's south end is **Carrie Bow Caye**, where the Smithsonian Institute has a research station; you can ask your hotel to arrange a visit, but there's no overnight accommodation.

Glover's Reef

30 miles east of Dangriga

The southernmost of Belize's three coral atolls, **Glover's Reef** lies twenty miles beyond the Tobacco range. Named after British pirate John Glover, the reef stretches about twenty miles from north to south, and eight miles east to west. Physically this is the best-developed atoll in the Caribbean, rising from depths of 3000ft, with the reef wall starting less than ten yards offshore. It offers some of the most spectacular **wall diving** in the world – the fantastic Long Caye Wall is less than 300ft offshore – with visibility of over 900ft.

Glover's Reef is home to rare **seabirds** such as the white-capped noddy, all its cayes have nesting ospreys, and Belize's **marine turtles** lay their eggs on the beaches. The vitally important snapper spawning grounds on the atoll attract dozens of immense **whale sharks**, which congregate during the late spring full moons to feast on snapper eggs. Within the aquamarine lagoon are hundreds of smaller **patch reefs** – a snorkelling wonderland.

These unique features led to the atoll being protected as the **Glover's Reef Marine Reserve**, further enhanced by its designation as a World Heritage Site in 1996. Fishing is not allowed from the cayes themselves, but it is permitted in certain specified zones.

The cayes of Glover's Reef

The principal cayes along Glover's Reef lie in the atoll's southeastern section. **Northeast Caye**, covered in thick coconut and broadleaf forest and with evidence of Maya fishing camps, lies just across the channel from **Long Caye**. Just under three miles southwest, **Middle Caye** is a wilderness zone, with a marine research and monitoring station run by the Wildlife Conservation Society (ⓦwcsgloversreef.org). Fisheries Department conservation officers are based here, rigorously patrolling the reserve. Only staff, scientists and students stay on the caye, but you can usually visit with permission; the ecology of the atoll is explained in interesting displays, and you may see research in progress. Contribute to conservation efforts by purchasing a T-shirt here, available only on the caye.

Southwest Caye, three miles beyond Middle Caye, was sliced by Hurricane Hattie in 1961 into two distinct islands, separated by a narrow, swimmable channel.

ARRIVAL AND DEPARTURE

TOBACCO CAYE

By boat Boats generally leave from near the bridge in Dangriga between 9am and 1pm, but there are no regular departures; check at the *Riverside Cafe* (see p.183), where you can meet the skippers (who sometimes require a minimum of three or four passengers before setting off). Captain Buck runs a reliable daily service leaving the caye at 9am and returning later, though any of the island lodge owners will take you if they're in town. It's a 30min trip and the one-way fare is about Bz$40/person.

SOUTH WATER CAYE

By boat There is no scheduled service between Dangriga and South Water Caye. If you're planning to stay on the island, it's essential to reserve accommodation in advance, in which

THE CENTRAL CAYES

case your hotel will provide a transfer. Otherwise, it's possible to arrive here under your own steam, by boat or kayak, or you could ask at the *Riverside Cafe* (see p.183) if there's a skipper around who will take you. Be warned, hotels and private boats alike tend to have a minimum charge per boat, based on four passengers, so a couple can pay as much as US$175 per person for the return trip.

GLOVER'S REEF

By boat Since a chartered boat from Dangriga or Hopkins/Sittee River will cost you US$350 each way, package transport from your hotel is the best way to arrive and depart. For charters, ask at your hotel or try Michael Jackson (ⓣ620 8913), who may be inclined to give a *Rough Guides* discount.

ACTIVITIES

Diving The dive centre based at *Reef's End Lodge* (ⓣ676 8363) offers single (US$75) and double (US$125) dives, including gear. Trips to sites further afield include Glover's Reef atoll (two dives for US$150) and Lighthouse Reef (two for US$250); prices include gear and a packed lunch.

ACCOMMODATION

THATCH CAYE

Thatch Caye Resort ⓣ603 2414, in the US ⓣ800 435 3145, ⓦthatchcaye.com. Luxury resort on a tiny private island, just 8 miles from Dangriga, with five *cabañas*, propped on stilts above the water and cooled by the breeze, plus four bungalows with open roof decks, and a family villa. No children under 12. Rates include all meals and transfers, plus use of kayaks and paddle boards. US$349

TOBACCO CAYE

Blue Dolphin Lodge ⓣ542 2032. Simple cabins on the sand on the eastern side of the island, and rooms in a main wooden building, with and without private baths. Most of

the hotel is run by solar power, and there's a thatched shelter with hammocks and snorkel equipment for rent. US$100
Reef's End Lodge ⓣ676 8363, ⓦreefsendlodge.com. Dive and adventure resort beside the jetty at the southern tip of the island. Stay right on the shore in the large wooden building, where the simple rooms are all en suite and share a balcony; in separate *cabañas* (US$150) or in the smarter, stand-alone a/c honeymoon cottage (US$150), lapped by the waves. The restaurant/bar, perched on stilts over the sea, with a spacious open deck, serves delicious food and makes a fantastic place to enjoy the sunset. Rates include all meals; multi-day dive packages available. US$130

6

6

Tobacco Caye Lodge ☎ 532 2033, ⓦ tclodgebelize .com. Self-contained little enclave at the north end of the island, with a good beach bar beside its own dock, six two- or three-bedded sea-view cabins with hot-water showers, deck with hammocks and solar lights. Rates include all meals at the cosy restaurant, serving great seafood, bbq and fresh fruit. U$$110

Tobacco Caye Paradise ☎ 532 2101, ⓦ tobaccocaye paradisecabin.com. Well cared-for family-owned property holding six basic yet attractive thatched, stilted *cabañas* with private bath and verandas with hammocks over the sea, plus its own little dining room, where lunch and breakfast cost US$10 each, dinner US$15. U$$70

SOUTH WATER CAYE

Blue Marlin Lodge ☎ 522 2243, in the US ☎ 800 798 1558, ⓦ bluemarlinlodge.com. Luxurious, Belizean-owned property on raked white sand under coconut trees, with appealing rooms in a traditional "caye house" plus assorted carpeted a/c cabins (US$335) with beautiful bathrooms – some are dome-shaped "igloos", others have a deck over the sea. A thatched dining room serves delicious meals, included in the price, and a fleet of boats offers diving (US$150 for a two-tank dive) and fishing (from US$100/hr). Boat transfer US$67.50 one way. U$$265

IZE Belize ☎ 580 2000, in the US ☎ 1 508 655 1461, ⓦ izebelize.com. Run by the US-based International Zoological Expeditions, this attractive resort caters primarily to students of reef ecology, but it's a wonderful option for anyone. As well as very comfortable private-bath cabins, nestled into the mangrove forest with wrap-around decks and views out to the reef, it also holds three shared-bath dorm rooms, available to independent travellers when not booked by student groups; all are fan-cooled. Closed Aug to early Dec. Dorms U$$50, cabins U$$375

★ Pelican Beach Resort ☎ 522 2024, ⓦ pelicanbeach belize.com. Idyllic oceanfront resort in a stunning location, centred on what was once a colonial convent, with a charmingly relaxed old-world atmosphere and an enticing array of hammocks suspended between the palm trees along its own private beach. Accommodation is in five sea-view rooms in the main building, plus eight large and luxurious "cottages", in stand-alone and duplex units (US$450); rates include all the excellent meals served on the breezy veranda, as well as snorkel gear; there's solar electricity and composting toilets. The attached *Pelican's University*, which holds dormitories and shared bathrooms, is only available to groups of ten or more students or travellers; rates are by negotiation. Boat transfer from the sister property at the north end of Dangriga (see p.183) costs US$68.75/person one way. Three-night minimum stay is usually required. U$$375

GLOVER'S REEF

★ Glover's Atoll Resort Northeast Caye ☎ 532 2916, ⓦ glovers.com.bz. Indulge your Robinson Crusoe "desert island" fantasy right here, by staying in one of twelve simple stilted wood-and-thatch cabins, over the water or on the beach, overlooking the reef; a dorm bed in the main wooden house; or simply camping out. Nightly rates are available, but unless you come for a full week on the resort's catamaran, which leaves the Sittee River (see p.192) on Sunday at 9am and returns the next Saturday, the boat trip here can be prohibitively expensive. Meals are not included, but there's an excellent restaurant, as well as kerosene stoves in the cabins, and open-air bbq grills. You can bring your own food and drink, or buy essentials such as bread, fish and lobster. The staff pretty much leave you to your own devices, but activities like sea-kayaking, fishing, snorkelling and scuba diving (with bargain PADI certification) are available with expert guides, some born and raised on the atoll. Per person per week (includes transfer): camping U$$109, dorms U$$164, cabins U$$274

Isla Marisol Resort Usher Caye ☎ 610 4204, ⓦ islamarisolresort.com. Twelve attractive wooden *cabañas* on the beach, each with ceiling fan, private hot-water shower and a shady veranda with hammocks. The food is excellent and the bar is built on a deck over the water. Rates include all meals, plus boat transfers from Dangriga (Wed or Sat). Potential activities, charged separately, include diving, with PADI certification available, fly-fishing, kayaking and snorkelling. Three-night package for two people U$$1750

Island Expeditions Southwest Caye ☎ 800 667 1630 (US), ⓦ islandexpeditions.com. A Vancouver-based, experienced sea-kayaking and snorkelling outfitter with superb guides and an exemplary environmental record. Guests are taken by fast skiff from Dangriga to the caye, where they sleep in spacious, comfortable white tents with proper beds, and eat gourmet meals in the screened dining room. Beginners receive kayak training, and veterans can visit the other cayes or take part in overnight camping expeditions to uninhabited islands. Excellent, biologist-led educational trips are also available. Three nights on Southwest Caye, for two people U$$1198

★ Off the Wall Dive Center and Resort Long Caye ☎ 532 2929, ⓦ offthewallbelize.com. A well-managed dive resort where guests stay in charming wooden *cabañas* with separate showers, and rates include all meals plus boat transfer from Dangriga. Two dives cost US$90, and there's a full range of responsible and professional PADI certification courses, while snorkelling and fishing are also available. Saturday pick-up and drop off at the Dangriga airport. Seven nights for two people U$$3000

Slickrock Adventures Long Caye ☎ 800 390 5715 (US), ⓦ slickrock.com. Multi-sport adventures with an emphasis on sea-kayaking but also including kite- and paddle-boarding, kayak surfing, fishing and windsurfing. Accommodation is in sixteen sturdy, comfortable stilted cabins, with a deck and hammock overlooking the reef, and varied, filling meals served in the spacious dining room. The all-inclusive packages include accommodation in Belize City before and after your stay, plus transfer by fast launch from Belize City on Wednesday or Saturday only. Five-night package, with two nights in Belize City, for two US$2790

Mayflower Bocawina National Park

Southern Hwy, 18 miles southwest of Dangriga • Daily 8am–4pm • Bz$10 • ⓦ duartedellarole.wixsite.com

One of Belize's loveliest rainforest parks lies four miles along an unpaved road that branches west from the Southern Highway six miles south of the Dangriga turn-off. Set beyond the citrus groves in the foothills of the Maya Mountains, the 7000-acre **Mayflower Bocawina National Park** focuses on small and minimally excavated ancient **Maya ruins**, but also offers fabulous **birdwatching** and wonderful **hikes**, as well as **zip-lining** and excellent **accommodation**.

The most accessible of the park's three main Maya sites is the Late Classic **Mayflower** itself, dating to around 900 AD and sited immediately across from the entrance station, which consists of a small open plaza surrounded by stone mounds, some of them all but covered by trees. Rudimentary footpaths lead south from here through the forest to the temple of **T'au Witz** ("dwelling-place of the mountain god"), while an acropolis complex known as **Maintzunun** ("hummingbird") looms above the far bank of Silk Grass Creek, a short walk in the opposite direction.

A large and impossibly lush meadow-like clearing a short way further along the access road holds *Bocawina Rainforest Resort* (see below) and the zip-lining headquarters (see below). The easiest hike in the park continues west along the road, which swiftly becomes impassable to ordinary vehicles beyond this point. Keep following the muddy creekside trail when the road finally peters out, and after a total of 1.5 miles you'll come to the broad cascade of **Bocawina Falls**, tumbling down the hillside. The waterfall is actually in two parts, with a pool below the upper falls that offers the chance to cool off.

A much steeper trail starts from the entrance station and leads across Silk Grass Creek, beyond the Maintzunun site, to the 100ft **Antelope Falls**, where you're rewarded with spectacular long-range views. Allow at least two hours for the round-trip hike of almost four miles.

ACTIVITIES · MAYFLOWER BOCAWINA NATIONAL PARK

Zip-lining Bocawina Adventures and Eco-tours (ⓣ670 8019, ⓦ bocawinaadventures.com) operate what's said to be the longest zip-line in Central America (daily 7am–7pm), with twelve separate platforms and one section that stretches almost half a mile through the jungle. The company also offers waterfall rappelling.

ACCOMMODATION

★**Bocawina Rainforest Resort** ⓣ670 8019, in the US ⓣ1 844 894 2311, ⓦbocawina.com. Absolutely delightful lodge, in the clearing in the middle of Mayflower Bocawina National Park. Accommodation is in rooms in a wheelchair-accessible lodge or in thatched, family-sized *cabañas* (US$179), some of which hold two separate units; all are large, with fresh modern furnishings, private bath, fan, electricity, wi-fi and balconies. The central building holds a restaurant that serves delicious food, using organic vegetables; guests pay US$45 extra for full board, and it's open to non-guests for breakfast and lunch. There's also a short self-guided nature trail, and excellent early-morning guided birding. US$119

Hopkins

Stretching for two miles along a shallow, gently curving bay, four miles east of the Southern Highway, the Garifuna village of **HOPKINS** has, thanks to its sumptuous **beach**, turned almost entirely to tourism. Its single unnamed main street, running north–south roughly a hundred yards inland from the sea, is lined with little guesthouses and cafés, largely catering to independent travellers. These form a continuous strip all the way south to what used to be a separate community known as **False Suttee Point**, but is now effectively an upscale annexe of Hopkins and is home to a succession of luxury resorts and condo developments.

Named for a Catholic bishop who drowned nearby in 1923, Hopkins was first settled in 1942 after a hurricane levelled its predecessor, Newtown, just to the north. The

6

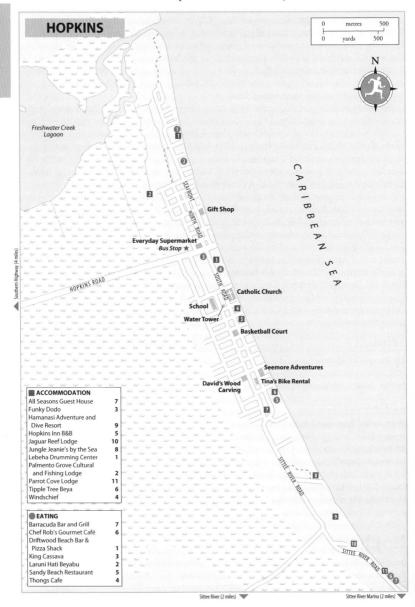

HOPKINS

Freshwater Creek Lagoon

CARIBBEAN SEA

Southern Highway (4 miles)

HOPKINS ROAD

SEAFRONT

NORTH ROAD

SOUTH ROAD

Gift Shop

Everyday Supermarket
Bus Stop ★

Catholic Church

School

Water Tower

Basketball Court

Seemore Adventures

Tina's Bike Rental

David's Wood Carving

SITTEE RIVER ROAD

SITTEE RIVER ROAD

Sittee River (2 miles)

Sittee River Marina (2 miles)

ACCOMMODATION	
All Seasons Guest House	7
Funky Dodo	3
Hamanasi Adventure and Dive Resort	9
Hopkins Inn B&B	5
Jaguar Reef Lodge	10
Jungle Jeanie's by the Sea	8
Lebeha Drumming Center	1
Palmento Grove Cultural and Fishing Lodge	2
Parrot Cove Lodge	11
Tipple Tree Beya	6
Windschief	4

EATING	
Barracuda Bar and Grill	7
Chef Rob's Gourmet Café	6
Driftwood Beach Bar & Pizza Shack	1
King Cassava	3
Laruni Hati Beyabu	2
Sandy Beach Restaurant	5
Thongs Cafe	4

Garifuna here, whose homes these days tend to be secure concrete structures rather than traditional wood-and-thatch houses, lived from small-scale farming, fishing with baited handlines, or paddling dugout canoes to pull up fish traps. They remain proud of their culture– most speak Garifuna as a first language – and **Garifuna Settlement Day** on November 19 (see box, p.182) is celebrated enthusiastically with singing, dancing and the beating of drums.

Great beaches and delicious food and accommodation in all price ranges make Hopkins a pleasant place to spend a few days relaxing, but it's also well equipped for numerous **outdoor activities**, from diving and snorkelling to kayaking and windsurfing. Just north of the village, a narrow creek gives way to a large, peaceful lagoon – great for kayaking – but construction of timeshares and condominiums threatens its accessibility. Still, the view inland from here, with the village and the high ridges of the Maya Mountains behind, is breathtaking.

As there are no street names in Hopkins, the best way to locate anything is in relation to the point where the road from the Southern Highway enters the village centre. The Belize Bank at the junction has a 24hr ATM, in a little air-conditioned booth.

6

ARRIVAL AND GETTING AROUND   HOPKINS

By bus Buses from Dangriga (Mon–Sat 7am & 2pm; 30min) loop around Hopkins before heading south to the Sittee River; let the bus driver know where you want to get off. Any bus on the Southern Hwy can drop you at the turn-off 4 miles west of the village. From here it's quite easy and common to hitch a ride into town; a taxi may also be waiting by the bus stop to run tourists into town for Bz$10.

Bike/motorbike rental Several hotels supply free bikes for guests. Otherwise, you can rent bicycles for around Bz$20/day from Fred's Bikes (☏ 660 5354) or Tina's Bicycles (☏ 662 8204), both at the southern end of the village. Motorbike Rentals (☏ 665 6292, ⓦ alternateadventures .com), opposite *Thongs Cafe*, rents motorbikes from US$60/day.

ACTIVITIES

Kayaking and windsurfing At the southern end of the village, you can rent kayaks for Bz$15/hr at *Tipple Tree Beya* (☏ 615 7006, ⓦ tippletreebelize.com), and windsurfers for Bz$60/day at *Windshief* (☏ 523 7249, ⓦ windsurfing-belize .com), which also offers windsurfing lessons for Bz$60/hr.
Snorkelling, diving and boat tours Most hotels can arrange snorkelling trips to the reef. *Hamanasi Resort* (see p.190) is the main dive operator, while *Parrot Cove Lodge*

also runs diving trips to South Water and other cayes (from US$150 for two dives, including equipment rental). The highly regarded Seemore Adventures (☏ 667 5779 or ☏ 602 4985, ⓦ seemoreadventures.com) offers diving (two-tank reef dives from US$145 including gear, park fees and snacks), certification courses, snorkelling (from US$70 per half-day) fishing charters (from US$280 for a half day) and snorkel gear rental (US$7/day).

ACCOMMODATION

Hopkins holds abundant accommodation to suit all budgets; many places only have a handful of rooms, however, so it's worth reserving your preferred option well in advance. Note that while Hopkins now forms an unbroken strip along the beach with the previously separate area known as **Sittee Point**, further south, the village's bars, shops and restaurants are very much concentrated towards the north.

HOPKINS VILLAGE
All Seasons Guest House South end of the village ☏ 666 4900, ⓦ belizeallseasons.com. Four beautifully decorated rooms with a/c, private bath, coffeemaker and fridge, in a lovely, tranquil garden with patio, plus three green two-bedroom *cabañas* alongside. Dune buggy rental available; German and Dutch spoken; long-term rentals are possible. Doubles US$60, *cabañas* US$100
Funky Dodo Just south of the central intersection ☏ 667 0558, ⓦ thefunkydodo.com. Friendly Brit-owned place with a reputation as a party hostel, very close to the beach and main bus stop, with very basic shared-bath

dorms plus private rooms, with a mix of shared (US$25) and private (US$40) bathrooms. Amenities include a bar, communal kitchen, laundry services, free wi-fi and cosy chill-out spots, and they also run inexpensive tours to destinations like the Cockscomb Jaguar Reserve. Dorms US$11, doubles US$25
★ **Hopkins Inn B&B** On the beach, near the village centre ☏ 665 0411, ⓦ hopkinsinn.com. Friendly place with four immaculate, whitewashed *cabañas* with veranda, private bath, fridge and coffeemaker. Local guides are available. Large continental breakfast included. German spoken. US$85

6

Jungle Jeanie's by the Sea South end of the village ☎ 533 7047, ⓦ junglebythesea.com. Eight hardwood *cabañas* sleeping up to four, some on stilts, one wonderful treehouse (US$120); all have private bath, some a fridge. Located at the edge of a patch of jungle by the beach in a shady, relaxed setting. The friendly owners serve international food (stir-fries, crêpes) and rent kayaks. Camping available. US$60

Lebeha Drumming Center North end of the village ☎ 665 9305, ⓦ lebeha.com. Set up to help perpetuate Garifuna drumming traditions, offering very basic shared-bath dorms for students and travellers, this has expanded to provide a broader range of accommodation, including private huts by the road (US$15) and some lovely wooden beach *cabañas* with private bath (US$49). Drumming lessons by request, and wi-fi available. Dorms US$8

Palmento Grove Cultural and Fishing Lodge Village centre ☎ 636 3247, ⓦ palmentogrovebelize.com. Strewn among the garden setting are a range of accommodation options including a private lovers' cabin with a sofa (US$50) or a lake-view family room with a double bed and bunk beds (US$60); all rooms have fans and a private bath with hot water. The property has a full-service restaurant and bar, along with room service, plus a TV and karaoke lounge, with wi-fi in common areas. The helpful tour desk can arrange various water activities available on site. US$40

Tipple Tree Beya On the beach, south end of the village ☎ 615 7006, ⓦ tippletreebelize.com. Comfortable rooms in a wooden building have private bath, hammocks, fridge and coffeemaker; one private cabin has a kitchen (US$55). The beautifully kept beachside location makes it well worth the price. US$45

Windschief On the beach, south of the centre ☎ 523 7249, ⓦ windsurfing-belize.com. Two cabins, one with a double bed and the other with two double beds, and both offering private bath, fridge, coffeemaker and access to the well-stocked beach bar, steps away from the sea. Windsurfing available. Smaller cabin US$35, larger cabin US$47.50

SITTEE POINT

Hamanasi Adventure and Dive Resort Immediately north of the road junction, Sittee Point ☎ 533 7073, in the US ☎ 1 844 235 4930, ⓦ hamanasi.com. One of the country's top dive resorts, with a range of luxuriously appointed suites and rooms on 1000ft of ocean, plus thirteen opulent "treehouse" *cabañas* (US$590) propped on stilts and set back from the sea amid the mangrove forest; all have a/c, fans, king- or queen-size beds, Belizean hardwood furniture, attractive bathrooms and private porches. Wi-fi is available in the lobby area only. For divers, *Hamanasi* offers fast modern dive boats and superb equipment, with tours around the reef and atolls, and there's also a programme of inland adventures. US$398

Jaguar Reef Lodge Just south of road junction, Sittee Point ☎ 822 3851, in the US ☎ 1 786 472 9664, ⓦ jaguarreef.com. Luxury resort with large thatched *cabañas* as well as two-bedroom suites (US$399) in the modern resort building, all a/c and set within beautifully landscaped beachfront grounds that also hold kids' and adult pools. The restaurant, under a huge, thatched roof overlooking the beach and pool, is highly rated. There is also a spa and coffee shop, and free kayaks and bikes are available. US$299

Parrot Cove Lodge South of the road junction, Sittee Point ☎ 523 7225, ⓦ parrotcovelodge.com. Smaller-scale adventure resort, offering bright tropical-themed a/c rooms, plus two larger and more luxurious apartments (US$400), each sleeping up to six, in an imposing two-level beach house, as well as a bar and Chef Rob's excellent restaurant (see p.192). US$169

EATING

Though your choice may be limited outside the tourist season, Hopkins has a good selection of **restaurants**. You'll always find delicious **Garifuna** and Creole meals, and usually very good seafood. Typical Garifuna dishes feature fish and vegetables like yam, plantain, okra and cassava, often served in *sere*, a rich, thick, coconut-milk sauce similar in consistency to a chowder, accompanied by rice or the Garifuna staple of thin, crispy cassava bread, baked on a metal sheet over an open fire. Service can be slow at inexpensive places, so be prepared to wait – at least you'll know it's fresh.

HOPKINS VILLAGE

★Driftwood Beach Bar & Pizza Shack At the northern end of the village on the beach ☎ 667 4872, ⓦ driftwoodpizza.com. Set on a gorgeous strip of sand, this laidback beach bar serves delicious pizzas (Bz$26–49) and daily dinner specials, and also hosts regular bbqs, full moon parties, drumming nights, volleyball games and jam sessions. 11am–10pm; closed Wed.

King Cassava At the central junction ☎ 503 7305. This lively, largely open-air bar/restaurant is likely to be the first building you see in Hopkins, and serves as the social hub of the village. The kitchen serves Mexican food (BZ$10–16) and fry-jacks for breakfast, while the bar usually stays open until midnight, and often puts on live music or drumming at weekends; this was the last place award-winning musician Andy Palacio (see p.255) played

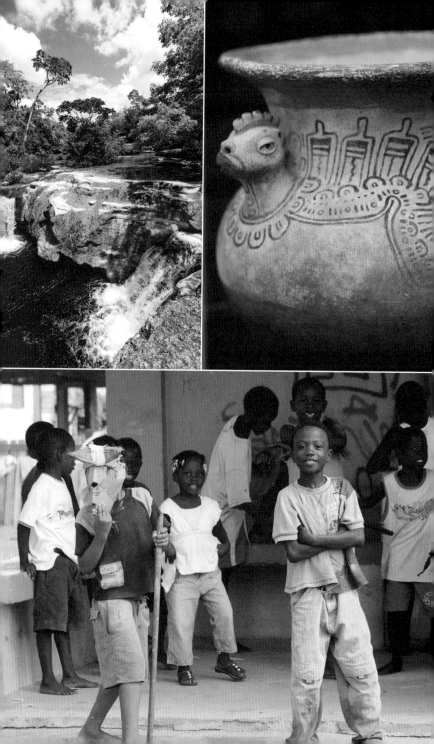

in before he died in 2008. 9am–9pm; closed Tues.

★**Laruni Hati Beyabu** On the beach, north of the centre ☎ 663 0720. Belizean-owned bar/restaurant with a beachfront view, serving a broad range of delicious local foods, from stew chicken or beans and rice to whole grilled fish, with most dishes priced at around Bz$10. A favourite among locals. Daily 10am–9pm.

Sandy Beach Restaurant On the beach, south end of village ☎ 650 9183, ⓦ sandybeachhopkins.com. Run by the Sandy Beach Women's Cooperative, this low-slung green hut serves all kinds of Garifuna specialities, best enjoyed on the beach veranda. The menu changes daily, but look out for dishes like *hudut*, fish cooked in coconut milk and served atop mashed plantains (Bz$15), and the sticky coconut crust dessert, cooked outdoors on an open fire. Mon–Sat 11am–9pm, Sun 10am–3pm.

Thongs Cafe Two blocks south of central junction ☎ 662 0110. International breakfasts, baked goodies and salads and sandwiches for less than Bz$15, in a cosy coffee-shop setting. Dinners are served at the weekend, and

there's a small gift shop and free wi-fi. Wed, Thurs & Sun 8am–2pm, Fri & Sat 8am–2pm & 6–9pm.

SITTEE POINT

★**Barracuda Bar and Grill** At the Beaches and Dreams Hotel ☎ 523 7259, ⓦ beachesanddreams.com. Superb, creative Mediterranean and Caribbean food at this beachside restaurant/lounge bar run by Alaskan chef Tony. Main courses such as pesto-baked snapper, chicken marsala or shrimp and chicken pasta cost around Bz$40, while a mixed seafood sampler that includes lobster is Bz$60. The chocolate pecan pie is to die for. 4–10pm; closed Tues.

★**Chef Rob's Gourmet Café** Parrot Cove Lodge, south of the road junction ☎ 670 1529, ⓦ parrotcovelodge.com. Dine beachside, tuck into a rib-eye steak with spiced rum sauce or red snapper fillet with lobster sauce, and enjoy a peaceful Hopkins evening. Freshly sourced, with an emphasis on local produce, Rob's creative four-course set menu changes daily, and costs Bz$59, or Bz$79 if you opt for a luxury dish like his Caribbean bouillabaise. Tues–Sun 12.15–9pm.

Sittee River

The pleasant village of **SITTEE RIVER** sits prettily on the north bank of its namesake stream, a mile or so inland from the southern end of Hopkins, or five miles east of the Southern Highway along its own unpaved access road. The river is a **wildlife** hotspot, with excellent birding and a number of creeks and pristine lagoons revealing freshwater crocodiles and turtles basking along the riverbanks. Should you spend much time in the village, be warned that the **sandflies** can be atrocious; guesthouses provide screens and mosquito nets for good reason.

Serpon Sugar Mill

1 mile off Southern Hwy, towards Sittee River • Daily 8am–5pm • Bz$10

Preserved as a roadside park with a small museum, the long-abandoned **Serpon Sugar Mill** dates back to 1863, not long after sugar production had been introduced to Belize by Maya refugees from Yucatán, and when demand was boosted thanks to the Civil War in the US. It lasted until 1910, by which time it was clear northern Belize offered much better conditions for growing sugar.

Now the site has largely returned to the forest, and what remains of the mill is rusting and rotting amid the trees. Larger chunks of machinery stand crumbling on their original brick foundations, while smaller bits and pieces have been strewn artistically along the trails or arrayed on logs. Strolling around is enjoyable, but the primary reason to stop here is not so much the mill itself as **birdwatching**; the woods here are alive with birds of all kinds.

ARRIVAL AND ACCOMMODATION   SITTEE RIVER

By bus Three daily buses between Dangriga and Placencia leave the highway to pass through Hopkins and Sittee River.

Glover's Guest House ☎ 520 5016, ⓦ glovers.com.bz. This very basic budget option serves chiefly as the base for travellers taking the Sunday-morning boat out to its sister

property, *Glover's Atoll Resort* on Glover's Reef (see p.186). Walk-ins are also welcome though, and there's a choice between camping, a bunk bed in the dorm, or a room with shared bath. Staying two nights earns you a third free, while there's a restaurant and open-air kitchen right on the riverbank. Camping US$12, dorms US$20, doubles US$30

The Cockscomb Basin

Cupped beneath the sharp ridges of the Maya Mountains, and watered by torrential rains, the **Cockscomb Basin** is a vast natural bowl that holds some of the most accessible yet unspoiled **rainforest** in Belize. Since 1986, it has been home to the **Cockscomb Basin Wildlife Sanctuary**, the world's only dedicated **jaguar reserve**, located seven miles west of the Southern Highway. For much longer than that, however, the basin has been home to the **Maya**; the ruins of **Kuchil Balam**, a Classic-period ceremonial centre, still lie hidden in the forest, while the modern village of **Maya Center** now marks the approach to the sanctuary from the highway. During the twentieth century, the forest was also exploited by mahogany loggers; the names of their abandoned camps, such as Leave If You Can and Go to Hell, illustrate how they felt about life in the forest.

6

Maya Center

When the jaguar reserve was created, the Mopan Maya residents of the village of Quam Bank, where the sanctuary's visitor centre now stands, were forcibly moved seven miles east to the new community of **MAYA CENTER** on the Southern Highway. Traditionally farmers, the inhabitants have since been persuaded of the virtues of ecotourism, and Maya Center has become the place to pick up information, find accommodation or hire a guide before you venture into the sanctuary itself.

All independent visitors should stop to pay the reserve admission fee of Bz$10 at the roadside **craft centre** (daily 7.30am–4.30pm), which is run by the village women's group, and also sells inexpensive wood and slate carvings and embroidery. A grocery store nearby sells basic supplies; nothing is available inside the sanctuary.

Cockscomb Basin Wildlife Sanctuary

6.6 miles west of Maya Center on the Southern Hwy, around 20 miles southwest of Dangriga, or 37 miles northwest of Placencia • Daily 8am–4.30pm • Bz$10 • ☎ 223 4988 (Belize Audubon main office), ⓦ belizeaudubon.org

Informally known throughout Belize as the **Jaguar Reserve**, the **Cockscomb Basin Wildlife Sanctuary** covers an area of around 200 square miles. While that's not in itself enough to support a healthy population of jaguars, it stands at the core of a much larger wilderness corridor stretching all the way to Guatemala. Current estimates of the actual number of jaguars in the reserve vary between around sixty and eighty, but very few visitors ever see one. Conservation group Panthera managed to track 131 different animals over the course of eleven years, and one ranger reported he hadn't seen a single jaguar in the three years he'd worked there. Even so, for wildlife enthusiasts the sanctuary is an absolute must-see destination, with the finest **hiking trails** of any protected area in Belize.

THE FOREST OF THE COCKSCOMB

Technically, the verdant habitat preserved in the Cockscomb Basin Wildlife Sanctuary is a **tropical moist forest**, made up of plant species including orchids, giant tree ferns, air plants (epiphytes) and trees such as banak, cohune, mahogany and ceiba. An annual rainfall of up to 118in feeds a network of wonderfully clear streams.

A sizeable proportion of Belize's plant and animal species live here, with mammals including tapirs, howler monkeys, otters, coatis, deer, anteaters, armadillos and, of course, jaguars, as well as other cat species. Three hundred bird species have also been recorded, including endangered scarlet macaws, great curassows, keel-billed toucans and king vultures, and the refuge also serves as a haven for large raptors like harpy, solitary and white hawk eagles. Reptiles and amphibians abound, including red-eyed tree frogs, boa constrictors and the deadly fer-de-lance snake, known in Belize as "yellow-jaw tommy-goff".

6

The rough but passable jeep road that leaves the highway at Maya Center takes five miles to reach the park boundary, fording streams and crossing the Cabbage Haul Gap, and then another 1.6 miles before it comes to an end at the sanctuary headquarters. Set in a grassy area, surrounded by beautiful foliage, the small compound here holds an informative **visitor centre**, with maps of the park trails, plus accommodation for rangers and visitors.

Short trails lead through the forest to the riverbank or to **Tiger Fern Falls**, a picturesque, two-tiered waterfall with a pool at the upper level. **Ben's Bluff Trail** is a more strenuous 2.5-mile hike to a forested ridge, with a great view of the entire Cockscomb Basin and a chance to cool off in a rocky pool. **Inner tube and kayak** rental is available; follow the marked trail upstream and tube down South Stann Creek for a soothing, tranquil view. If you're prepared, you can climb **Victoria Peak**; two miles along the route, a trail leads to Outlier Overlook – a great challenging day-hike or overnight camp.

THE VICTORIA PEAK TRAIL

Viewed from the sea, the jagged granite peaks of the Cockscomb range take on the appearance of a colossal, recumbent head, whose sloping forehead, eyebrows, nose, mouth and chin have earned the range the nickname of "The Sleeping Maya". **Victoria Peak**, the highest point in the Cockscomb, stands 3675ft tall, which makes it the second-highest mountain in Belize after 3687ft-high Doyle's Delight (see p.215).

The first recorded climb to the summit was in 1888, but it's reasonably certain that the ancient Maya were first to make it to the top. While it's no giant by world standards, the multi-day **Victoria Peak Trail** should not be undertaken lightly; it involves scaling some of the rock faces below the peak using climbing equipment, and being able to carry supplies for three to five days. Maya Guide Adventures (☎600 3116, ⊛mayaguide.bz) offer four-day **guided trips** during the dry season only (Feb–June; US$750/person), with a minimum group size of five.

You'll need to begin each day's walk at first light to minimize the danger of **heat exhaustion** later in the day. Creeks cross the trail regularly and the water is generally safe to drink, though you may prefer to purify it. Simple **shelters** along the way mean it's not necessary to bring a tent, but they do offer protection from biting insects. There's no charge for using the trail – you just pay the Jaguar Reserve entrance fee and backcountry campsite charges.

ALONG THE TRAIL

The Victoria Peak Trail starts by following a level, abandoned logging road from the Jaguar Reserve headquarters, through secondary forest. It's marked in kilometres, and the first rest point comes after 12km, where the **Sittee Branch River** beckons with the chance of a cooling swim. On the far bank, a thatched shelter with kitchen and pit toilets provides the **first campsite**. Beyond, the trail climbs and descends steeply in a series of energy-sapping undulations until you reach km 17, where you walk along a steep ridge before descending to the **second campsite**, at km 19. A **helipad** hacked out of the forest at km 18 offers the first real views of the peak. If you've set off early and are fit you can reach the second campsite in one day, but be warned that the 7km between the two campsites are extremely rigorous. Here, you can hang hammocks in an open-sided wooden shelter; your shower is a small waterfall cascading over smooth rocks.

The final stretch to the peak is four relentless uphill hours, at inclines of about 60 degrees, with much of the trail along a rocky creek bed that's too dangerous to attempt in heavy rain. As the ascent becomes ever more vertical and you rise above the forest canopy, the views increase in splendour. Closer to the ground, wildflowers cling to rock crevices. Just below the peak, you haul yourself up through a narrow gully on a rope; above here the track along the final ridge passes though elfin **cloud forest**, with gnarled tree limbs draped in filmy moss and tiny ferns, before reaching the **summit**. Low, waxy-leaved bushes offer only scraps of shade, and the Belize flag flutters in the breeze. An exercise book recording the names of successful climbers is tethered to the rock that marks the peak. Spread beneath you are a series of deep green, thickly forested ridges and valleys – on a very clear day you can see to the Caribbean – and not a sign of humanity's impact.

The trek down is almost as arduous, taking about an hour less to reach the campsite. With an early start, you can walk all the way out to the sanctuary headquarters the following day.

ARRIVAL AND TOURS | COCKSCOMB BASIN

Almost all visitors to the jaguar reserve arrive on **guided tours**, arranged through their hotels or local operators. It is possible, however to come here independently, either with your own vehicle or, much more laboriously, using a combination of buses, taxis and walking.

By bus All buses between Dangriga and Placencia or Punta Gorda pass through Maya Center. If visiting the reserve, you need to sign in and pay the entrance fee at the craft centre at the junction of the road leading up to the Cockscomb. From the craft centre, you can catch a ride with a taxi or truck to the reserve headquarters; this usually costs about Bz$30–40 each way for up to five people.

Tours Roam Belize offers full-day guided tours into the reserve from Hopkins, Dangriga or Placencia (☎ 522 2328, ⓦ roambelize.com, US$85/person), and *Nu'uk Che'il Cottages*, just up the access road (☎ 670 7043, ⓦ nuukcheilcottages.com), offer guided tours (half-day Bz$80, full-day Bz$150) or a simple taxi service (Bz$30 each way, per car) into the reserve.

ACCOMMODATION

COCKSCOMB BASIN WILDLIFE SANCTUARY
Reserve headquarters ⓦ belizeaudubon.org. If you fancy experiencing Cockscomb at night, the Belize Audubon Society offers a wide range of accommodation in the park itself, including private furnished cabins for four or six people, wooden dorms and camping space close to the visitor centre; private and shared bathrooms in a house that also holds a shared kitchen, at the park entrance 5 miles off the highway; and additional camping at two designated sites along the trails. There is no restaurant at the headquarters, so bring supplies. Camping US$10, dorms US$20, cabins US$55

MAYA CENTER
Nu'uk Che'il Cottages 500yd off the highway in the direction of the reserve ☎ 670 7043,

ⓦ nuukcheilcottages.com. Maya family compound where visitors can camp in the garden or sleep either in spartan rooms with private bath or a large wooden cabin that holds shared showers and dorm beds. The restaurant serves Maya cuisine (Bz$15–20), and the owner Aurora, who is one of the Garcia sisters from San Antonio in Cayo, has developed a medicinal plant trail out back. Camping Bz$10, dorms Bz$30, double or triple rooms Bz$80

★ **Tutzil Nah Cottages** Southern Hwy at the Maya Center speed bump ☎ 533 7045, ⓦ mayacenter.com. Two clean, flower-framed cabins, one wood and one concrete, housing four rooms with a choice of shared bathrooms or private bath (US$22); you can also rent a whole house for US$55. Run by the Chun brothers, who also own a small grocery store at the front and offer excellent guided tours of the reserve. US$18

The Placencia peninsula

A long, crooked finger of land that juts out from mainland Belize to shelter the Placencia Lagoon from the sea, the **Placencia peninsula** has turned during the last few years from a little-known backwater into the main centre for tourism in southern Belize. Where once were only tiny, scattered villages is now an all-but-unbroken fourteen-mile strip of hotels and resorts. If that doesn't sound to your taste, however, you may be pleasantly surprised. So far at least, the peninsula remains appealingly low-key and laidback. That may well change if the developers have their way – and clearly will if the long-promised new international airport ever manages to open – but for the moment there's still a lot to like about the area. Most of all its **beaches**, or rather its beach, for the entire eastern seaboard is lined with a continuous strand of deep, even white sand.

The prime destination for visitors, the village of **Placencia** itself, dangles from the very tip of the peninsula, a total of 24 miles south off the Southern Highway. Still recognizable as the fishing village it used to be, it's a friendly, laidback place that holds abundant lodging and dining options for budget travellers. More affluent visitors, including increasing numbers of honeymooners, tend to stay in the plusher hotels further north, which include some of the country's most opulent resorts, but also a cluster of charming, good-value boutique hotels along the beautiful stretch known as **Maya Beach**, nine miles north of Placencia.

The **Barrier Reef** that lies on average eighteen miles offshore from Placencia is wider than in the north of the country, and breaks into several smaller reefs and cayes that evolve into more coral canyons and drop-offs. Thanks to the distances involved, **snorkelling and diving** trips are more expensive here than elsewhere; the upside is that there are mangrove islands and coral heads closer to the coast, and you can still see a lot of fish and some coral by snorkelling just offshore.

6 Maya Beach

While the ten-mile stretch of road that runs from the Southern Highway to the sea is blissfully rural, development starts as soon as you reach the northern end of the Placencia Peninsula. First you pass the site of the proposed new airport, followed immediately by the enormous, eyesore *Placencia Hotel*, and successive new condo blocks, many of which remain unoccupied and incomplete.

This unpromising start belies the genuine charm of **Maya Beach** immediately beyond, not so much a village as a string of relaxed, low-key accommodation options and restaurants, arrayed along a particularly gorgeous section of sandy Caribbean shore. The peninsula is so narrow at this point that most of the resorts also offer access to Placencia Lagoon on its western side. As well as arranging fishing and diving trips, many also have bikes and kayaks for guests, and it's a relatively easy paddle out to False Caye.

Seine Bight

The Garifuna village of **SEINE BIGHT**, two miles south of Maya Beach, is still very much an authentic community, characterized by often-dilapidated roadside shacks. Supposedly founded by privateers in 1629, Seine Bight may have been given its present name by French fishermen deported from Newfoundland after Britain gained control of Canada. Its present inhabitants are descendants of the Garifuna settlers who arrived here around 1869.

Placencia

Shaded by palm trees and cooled by the sea breeze, **PLACENCIA** holds some of the most beautiful **beaches** in Belize, and these, together with the abundant accommodation for all budgets, make it a great place to relax.

There's no real centre to the village; the main road meanders its way through from north to south, passing all manner of shops, restaurants and little hotels, before finally coming to an end at a smart new pier. A short way east, connected by countless unpaved lanes and footpaths, a slender strip of wooden boardwalk, open only to pedestrians and known as the **Sidewalk**, runs parallel to the beach. Once listed in the *Guinness Book of Records* as the narrowest street in the world, it connects a string of somewhat larger hotels, B&Bs and beach bars.

The villagers enjoy the easy life as much as visitors – as you'll find out during **Lobsterfest**, celebrated over a fun-filled weekend in late June. You could also try to visit during the **Sidewalk Arts Festival**, held around Valentine's Day in early February. At the festival, you can meet some of the artists and musicians of Belize's vibrant arts scene. If Placencia has one drawback, it might be that its distance from the reef puts some tours out of the reach of budget travellers – but more options are becoming available.

ARRIVAL AND DEPARTURE	THE PLACENCIA PENINSULA

By plane Placencia's airport, barely 2 miles north of Placencia village, is served by at least a dozen daily flights in each direction on the Belize City–Punta Gorda run (typical one-way fares US$120 to Belize City, US$60 to Punta Gorda; ⓦtropicair.com and ⓦmayaislandair.com). Taxis are usually waiting to take passengers into Placencia village (BZ$12–16). A new international airport has been under construction on the north end of the peninsula for several years, but at the

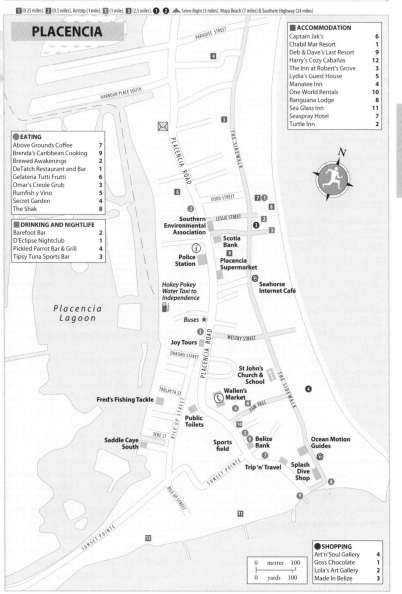

PLACENCIA

■ ACCOMMODATION	
Captain Jak's	6
Chabil Mar Resort	1
Deb & Dave's Last Resort	9
Harry's Cozy Cabañas	12
The Inn at Robert's Grove	3
Lydia's Guest House	5
Manatee Inn	4
One World Rentals	10
Ranguana Lodge	8
Sea Glass Inn	11
Seaspray Hotel	7
Turtle Inn	2

● EATING	
Above Grounds Coffee	7
Brenda's Caribbean Cooking	9
Brewed Awakenings	2
DeTatch Restaurant and Bar	1
Gelateria Tutti Frutti	6
Omar's Creole Grub	3
Rumfish y Vino	5
Secret Garden	4
The Shak	8

■ DRINKING AND NIGHTLIFE	
Barefoot Bar	2
D'Eclipse Nightclub	1
Pickled Parrot Bar & Grill	4
Tipsy Tuna Sports Bar	3

● SHOPPING	
Art'n'Soul Gallery	4
Goss Chocolate	1
Lola's Art Gallery	2
Made In Belize	3

time of writing it's still years away from operating as a full-scale alternative to Philip Goldson International Airport.

By bus Buses from Dangriga (4–6 daily; 1hr 45min) pull in at the petrol station near the beach at the southern end of the village. In addition, all buses between Dangriga and Punta Gorda stop at Independence/Mango Creek, from where you can take the Hokey Pokey ferry for the short ride to Placencia.

By boat The Hokey Pokey ferry (☎ 523 2376) departs for Independence/Mango Creek from the Main Dock on the northwest edge of the village, where buses on the Dangriga–Punta Gorda line are usually timed to meet the ferry. De Express (☎ 626 8835) provides a weekly shuttle between Placencia and Puerto Cortés, Honduras, departing from the Main Dock on Friday morning at 9am, and returning from Honduras on Monday; you can buy tickets in advance from the Barefoot Bar (see p.201).

Destinations Independence (7–8 daily; last boat from Placencia Mon–Sat 6pm, Sun 5pm; last boat from Independence daily 4.30pm; 20min; Bz$10); Puerto Cortés, Honduras (Fri 9am; 4hr 30min; US$60).

GETTING AROUND

By taxi A taxi between Placencia village and Maya Beach will cost at least Bz$30. Local taxi firms include Noel's (☎ 600 6047) and Travelling Gecko (☎ 523 4078).

Car rental Barefoot Services, on the main road in Placencia village (☎ 523 3066, ⓦ barefootservicesbelize .com), rents cars from around US$65/day, golf carts from US$39 for 8hr, and scooters from US$19 for 4hr (Mon–Fri & Sun 9am–5pm).

INFORMATION

Tourist information The Placencia Tourism Center is near the northern end of the main road in Placencia village, (Mon–Fri 9–5pm; ☎ 523 4045, ⓦ placencia.com). It produces the excellent free *Placencia Breeze* newspaper, with full local listings, transport schedules and a good map, and also stocks brochures for accommodation and tour operators.

TOURS AND ACTIVITIES

Diving and snorkelling Splash Dive Shop, in the marina north of the village, and with a central office across from Scotia Bank (☎ 523 3080, ⓦ splashbelize.com), is the best-equipped diving operation in Placencia. Sea Horse Dive Shop, in town near the petrol station (☎ 523 3166, ⓦ belizescuba.com), also offers instruction and excursions at competitive rates. Diving trips start around US$130 for a two-tank dive, and US$450 for open-water certification; snorkelling trips start at about US$85/person including equipment, transport and a snack. Pirate's Point Tours (☎ 623 8399, ⓦ tourbelize.org) and Ocean Motion Guides (☎ 523 3363, ⓦ oceanmotionplacencia.com) both offer snorkelling and manatee-watching trips.

Reef research trips The research organization ReefCI (☎ 626 1429, ⓦ reefci.com) offers divers the chance to participate in two- or four-week scientific programmes on the Barrier Reef, most notably on diving trips to Sapodilla Caye to help tackle the lionfish problem (see box, p.207) and on lobster and queen conch surveys.

Fishing World-class fishing draws anglers eager to catch tarpon, snook and bonefish that abound in the waters off Placencia. A day out with a boat and guide will set you back around US$300; any of the dive or snorkel places can arrange this, as can Trip'n'Travel (☎ 660 7189, ⓦ tripntravel .bz). Rods, flies and tackle are available from Fred's Fishing

Gear (daily 8am–5pm; ☎ 523 3304, ⓦ fredsfishing.tripod .com).

Sea-kayaking Saddle Caye South (☎ 615 9973, ⓦ kayakbelize.com) offers excellent kayak rental (single Bz$60/day, double Bz$100/day), as well as guided and self-guided four- to six-day river- and sea-kayaking trips.

Sailing The cayes off Placencia offer even more beautiful sailing than the northern cayes, and the village is a base for top-tier catamaran charters. For a week's sailing you'll need to book well in advance. Some resorts also have Hobie Cats (small catamarans) for rent.

Nature tours Trip'n'Travel, based at Placencia Office Supply at the southern end of the village (☎ 660 7189, ⓦ tripntravel.bz), and Barebones Tours (☎ 677 9303, ⓦ barebonestours.com), who have a base in Monkey River, organize nature tours, overnight jungle adventures and trips down the Monkey River.

Culinary tours The food and cultural offerings at the tiny operation of Taste Belize (☎ 664 8699, ⓦ tastebelize.com) are fun and well organized. The surprisingly comprehensive list of options, with an emphasis on sustainable tourism, includes days oriented around chocolate, Maya/Creole/Garifuna cooking, a lesson on Belizean bitters, and a jaunt that combines visits to Marie Sharp's factory (see p.181) and a banana farm. Payment is by cash only.

ACCOMMODATION

As the **beach** that lines the eastern side of the Placencia Peninsula is consistently enjoyable all the way along, the major issue in choosing **accommodation** is whether you'd rather be in Placencia itself or in the more upscale resorts and hotels further north. While the options in **Placencia Village** tend to be less fancy, less private and squeezed up closer together, it's simple to stroll around and sample the village's many cafés, bars and restaurants. If, on the other hand, you stay in the luxury resorts a couple of miles north, or in the boutique-style hotels of **Maya Beach** 9 miles out of the village, you'll almost certainly have a nicer room, a quieter stretch of beach and a good restaurant on site, but you may well start to feel isolated.

MAYA BEACH

Barnacle Bill's Beach Bungalows 23 Maya Beach Way ☎ 533 8110, ⓦ barnaclebills-belize.com. Two well-equipped self-catering rentals, propped on stilts on a

beautiful sandy stretch of beach. Each of these wooden bungalows has a double bedroom, bathroom with tub, living room with sofa bed and kitchenette with microwave, grill, coffeemaker and fridge; call ahead and they'll stop to pick your groceries with you after picking you up from the airstrip. Kayaks and bikes included for guests. US$115

Green Parrot Beach Houses 1 Maya Beach Way ☎ 533 8188, ⊛ greenparrot-belize.com. Choose from six open-plan wooden houses (each sleeping up to five) raised on stilts, and two thatched "honeymoon" cabins on the beach. Each house has a living room, a loft with queen and single bed, kitchen and deck with hammock. Great restaurant. Rates include transport from Placencia airstrip, breakfast and kayaks. US$170

★ **Maya Beach Hotel** Maya Beach Way ☎ 533 8040, ⊛ mayabeachhotel.com. Eco-sensitive and quiet resort where assorted rooms and apartments (US$180), private units and others are arrayed around an infinity pool yards from the sea. There are stylish soft colours, wooden furniture and atmospheric artwork throughout. All rooms have a/c, private bath and queen beds, and there's a superb restaurant (see p.200). US$110

Singing Sands Inn 714 Maya Beach Way ☎ 533 3022, ⊛ singingsands.com. Very stylish mahogany and thatch *cabañas* with queen-sized bed, porch, hammock and in-room bathroom with mosaic washbasin. There's also a good-value family-sized bungalow (US$275) overlooking a wonderful deck-surrounded pool, complete with fountain. It's extremely romantic at night, when the whole property is lit up, and the *Bonefish Grille* restaurant is recommended (see p.200). Snorkel from the bar out on the jetty. Kayaks and fishing charters available. US$110

SEINE BIGHT

★ **The Inn at Robert's Grove** Half a mile south of Seine Bight ☎ 523 3565, ⊛ robertsgrove.com. Well-managed luxury resort 5 miles north of Placencia Village, with 72 spacious, elegant a/c rooms and suites (US$300), all with sea balconies; the largest villa suites have three bedrooms. Also comes with three pools, several rooftop jacuzzis and an oceanfront spa. The *Seaside Restaurant*, with tables on a wooden deck on the beach, serves superb international and local dishes; *Habañeros Mexican Café* is great for snacks and drinks by the lagoon; and the Belizean café *Sweet Mama's* stands by the highway. On site there's also a spa and dive centre, plus snorkelling, fishing, sailing, kayaking, windsurfing and organic garden. Three tiny cayes for guests to visit lie offshore. US$240

PLACENCIA VILLAGE

Captain Jak's Main Rd ☎ 622 7104, ⊛ captainjaks.com. Lagoon-side compound holding *cabañas* with kitchenettes, two-storey cottages (US$125) with living rooms downstairs and two bedrooms upstairs, and an entire private villa that sleeps eight (US$315). The property's own waterfront dock has loungers, thatched shelters and hammocks, and there are also lush tropical gardens. Bikes, kayaks, scooters and golf carts available to rent. US$95

Chabil Mar Resort 2284 Placencia Peninsula Rd ☎ 523 3606, ⊛ chabilmarvillas.com. Luxury, lushly landscaped property with huge one- or two-bedroom villas with verandas and a/c. *Chabil Mar* is kitted out with two infinity pools, 400ft of beachfront, private pier and free use of bikes, paddleboards and kayaks, plus a raft of other activities, as well as a concierge to attend to your every wish. You can sign up for the three meal per day full plan (US$73) or individual meals. US$410

Deb & Dave's Last Resort Main Rd ☎ 523 3207, ✉ debanddave@btl.net. Four clean, wooden budget rooms in the heart of the village, with shared hot-water bath, in a secluded annexe to the family home, all set within beautiful gardens. Kayaks for rent. US$27.50

Harry's Cozy Cabañas Bile Up St ☎ 523 3155, ⊛ cozycabanas.com. Spacious, varnished wooden cabins on stilts on the beach, at the southern tip of the peninsula 300yd west of the dock. Newly renovated and restored, each has a screened porch, double and single bed, fridge and coffeemaker; one has a small kitchen (US$80). The plant-filled gardens are home to iguanas. According to Harry, kicking back with a Belikin beer under his "Tree of Knowledge" imparts wisdom. Two-night minimum stay. US$65

Lydia's Guest House Near the north end of the Sidewalk ☎ 523 3117, ⊛ lydiasguesthouse.com. Twelve clean, secure budget rooms, sharing five bathrooms and a kitchen, in a quiet location near the beach, plus four private beach cottages (US$50), each with kitchenette and porch. US$30

★ **Manatee Inn** At the north end of the Sidewalk ☎ 523 4083, ⊛ manateeinn.com. Modern timber-frame budget inn, facing the beach, where the two storeys hold six simple but comfortable en-suite rooms, with hardwood floors and ceiling fans. A full programme of local tours is available, inland and out to sea. US$40

One World Rentals Main Rd ☎ 523 3103, ⊛ oneworldplacencia.com. Clean, bright, a/c self-catering rentals, tucked away amid gardens in the middle of the village. Six studios, with kitchenettes, and three larger apartments with kitchens, living rooms and a screened porch equipped with hammocks (US$100). There's also an on-site laundry and gift shop. US$75

★ **Ranguana Lodge** Sidewalk ☎ 523 3112, ⊛ ranguanabelize.com. Five white *cabañas*, set in a beautiful tropical garden, each with hammocks on the porch and optional a/c, all close to or on the beach (beachfront *cabañas* US$150) near the village centre. Comfortably furnished with hardwood floors and fittings, fridge and coffeemaker; bathrooms have tubs. Beach *palapas* for relaxing. US$89

Sea Glass Inn Garden Grove ☎ 523 3098, ⊛ seaglassinnbelize.com. A very comfortable two-storey hotel with clean, well-furnished rooms, all with private bathroom, a/c, fridge and coffeemaker. The wide, breezy verandas with hammocks are great for relaxing and you

6

6

can borrow a cooler to take to the beach. Laundry service and local tours, plus kayaks and bikes for rent. US$79

Seaspray Hotel Sidewalk ☎ 523 3148, ⓦ seasprayhotel.com. Placencia's first hotel, built in 1964 and still run by the same family, the Leslies. Popular and well run, in a great location, it holds assorted excellent accommodation options that range from economy rooms set well back from the beach to a seafront *cabaña* complete with veranda and swinging hammock (US$85). All have private bath and fridge, some also TV, kitchenette and balcony. Don't miss *DeTatch* restaurant on the beach (see below). Economy doubles US$27, standard doubles US$55

Turtle Inn 1 mile north of Placencia Village

☎ 523 3244, in the US ☎ 1 800 746 374, ⓦ turtleinn.com. Francis Ford Coppola's Caribbean resort is every bit as sumptuous as his *Blancaneaux Lodge* in Cayo (see p.132) and *La Lancha* in Guatemala (see p.159). The thatched seafront "cottages" (US$539) have lots of varnished wood and Indonesian art, plus fabulous bathrooms and a screened deck. Garden cottages are just as comfortable and less expensive, while beachfront villas (US$919) hold up to three bedrooms. The atmosphere is more relaxed than at *Blancaneaux*, and there's a soothing spa as well as a pool and dive shop, plus three restaurants, two bars, wine cellar and gelato bar for the kids; complimentary kayaks and bikes. US$499

EATING

MAYA BEACH

Bonefish Grille Singing Sands Inn ☎ 533 3022, ⓦ singingsands.com. Intimate beachside restaurant, owned by two Korean sisters, with exceptionally romantic lighting and superb, creative Southeast Asian food. Try the Korean beef, Thai fish or rice noodles with shrimp; a table-top mixed Korean grill for two costs Bz$85. The breakfast menu is also good. Daily 7.30am–9.30pm.

★**Maya Beach Bistro** Maya Beach Hotel ☎ 533 8040, ⓦ mayabeachhotel.com. Charming and delightful beachfront restaurant, romantically open to the ocean breezes and specializing in delicious, creative Caribbean seafood such as grilled or nut-crusted fish fillets, shrimp and lobster, typically priced around Bz$39–42. Smaller tapas-style starters cost Bz$19–25, while meatier options include pork rib and roast chicken. Entirely unpretentious, and also great for breakfast or evening cocktails. Daily 7am–7pm.

PLACENCIA VILLAGE

Above Grounds Coffee South end of Main Rd ☎ 634 3212, ⓦ abovegroundscoffee.com. Nestle into a window seat in this cosy treehouse café, near the south end of the village, and watch the world go by down below. Freshly baked cakes and cookies, free wi-fi, book exchange and, above all, great Guatemalan coffees (from regular brews at Bz$3 to a large mocha at Bz$9). Mon–Sat 7am–4pm, Sun 7am–noon.

Brenda's Caribbean Cooking Beside the pier. Simple barbecue shack right by the sea, with shaded-open-air seating alongside the grill. Brenda herself, a big local character, will prepare a full meal of jerk chicken or seafood gumbo for Bz$15–18, including dessert, and also offers irresistible coconut cookies. Hours vary, but generally daily 9am–2pm.

Brewed Awakenings Main Rd ☎ 635 5312. Friendly, colourful roadside stall, attached to a little farmers' market at the northern end of the village, serving excellent fresh espresso coffees and smoothies for Bz$5–6. Mon–Sat 6am–6pm.

DeTatch Restaurant and Bar Seaspray Hotel Sidewalk ☎ 503 3385, ⓦ seasprayhotel.com. The best Belizean-owned restaurant in town is right on the beach, just north of the centre, with a lovely, thatched open-air dining room and a scenic view of the ocean. *DeTatch* serves Caribbean cuisine at very affordable rates – the Bz$12 lunch specials, such as fish balls with rice and beans, are a real bargain – and delicious seafood mains (Bz$25–30) at all hours, while the fry-jacks are especially good at breakfast. Daily 7am–10pm.

★**Gelateria Tutti Frutti** Main Rd ☎ 523 4055. Genuine Italian ice cream, made by genuine Italians, and quite simply the best in Belize. It's available in dozens of flavours and you should try at least one every day you're in town (make one the extra minty chocolate chip, or the lavender). One scoop costs Bz$3.75, shakes start at Bz$6. 9am–9pm; closed Wed.

Omar's Creole Grub Main Rd ☎ 624 7168. Long-standing local favourite, recently moved to larger premises, with seating on a large open-air deck. Omar being a fisherman, the speciality here is ultra-fresh seafood, grilled or served with Caribbean or coconut curry; shrimp dishes cost Bz$25, whole lobsters are Bz$45. Lunchtime burritos and burgers cost more like Bz$8–12. 8am–9pm; closed Sat.

Rumfish y Vino Main Rd ☎ 523 3293, ⓦ rumfishyvino.com. Swish rooftop "gastro-bar", opposite the sports field, where the inventive tapas menu (Bz$16–22) is complemented by burgers and flatbreads for more like Bz$30, full-sized mains such as fish stew or short-rib lasagne for Bz$35 and an extensive drinks list. The candlelit surroundings and atmospheric veranda are as enjoyable as the food. Daily 2–10pm.

Secret Garden Main Rd ☎ 523 3617, ⓦ secretgardenplacencia.com. Attached to a spa and tucked, as the name implies, into a hidden enclave across from the sports field, this courtyard café/restaurant offers a peaceful respite from the bustle of Placencia, serving great breakfasts and anything from Thai curry (Bz$28) to jambalaya (Bz$35) or grilled grouper (Bz$40). Mon–Sat 5–9pm.

The Shak Sidewalk ☎ 523 3252. Small restaurant, facing the pier at the south end of the Sidewalk, serving fabulous fresh-fruit juices (Bz$5) and smoothies (Bz$7), good all-day breakfasts for Bz$12 and salads, sandwiches and curries for Bz$15–20. 7am–6pm; closed Tues.

DRINKING AND NIGHTLIFE

Although most of Placencia's restaurants also serve drinks, and many encourage diners to linger into the night, there are a few places with **live music** and more of a bar atmosphere. Almost everywhere you can drink offers an early-evening happy hour.

6

MAYA BEACH
Jaguar Lanes & Jungle Bar Main Rd ☎ 629 3145. An unlikely sight in sleepy Maya Beach, this four-lane bowling alley makes a fun early-evening rendezvous, serving snacks like hot dogs and pizzas (Bz$15–35) in the adjoining open-air bar. Daily 2pm to around 10pm.

PLACENCIA VILLAGE
Barefoot Bar Sidewalk ☎ 523 3515. Old favourite in a brightly decorated and prominent location. Very popular bar, right on the beach, with primary-coloured tables and loungers and live music five nights a week, plus great cocktails (happy hour 5–6pm), and surprisingly good bar food (plus, once in a great while, fire dancers). Daily 11am–midnight.
D'Eclipse Nightclub Near the airstrip, north of Placencia Village ☎ 523 3288. With its predominantly Caribbean sounds, the peninsula's only true clubbing experience, a couple of miles north of the village, attracts a good mix of locals and visitors. Busy at weekends from midnight. Thurs–Sun 9pm–2am.
Pickled Parrot Bar & Grill Pickled Parrot Cabañas ☎ 636 7068. Friendly bar/restaurant, set back from the main road under a big thatched roof, with wonderful blended tropical drinks, pool tables and a pretty decent food menu. Mon & Wed–Sun 11am–midnight.
Tipsy Tuna Sports Bar Sidewalk ☎ 523 3089. This lively beachfront bar and restaurant is often packed and regularly hosts live reggae, soca and punta music. Happy hour (daily 5–7pm) includes free banana chips. Free wi-fi available. Mon, Tues, Wed & Sun 11.30am–midnight, Thurs–Sat 11.30am–2am.

SHOPPING

SEINE BIGHT
Goss Chocolate Blue Crab Resort, just north of Seine Bight ☎ 523 3544, ⊛ gosschocolate.homestead.com. This tiny little chocolate factory is Seine Bight's chief claim to fame. Visitors can buy truffles, bars and boxes of superb organic dark, white and milk chocolate. Mon–Fri 9am–5pm, Sat 10am–5pm.
Lola's Art Gallery Seine Bight ☎ 601 1913, ⊛ jcasadart.com. Lola Delgado's studio/showroom, just behind the soccer field in Seine Bight, offers visitors the chance to buy her superb (and affordable) oil and acrylic paintings of village life. Specializing in beach scenes, flora and fauna, and (faceless) portraits of the Garifuna, she also does overnight commissions. Daily 7am–6pm.

PLACENCIA VILLAGE
Art'n'Soul Gallery Sidewalk, Placencia Village ☎ 503 3088. This little beachfront gallery sells a fine assortment of paintings and crafts by more than three dozen local artists, with a special emphasis on Garifuna themes and culture. Daily 9am–6pm.
Made In Belize Sidewalk, Placencia Village. Run by local woodcarver Leo, this ramshackle gift shop, near the *Tipsy Tuna* on the Sidewalk, holds an intriguing array of Belizean woodcarvings of birds and sea creatures. Daily 9am–5pm.

Monkey River

A fabulous day-trip by boat from Placencia would take you twelve miles southwest along the coast to **Monkey River**, teeming with fish, birdlife and **howler monkeys**. Tours set off by 8am from the Main Dock, and consist of a thirty-minute dash through the waves and amid the mangrove swamps as far as the rivermouth, followed by a leisurely glide up the river and a walk along forest trails.

Be sure to bring binoculars, as they're essential to make the most of amazing **birding** as well as the chance to see turtles, iguanas, crocodiles and howler monkeys. You'll be glad, too, of insect repellent once you leave your boat and hike into the forest; there aren't many precautions you can take, however, against the monkeys' unfortunate habit of attempting to splatter intruders with fresh excrement.

Either before or after your tour, you'll probably stop off in **Monkey River Town**, the tiny village at the mouth of the river on its south bank. This was one of the last communities in Belize to be hooked up to the national electricity grid in 2009, and it still has the romantic yet slightly unsettling feel of a frontier outpost. As well as a handful of restaurants, it also holds a couple of simple accommodation options.

ARRIVAL AND TOURS   MONKEY RIVER

By car Most visitors to Monkey River arrive on boat tours from Placencia, but it's also possible to drive to the river, by following a 14-mile dirt road that branches off the Southern Hwy south of Independence. The road ends on the opposite bank of the river to the village, but just call out and someone will give you a ride over in a boat.

Tours The best tours from Placencia are run by Monkey

River Magic (US$75/person, minimum four people; contact Trip 'n' Travel ☎ 523 3205, ⓦ tripntravel.bz), and led by experienced local guide Evaristo Muschamp. If you arrive here under your own steam and want to take a tour, or simply rent a canoe for US$10, contact Clive at the *Sunset Inn* (☎ 709 2028, ⓦ monkeyriverbelize.com).

ACCOMMODATION

Enna's Guest House Monkey River Town ☎ 520 2033. Basic rooms with shared bath, and a panoramic river view. Enna's brothers are tour guides. US$25

Sunset Inn Monkey River Town ☎ 709 2028, ⓦ meweb .net/monkeyriver. Two-storey wooden building, set on a tiny bay at the back of the village. Offers eight simple

rooms, five of which are a/c, with comfortable beds, hot and cold running water and private showers, plus tasty Creole food in the dining room (full board US$15/person), and a wide veranda overlooking the river. Owner Clive Garbutt is an excellent guide, and also has canoes for rent. No credit cards. US$30

EATING AND DRINKING

Alice's Restaurant Monkey River Town. The choice at this simple lunch spot, according to friendly owner Alice, boils down to rice and beans, or beans with rice; either will set you back Bz$15, with a soda thrown in. Daily noon–3pm.

Ivan's Cool Spot Monkey River Town. The nicest bar in the village, right where the river meets the sea, with tables under the trees and an open-air thatched shelter. Daily 10am–8pm.

The cayes off Placencia

Any number of idyllic **islands** are scattered along and around the **Barrier Reef**, which stretches parallel to the coast an average of eighteen miles off the Placencia Peninsula. Boat trips available from Placencia range from a straightforward day on the water up to a week of camping, fishing, snorkelling or sailing.

Diving or **snorkelling** along the reef is excellent, with shallow fringing and patch reefs, and some fantastic wall diving. You can visit several virtually pristine protected areas, including **Laughing Bird Caye National Park** and **Gladden Spit and Silk Cayes Marine Reserve**.

In addition, **Placencia lagoon** is ideal for exploring in a **canoe or kayak**; you may even spot a manatee, though it's more likely to be a series of ripples as the shy giant swims for cover. The reefs and shallows off Placencia are rich **fishing** grounds too, and the village is home to several renowned fly-fishing guides (see p.198).

Coral Caye

8 miles northeast of Placencia • ☎ 824 4914, ⓦ thefamilycoppolaresorts.com/en/turtle-inn

What was formerly known as **French Louie Caye** is now **Coral Caye** since being taken over by the Coppola group, but it remains a beautiful, tiny island just eight miles off Placencia. There's fantastic snorkelling, with hard and soft corals, sea anemones and schools of tiny fish among the mangroves here; you can also visit half a dozen uninhabited cayes nearby. The cave also boasts a resident pair of ospreys who successfully rear chicks every year. Accommodation is available (see opposite).

Whipray Caye

8 miles northeast of Placencia

The small, idyllic island of **Whipray Caye** lies surrounded by reef and coral heads eight miles northeast of Placencia. Shown on some maps as Wippari Caye, it offered fabulous fishing. For the past decade or two it could only be visited by arrangement with the owners of the accommodation on the island, but with this closing in 2017, it's not clear what lies ahead in terms of visitor access.

Laughing Bird Caye National Park

11 miles east of Placencia • Day tours from Placencia cost US$40–100 • ☎ 523 3565, ⓦ laughingbird.org

The most popular destination for day-trips from Placencia is the uninhabited **Laughing Bird Caye National Park**. A World Heritage Site, located thirteen miles offshore, the long, narrow caye itself sits atop a "faro", a limestone reef rising steeply from the seabed. Its outer rim encloses a lagoon, making it similar to an atoll.

Named for the laughing gull, the caye covers less than 1.5 acres, and gulls no longer nest here, but it's the centre of a national park that protects over ten thousand acres of sea as a "no take zone" (no fishing). There's a ranger station, and many tours stop for lunch on the beach. The northern tip of the caye protects native vegetation and nesting birds and turtles, and is off-limits.

Gladden Spit and Silk Cayes Marine Reserve

23 miles east of Placencia • Day tours from Placencia typically cost US$100

The exquisitely beautiful Silk Cayes, set twelve miles beyond Laughing Bird Caye, form part of the **Gladden Spit and Silk Cayes Marine Reserve**, a large protected area designated to safeguard the seasonal visitation of the enormous yet graceful **whale shark**.

These migratory fish, found throughout tropical waters, are attracted to Gladden Spit during the full moons of April, May and June by huge numbers of spawning snapper. The sharks are filter-feeders, so it's the protein-rich spawn they're after, not the fish themselves. Research conducted by the University of York and the Nature Conservancy indicates that this is one of the largest and most predictable aggregations of whale sharks in the world; radio-tracking shows that they travel as far as Cancún in Mexico and down to Honduras – and probably further. All guides taking you to see the sharks will have undergone training not to disturb their feeding; boats should stay 15yd away, and snorkellers and divers at least 3 yd away.

Ranguana Caye

20 miles southeast of Placencia • Accessible on tours (about US$125) from Placencia or via *Ranguana Caye Cabañas* (see below)

Ranguana Caye, which is visited by some snorkel trips, is a jewel of an island just 120yd long by 25yd wide, surrounded by perfect patch reefs. For divers, the 2400ft drop-off begins 750yd offshore. The sand on Ranguana is softer than in Placencia, the palm trees taller and the sunsets glorious, silhouetting mountain ranges in the distance.

ACCOMMODATION   THE CAYES OFF PLACENCIA

CORAL CAYE
Coral Caye ☎ 824 4914, ⓦ thefamilycoppolaresorts .com/en/turtle-inn. Guests on this privately owned island have the entire place to themselves, and sleep in one of two comfortable, unfussy cottages; along with the Great House, which houses a kitchen, games room and bar, these are the only buildings on the island. As you'd expect, all meals and any desired activity – be it a birthday party, private chef or

a massage – can be catered for effortlessly. Delicious meals are served by the resident caretaker. Rates include continental breakfast only. US$895

RANGUANA CAYE
Ranguana Caye Cabanas ☎ 674 7264, ⓦ ranguanacaye.com. Beautiful wooden cabins facing into the breeze, with meals served in a *palapa*-covered

dining area. The cabins are available to guests for single nights, or in a package that combines two nights here with two in Placencia. Rates include transport, meals, drinks, use of kayaks and snorkel gear. Per cabin, per night US$599; four-night package US$2399

Punta Gorda

6

South of the Placencia and Independence junctions, the Southern Highway twists through pine forests and neat ranks of citrus trees and crosses numerous creeks through **Toledo District** – with only a few villages along the way. The highway ends at likeable little **PUNTA GORDA**, the southernmost town in Belize. As well as being the base for rewarding visits both to inland **Maya villages** and the little-visited southern **cayes and marine reserves**, it also offers daily skiffs to **Puerto Barrios** in Guatemala and **Livingston** in Honduras.

Punta Gorda itself is an appealing blend of village, provincial capital and international ferry port. Commonly known as "**PG**", and set at the spot where the Southern Highway finally reaches the sea and promptly comes to an end, it's a small, unhurried and hassle-free place. Admittedly on first impression it's not immediately obvious what there is to do all day, and there's not really a beach to speak of, but with a fine crop of hotels and restaurants, and plentiful tours and activities in the vicinity, PG makes a perfect base for a stay in Toledo District. Cooling sea breezes here reduce the worst of the heat and, though this is undeniably the **wettest** area of Belize, most of the extra rain falls at night, leaving the daytime no wetter than Cayo District.

As well as being home to a population of around eight thousand, including Garifuna, Maya, East Indians, Creoles and some Lebanese and Chinese, PG is the business centre for nearby villages and farming settlements, with Saturday as its most animated **market day**. Whichever day you visit, you'll almost certainly be approached by polite Maya women and girls, imploring you to buy the small and attractive **decorative baskets** they make from local vines.

ARRIVAL AND DEPARTURE   PUNTA GORDA

Current **schedules** for all local transport, including buses to the Maya villages and boats to Guatemala, are printed in the free local newspaper, the *Toledo Howler*.

By bus Buses to and from Belize City stop outside the James Buses office just off Front St, though the express bus departs at 6am from the petrol station at the northeast edge of the centre. Buses to the Maya villages leave from the market area, with only a minimal service on Sundays.

Destinations Belize City via Belmopan and Dangriga (10 daily, express service at 6am; 5hr 30min–6hr 30min); Jalacte

---

CONFEDERATES AND METHODISTS IN PUNTA GORDA

The **Toledo settlement**, the ruins of which still stand north of Punta Gorda, was founded in 1867 by **Confederate** emigrants from the US who hoped to recreate the antebellum South in what was then British Honduras. Since slavery was abolished hereabouts decades earlier, and the resident Garifuna and Creoles were not inclined to work for former slave owners, the settlers brought over indentured labourers from India. They called these labourers "coolies", and their descendants still live in Punta Gorda and along the Southern Highway; though long since fully assimilated into Belizean culture, they're still referred to as "coolies" by other ethnic groups, though rarely in a derogatory way.

Many Confederate settlers drifted back to the US, discouraged by the torrential downpours and the rigours of frontier life, but those who stayed were soon joined by **Methodists** from Mississippi. The Methodists were deeply committed to the settlement and, despite a cholera epidemic in 1868, managed to clear 160 acres. Between 1870 and 1890 **sugar** became the main product, with twelve separate estates running their own mills. After this, falling sugar prices pushed the farmers into alcohol production instead, but this was out of the question for the teetotal Methodists. By 1910 their community was destitute, although it was largely thanks to their struggle that Toledo was permanently settled.

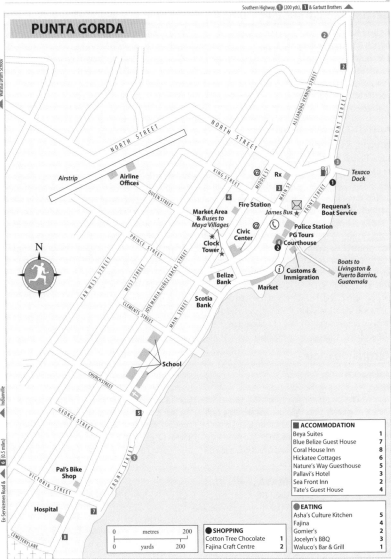

PUNTA GORDA

6

via San Antonio, Rio Blanco and Pueblo Viejo (Mon–Sat 3–4 daily, Sun 6am only; 3hr); San Benito Poite, via Blue Creek (4 weekly; 2hr 30min); Silver Creek via San Pedro Columbia (for Lubaantun) and San Miguel (Mon–Sat 4–5 daily; 2hr).

By plane Maya Island Air and Tropic Air operate several daily flights from Belize City (via Dangriga and Placencia), landing at the rudimentary airstrip five blocks west of the main dock, which is a 5–10min walk from most of the town's hotels. The hour-long flight usually costs US$135–150 one way.

By boat Three boats sail each day from the main dock near the centre of the seafront to Puerto Barrios in Guatemala. Requena's Charter Service leaves at 9.30am (☎722 2070, ✉watertaxi@btl.net); *Pichilingo* at 2pm (☎7948 5525); and *Marisol* at 4pm (☎722 2870). There's also a ferry to Livingston (departing Tues & Fri at 10am). There's no need to buy your ticket in advance; just turn up at the dock half an hour before departure.

Destinations Puerto Barrios, Guatemala (4 daily; 1hr; Bz$50); Livingston, Guatemala (2 weekly; 10am Tues & Fri; 1hr; Bz$60).

6

GETTING AROUND AND INFORMATION

By bike Many accommodation properties have free use of bicycles or inexpensive bike rental on site.

Car rental Barefoot Services, in Placencia (☎ 523 3066, ⓦ barefootservicesbelize.com), will deliver rental cars to Punta Gorda. Rates start around US$65/day. It's also possible to rent a car through *Sun Creek Lodge* (☎ 604 2124, ⓦ suncreeklodge.de).

Tourist information The Belize Tourism Industry Association (BTIA) has a large office in a pretty colonial building just south of the dock on Front St (Mon–Fri 8am–noon & 1–5pm; ☎ 722 2531); staff can help with transport schedules and in setting up tours of the outlying cayes and sites in Toledo District.

ACTIVITIES AND OPERATORS

DIVING, SNORKELLING AND FISHING

Blue Belize Dan Castellanos, a traditional fisherman turned tour guide and PADI Divemaster, offers expert marine tours from fishing to snorkelling. He's based at the *Blue Belize Guest House* (see opposite).

Garbutt Brothers ☎ 604 3548, ⓦ garbuttsfishinglodge.com. Based at the small marina at the entrance to town, the Garbutt brothers run scuba, snorkel and marine tours – they're especially adept at fly-fishing – as well as affordable trips to the pristine Lime Caye. They also rent kayaks and seaside cabins.

TIDE ☎ 722 2129, ⓦ tidetours.org. The Toledo Institute for Development and the Environment, based on the main road a mile out of town, close to *Waluco's*, is involved in many conservation projects, and also offers trips to the cayes and marine reserves, cacao, mountain-bike and kayak tours and camping trips to Payne's Creek National Park.

OTHER ACTIVITIES

Maroon Creole Drum School 1 mile out of town, just after the Joe Taylor Bridge ☎ 668 7733. Emmeth Young offers classes (US$10/hr) and workshops in making as well as playing a drum in a creekside camp. See their Facebook page for more information.

PG Tours Front St ☎ 636 6162, ⓦ pgtoursbelize.com. Offers a wide range of tours from the active (tubing, hiking, snorkelling) to the more sedate (birding), with some authentic cultural options, including cooking. They can also book local accommodation.

Warasa Drum School New Rd ☎ 632 7701, ⓦ warasadrumschool.com. Classes, workshops and occasional performances (from Bz$25 for private lesson).

ACCOMMODATION

★**Belcampo Lodge** Wilson Rd, 5 miles north of Punta Gorda ☎ 1 888 299 9940 (US), ⓦ belcampobz.com. Super-upscale resort enjoying wonderful views over landscaped grounds from a glorious hilltop setting high above the Río Grande. The unpaved turn-off is 4 miles south of Jacintoville on the Southern Hwy. Guests stay in spacious, beautifully furnished wooden *cabañas*, each with a private glass-screened deck shaded by trees, and enormous shower rooms. Meals in the main lodge building are mostly put together from ingredients grown on-site. Enjoy the spa, or take the cable car down to the river, which must rate as one of Belize's most spectacular jungle settings. Spend time fishing or just relaxing at the hilltop pool, enjoy a breathtaking panorama from the main lodge or walk the

---

CACAO AND THE MAYA

The ancient Maya, who were the first to process cacao into **chocolate**, assigned great value to the beans which could be used as money and traded over vast distances. These days, commercial production and cacao-related ecotourism continue to generate financial benefit. The environment of Toledo provides ideal growing conditions, and anyone passing through the local villages is likely to see cacao beans drying on special concrete pads. The Toledo Cacao Growers' Association was established in conjunction with chocolate company Green & Black's, and the UK's first Fair Trade product was born. Almost all of the crop is organically produced and used to make the company's delicious **Maya Gold** imprint sold abroad.

New, local entrepreneurs have started up, too, including **Cotton Tree Chocolate** in Punta Gorda (see p.208), **Ixcacao**, a short distance north (see p.219), and **Goss Chocolate** on the Placencia Peninsula (see p.201). You can also get hands-on during a **tour** of a working establishment at Agouti Cacao Farm (Mon–Sat 8.30am–4pm, US$25; ☎ 624 0166, ⓦ agouticacaofarm.wordpress.com).

The **Chocolate Festival of Belize**, held at the end of May each year during Commonwealth Holiday weekend, features a Saturday programme of sweet and savoury cook-offs, street events and concerts in Punta Gorda; weekend festivities may also include Maya dance and cultural activities at Lubaantun on Sunday (ⓦ chocolatefestivalofbelize.com).

THE LOATHSOME LIONFISH

The waters of the Caribbean have been invaded by a dangerous predator – the fearsome-looking **lionfish**, which has in the last few decades had a devastating impact on the already fragile ecosystems of Belize's Barrier Reef. Not only does each lionfish eat colossal quantities of the eggs and young of other species, but none of the larger local fish recognize the lionfish as being potentially edible. That allows them to breed at an astonishing rate; a single female lionfish can lay as many as twenty thousand eggs every four days.

The lionfish is originally from the Red Sea, where it occupies a stable position in the food chain, and is preyed on in turn by other species. It's thought that the problem began in Florida in the mid-1980s with the release into the ocean of perhaps a dozen fish that had been imported as pets, but then overgrown their aquariums.

Efforts to alleviate the situation in Belize include hunting them, or more simply, **eating** them. The *Chabil Mar Resort* (see p.199) sponsors **hunting excursions**, and to a greater end, local restaurants are being encouraged to add them to their menus – the silver lining being that they're delicious, and also serve as an alternative to conch, which are becoming less plentiful.

MONITORING THE SITUATION

Working in conjunction with Belize's Ministry of Fisheries and local NGOs, **Reef Conservation International** (ReefCI; ☎ 629 4266, ⊕ reefci.com) is helping to tackle the lionfish problem by monitoring the populations of conch, lobster and lionfish on the reef off Toledo. Participants in its weekly programme leave Punta Gorda on Monday morning to spend four nights on Sapodilla Cayes. Acccomodation is in individual *cabañas*; a couple are en suite, the rest share bathrooms. The all-inclusive price for four nights and five days, with three dives per day (and free PADI qualification if you don't already have it), is US$1330 per person (or US$1025 for non-divers who wish to participate).

---

nature trails through the forest. Packages available. US$514
Beya Suites Front St, 0.5 mile north of the centre ☎ 722 2188, ⊕ beyasuites.com. A former winner of Belize's "Small Hotel of the Year" award, this bright pink house on the seafront is a good Belizean-owned option. All rooms offer a/c, TV and private bath. Most have balconies, and there's a rooftop sun deck. Laundry and breakfast available. Bar downstairs. US$87
Blue Belize Guest House 139 Front St ☎ 722 2678, ⊕ bluebelize.com. Impressive, friendly guesthouse, set amid flowering seafront gardens at the south end of town. Two buildings, linked by a raised boardwalk, hold four one-bedroom kitchenette units plus two two-bedroom honeymoon suites with full kitchens (US$155). All are bright and colourfully decorated, and share access to spacious seaview terraces. Breakfast and bicycles included. US$85
Coral House Inn 151 Main St ☎ 722 2878, ⊕ coralhouseinn.com. This smart and attractive columned guesthouse makes you feel truly at home, in comfortable a/c rooms or a self-contained cottage (US$145), featuring decor from local artisans. Gorgeous pool with thatched bar, and hammocks on the ground's verandas. Complimentary breakfast and bicycles. US$110
Hickatee Cottages Ex-Servicemen Rd, beyond Cemetery Lane ☎ 662 4475, ⊕ hickatee.com. This small B&B, around a mile west of downtown Punta Gorda, consists of four rustic-chic private cottages set amid twenty acres of lush jungle and drawing numerous butterflies, birds and monkeys each day. The cottages are equipped with solar-powered ceiling fans and hot-water showers, and there's a small pool, abundant nature trails and free bicycles; local tours are easily arranged. Rates include breakfast plus transfers to and from town; excellent dinners in the on-site dining room (closed Wed & Sat) cost US$20. US$90
Nature's Way Guesthouse 65 Front St ☎ 702 2119. Rustic, somewhat ramshackle place, set in an overgrown garden, where eight clean rooms overlooking the sea have shared baths and cold showers. It's a good spot to meet other travellers and get information. Decent breakfast (US$6) and a book exchange also available. The owner promotes eco-tourism and can arrange trips to Maya villages. US$35
Pallavi's Hotel 21 Main St ☎ 702 2414, ⊕ puntagordabelize.com/graces. Functional, clean rooms with private bath in the centre of town; those with a/c cost twice as much. The restaurant, open daily, features a large menu including hearty Belizean dishes for less than Bz$15. US$32
Sea Front Inn 4 Front St ☎ 722 2300, ⊕ seafrontinn.com. Two imposing eccentric stone buildings with steep Alpine-style eaves, 600yd north of the centre. Spacious rooms have tiled floors, a/c and TV; some have a balcony. The triple (Bz$190) is good for longer stays. Breakfast and tours available. Bz$165
Tate's Guest House 34 José María Nuñez St ☎ 722 0147, ✉ tatesguesthouse@yahoo.com. Quiet, friendly family-run hotel, two blocks west of the town centre. Simple but clean rooms have private bath and TV; some have a/c; and there's access to a shared kitchen. Bz$75

6

MAYA SEA SALTS

The cayes and coastline of Toledo were once home to ancient **Maya sea traders** and salt plant workers. Archeological fieldwork by Heather McKillop (through Louisiana State University) has documented sea-level rises since the end of the Classic period (900 AD), which submerged ancient sites and created the modern mangrove landscape. The Maya port of **Wild Cane Cay**, a mangrove-covered caye twelve miles north of PG, was once responsible for the trade in salt (produced in nearby Punta Ycacos Lagoon) – a necessity for the inhabitants of the great inland cities.

Although the works were abandoned with the Classic Maya collapse, Wild Cane Caye continued to participate in sea trade with Postclassic cities as far away as Chichén Itzá in Mexico's Yucatán. McKillop's project also documented unique **coral architecture**, in which coral rock was mined from the sea to build platforms for structures of perishable material. The coastal area is managed by TIDE (see p.206); anyone planning to visit the site must check in at the **ranger station** on nearby **Abalone Caye**.

EATING

Asha's Culture Kitchen 74 Front St ☎ 722 2742, ⓦ facebook.com/AshasCultureKitchen. Welcoming local restaurant in a sleepy seafront spot south of the centre, serving fresh seafood and bbq either in the main bar, which hosts live music and/or drumming most nights, or under the starlight on the large deck over the water. Typical fish dishes include lionfish (Bz$25) and lobster (Bz$40); curried, grilled or baked chicken is just Bz$12. Daily 11am–midnight.

Fajina Front St ☎ 601 4838. This tiny upstairs restaurant, opposite the entrance to the docks and, like the crafts shop below (see below), run by the Fajina Maya Women's Coop, is a popular local choice, serving hearty portions of Maya cuisine for Bz$5–10. Daily 7am–8pm.

★**Gomier's** Front St, before the Joe Taylor Bridge next to Beya Suites, ⓦ facebook.com/Gomiers. Simple thatched *palapa*, across from the sea at the north end of town, where the genial chef/owner Gomier, originally from St Lucia, cooks up wonderful vegetarian dishes and seafood to a gentle reggae soundtrack. Exotic fruit juices and seaweed shakes for Bz$6–8, fish or tofu burgers for Bz$8 and garlic shrimp or whole fish for Bz$16–18. Gomier can also teach you how to make your own tofu (Bz$75/person). Mon–Sat 8am–2pm and 6–9pm.

Jocelyn's BBQ Front St ☎ 607 2877. This green shack, recently expanded with a pleasant deck and some outdoor plastic tables and chairs scattered at the sea's edge across from the petrol station, serves great dishes like jerk chicken and fried fish (with coco-rice and beans) for Bz$6–12. Daily 8am–midnight.

Waluco's Bar & Grill Front St by Tide Pier ☎ 670 3672. This large, thatched seafront bar, on the main road a mile short of town, is renowned for its bbq, as well as the live music and/or Garifuna drumming it puts on, at the weekends especially. Tues–Thurs 11am–10pm, Fri–Sun 11am–midnight.

SHOPPING

Cotton Tree Chocolate 2 Front St ☎ 621 8776, ⓦ cottontreechocolate.com. Take a free tour (daily at 10am) of this tiny chocolate factory, in the northernmost house on Front St downtown, to see mighty pots of fresh chocolate, made with locally grown, organic "fine flavour cacao", churning on the stove, then dive right in (figuratively, of course). What's not to like? Mon–Fri 8.30am–noon & 1.30–5pm, Sat 8.30am–noon.

Fajina Craft Centre Front St ☎ 666 6141. Run by a Maya women's cooperative whose members come from rural villages all over Toledo, this central crafts shop sells a fine assortment of baskets, bags, jewellery, carvings and even cookbooks. Mon–Sat 8–11am & noon–4pm.

The cayes off Toledo

Marking the southern tip of Belize's Barrier Reef, the **cayes and reefs** off Punta Gorda get relatively little attention from visitors. Roughly 130 low-lying mangrove cayes clustered in the mouth of a large bay north of PG are protected in the **Port Honduras Marine Reserve**, which was established in part to safeguard **manatees** living in the shallow water. Further out to sea, the **Sapodilla Cayes Marine Reserve** incorporates another group of irresistible islands.

Snake Cayes

The first real **beaches** north of Punta Gorda appear on the idyllic **Snake Cayes**, a group of four islands seventeen miles northeast of PG. Surrounded by glorious white coral sand beaches, they're quite easy to visit on day-trips. Beyond here the main reef is fragmented into several clusters of cayes, each surrounded by a small independent reef.

Sapodilla Cayes

6

The most easterly of the caye clusters at the southern end of the barrier reef are the stunningly beautiful **Sapodilla Cayes**. Each of this chain, which consists of five main islands, is encircled by coral and holds gorgeous soft-sand **beaches**. Some cayes have accommodation and others have even been used by refugees; the area faces increasing visitor pressure, though a management plan co-devised by the **Southern Environmental Association** (SEA; ☎ 523 3377, ⓦseabelize.org) aims to limit damage. SEA is active in environmental education, taking boatloads of schoolchildren to the **Sapodilla Cayes Marine Reserve** to learn about marine ecosystems and participate in beach clean-ups; committed **volunteers** can contact their office at Joe Taylor Creek in PG.

These days, day-trippers from Guatemala and Honduras as well as Belize are challenging the already thinly stretched conservation agencies. Uninhabited **Northeast Caye**, thickly covered with coconut trees and under government ownership, is the **core zone** of the reserve, to be left undeveloped. A Bz$20 reserve entrance fee is levied at **Hunting Caye**, an immigration post that handles foreign visitors, and also has limited camping and picnic facilities. The sand at stunning Crescent Moon Beach on the caye's east side attracts hawksbill turtles to nest. **Nicolas Caye** has an abandoned resort, where visitors can camp or ask the caretaker for permission to sleep in a basic cabin.

The most southerly main island, **Lime Caye**, is a fantastic place to savour glorious isolation, with rudimentary cabins available to rent from *Garbutt's Fishing Lodge* (see p.206), and snorkelling available on the reef just offshore.

Inland Toledo

Exploring **inland Toledo** can be a true highlight of a trip to Belize. Tourism here is distinctly low-impact – providing additional income without destroying the communities' traditional ways of life. This region is the heartland for the **Maya** of Belize. The Maya constitute a small minority of Belizeans – around ten percent of the population. In Toledo, however, roughly half the inhabitants are descended from the Maya refugees who have fled repression and land shortages in Guatemala since the late nineteenth century. For the most part, the **Mopan Maya** from Petén and the **Kekchí** speakers from the Verapaz highlands keep to their own distinct villages, which look much like their counterparts in Guatemala. Very few speak Spanish, maintaining instead their indigenous languages and Belizean Kriol.

RANGER FOR A DAY

The **Ya'axché Conservation Trust** (☎722 0108, ⓦyaaxche.org) runs an interesting "**ranger for a day**" programme from its Toledo HQ, on the Southern Highway halfway between Independence and Punta Gorda; its website gives access details. Guests spend the day patrolling the 15,000 acre Golden Stream Corridor Preserve, learning about medicinal plants, checking for signs of illegal activity and monitoring the region's biodiversity. The US$50 fee (if your patrol is on foot, US$95 if it's by boat along the river itself) includes lunch and directly funds the locally staffed park-ranger programme.

The largest villages are **San Antonio** and **San Pedro Columbia**. Simple guesthouses and Maya homestays are available in the rural areas, though a few more luxurious **lodges** have opened their doors in recent years.

Of course the ancient Maya lived here too, with ruins scattered throughout. The best-known sites are **Lubaantun**, the supposed home of the famous Crystal Skull, and **Nim Li Punit**, with its impressive stelae. **Pusilhá**, harder to reach, near the Guatemalan border, contains the finest Maya bridge to be found anywhere.

6

The Southern Highway to Dump

The only road access to Toledo is along the **Southern Highway**, which enters the region a mile or so south of the Independence junction. It then runs for roughly 45 miles southwest to a dismally named speck on the map called **Dump**, where it turns sharply southeast for the last fourteen miles to Punta Gorda and the sea. The first thirty or so miles of the route pass through a patchwork of forest reserves, with barely a dwelling in sight. After that comes a quick succession of little **Maya villages**, with the most obvious first stop being the ancient site of **Nim Li Punit**.

Nim Li Punit

Southern Hwy, 5 miles north of Big Falls • Daily 8am–4pm • Bz$10 • Buses along Southern Hwy will stop at the entrance

The Late Classic Maya site of **NIM LI PUNIT**, just west of the Southern Highway, occupies a commanding position on a ridge above the Kekchí Maya village of **Indian Creek**, with views over the maize fields to the coastal plain. The scene can barely have changed since ancient times. Discovered only in 1976, Nim Li Punit is thought to have been allied to nearby Lubaantun (see p.212), and to have had some sort of long-term connection with Copán in Honduras.

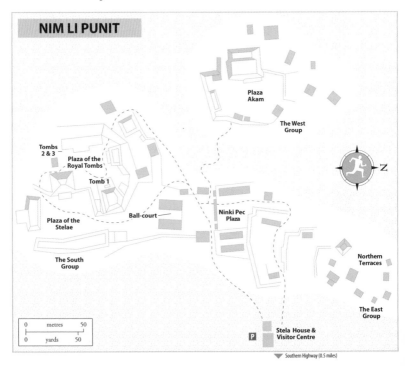

NIM LI PUNIT

Plaza Akam

The West Group

Tombs 2 & 3

Plaza of the Royal Tombs

Tomb 1

Ball-court

Ninki Pec Plaza

Plaza of the Stelae

The South Group

Northern Terraces

The East Group

Stela House & Visitor Centre

P

0   metres   50

0   yards   50

Southern Highway (0.5 miles)

Stela House

Steps lead up from the site car park to its **visitor centre**. Nim Li Punit is chiefly noteworthy as home to some of the largest and best-preserved **stelae** in Belize, which are now sheltered in the adjoining **Stela House**. A total of 26 stelae were found here, eight of them carved. The tallest of the lot, and one of the tallest anywhere in the Maya world, is **Stela 14**, at almost 30ft high. Never actually erected, it's a magnificent spectacle, with panels of glyphs above and a richly attired ruler. His elaborate headgear is responsible for Nim Li Punit's modern name, Kekchí for "big hat". Although the "name glyph" that signifies its ancient name has been identified, the name itself remains unknown.

6

    Stela 15, dated to 721 AD and the earliest here, is even more impressive. Carvings on this great slab depict a ruler in the act of dropping an offering – perhaps *copal* incense or corn kernels – into a burning brazier supported on the back of a monster, in order to conjure up a vision of **Waxaklahun Ubah Kan**, or "Mosaic War Serpent", the ruler's battle standard. To the right, a smaller figure also makes an offering, while on the left side a column of very clear glyphs separates the main figure from a guard.

The site

Beyond the visitor centre, you enter **the site** itself through a plaza surrounded by walls and buildings of cut stones held together without mortar. While few of the structures have been excavated to any great extent, the open areas between them have been cleared and maintained as rich green lawns, making it a delightful place to stroll around. Pass through the beautiful **walled ball-court** to reach the **South Group**, which may have functioned as an observatory to record the sunrise at the solstices and equinoxes. The **West Group**, by contrast, remains very much overgrown, allowing you to feel as though you're exploring all-but-virgin jungle.

    Note that cruise lines bring their passengers here on sightseeing tours, currently from Wednesday to Friday; if you want to avoid the crowds, ask the locals for advice on the best time to come.

Big Falls

The Southern Highway crosses the Río Grande a couple of miles southwest of the Silver Creek Road turnoff. The village of **BIG FALLS** here holds a petrol station, store, a couple of bars and a luxury resort. It's not a particularly pretty place, but it does boast Belize's only **hot spring**, a sumptuous spot for a warm bath. The spring feeds a creek that flows into the Río Grande, just upstream of the bridge in the village centre.

Dump

The unfortunately named village of **DUMP**, four miles southwest of Big Falls, amounts to little more than a petrol station. It marks the road junction where the Southern Highway makes an abrupt ninety-degree turn for its final fourteen-mile run to meet the sea at **Punta Gorda**. A separate road continues west from here towards the border town of **Jalacte** (see p.213).

Silver Creek Road

The unpaved **Silver Creek Road** branches off the Southern Highway just under five miles southwest of Nim Li Punit, then curves first west, and then south, for nine miles to join the road to Jalacte, two miles west of Dump. While primarily of interest as offering the only access to the Maya site of **Lubaantun** (see p.212), it's also a very attractive route in its own right, passing through the modern Maya villages of **San Miguel** and **San Pedro Columbia**.

San Miguel

Sprawling across a verdant clearing in the rolling foothills of the Maya Mountains, the attractive village of **San Miguel** was settled in 1950 by Kekchí Maya migrants from Santa Teresa, to the southwest. As well as holding a TEA guesthouse (see box, p.219), it's also home to the *Back-a-Bush* budget lodge (see p.220).

Lubaantun

1.3 miles north of the road between San Pedro Columbia and San Miguel • Daily 8am–4pm • Bz$10

Set on a high ridge two miles north of San Pedro Columbia, the Late Classic city of **Lubaantun** is the best-restored ancient Maya site in southern Belize. Impressive though it is today, it covered a much larger area during its brief heyday, between around 730 AD and 860 AD. Its original name being unknown, the modern Maya "Lubaantun", which means "place of the fallen stones", seems appropriate in view of its ruined state. While many structures remain topped and entangled by mighty trees, however, this is still a spectacular and compellingly beautiful site. Essentially it's a single **acropolis**, holding eleven major structures, five plazas and three ball-courts. Climbing the high pyramids is not allowed, but the view over the forest is staggering nonetheless.

Brief history

Lubaantun came to the attention of **colonial authorities** in 1903, and archeologist Thomas Gann was sent to investigate. A **survey** in 1915 revealed many structures, and three ball-court markers were removed and taken to the Peabody Museum at Harvard. The British Museum expedition of 1926 was joined in 1927 by J. Eric S. Thompson, who became a renowned Maya expert, though no further excavations took place until Norman Hammond mapped the site in 1970, showing trading links with communities on the coast and inland – relationships likely enhanced by Lubaantun's wealth of cacao.

Buildings here were constructed by layering and fitting together precisely carved **stone blocks**, Inca-style, with nothing to bind them. This technique, and the fact that most of the main buildings have **rounded corners**, give Lubaantun an elegance

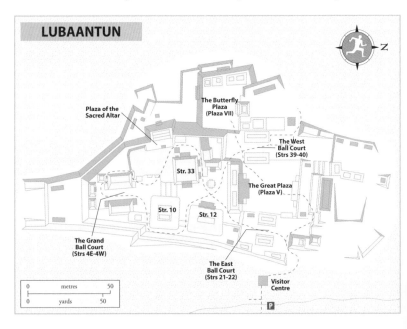

LUBAANTUN

The Butterfly Plaza (Plaza VII)

Plaza of the Sacred Altar

The West Ball Court (Strs 39-40)

Str. 33

The Great Plaza (Plaza V)

Str. 10

Str. 12

The Grand Ball Court (Strs 4E-4W)

The East Ball Court (Strs 21-22)

Visitor Centre

0   metres   50
0   yards   50

THE CRYSTAL SKULL OF LUBAANTUN

The famous **Crystal Skull of Lubaantun** was supposedly discovered beneath an altar in 1924 by Anna Mitchell-Hedges, the adopted daughter of a British Museum expedition leader, F.A. Mitchell-Hedges. So the story goes, the find happened to coincide with her seventeenth birthday, and the skull was then given to the local Maya, who in turn presented it to Anna's father in gratitude for his assistance. According to assorted New Age mystics, the skull has mysterious supernatural properties; Anna herself, who always refused to let it be tested, stated that it was used by ancient Maya priests to will death on unfortunate victims.

Although the skull is indeed fashioned from a single piece of pure rock crystal, none of the legend is now thought to be true. There's no contemporary record of its discovery, or even that Anna was ever in Belize; Mitchell-Hedges probably bought it in an **auction** at Sotheby's in 1943. More to the point, when the skull was finally examined by Smithsonian scientists after Anna died, aged 100, in 2007, it was conclusively proved to have been carved using high-speed diamond-tipped metal rotary tools, perhaps as recently as the 1930s.

The same goes for an almost identical skull owned by the British Museum, of which the Lubaantun skull may have been a direct copy. Both seem to have been modelled on the same actual human head, which forensic scientists have identified as displaying European rather than Indo-American facial characteristics.

6

sometimes missing from larger sites. Another anomaly is that no stelae were found; it's conjectured that Lubaantun was the regional administrative centre while Nim Li Punit, only eleven miles away and with numerous stelae, had a more ceremonial function. The plainness and monumentality of Lubaantun's architecture is also similar to the buildings at Quiriguá in Guatemala (which has numerous stelae), and there may have been a connection between them.

Lubaantun's relics

Glass cases in the **visitor centre** display distinctive **flints** (symbols of a ruler's power) and **ceramics**, while wall panels describe the various digs and depict life in a modern Maya village. The knowledgeable head caretaker, Santiago Coc, or his son, Kenan, may be able to give you a guided tour. They also make working replicas of the ocarinas – clay whistles in the shape of animals – that have been found here; their evocative notes occasionally float through the ruins. Dozens of mass-produced ceramic **figurines** litter the site, often depicting ball-players – items found nowhere else in such quantities.

San Pedro Columbia

In the predominantly Kekchí village of **San Pedro Columbia**, the Silver Creek Road crosses a bridge over the **Columbia River**. The Maya city of Lubaantun lies within walking distance to the north, while from the village itself it's possible, with a local guide, to paddle to the "source" of the Columbia – a gorgeous spot a mile or two upstream where the river re-emerges from an underground section, gushing forth among the rocks in an enormous, crystal-clear spring overhung with jungle foliage.

The road to Jalacte

From **Dump** (see p.211), where the Southern Highway makes its final dogleg turn towards the sea, another road heads directly west towards the border with Guatemala. In the absence of any official name, it's colloquially known as **the road to Jalacte**. Thanks to funding from the government of Taiwan, work to widen, flatten and above all **pave** it started in 2011, with the ultimate aim of opening a **new border crossing** between Belize and Guatemala. That prospect alarms many of the local Maya villagers, who fear marginalization once a new through highway opens.

Thus far, however, progress has been slow; at the time of writing, only the first eleven miles beyond Dump had been paved, and the road was only negotiable in an ordinary vehicle as far as **Pueblo Viejo**, another five miles on. Up to three daily buses from Punta Gorda make it all the way to Jalacte itself, five miles further still, but it's not a route to attempt on your own. In any case, there's no corresponding highway on the Guatemala side of the border; lone cyclists have reported managing to continue from Toledo into Guatemala, but as yet the crossing is not a legal exit point.

For visitors, the road offers access to attractions including villages like **San Antonio**, **waterfalls** at Río Blanco National Park and Pueblo Viejo and the Maya ruins of **Uxbenká**. In addition, a separate road that branches south at Mafredi, four miles west of Dump, leads to the village of **Blue Creek** and, eventually, southern Belize's largest Maya site, **Pusilhá**.

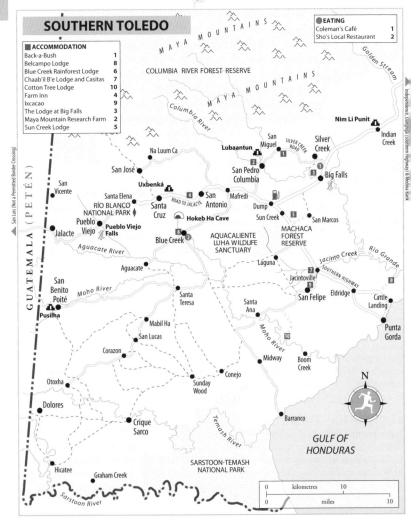

SOUTHERN TOLEDO

● EATING
Coleman's Café	1
Sho's Local Restaurant	2

■ ACCOMMODATION
Back-a-Bush	1
Belcampo Lodge	8
Blue Creek Rainforest Lodge	6
Chaab'il B'e Lodge and Casitas	7
Cotton Tree Lodge	10
Farm Inn	4
Ixcacao	9
The Lodge at Big Falls	3
Maya Mountain Research Farm	2
Sun Creek Lodge	5

San Antonio
6 miles west of Dump, 20 miles northwest of Punta Gorda

The founders of the Mopan Maya village of **SAN ANTONIO**, perched on a small hilltop and surrounded by jungle-clad hills and swiftly flowing rivers, came from the Guatemalan town of San Luis. It's now the largest Maya settlement in Belize, home to around two thousand villagers, who maintain many traditions, including the worship of their patron saint in the beautiful **stone church** of San Luis Rey. It's the third such church to stand here, its two predecessors having been destroyed by fire, and features a set of **stained-glass windows** depicting the twelve apostles and other saints, donated by St Louis, Missouri.

San Antonio is also home to a couple of shops and a TEA guesthouse (see box, p.219). Locals continue to observe pre-Columbian traditions, with a fiesta taking place around August 25, featuring *marimba* music, masked dances and much heavy drinking.

San José

A sinuous track leads for ten miles northwest from a junction a mile east of San Antonio to the village of **SAN JOSÉ**, nestled amid the lower slopes of the Maya Mountains. Active-minded visitors can hike from San José higher into the mountains. Ask for Alfredo Sho or Emelino Cho, who will guide you as far as **Little Quartz Ridge**, a steep and isolated plateau with an ecosystem unique to Belize, or even to (at least) the lower slopes of **Doyle's Delight**, the highest peak in Belize. For either trip, you'll need camping gear and supplies for at least three days, plus a great deal of stamina.

An even more adventurous hike, the arduous eight-day **Maya Mountain Divide Trail**, leads from San José to **Las Cuevas**, at the end of the Chiquibul Road in Cayo; if you're interested, contact Marcos Cucul (see p.121).

Uxbenká
Just east of Santa Cruz, 4 miles west of San Antonio

The ruins of little **UXBENKÁ** ("ancient place") are superbly positioned on an exposed hilltop on the eastern fringes of the village of **Santa Cruz**. There are no signs to the site; look out for a thatched *palapa* above the southern side of the road. Neither is there a visitor centre or caretaker, so to understand its minimally excavated structures it's best to ask in the village for a guided tour from someone associated with the TEA guesthouse (see box, p.219).

An early Maya political centre from the Early Classic period, Uxbenká may even have existed in the Preclassic era, and had links to Tikal. It's believed to have been a major agricultural centre, engaged in cultivating **cacao** on terraces nearby. The core area consists of seven architectural plazas spread across three ridges. Appearing to contain the civic, ceremonial and elite residences of Maya society, it has been grouped into three clusters: the **Stela Plaza** (Group A), an "**acropolis**" residential group (Group G), located atop the highest hill, and a set of five conjoined **plazas** (Groups B–F), the site's main ceremonial groups.

The star finding at Uxbenká is what may be the oldest **canoe** ever discovered in Mesoamerica. Possibly a stylized rendition rather than a functional canoe, it was found in a cliff-top cave, and has been carbon dated to somewhere between 120 and 240 AD.

Río Blanco National Park
5 miles west of San Antonio, 12 miles west of Dump • Daily 8am–5pm • Bz$5 • ⓦ belizeit.com

The roadside **Río Blanco National Park** offers easy access to a broad cascade in the Río Blanco. From the wooden visitor centre – a simple hut propped on stilts and set just back from the highway – a short trail leads down through the forest to the spot where the **Río Blanco Falls** tumble 20ft over a 100ft wide rocky ledge into a deep pool. Taking a quick dip is all but irresistible – there's even a little changing cabin alongside.

A network of hiking trails used to extend into the wilderness on the far side of the river, but sadly the swaying plank bridge has collapsed, so there's now nothing more to the park than the waterfall.

Pueblo Viejo

In the village of **Pueblo Viejo**, four miles west of Río Blanco National Park (and sixteen miles west of Dump), an impressive series of **waterfalls** on Pueblo Creek make a dramatic spectacle. Above the cascades, a steep trail leads through orchid-laden rainforest to a mountaintop overlook; ask in the village for a guide.

Blue Creek

Buses to Blue Creek leave Punta Gorda at noon on Mon, Wed, Fri & Sat (1hr 30min)

At the tiny village of **Mafredi**, about 5.5 miles from San Pedro Columbia, a branch road heads south and west to **BLUE CREEK** (located fourteen miles west of Dump, and thirty miles northwest of Punta Gorda). The main attraction here is the village's namesake **stream** – a beautiful stretch of water that emerges from magnificent rainforest to flow through the heart of the village. As well as holding the *Blue Creek Rainforest Lodge* (see p.220), Blue Creek also offers activities such as hiking and caving under the TEA programme (see box, p.219). Ask at the roadside *Sho's Local Restaurant* for a reliable **guide**.

The **Tumul K'in Center of Learning** (☎608 1070, ⓦtumulkinbelize.org) is an active community development organization with programmes in Maya culture, philosophy, cultivation and food processing (try the mango or papaya jam), plus a radio station. Ecotourism activities are run by Rosemary Salam, including tours to Maya sites and cultural nights with food provided – book in advance.

Hokeb Ha Cave

Thirty minutes' walk upriver from the well-signposted *Blue Creek Rainforest Lodge*, outside Blue Creek village, you reach the **source of Blue Creek**, where the water gushes from beneath a mossy rock face. Alongside is the entrance to **Hokeb Ha Cave**, which is fairly easy to explore, and often busy on Sundays with visitors and children trying to sell souvenirs. As well as being festooned with huge stalactites and stalagmites, its inner recesses shelter a Maya altar. This entire area is made of limestone bedrock honeycombed with caves, many of which were sacred to the Maya, and plenty of others are doubtless waiting to be rediscovered. It's best visited with a **guide** to explore the cave's inner sanctum; ask around in Blue Creek village.

Aguacate

Five miles west of Blue Creek, the undeveloped yet sublimely pretty Kekchí village of **Aguacate** is an ideal place to learn the traditional methods of cooking wild meat and freshly caught river shrimp. It's home to a few families in the Maya Homestay programme (see box, p.219).

San Benito Poité

Buses to San Benito Poité leave Punta Gorda at noon on Mon, Wed, Fri & Sat (2hr 30min)

West of Blue Creek, the rough, unpaved road climbs a ridge to the valley of the Moho River, passing through the community of **Santa Teresa** before reaching **San Benito Poité** (fourteen miles west of Blue Creek, and forty miles west of Punta Gorda). Most of the inhabitants of this very traditional village speak only Kekchí, plus a smattering of Spanish, and they may not be as immediately welcoming as in other Toledo villages. The few visitors who make their way this far up the valley, almost to the Guatemalan border, come not so much to see San Benito Poité itself, as the ancient Maya city of **Pusilhá**, the ruins of which are located in and around the village. If you want to visit

the site, it's essential to **ask permission** from the *alcalde* (similar to a mayor) as soon as you arrive.

At the entrance to the village, a bridge crosses the fast-flowing Pusilhá (Machaca) River, with a lovely **camping** spot nearby. Just downstream, the Pusilhá and Poité rivers meet to form the **Moho River**, the middle stretch of which holds some of the most exhilarating **whitewater rapids** in Central America – occasionally paddled by raft and kayak expedition groups from overseas.

6

Pusilhá

In San Benito Poité, 14 miles west of Blue Creek, on the banks of the Moho River • No fixed hours or admission; ask for permission to visit and a guide in San Benito Poité Village

The largest Maya site in southern Belize, **Pusilhá** remains only minimally excavated. To make sense of what you see, you're strongly recommended to go with a Kekchí-speaking **guide**, arranged either in advance through the BTIA office in Punta Gorda (see p.206), or on the spot with the *alcalde* of San Benito Poité.

Strategically built on high land between the confluence of two rivers, the site has yielded an astonishing number of carved monuments, including **zoomorphic altars** – great, rounded stone tablets carved with stylized animals – similar to those at Quiriguá in Guatemala. Archeologists originally believed that Pusilhá was under Quirigua's control, but recent studies indicate a closer connection with Copán in Honduras. Although many monuments were removed to the British Museum during expeditions in the late 1920s, the **Stela Plaza** – the city's sacred centre – still holds a few eroded stelae and three zoomorphic altars that resemble frogs. Nearby you can see the remains of a **walled ball-court**.

The highlight, however, is the finest **Maya bridge** to survive anywhere in the Maya world, built at a narrow point over the Pusilhá River. Clearly visible are the remains of the main abutments, solid vertical walls of cut stones and supported by ramps of rock. In ancient times the bridge supports would have been spanned by beams of sapodilla wood, carrying the road to the **Gateway Hill Acropolis**. Both the palace of Pusilhá's rulers and the city's administrative centre, this awe-inspiring edifice soars 240ft above the river in a series of pyramidal platforms, terraces and facades. As for why the bridge was constructed at all – the ancient Maya usually crossed rivers by canoe – it seems likely that this feat of engineering was created solely to form an impressive processional route to the acropolis.

The Southern Highway south of Dump

The final fourteen miles of the Southern Highway, heading southeast from Dump to meet the sea at Punta Gorda, is punctuated only by a handful of little villages. Both **Sun Creek**, two miles south of Dump, and **Jacintoville**, five miles after that, hold appealing accommodation options. Otherwise, the only potential diversion is to head down the unpaved road that branches southwest into the rainforest at Jacintoville, to

SARSTOON TEMASH NATIONAL PARK

The Belizean coastline south of Punta Gorda is flat, with tidal rivers meandering across a coastal plain covered with thick tropical rainforest, forming a unique ecosystem with numerous orchids and palms. The **Temash River** is lined with the tallest mangrove forest in the country, **black mangroves** towering more than 90ft above the riverbanks, while in the far south the **Sarstoon River**, navigable by small boats, forms the border with Guatemala. Nominally protected as **Sarstoon Temash National Park**, the land has, to the dismay of the local Maya, nonetheless been authorized by the Belizean government for oil exploration; for the latest news, visit Ⓦ satiim.org.bz. It's possible to arrange **tours** through operators in Punta Gorda; some companies paddle the rivers using inflatable kayaks.

reach the **Ixcacao** chocolate farm at San Felipe after three miles, or the coastal town of **Barranco** after fifteen more.

Ixcacao

Barranco Rd, San Felipe • No fixed hours; tours and visits by reservation • 1hr chocolate making session US$30/person • ☎ 742 4050, ⓦ ixcacaomayabelizeanchocolate.com

Under the irresistible slogan "Chocolate Will Save The Rainforest", the dynamic and very welcoming Juan and Abelina Cho have turned their small cacao farm, **Ixcacao**, into a museum-cum-factory-cum-all-round-inspiration. Located on the edge of the village of San Felipe, it offers a range of visitor options, from a quick scoot around a grove of cacao trees, followed by a chance to watch the beans become chocolate in the simple kitchen; an in-depth tour of the farm; or a wide-ranging programme of hikes and local visits.

Underlying the whole enterprise is a passionate belief in the importance of organic farming and sustainable agriculture; most of the cacao grown here ends up in Green & Black's Maya Gold brand. You can also, of course, buy home-made chocolate, and even drink **chocolate wine**, while the kitchen serves chocolate-based meals, and budget **accommodation** is available (see p.221).

Barranco

Buses to Barranco leave Punta Gorda at noon on Mon, Wed, Fri & Sat (1hr)

Set amid forest and savannah, the small and traditional **Garifuna** village of **BARRANCO** lies 26 miles by road from Punta Gorda. Belize's southernmost coastal settlement, it is home to around 150 people, mostly children and the elderly, with Garifuna regularly spoken only by older people. The culture lives on, however: although virtually all the villagers are Catholics, the village boasts the country's largest *dabuyaba* (a Garifuna temple, built of poles with a thatched roof). It's occasionally used for *dugu* rites, when family members honour the spirits of their ancestors. Preparation takes many months and the **ceremonies** – comprising prayers, drumming, singing, dancing and offerings of food – last four days.

The only accommodation here is at the simple TEA guesthouse (see box, p.219). Several jungle trails can be explored on foot or horseback, and local **guides** can show you excellent birding spots; check with village chairman Dr. Joseph Palacio.

MAYA VILLAGE GUESTHOUSES AND HOMESTAYS

Five Mopan or Kekchí Maya villages in Toledo – Laguna, San Antonio, Santa Elena, San José and San Miguel – have built basic but clean eight-bed **guesthouses**, which accommodate overnight guests for Bz$22 per person. Visitors can **eat** with local families for Bz$8–10 per meal. Each location has its own attraction, be it a cave, waterfall, river or ruin, and offers **activities** such as guided walks or tours (Bz$10–25) or rental kayaks (Bz$10/half day, Bz$15/full day). In a further five villages – Barranco, Blue Creek, Medina Bank, Pueblo Viejo and San Pedro Columbia – a similar range of activities is available, but there's no overnight accommodation. The programme is organized by the **Toledo Ecotourism Association**, or **TEA** (☎629 4280, ⓦ teabelize.org). Look out for its logo as you travel around; it's extremely unusual for the guesthouses to be booked up so in most cases you can just show up in the village and stay. TEA also arranges packages, including accommodation plus all meals and activities, for Bz$100 per person per day, while its website details **bus timetables** for the villages.

In addition, the homestay program run by **Maguacate Belize** (US$11/person/night; ☎633 9554, ⓔ cucullouis@gmail.com), enables visitors to stay with a Mopan or Kekchí Maya family. It's an excellent way to experience Maya life and culture without feeling like an intruder: guests participate in family activities (perhaps working the milpa or cooking tortillas and the like), learn about medicinal plants and ancient myths, bathe in the creek, eat typical meals (US$3.50 per meal) and sleep in a hammock or on a foam mattress in the same building as family members. Local bus transport is available from and to Punta Gorda (1 daily Mon, Wed, Fri & Sat).

Barranco was also the birthplace of celebrated musician **Andy Palacio** (see p.255), who was buried here following his sudden death in 2008.

ACCOMMODATION INLAND TOLEDO

BIG FALLS

The Lodge at Big Falls ☏ 732 4444, ⓦ thelodgeatbigfalls .com. Smart, comfortable and very spacious thatched *cabañas*, set in 29 landscaped and flower-filled acres on a meandering bend of the Río Grande. All are fully screened, with tiled floors, ceiling fans, roomy bathrooms, hardwood furniture and a large deck with hammocks; three have a/c and kitchenettes. Two hundred species of birds have been recorded here, and butterflies are everywhere along the trails by the riverbank; kayaks and inner tubes also available – put in at San Miguel, 5 miles upstream, for a wonderful float back home. Fresh juices from the citrus orchard are served in the restaurant, or at an outdoor grill by the swimming pool, and activities are available. Rates do not include meals, at US$66 per person per day. US$221

SAN MIGUEL

Back-a-Bush Just off the road to Lubaantun ☏ 631 1731, ⓦ back-a-bush.com. Very simple rooms in a working organic farm (loofah, aloe vera, fruits and vegetables) and garden compound, run by friendly Dutch owner, long-time resident Elsbeth. As well as a dorm holding six bunks, there's also one private room with its own shower (US$30), a more comfortable cabin (US$80) and space for camping. Meals (with veggie options) are also available at US$5–7.50. Cash only. Camping US$5, dorms US$12.50

SAN PEDRO COLUMBIA

Maya Mountain Research Farm 2 miles upriver from San Pedro Columbia ☏ 630 4386, ⓦ mmrfbz.org. Concealed within the folds of the namesake mountains, this unique set-up offers permaculture students, volunteers and anyone with a taste for wilderness to fall off the grid. Getting here is an adventure in itself – with the help of a guide from San Pedro Columbia, you either hike or paddle in on a canoe. The rustic wooden cabins barely interfere with the engulfing jungle cacao farm, which borders a pristine stretch of the Río Grande, and meals are cooked on a wood-fired stove and shared in a large *palapa*; wi-fi is available, and other activities include hiking – Lubaantun is less than 2 miles away – tubing, and exploring unexcavated ruins. They prefer visitors to stay for at least a week. Per person per day, three meals included US$50

SAN ANTONIO

★**Farm Inn** Santa Cruz Rd, 2 miles west of San Antonio ☏ 732 4781, ⓦ thefarminnbelize.com. Very comfortable accommodation on a lush, working chocolate farm. All the six guest rooms are en suite, with hardwood floors and hammocks on open decks; two hold kitchenettes (but note that there's no a/c, and the fans only run when generators are on). The property hosts four thousand cacao trees, and the owners also grow coffee (a thousand bushes), fruit and medicinal plants; the 52-acre site also holds creeks and several hiking trails. The on-site bar/restaurant is open for all meals daily (reservations required for dinner), and usually serves one main dish, such as African *potjie* (one-pot stew) or bbq. Most guests drive, but pick-ups can be arranged. Rates include breakfast. US$95

BLUE CREEK

Blue Creek Rainforest Lodge ☏ 580 2000, in the US ☏ 1508 655 1461, ⓦ izebelize.com. This rainforest lodge, set beside a lovely turquoise pool, a 10min walk along the right-hand bank upriver from Blue Creek and not far from Hokeb Ha cave, is the sister property of the IZE Belize resort on South Water Caye (see p.186), and doubles as an ecology study centre. The lodge itself has a large river-view deck, while accommodation is in wooden cabins, set among the trees, with electricity and porches, and a couple of two-bedroom treehouses. Per person per day, three meals and two activities included US$120

SUN CREEK

★**Sun Creek Lodge** Mile 12 Southern Hwy, 2 miles south of the Dump junction ☏ 607 3636, ⓦ facebook .com/Suncreeklodge. A naturalist's paradise, providing necessary modern conveniences while maintaining a rustic feel. The four beautiful thatched *cabañas* all come with electricity; two have double beds and private bathrooms, and there's a grander villa with separate living room (US$95). The innovative jungle bucket showers make you feel as though you're standing under a waterfall. Belizean/German owner Bruno knows Toledo District and the entire country exceptionally well and runs International Belize Tourism Marketing, which offers tours and jeep rental (from US$60/day). Rates include breakfast. US$60

JACINTOVILLE

Chaab'il B'e Lodge and Casitas Barranco Rd ☏ 677 9921, ⓦ chaabilbe.com. On the bank of beautiful Jacinto Creek, 300yd off the highway, this relaxing retreat offers a/c comfort in four spacious, tiled, en-suite rooms with soft and earthy colours (and flat screen TVs), or in three thatched *casitas* (with fans), all surrounded by three acres of orchid-laden gardens (and curious howler monkeys). The wonderful fully screened thatched restaurant serves excellent meals (lunch US$10, dinner US$25), and features a great view. The place is very popular with birders, with scores of species seen along its forested trails, while the natural, rock-lined pool in the creek is perfect for a refreshing dip. Rates include breakfast. $\underline{\text{US\$100}}$

SAN FELIPE
★**Cotton Tree Lodge** Moho River ☎ 670 0557, in the US ☎ 1212 529 8622, ⊛ cottontreelodge.com. Impressive riverside property, accessible by road from San Felipe village, and holding eleven smart thatched *cabañas* (US\$207) set on stilts and connected by a raised boardwalk lined with cacao and mango trees, as well as five individual rooms. All have a chic feel while offering varying levels of comfort; more expensive units have a veranda with hammocks, while the honeymoon suite (US\$273) has a

jacuzzi and plunge slide straight into the river. The giant ten-sided *palapa*-restaurant flaunts imaginative local artwork, while the location is ideal for exploring sites inland, kayaking the river or sunset boat cruises straight out to the cayes. Chocolate tours are a speciality. Rates shown here do not include meals, which total US\$52 per person per day; packages with meals and tours are available. $\underline{\text{US\$196}}$

Ixcacao Barranco Rd ☎ 742 4050, ⊛ ixcacaomaya belizeanchocolate.com. Simple accommodation in a sixteen-bunk dormitory on a very friendly working chocolate farm (see p.219), with electricity, ceiling fan, mosquito net and shared shower room. Rates include chocolate-making, breakfast and dinner. $\underline{\text{US\$60}}$

EATING

BIG FALLS
★**Coleman's Café** Southern Hwy ☎ 630 4069, ⊛ facebook.com/colemanscafe. The ideal place for a break as you tour inland Toledo, this friendly café, just off the highway, serves delicious Belizean (or rather, Belizean-East Indian) food. Lunch is a one-visit self-serve buffet for Bz\$15, while a full dinner costs Bz\$10 for chicken, Bz\$20 for fish or

shrimp, with wine available. Daily 10.30am–4.30pm.

BLUE CREEK
Sho's Local Restaurant ☎ 630 4267. Simple restaurant at the entrance to Blue Creek village, where Delphina Sho serves basic, tasty Belizean staples and local dishes for less than Bz\$10. Mon–Sat 7am–8pm.

GREEN IGUANA

Contexts

History

Belize is the youngest nation in Central America, only gaining independence from Britain in 1981, and its history has been markedly different from the surrounding republics since at least the mid-seventeenth century. Although the whole region was (to a greater or lesser degree) colonized by Spain in the sixteenth century, it was the entanglement with Britain that gave Belize its present cultural, social and political structures.

Delving far back into the past, prior to the advent of Maya civilization, scattered archeological remains and a handful of written texts provide very little concrete knowledge, and excavations could throw up new information at any time. It's generally thought that the region's first human inhabitants were **Stone Age hunter-gatherers** who crossed the Bering land bridge from Asia, beginning probably around 25,000 BC. They spread rapidly southwards, developing the **Clovis** culture (named after stone projectile points found in New Mexico) at least 11,000 years ago, and subsisted on hunting large mammals like mammoths, mastodons, deer and horses. By 9000 years ago, scarcity of game due to climatic change forced a different way of life, with more intensive use of plants. This **Archaic** period saw the cultivation of peppers, squash, beans and, importantly, maize, with more settled societies enabling an identifiable culture – broadly known as **Proto-Maya**. Archeological evidence suggests Archaic sequences in Belize until later than 2000 BC, and an early Proto-Maya language was also in use.

Belize is thought to have been an area of savannahs and broad-leaved woodland throughout this time, with tropical forests not appearing until the Classic period. The country was part of a vast region known to archeologists as **Mesoamerica**, stretching from north-central Mexico to El Salvador and Honduras. The cultures that developed throughout the region shared several characteristics, including a complex calendar, hieroglyphic writing, a similar cosmology and religion and a highly organized, stratified society – possibly having a common origin in the **Olmec** civilization of southern Mexico. For Belize, the most important group were the **Maya**, whose culture emerged here as early as 2500 BC and whose cities were at the height of their power between 250 and 900 AD.

The Maya in Belize

The development of the culture recognized as distinctly Maya began in what's known as the **Preclassic** (or Formative) period, from 2000 BC to 250 AD. The phase is subdivided into Early, Middle and Late periods, with boundaries not marked by exact dates, but understood as cultural and technological milestones; for example, when advances were made in architecture or administration. Current excavations appear to be pushing back the date when the earliest breakthroughs were made.

The **Early Preclassic** (roughly 2000 BC–1000 BC) marks the beginning of agriculture, notably the annual cutting and burning of forest in order to plant maize. Food needs

25,000 BC	10,000 BC	7500 BC
First waves of nomadic Paleo-Indian hunters from Siberia to the Americas	Stone tools indicative of Clovis culture found throughout North and Central America	Archaic period: Beginnings of agricultural communities throughout Mesoamerica; maize and other crops cultivated

were supplemented by hunting, fishing and foraging, and though there's no evidence of structures larger than dwellings during the period, ceramics were produced; pottery found at **Cuello**, near Orange Walk, dates from around 1000 BC – among the earliest in the Maya lowlands. Elsewhere in Mesoamerica, the emergence of the great Olmec civilization was to have a far-reaching impact, originating in the coastal plain of Veracruz. Often regarded as the true ancestors of Maya culture, the Olmecs developed a complex polytheistic religion, a writing system and a calendar known as the "long count", later adopted by the Maya.

By the **Middle Preclassic** (1000 BC–300 BC) there was a substantial increase in population – evidence of numerous settlements can be found from southern Guatemala to northern Yucatán, including almost all of Belize, in particular the main river valleys. All the settlements produced Mamóm-style red or orange monochrome pottery and stone metates for grinding corn, and it's thought that a common Maya language was spoken throughout the area. A universal belief system, practised from a very early date, may have provided the stimulus and social cohesion to build bigger towns. As in all early agricultural communities, food surpluses would have eventually freed some people to become seers, priests and astronomers. By 750 BC Nakbé, in northern Petén, was a large city, perhaps the first one in the Maya world, evidence that the Maya had progressed far beyond a simple peasant society.

The explosion in Maya architecture, culture and population came in the **Late Preclassic** (300 BC–250 AD), when **Chicanel culture** dominated the Maya world. The famous Maya corbelled arch (without a keystone, but consisting of two sides, each with stones overlapping until they eventually met, thus able to span only a narrow gap) was developed, and hugely ambitious large pyramids with elaborate temples were built at Tikal, El Mirador and Río Azul in Petén. In northern Belize, Cuello, Nohmul, Lamanai and Cerros were the great centres, all featuring major examples of public architecture. Lamanai and Cerros controlled trade routes right through the Classic and into the Postclassic periods. The Belize River valley was fully settled, with local centres such as Cahal Pech, Pacbitún and El Pilar consolidating their power.

The question of what sparked this phase of rapid development is a subject of much debate. Most archeologists agree that the catalyst was the Olmec culture, which the Maya adopted and adapted, developing complex administrative mechanisms to feed and control the growing population. A hierarchical structure evolved, with ultimate military and spiritual power vested in Maya kings, who established ruling dynasties and communicated with the gods by spilling their own blood at propitious festivals.

Building the Maya cities

The start of the greatest phase of Maya achievement, the **Early Classic** period (250 AD–600 AD), is marked by the introduction of both the long count calendar and a recognizable form of writing, which took place before the fourth century AD. The cultural influence of the Olmecs was replaced by that of **Teotihuacán**, which dominated central Mexico during the early Classic period. Armed merchants spread the power of Teotihuacán as far as Yucatán, Petén and Belize, bringing new styles of ceramics and alternative religious beliefs. While complete subjugation remained unlikely, in around 400 AD the overwhelming power of Teotihuacán did radically alter Maya life: in Petén, **Tikal**'s rise was helped by close links with Teotihuacán, and

4500 BC	**2000 BC–250 AD**	**250 AD**
Proto-Maya period: First Mayan-speaking groups settle in western Guatemala	Preclassic or Formative period: Maya begin building centres which develop into great cities, including Lamanai and Cahal Pech	Classic period: Maya culture reaches its height, with use of long count calendar; Caracol is Belize's largest Maya city

both cities prospered greatly; Tikal has a stela (a freestanding carved monument) depicting a Tikal lord on one side and a warrior from Teotihuacán on the other.

Most of the now ruined cities that we see today were built during the Classic period, almost always over earlier structures. Elaborately carved stelae, bearing dates and emblem-glyphs, tell of actual events in rulers' lives – battles, marriages, dynastic succession and so on. The deciphering of these dates has provided confirmation (or otherwise) of archeological evidence and offers major insights. Made up of independent city-states, the Maya region was bound together by religion, culture and sophisticated trade. The cities jostled for power and influence, occasionally erupting into warfare, with three or four main centres dominating through a process of alliances. **Calakmul**, in Campeche, Mexico, and Tikal were the nearest of these "superstates" to Belize, and in 562 AD an alliance of Calakmul and Caracol, in southern Cayo District, defeated Tikal, as shown by an inscription on Altar 21 at Caracol. Other detailed carvings on wooden lintels and stone monuments at the site depict costumed lords trampling on bound captives. Victory of the subordinate state over the dominant regional power may well have caused the major upheaval that followed.

The collapse of Teotihuacán in the seventh century caused shock waves throughout the civilizations of Mesoamerica in what is known as the **Middle Classic Hiatus**. No stelae were erected in the Maya cities, and many existing monuments were defaced. Warfare raged as rival lords strove to win political power in the dominant Maya centres. But as new kings established dynasties, free of Teotihuacán's political control, Maya cities flourished as never before. Architecture, astronomy and art reached degrees of sophistication unequalled by any other pre-Columbian society. Many centres were larger than their contemporary Western European counterparts, then in their "Dark Ages": Caracol had an estimated 150,000 people.

The prosperity and grandeur of the **Late Classic period** (600 AD–850 AD) reached all across the Maya lands: from Bonampak and Palenque in the west, to Calakmul and Uxmal in the north, Altun Ha and Cerros in the east, and Copán and Quiriguá in the south. Masterpieces of painted pottery and carved jade (the Maya's most precious material) were crafted, often to be used as funerary offerings, while exquisite works of shell, bone and (rarely) marble also appeared. Temples were painted in brilliant colours, and though most pigments have faded, enough vestiges remain to vividly reconstruct the ancient cities.

Collapse of the Classic Maya

Though it was abrupt when the end came for each Maya centre, it took around a century (**Terminal Classic**; 800 AD–c.1000 AD) for Classic Maya civilization to be extinguished in Belize. By 750 AD alliances and trade links were breaking down, warfare increased and stelae were carved less frequently. The sacking of Dos Pilas, in the Petexbatún region of southwest Petén, by nearby Tamandarito in 761 AD is regarded as the first phase of the **Classic Maya collapse**. Strife and disorder spread throughout Mesoamerica, cities became depopulated, and new construction ceased over much of Belize by 830 AD. Bonampak, in Chiapas, was abandoned before its famous murals could be completed, and many of the great sites along the River Usumacinta (now the border between Guatemala and Mexico) were occupied by militaristic outsiders.

The decline and subsequent collapse of Classic Maya civilization had several probable causes. Strong evidence suggests that a prolonged drought in central Yucatán caused

800 AD	987 AD	1000 AD
Terminal Classic period: Decline of Classic Maya civilization, but some sites, notably Lamanai, survive	Yucatán sites show evidence of Toltec culture, which is grafted onto Maya culture, probably extending into Belize	Early Postclassic period: Toltec domination of the Guatemalan highlands

competition for scarce resources, with the effects rippling outwards. The massive increase in population may have put intolerable pressure on food production, ultimately exhausting the soil. But also, the growth and demands of an unproductive elite may well have led to a peasant revolt, leading to the abandonment of city life. By the tenth century, the Maya had largely abandoned their central cities and most of those that remained were reduced to a primitive state.

Not all Maya cities were deserted, however: many in northern Belize survived and even prospered, with Lamanai and others remaining occupied throughout the **Postclassic period** (c.900 AD–1540 AD). The Yucatán peninsula escaped the worst of the depopulation, and came under the influence (possibly by outright conquest) of the militaristic **Toltecs**, who came from central Mexico in 987 AD, creating a hybrid of Classic Maya culture.

From around 900 AD to the time of the Spanish Conquest the Yucatán peninsula and northern Belize consisted of over a dozen rival provinces, bound up in a cycle of competition and conflict. Northern Belize was part of the Maya province of **Chactemal** (later known as Chetumal), covering an area from around Maskall, near the site of Altun Ha, to Laguna Bacalar in southern Quintana Roo in Mexico, and with Santa Rita, near Corozal, as its likely capital. Chetumal was a wealthy province, producing cacao and honey; trade, alliances and wars kept it in contact with surrounding Maya states up to and beyond the Spanish conquest of Aztec Mexico. Further south, thick forests and the ridges of the Maya Mountains intruded, becoming known as **Dzuluinicob** to the Maya of Chetumal – "land of foreigners" – whose capital was Tipú, located at present-day Negroman on the Macal River. Here, the Maya controlled the upper Belize River valley, strenuously resisting attempts by the Spanish to subdue and convert them.

Arrival of the Europeans

The general assumption that Belize was practically deserted by the time Europeans arrived is now widely discredited. In 1500 AD the native population in the area which was to become Belize is estimated to have been around two hundred thousand – almost as high as it is today – and the Maya towns and provinces were still vigorously independent. **Spanish** sailors Pinzón and de Solis first set eyes on the mainland of Belize in the early sixteenth century, though a landing didn't occur until 1511, when a small group of shipwrecked Spanish sailors reached land on the southern coast of Yucatán: five were immediately sacrificed and the others became slaves. At least one of the slaves must have escaped and regained contact with his fellow countrymen, because when **Cortés** reached Cozumel in 1519 he knew of the existence of two other enslaved survivors, and sent gifts for their release. Geronimo de Aguilar immediately joined Cortés, but the other survivor, **Gonzalo Guerrero**, refused: Guerrero had married the daughter of Na Chan Kan, the chief of Chactemal, and preferred life among his former captors. Due to his knowledge of Spanish tactics he became a crucial military adviser to the Maya in their subsequent resistance to Spanish domination: the archeologist Eric Thompson calls him the first European to make Belize his home.

The Spanish made few reports of their early contact with the Maya in Belize, probably because they heard no stories of gold – their overriding obsession. In 1525 Cortés himself probably passed through southern Belize on his epic march from

1250	1511	1521
Rivalry and trade among the city-states of Petén, Yucatán and Belize. New, competitive power structures formed along trade routes	First Spanish contact with Maya in Yucatán; Spanish sailors are captured	Aztec capital Tenochtitlán falls to Spanish troops commanded by Cortés

Veracruz in Mexico to punish a rebellious subordinate in San Gil de Buena Vista, near the mouth of the Río Dulce on the Bay of Honduras. One hundred and forty Spanish soldiers and three thousand Indians marched across the Maya heartland, which still contained many thriving towns and cities. At Tayasal on Lake Petén Itzá, he was welcomed by Can Ek, chief of the Itzá, who had heard of Cortés's cruelty in conquering Mexico and decided not to oppose him. At the valley of the Sarstoon River, the present boundary with Guatemala, Cortés pacified rebels before sailing north to Mexico, apparently without realizing that Yucatán was not an island.

Attempted conquest and Maya resistance

For the Spanish it proved relatively simple to capture and kill the "living god" leaders of such highly organized empires as the Aztecs and Incas. However, the Maya provinces of present-day Yucatán and Belize were not united, and their rulers were accustomed to dealing with enemies by fighting or by forming temporary alliances – one reason why the Spanish found this region so difficult to subdue.

In 1528 **Francisco de Montejo**, granted permission by the Spanish Crown to colonize the "islands" of Cozumel and Yucatán, established a settlement called Salamanca on the mainland coast south of Cozumel, and his lieutenant, **Alonso Dávila**, led an expedition south. Neither was successful: both groups encountered hostile Maya, and Dávila was forced to turn away from Chetumal by Maya under the command of Gonzalo Guerrero. A second attempt by Dávila in 1531 was marginally more successful but nevertheless short-lived. On the advice of Guerrero – who realized they could not defeat the Spanish outright – the Maya abandoned Chetumal. Dávila occupied the town, renaming it **Villa Real**, but the Maya continually harassed his troops and they were driven out eighteen months later, fleeing south along the coast of Belize to Omoa in Honduras. For some years after, the Maya in Belize remained free from Spanish interference; Chetumal regained its trading links and became a powerful military ally, sending fifty war canoes to Omoa in 1542 to assist the local chief fighting the Spanish.

Montejo's vision of ruling a vast province of the Spanish empire comprising Yucatán, Belize and Honduras was not to be fulfilled, though his son, Montejo the Younger did complete the conquest of Yucatán, establishing a capital at Mérida in 1542. Late the following year, however, **Gaspar Pacheco**, his son Melchor and nephew Alonso began another chapter in the sickeningly familiar tale of Spanish atrocities, advancing on Chetumal, destroying crops and food stores and ruthlessly slaughtering the inhabitants. By 1544 the Pachecos had founded a town on Lake Bacalar, and claimed *encomienda* (tribute) from villages surrounding Chetumal. To the south, however, Tipú maintained alliances with other Maya provinces and continued in armed resistance.

During the second half of the sixteenth century missions were established, including one at Lamanai in 1570, and the Spanish, with difficulty, strengthened their hold over northern Belize. In 1618, Spanish priests Fuensalida and Orbita visited **Tipú**, on the Macal River, and punished the Maya for worshipping "idols". Resentment was always present, however, and the Maya burnt the church in defiance, before boiling over into total rebellion in 1638, which forced Spain to abandon Chetumal and Tipú completely and more or less permanently.

In the mid-seventeenth century the nearest permanent Spanish settlements to Belize were Salamanca de Bacalar in southern Yucatán and Lago de Izabal in Guatemala.

1528 & 1531	1543 & 1544	1570
Alonso Dávila attempts to capture and settle at Chetumal	Gaspar and Melchor Pacheco brutally conquer southern Yucatán and northern Belize	Spanish mission established at Lamanai; eight others built in northern Belize

Records are scarce, but it seems the Maya of Belize were under some form of Spanish influence even if not under direct rule: perhaps the determination of Maya resistance deterred Spain from full colonization; or perhaps the Maya fled to inaccessible forests to retain their independence. Repeated **expeditions** were nonetheless mounted by Spanish friars in an attempt to bring the heathen Maya of Tipú into the fold of the Catholic Church, though these were never more than partially successful.

In 1695 a Spanish mission met leaders of the Itzá to discuss the **surrender of the Itzá**. The negotiations were fruitless, and in 1697 Spanish troops attacked Tayasal, the Itzá capital on Lake Petén Itzá (near modern Flores). At Tipú, the struggle was to continue with simmering resentment until 1707, when the population was forcibly removed to Lake Petén Itzá. This cruel act effectively ended Spanish attempts to settle the west of Belize, as without labourers it would be impossible to establish a successful colony.

In the late seventeenth century Bacalar was abandoned after years of **Maya and pirate attacks**. Spain's forces were simply too stretched to secure the vast (and relatively gold-free) territory from Campeche to Nicaragua. British territorial ambitions now focused on the Caribbean, too, resulting in continuous conflict. The capture of Jamaica in 1655, after 150 years of Spanish rule, gave England a base from which it could harass Spanish shipping.

British incursions

The failure of the Spanish to dominate southern Yucatán allowed British **buccaneers** (or pirates) preying on Spanish treasure fleets to find refuge along the coastline, and in turn – much later – led to Guatemala's claim to British Honduras and refusal to recognize Belize's independence.

Some of the great Elizabethan sailors, such as Raleigh, Hawkins and Drake are known to have been in the Bay of Honduras, and they may have sought refuge on the coast of Belize after raids on Spanish ships, though there are no records to prove any kind of settlement or temporary camp until the 1700s. Certainly, there was no attempt by Britain to colonize Belize as it was doing elsewhere in the Caribbean, instead being content to let pirates like Blackbeard roam the region; he is thought to have camped on the Turneffe Atoll around 1718. Britain also competed with **France** and the **Netherlands** to establish a foothold in the Caribbean, each one setting up companies to equip privateers – really government-sanctioned pirates – to raid Spanish treasure fleets. In the periodic absences of bounty, they would plunder piles of **logwood**, ready cut and awaiting shipment to Spain. Hard and extremely heavy, it was worth £90–110 a ton back in Britain, where it helped to build up the textile industry as a black, red and grey dye for woollens. Such an abundance of convertible wealth attracted numerous British buccaneers, possibly as early as 1638, who settled along the Spanish Caribbean coastline, including at the mouth of the Belize River.

The various treaties signed between Britain and Spain from the late seventeenth to the mid-eighteenth century, attempted first to outlaw the buccaneers, but eventually allowed the British to establish logwood camps along the rivers in northern Belize. This was never intended to legitimize permanent British settlement of perceived Spanish imperial territory, thus the camps periodically came under attack. But the attention of European powers rarely rested long upon the humid and insect-ridden swamps where the logwood cutters, who were becoming known as **Baymen**, worked and lived. The British

1638	1660	1697
The Maya rebel, forcing Spanish to abandon Tipú on the Macal River and Chetumal	British pirate Bartholomew Sharpe harvests logwood in Belize, and British buccaneers and Baymen settle the coast	Conquest by Spanish troops of the Itzá Maya of Noh Petén (present-day Flores), last independent Maya kingdom

THE LIFE OF A BAYMAN

Life in the **logwood camps** was uncomfortable. Though the wood was mainly cut in the dry season, it was too heavy to float, and the men had to build rafts to float it down to the river mouth in the rainy season, where it awaited shipment. The **Baymen** lived in rough huts thatched with palm leaves (known as "Bay leaf" – still used today in tourist *cabañas*), and survived on provisions brought from Jamaica. These ships also brought rum, which the Baymen drank with relish. An English merchant (writing in 1726) reported: "Rum Punch is their Drink, which they'll sometimes sit for several Days…for while the Liquor is moving they don't care to leave it." Though many of the woodcutters "voluntarily" gave up buccaneering, raiding of Spanish ships still occurred throughout the seventeenth century, punished by Spain whenever it had the opportunity.

government, while profiting from the trade in logwood, preferred to avoid the question of whether or not the Baymen were British subjects and left them to their own devices.

As gangs of woodcutters advanced further into the forests in search of valuable **mahogany** (which overtook logwood as the principal export by the 1760s) for furniture making, they came into contact with the Maya. Although they had no wish to colonize or convert them, records show that early buccaneers took Maya captives to trade in the slave markets of Jamaica, and they also enslaved people to work in Belize. The Maya were so weakened by disease and depopulation that they only offered limited resistance.

Spanish attacks

There were Spanish attacks throughout the eighteenth century, with the Baymen driven out on several occasions. Increasingly though, Britain – at war with both Spain and France during the period 1739 to 1748 – began to admit a measure of responsibility for the protection of the settlers. In 1746, in response to requests, the governor of Jamaica sent troops to aid the Baymen, but this didn't stop the Spanish decimating the settlement in both 1747 and 1754. The **Paris Peace Treaty** of 1763 allowed the British to cut logwood, but since it did not define boundaries the governor of Yucatán sent troops from Bacalar to ensure that the cutters confined themselves to the Belize River. In 1765 Admiral Burnaby, the British commander-in-chief at Jamaica, visited Belize to ensure that the provisions of the treaty were upheld, finding them "in a state of Anarchy and Confusion". The admiral, recognizing that the Baymen would benefit from some form of regulation, drew up a simple set of laws concerning the maintenance of justice in what was a remote and uncouth area where the British government was only reluctantly involved. Known as **Burnaby's Code**, it gave authority to a bench of magistrates, supported by a jury, to hold quarterly courts with the power to impose fines. The Baymen attached a grand importance to the Code (though only sporadically obeyed it), and voted to increase its scope a year later.

A century of antagonism, boundary disputes and mutual suspicion between the Spanish and the Baymen meant that relations were never secure. The Spanish feared raids on their ships, while the Baymen fostered a spirit of defiance in the face of Spanish reprisals, leading to the realization that British rule was preferable – as long as they could choose which of its institutions to accept. Their tenure was nonetheless still very uncertain: in 1779 Spain (allied with France in the American War of Independence) sent a fleet and captured all the inhabitants of St George's Caye – the capital of the

1718	**1724**	**1746**
Famous pirate Blackbeard roams the coast and camps on Turneffe Atoll	First record of African slaves in Belize; they cut logwood and do domestic and farm work	Tensions simmer between Baymen and Spanish; Jamaica sends troops to aid Baymen, but Spanish decimate Baymen settlement in 1747

THE BATTLE OF ST GEORGE'S CAYE

September 10 is a national holiday in Belize, marking the date of one of the country's defining victories: the **Battle of St George's Caye**. This was the final showdown between the waning Spanish Empire and the Bay settlers, who were supported by a British warship and troops. The battle came as a result of the outbreak of war between Britain and Spain in 1796. Field Marshal **Arthur O'Neil**, an Irishman and the captain general of Yucatán (named **Don Arturo** by the Spanish), assembled ships and troops, determined to drive out the British settlers and this time to occupy Belize. Lord Balcarres, the governor of Jamaica, despatched **Lieutenant Colonel Barrow** to command the settlers in the event of hostilities. At a vital Public Meeting held on June 1, 1797, the Baymen decided by 65 votes to 51 to defend the settlement rather than evacuate. A few companies of troops were sent from Jamaica, and slaves were released and armed. The sloop **HMS Merlin**, under the command of Captain John Moss, was stationed in the Bay, local vessels were armed, gun rafts were built and an attack was expected at any time. Throughout the next year the mood of the defenders vacillated between aggression and despair, preparing for war with scant resources under the martial law supervision of Lieutenant Colonel Barrow.

The **Spanish fleet**, reported to consist of 32 vessels, including sixteen heavily armed men-of-war and two thousand troops, arrived just north of St George's Caye in early September 1798. On September 3 and 4 several of the Spanish warships attempted to force a passage over Montego Caye Shoals, between Long Caye and St George's Caye, but were repulsed by the Baymen's sloops. Stakes put down by the Spanish to mark the channels were removed by the defenders, who knew these waters well. Barrow and Moss correctly guessed that the Spanish would then try to seize St George's Caye. The *Merlin* and part of the Baymen's tiny fleet sailed there on the evening of September 5, securing it just as twelve Spanish warships were attempting to do the same.

The next few days passed anxiously: the Spanish with their massive firepower severely restricted by the shallow water; and the Baymen with their small but highly manoeuvrable fleet awaiting attack – and slaves apparently at least as eager to fight the Spanish as their masters were. On the morning of **September 10, 1798**, fourteen large Spanish ships sailed to within 1.5 miles of St George's Caye, keeping to the deep water to the east, and began firing. Captain Moss held his fire – the Spanish broadsides were falling short. At 1.30pm he gave the order to attack. Guns blazing, the *Merlin* and the Baymen's fleet swept forward, wreaking havoc among the heavy and crowded Spanish ships. The Spanish fleet, already weakened by desertions and yellow fever, suffered heavy losses and fled in disorder to Caye Chapel. There they remained for five days to bury their dead, and on the morning of September 16 they sailed for Bacalar, still harassed by the Baymen.

Though a victory was won against overwhelming odds, the Battle of St George's Caye was not by itself decisive as no one in Belize could be sure that the Spanish would not return. The territory remained as a timber-cutting settlement, but not within the British Empire. In practical terms, the power of the Spanish was lessening while that of the British was expanding, but in Belize the slaves were still slaves, and though they had fought valiantly, their owners expected them to go back to cutting mahogany. Indeed controversy still exists in Belize over the fact that the battle was fought between two European powers to establish rule, while also enabling slave owners to claim that the slaves were willing to fight on behalf of their masters. Whatever its legacy, 1798 was the last point at which Spain attempted to gain control; Britain gradually assumed a greater role in the government of Belize.

1786	**1798**	**1832**
In London, the Convention of Loggers is drawn up, which permits settlers to cut mahogany, though Spain still claims sovereignty	Battle of St George's Caye, between British-backed Baymen and Spanish troops; the scrappy Baymen are victors	The Garifuna from Honduras settle in southern Belize, in what is today Dangriga

Baymen – imprisoning them in Mérida and Havana. The **Versailles Peace Treaty** (1783) did little to resolve matters, but a convention signed three years later allowed timber to be cut as far south as the Sibun River – also stipulating that no system of government could be established without approval from Madrid. True to their "turbulent and unsettled disposition", the Baymen ignored it, cutting wood where they pleased, and after 1791, the British governor of Jamaica also failed to add authority to the settlement.

Settlers and slaves

A report by a Spanish missionary in 1724 mentions the ownership of **slaves** by English settlers, and it's possible that Africans were brought in (from Jamaica and Bermuda) even before that time. The British population in the Bay of Honduras had never been more than a few hundred, their livelihoods dependent on the attitude of authorities in the adjacent Spanish colonies. In order to gain concessions from Spain favourable to the Belize settlement, Britain agreed to relinquish claims to the Mosquito Coast (a British protectorate along the coasts of Honduras and Nicaragua) in the **Convention of London** in 1786. Many aggrieved displaced inhabitants settled in Belize, and by 1790 the population reached 2900, of whom over 2100 were slaves.

The often held view that slavery in Belize was somehow less harsh than elsewhere is a misconception that may have arisen due to the differences between plantation slavery in the West Indies and United States and the mainly forest labour that Africans in Belize were required to perform. The myth has been skilfully manipulated by apologists for colonialism, who maintain that during the pivotal Battle of St George's Caye black people voluntarily fought "shoulder to shoulder" with their white masters, and thus preferred slavery over the freedom offered by the Spanish authorities to any slave who escaped. Although some slaves did fight alongside their masters in 1798, they also continued to run away: in 1813 fifteen slaves belonging to Thomas Paslow, one of the heroes of the battle, escaped "because of ill-treatment and starvation", their desperation evidence enough to refute the myth. Many escaped slaves ended up in maroon settlements such as the one at **Gales Point** (see p.65). Records of **slave revolts** from 1745 to 1820 are further indication that relations were not as amicable as some would like to believe.

Belizean whites were always vastly outnumbered by blacks, and they feared rebellion at least as much as Spanish attack. The biggest (and arguably most successful) revolt occurred in 1773 when six white men were murdered and at least eleven slaves escaped across the Hondo River, where they received asylum from the Spanish authorities. This was not a display of altruism – encouraging slaves to flee was calculated to weaken the British settlement's economy.

Ironically, it was the **Abolition Act of 1807** – which made it illegal for British subjects to continue with the African slave trade but not illegal to transport slaves from one British colony to another – that gave the settlers in Belize recognition as **British subjects**. Belize was clearly not a colony, and therefore slaves could not be transported from Jamaica. Superintendent Arthur, the British government's representative in Belize, decided that the settlers were British subjects and therefore forbidden to engage in the slave trade. The **Abolition Act of 1833** ended slavery throughout the British Empire, and contained a special clause to include Belize. The Act, however, did not end slavery immediately: "freed" Africans were to be called "apprentices", required to work for forty hours per week for free before being allowed to work for payment. This abuse

1833	1847	1854
Abolition Act of 1833: Slavery officially ends in British Empire, with a special clause to include Belize	The Caste War of Yucatán begins between the Spanish, Maya and mestizo, sending many refugees into Belize	An elected Legislative Assembly is formed, presided over by a British superintendent

---

SLAVERY IN BELIZE

The nature of **slavery** in Belize was very different from that on the sugar plantations. The cutting of mahogany involved small gangs working in the forest on their own or on a fairly harmonious level with an overseer. The slaves were armed, with firearms in some cases, to hunt for food and for protection against the Maya. Skills developed in searching for the trees, cutting them down and transporting them to the coast involved a position of trust that slave masters depended on for the continuation of their own way of life. **Manumission**, whereby a slave would purchase freedom or be freed as a bequest in a will, or simply a gift, was much more frequent in Belize than in the Caribbean islands – perhaps an indication of the greater informality of Belizean society. However, treatment was still harsh, with no protection offered by the law. Owners could inflict up to 39 lashes or imprisonment, and if a slave was hanged for rebellion the owner could be compensated for financial loss.

---

continued until full freedom in 1838. Despite inherent immorality in the institution of slavery, the Act provided for **compensation** to be paid to the owners for the loss of property, rather than to former slaves for their suffering – and, at £53 per slave, the compensation paid in Belize was higher than in any formal British colony.

The Colony of British Honduras

The consolidation of British logging interests in the eighteenth century and the grudging steps towards recognition from Spain led to a form of **British colonial government** gradually becoming established in Belize. The **Public Meeting**, beginning in the early 1700s, was the settlers' initial efforts at a rudimentary form of government, assuming greater importance until the 1730s when they elected magistrates – though only property-owning white men could vote. Free black men could vote at the Public Meeting after 1808, though their franchise was limited through higher property requirements than that of whites. **Burnaby's Code** in 1765 had enlarged the jurisdiction of the magistrates and allowed laws passed at the Meeting to be enforced by a British naval captain, though officers' reports invariably commented on the lamentable inability of settlers to keep their own laws.

Britain's early acceptance of some form of responsibility to the settlers led to the arrival in 1786 of the first **superintendent**, Captain Despard. The office appears to have been difficult, often facing an unsupportive Public Meeting, which wanted to run the settlement without "interference" from London. But gradually, the powers of the superintendent grew, while the election of magistrates ceased altogether in 1832, when they were appointed by the superintendent. In 1854 an elected **Legislative Assembly** was formed, establishing the beginnings of colonial-rule parliamentary democracy. The assembly began petitioning for recognition as a colony, arguing that the settlement was in fact, if not in law, already a British colony. Earl Grey, at the Colonial Office, supported the assembly, and Palmerston, the British prime minister, agreed. On May 12, 1862, the Belize settlements, with the boundaries that still exist today, became the **Colony of British Honduras**. In 1871 the British government established a **Crown colony** assembly in line with colonial policy throughout the West Indies, under the control of a governor appointed by the Colonial Office.

1859	1862	1871	1893
In vain attempt to settle border dispute, Britain and Guatemala sign Anglo-Guatemalan Treaty	On May 12, the Belize settlements, with boundaries that still exist today, become the Colony of British Honduras	Belize became a Crown colony, with a nominated Legislative Council	Mexico renounces its claim to Belizean territory and signs peace treaty

Mexican and Guatemalan claims

After the Battle of St George's Caye in 1798 Spain maintained its claim to Belize, and the **Treaty of Amiens** in 1802 required Britain to hand back territory captured during the war which was taken by Spain to include Belize. The Baymen, however, had no intention of leaving, and in the face of increasing difficulties throughout the Spanish Empire, and Britain's willingness to assist the settlers, Spain's claim became insupportable.

Although **Mexico's independence**, achieved in 1821 and followed two years later by the colonies in Central America, marked the effective end of the Spanish Empire, it didn't signal the end of external claims to Belize. The nineteenth century was filled with claims and counter-claims and treaties made and broken. Mexico's claim to the northern half of British Honduras as an extension of Yucatán was unacceptable to the British government, and after numerous diplomatic exchanges an **Anglo-Mexican Treaty** was ratified in 1897.

Guatemala's claim was the source of more belligerent disagreement with Britain, and there's no doubt that the British government shares much of the blame for the confusion. In treaty after treaty Britain regarded Belize as a territory under Spanish sovereignty, and long after Spain's expulsion, Britain maintained the fiction of Spanish sovereignty. Guatemala's assertion rested upon the acceptance in international law of *uti possidetis* – the right of a colony that successfully gains independence from a colonial authority to inherit the rights and territory of that authority. For this to be valid, however (even if Britain accepted its premise – which was doubtful), the entire territory of Belize would have had to have been under Spanish control in 1821. Since this was clearly not the case Britain asserted that Guatemala's claim was invalid.

In a vain attempt to reach a settlement, Britain and Guatemala signed the **Anglo-Guatemalan Treaty** in 1859: the interpretation of its various clauses has been the source of dispute ever since. The treaty, which in the British view settled the boundaries of Guatemala and Belize in their existing positions, was interpreted by Guatemala as a disguised treaty of cession of the territory – if Article 7 was not implemented. Under the provisions of this crucial article, Britain agreed to fund and build a road from Guatemala City to the Atlantic coast and in return Guatemala would drop its claim to Belize. If the road was not built then the territory would revert to Guatemala. Although a route was surveyed in 1859, Britain considered the estimated £100,000 cost of construction too high a price to pay to secure the territory of Belize, and the road was never built. The dispute was no nearer resolution when the settlement became British Honduras in 1862, and Article 7 remained a cause of rancour and disagreement for decades. Finally, in 1940, Guatemala repudiated the treaty on the grounds that the provisions of Article 7 were not fulfilled, and the new constitution of 1945 declared Belize – *Belice* in Spanish – to be the 23rd department of Guatemala. In 1948 Guatemala made the first of several **threats to invade** to "recover" the territory; Britain responded by sending cruisers and troops, the first of many military deployments over the next four decades. In hindsight, £100,000 in 1859 would have been a comparative bargain.

The Caste Wars of Yucatán

The terrible, bloody **Caste Wars** of Yucatán began with a riot by Maya troops at Valladolid in 1847. They sacked the town, killing whites, spreading terror and coming within a hair's breadth of capturing the peninsula's capital, Mérida, and throwing off

1919	1931	1950
Riots in Belize City by black servicemen spark the "black consciousness" movement	2500 people die in the deadliest hurricane in Belizean history, which makes landfall in Belize City on September 10, the country's national holiday	George Price and the People's United Party (PUP) launch a pro-independence movement, spurred by the country's severe economic decline

white rule completely. From 1848, as Mexico sent troops to put down the rebellion, thousands of Maya and mestizo **refugees** fled to Belize, increasing the population of Orange Walk and Corozal districts. The superintendent in Belize encouraged them to stay as they cleared land for sugar cane and brought much-needed farming skills.

The rebellious **Cruzob Maya** (taking their name from a sacred "talking cross") occupied a virtually independent territory in the east of Yucatán. They established their capital at Chan Santa Cruz ("little holy cross" – they were also known as the **Santa Cruz Maya**), the modern town of Felipe Carillo Puerto, north of Belize. At this time, the border was not clearly defined, and Belizean woodcutters came into conflict with the Santa Cruz Maya, who attacked mahogany camps and took prisoners for ransom. Alarm spread and eventually a compromise was reached, with the prisoners' release secured by a ransom, and further royalties paid for the right to cut wood in Maya territory. In fact British merchants profited by selling the Santa Cruz Maya arms, which provoked strong protests from Mexico.

In 1851, the **Icaiché Maya**, who were not in rebellion, were attacked by the Santa Cruz Maya, leading the Mexican government to propose an alliance between themselves and the Icaiché against the Santa Cruz. Icaiché leaders requested British help in their negotiations, and, wanting to enter Icaiché lands to log mahogany, the Belizean timber companies were also signatories to the treaty. In the **treaty of 1853** the Icaiché were granted virtual autonomy in return for recognizing the authority of Mexico, and the British were allowed to cut wood under licence in the Icaiché lands, in what was to become the northwest of Belize. British woodcutters viewed the agreement as a means to expand their territory at the expense of both the Icaiché and a weakened Mexico.

It was now the turn of the Icaiché to demand rent from the British loggers, which was only paid after further **Maya attacks**. British arms-trading with the Santa Cruz Maya incensed the Icaiché, and the flames were fanned further after an attack by the Santa Cruz Maya. After years of broken agreements and betrayal the Icaiché, supported by Mexico and led by **Marcos Canul**, attacked mahogany camps on the Río Bravo and the New River in 1866, and captured dozens of prisoners. The lieutenant governor declared martial law and sent for reinforcements from Jamaica. Raids and counter-raids continued, with Belizean villages sacked and colonial troops retaliating. Canul briefly occupied Corozal in 1870, and after a battle at Orange Walk in 1872 Corozal became a fortified British base. Although the violence diminished, the danger of Maya attacks wasn't over until 1882 when the Icaiché leader, Santiago Pech, met the governor in Belize City to recognize British jurisdiction in the northwest.

The twentieth century

By 1900 Belize was an integral, if minor, colony of the British Empire. The population in the census of 1901 was 37,500, of whom 28,500 were born there. Comfortably complacent, white property owners could foresee no change to their rule, with workers in the forests and estates predominantly black, the descendants of former slaves, known as "Creoles". Wages were low and strict controls were maintained, stifling worker organization and with the power to imprison labourers for missing a day's work.

Belizeans rushed to defend the "mother country" in **World War I**, but black troops were not permitted to fight a white enemy and were instead placed in labour battalions

1954	1961	1964
A general election is held, with an overwhelming win by the People's United Party (PUP), led by George Price	Hurricane Hattie strikes Belize, demolishing Belize City, killing hundreds and leaving thousands homeless	A new constitution gives Belize autonomy, ushering in a two-chamber parliament

in British-held Mesopotamia. On their return in 1919, humiliated and disillusioned, their bitterness exploded into violence, and the troops were joined by thousands of Belize City's population (including the police) in looting and rioting, an event which marked the onset of **black consciousness** and the beginnings of the independence movement. The ideas of **Marcus Garvey**, a phenomenally industrious and charismatic black Jamaican leader, and founder of the Universal Negro Improvement Association (UNIA), were already known in Belize – the government's ban on *Negro World*, the UNIA's magazine, contributed to the severity of the 1919 riot – and in 1920 a branch of the UNIA opened in Belize City. Garvey believed that the "Negro needs a nation and a country of his own" – a sentiment which found increasing support among all sectors of black society in Belize. Garvey himself visited Belize in 1921.

The status of workers had improved little over the previous century, and the Depression years of the 1930s brought extreme hardship, the disastrous hurricane of 1931 compounding the misery. The disaster prompted workers to organize in 1934 after an unemployment relief programme initiated by the governor was a dismal failure. **Antonio Soberanis** emerged as a leader, founding the Labourers and Unemployed Association (LUA), and holding regular meetings in the "Battlefield" – outside the colonial administration in Belize City. Soberanis was arrested in October 1934 while arranging bail for pickets at a sawmill who had been arrested. He was released a month later and meetings resumed, but the government passed restrictive laws, banning marches and increasing the governor's power to deal with disturbances.

World War II gave a boost to forestry and the opportunity for Belizeans to work abroad, though conditions for returning soldiers and workers were no better than they had been following World War I. In 1946 political power still lay with the tiny wealthy elite and with the governor, a Foreign Office appointee. The devaluation of the British Honduras dollar in 1949 caused even greater hardship. A new constitution emerged in 1951, and in 1954 a **general election** was held in which all literate adults over the age of 21 could vote. The election was won with an overwhelming majority by the **People's United Party** (PUP), led by **George Price**, ushering in a semblance of ministerial government. Belize became an **internally self-governing** colony in 1964, a step intended to lead to full independence after a relatively short time, as was the policy throughout the Caribbean. Until then, the British government, through the governor, remained responsible for defence, foreign affairs and security. The National Assembly became a bicameral system with an appointed Senate and an elected House of Representatives.

The delay in achieving independence was caused largely by the still unresolved **dispute with Guatemala**. Twice, in 1972 and 1977, Guatemala moved troops to the border and threatened to invade, but British reinforcements were an effective dissuasion. The situation remained tense, but international opinion moved in favour of Belizean independence.

Independence and the border dispute

The **UN resolution** of 1980 unequivocally endorsed Belize's right to self-determination, with all territory intact, before the next session. Further negotiations with Guatemala began but Belize's neighbour still insisted on territorial concessions. In March 1981, Britain, Guatemala and Belize released the "Heads of Agreement", which, they hoped, would result in a peaceful solution; accordingly, on September 21, 1981, Belize became

1971	**1973**	**1981**
The country's new capital is established in inland Belmopan	The country officially changes its name from British Honduras to Belize	On September 21, Belize becomes an independent country within the British Commonwealth

BELIZEAN ETHNIC GROUPS AND LANGUAGES

Belize today has a very mixed cultural background, with thirteen recognized **ethnic groups** – though the two largest, Creoles and mestizos, form 75 percent of the total population (currently around 330,000).

THE MESTIZOS

The largest ethnic group (around fifty percent) are **mestizos**, descended from Amerindians and early Spanish settlers, most of whom speak **Spanish** as their first language. Mainly located in the north, Ambergris Caye and Caye Caulker, with a sizeable population in Cayo, many of their ancestors fled to Belize during the Caste Wars of Yucatán (see p.233). During the 1980s, the arrival of an estimated forty thousand mestizos – most referring to themselves as **Ladinos** – added permanently to Belize's Spanish-speaking population. Causing the greatest shift in Belize's demography for centuries, most were fleeing conflicts and repression in El Salvador, Guatemala and Honduras. Those granted refugee status were settled in camps, mostly in Cayo, and allowed to farm small plots, though many, especially those undocumented, still provide convenient cheap labour. These immigrants are tolerated, if not exactly welcomed – few countries could absorb a sudden twenty percent population increase without a certain amount of turmoil – and many have integrated and learnt Kriol, if not English. Most original refugees have received Belizean nationality, and their children are Belizean citizens.

THE CREOLES

Creoles, descended from Africans brought to the West Indies as slaves and early white settlers, comprise just under a quarter of the population, though they make up a large proportion of Belize City, with scattered settlements elsewhere. **Kriol** (from "Creole") is the common language in Belize, a dialect of English similar to that spoken across the West Indies. Kriol underwent a recent formalization, with a more or less standardized written language. Controversy rages over whether or not Kriol should be taught in schools alongside English and become the country's official language.

an independent country within the British Commonwealth, with Queen Elizabeth II as head of state. British troops remained in Belize to ensure its territorial integrity.

The new government of Belize, formed by the PUP with George Price as premier, continued in power until 1984, when the United Democratic Party (UDP), led by **Manuel Esquivel**, won Belize's first general election. The new government encouraged private enterprise and foreign investment, and began a programme of neo-liberal economic reforms which privatized much of the public sector – unpopular changes that assured the PUP's return to power in 1989.

In 1988 Guatemala and Belize established a joint commission to work towards a "just and honourable" solution to the **border dispute**, and in 1990 Guatemala agreed in principle to accept the existing border. The only sticking point was the common boundary of the territorial waters between Belize and Honduras, making it theoretically possible for Guatemalan ships to be excluded from their own Caribbean ports. The PUP's response was to draft the **Maritime Areas Bill** in 1991, which allowed Guatemala access to the sea by restricting Belize's territory between the Sarstoon River and Ranguana Caye, sixty miles to the northeast. This measure proved acceptable to Guatemala's President Serrano, and on September 11, with just ten days to go before Belize's tenth anniversary celebrations, Guatemala and Belize established full diplomatic relations for the first time.

1984	1992	1993
United Democratic Party (UDP), led by Manuel Esquivel, wins Belize's first post-independence election	Guatemala recognizes Belize as a sovereign state	The UDP wins a tight election, and Esquivel again assumes leadership as prime minister

THE MAYA

The **Maya** in Belize are from three groups – Yucatec, Mopan and Kekchí – and make up around eleven percent of the population. The Yucatecan Maya also entered Belize to escape the fighting in the Caste Wars, and most were soon acculturated into the mestizo way of life as small-scale farmers. The Mopan Maya came to Belize in the 1880s and settled in the hills of Toledo and the area of Benque Viejo. The last and largest group, the Kekchí, came from the area around Cobán in Guatemala to work in cacao plantations in southern Belize. Small numbers still arrive in Belize each year, boosting villages in Toledo.

THE GARIFUNA

The **Garifuna** (see box, p.182) form just over six percent of the population and live mainly in Dangriga and the villages on the south coast. They are descended from shipwrecked and escaped African slaves who mingled with the last of the Caribs on the island of St Vincent and eventually settled in Belize in the years after 1832.

OTHER ETHNIC GROUPS

Another significant group are **East Indians**, established mainly in southern Toledo District, the descendants of indentured labourers brought over in the late 1860s by a small number of Confederate refugees seeking to re-establish the plantocracy following defeat in the American Civil War. More recent Indian immigration has occurred in Belize City.

Though the white, German-speaking **Mennonites** (see box, p.71) form only around four percent of the population, they undertake the vast majority of agriculture in Belize. Their opposition to government interference in their religion has over centuries forced them to move on, but in Belize they appear to have found a secure and permanent home.

The **Chinese** are a small ethnic group, many arriving in the nineteenth century as labourers on sugar estates in the south. Many more (Taiwanese and Cantonese) arrived in the 1980s.

An excellent TV **documentary series**, *Simply Belize: A Cultural Diary*, covers all thirteen ethnic groups; it is available at the Belize City Museum and some gift shops (see ⓦsimplybelize.org).

In 2008, Prime Minister Dean Barrow stated that resolving the border dispute was one of his leading goals while in office. In December 2008, Belize and Guatemala signed a special agreement to submit the border issue to the International Court of Justice (ICJ), but in October 2013 this agreement was suspended. The reality today is that though both countries are committed to **negotiation**, the failure to reach a watertight agreement means that the issue will continue to resurface.

Belize in the twenty-first century

A major twenty-first-century event with the potential to dramatically alter the course of Belize's future was the discovery of **oil** at Spanish Lookout in Cayo District (see p.126). Modest extraction began in 2005, and the country then granted eight-year concessions for petroleum research to eighteen other companies, with the Taiwanese state Chinese Petroleum Corporation (OPIC) pursuing drilling exploration offshore, and US Capital undertaking seismic testing in Sarstoon Temash National Park (STNP) in coastal Toledo. A further oil field at Never Delay near Belmopan was declared commercial in January 2010, but the movement against oil production has become more vociferous in the last few years and after the tragic BP oil spill in the Gulf of Mexico in 2010,

1998	2000	2001
The People's United Party (PUP) wins the national election, and party leader Said Musa becomes prime minister	Hurricane Keith roars through in October, causing destruction in its wake	Hurricane Iris hits the country, becoming the most damaging hurricane in Belize since Hattie in 1961

environmental organizations led the way in pushing for a ban on offshore drilling. In April 2013, they had a major victory: Belize's Supreme Court declared offshore drilling contracts previously issued by the government to be null and void, which effectively ends drilling in the reef. But there are also other pressing concerns. Even if oil-drilling continues in any capacity in the future, commentators are rightly saying that the Belizean government's tiny administration does not have the resources to either monitor a domestic oil industry or to ensure that its revenues are used in the country's best interests. Furthermore, explorations in sensitive areas like Toledo risk disrupting agreements brokered over **Maya land rights**. Licences for logging and resource extraction in the 1990s were deemed to have adversely affected both local environment and culture, and a further dispute over land use will open up old wounds and divisions.

Moreover, with the Belize–Guatemala border issues remaining unresolved, tensions continue to simmer on. Guatemalan peasant farmers regularly clear land just inside Belize's western border: they are regarded as illegal immigrants, and the official policy is expulsion, while small groups of soldiers from each country also occasionally stray across the other's border. In April 2016, the border dispute spiked after a Guatemalan teen was shot by Belizean troops. Guatemala deployed 3000 troops to the border. However, the two countries have also come together in key instances in recent years, notably in 2014, when they launched a joint effort to minimize illegal logging.

Political parties

Politically, Belize today is firmly **democratic**. The nominally left-of-centre **People's United Party (PUP)** has alternated with the perceived-to-be more market-led **United Democratic Party (UDP)**. In 2003, the PUP under Prime Minister **Said Musa** proved an exception to the rule by winning an unprecedented second term in a landslide victory – though following a storm of corruption allegations including over government misuse of pension funds, the UDP were returned to power in 2008 under **Dean Barrow**.

THE MYSTERY OF MCAFEE

Tech pioneer **John McAfee** made his name – and his multimillions – developing software that tracks down computer viruses. But in 2012, he became the one who was being tracked down – through the jungles of Belize. British-American expat McAfee fled his compound on Ambergris Caye in the autumn of 2012 after Belizean police wanted to question him as a "person of interest" in the death of his neighbour, a Florida retiree who was found with a bullet in his head. The two men had apparently been quarrelling over McAfee's many dogs, several of which had been poisoned. The death made news on the island, but it was what happened afterwards that took this case from "local crime story to worldwide news", as the *New York Times* put it. McAfee didn't just go on the run – he mocked Belizean officials while doing so. He became a gleeful "cyberdissident", posting on Twitter and websites as he trekked to Guatemala, wearing disguises along the way, including that of a "drunk German tourist", as he wrote on his blog. Even Belizean Prime Minister Dean Barrow weighed in, branding McAfee "bonkers". McAfee was deported by Guatemala to Florida, and then spent time in Oregon, California, and now in Lexington, Tennessee. He has said that he'll cooperate with Belizean police as long as he can do so on his own turf, in the US – but thus far Belize has presented no new plans to pursue him. If you think this is a story made for the movies, you're right – McAfee's fugitive tale has been optioned by Warner Brothers.

2002	2003	2005	2006
In response to the growing cruise-ship industry, Belize City builds the Tourism Village, catering to cruise passengers	The People's United Party (PUP) under Prime Minister Said Musa wins unprecedented second term in landslide victory	Discovery and extraction of oil at Spanish Lookout in Cayo District	Belize begins commercial production with its oil reserves

In March 2012, Barrow started his second term after the UDP won the election again. Barrow has proven to have staying power: in November 2015, he embarked on his third term, as the UDP were voted in again. Belizean politics are both lively and divisive, which comes across quite vividly in the media coverage, including in the main newspapers, TV channels and radio stations.

The tourist industry

The booming **tourist industry**, bringing in well over US$400 million a year out of Belize's US$2.3 billion GDP and employing almost a third of the country's workforce, is now the mainstay of Belize's **economy**, pushing agriculture and fisheries into a close second place. The **cruise industry** continues to grow, which, of course, affects the country's conservation efforts (see p.247) and also, according to some, Belize's overall cultural direction. In the last few years especially, tour operators, in order to appeal to cruise ship day-trippers, have had to incorporate a sometimes frivolous, entertaining-at-all-costs approach to guiding at venerated sights. This can add an "amusement park" feel to some of the popular Maya temples, where you'll regularly see big buses disgorging passengers. Of course, proponents state that the cruise industry brings in the bucks, and for many Belizeans, that's key to a rosy future. In 2013, Norwegian Cruise Line (NCL) purchased an island from the Belizean government – **Harvest Caye**, which lies just three miles from the village of Placencia, in southern Belize. After three years – and millions of dollars – NCL unveiled its new island port in November 2016. Unlike in Belize City, where passengers need to travel ashore on tender boats, here, the cruises can pull right up to the island, so passengers can step off onto a pier and walk to land. While there are many who feel that the new cruise port will engulf relatively quiet southern Belize with massive crowds (potentially endangering flora and fauna in the process), there are also numerous proponents, who highlight the fact that Norwegian took great pains to preserve Belizean culture and nature. For example, instead of the usual chain shops found at most cruise ports, the shopping at Harvest Caye is rooted in local arts and crafts. Time will tell, of course, as to how well this new port is integrated into the flow of Belizean society, but for now, it's being held up as a shining cruise port example in the Caribbean, which may well inspire many others like it.

Annual growth in Belize hovers around three percent, with inflation at four percent, and unemployment a steady ten percent. Per capita income is high for Central America, at about US$8400, boosted by remittances many Belizeans receive from relatives abroad. This apparent advantage is offset by the fact that many of the brightest and most highly trained citizens leave, fitting in well in English-speaking North America, though some graduates do return.

A flip side to increased tourism has been **expat immigration** to Belize from North America and Europe, which continues to rise. In recent years, Belize's north, around Corozal, Orange Walk and Sarteneja, has become fertile ground for expats, because real estate is still a relative bargain – and proximity to Mexico means more (and often better) health-care options just across the border. But, though expats bring in much-needed capital, you'll hear Belizeans raise concerns about the domination of business by foreigners, which is evident throughout the cayes.

Figures are obviously not available for Belize's income from the lucrative drug trans-shipment business, but this illicit economy is certainly a sizeable fraction of the

2008	**2012**	**2013**
Following PUP corruption allegations, UDP returns to power in 2008 under Prime Minister Dean Barrow	In March 2012, UDP wins again, and Barrow kicks off his second term	Belize's Supreme Court declares previous offshore oil-drilling contracts issued by government to be null and void

SIMONE BILES SOMERSAULTS INTO FAME

Belize has a new star. In 2016, Belize received worldwide recognition thanks to **gymnast Simone Biles**, a dual citizen of Belize and the US who lovingly calls Belize her second home. Biles won four gold medals in the Río summer Olympic Games, setting a new American record for most gold medals in women's gymnastics at a single Games. Her fame spread in quickly: in 2016, Biles was chosen as one of the BBC's 100 Women, and was a finalist for *Time Magazine's* 2016 Person of the Year. Biles was also celebrated by her fellow Olympians: she was selected by Team USA to be the flag bearer for the closing ceremony, making her the first American female gymnast to be given this honour.

country's official income. Drug-related crime has been on the rise in Belize for thirty years – particularly in Belize City, which since the early 2000s has seen robberies and murders reach out-of-hand proportions, especially gang-on-gang ghetto violence. The government response has been to join Belize Defence Force (BDF) personnel with police on the city streets, and to introduce **checkpoints** on roads across the country. This increased **militarization** has yet to have an impact on crime levels, though accusations of abuse of power are commonplace – while not affecting tourists. A high murder rate also means that the **death penalty** remains popular, even though no one has been executed since 1985. The campaign to replace the British-based **Privy Council** with the **Caribbean Court of Justice** (established in 2005) as the highest court of appeal owes itself to the perception that more executions will be approved. While on the face of it removing this bastion of direct colonial authority seems a positive step, the fear in some quarters is of a lower standard of justice and an inability to uphold democratic principles.

Though Belize's traditional links with Britain and the Commonwealth countries in the West Indies remain strong, the **United States** is by far its largest trading partner and supplies much of the **foreign aid** on which Belize still depends – though multilateral organizations like the EU have also funded significant infra-structural projects. Belize has also joined the **Free Trade Area of the Americas** (FTAA), aimed at establishing the largest free trade area in the world. Concerns over a depression in agricultural prices and a manufacturing base unable to compete with imports are commonplace, though the idea that the agreement might signal an end to the **fixed rate of exchange** with the US$ has yet to be realized. The reality is that Belize continues to be firmly linked to US designs for the region and will face increasing challenges from global competition.

2015	2015	2016
Prime Minister Barrow, at the helm of the UDP, wins a record third consecutive term	Gymnast Simone Biles – a dual citizen of Belize and the US – wins four gold medals in the Rio Summer Olympic Games	Norwegian Cruise Line (NCL) unveils its custom-made port and resort on Harvest Caye, which it purchased in 2013

Maya life and society

For some three thousand years before the arrival of the Spanish, Maya civilization dominated Central America, with a complex and sophisticated culture. While remains of the great Maya centres, which tower above the forest roof, are testament to the scale and sophistication of Maya civilization, they offer little insight into daily life. Archeologists have instead turned to the residential groups that surround each site, littered with the remains of household utensils, pottery, bones and farming tools. These wattle-and-daub structures were each home to a single family, within a larger group housing the extended family who farmed and hunted together and specialized in some trade or craft. Dependent on agriculture, they farmed maize, beans, cacao, squash, chillies and fruit trees in raised and irrigated fields, while wild fruits were also harvested from the forest. Much of the land was communally owned and groups of around twenty men worked in the fields together. The early practice of slash-and-burn was soon replaced by more intensive farming methods to meet the needs of a growing population. Sophisticated processes of terracing, drainage and irrigation improved soil fertility, with each large city – today hemmed in by forest – once surrounded by open fields, canals and residential compounds. Most people would have bought some of their food in markets, though all households had a kitchen garden where they grew herbs and fruit.

The main sites represent larger versions of the basic residential groups, housing the most powerful families and their assorted retainers. They took on larger political, religious and administrative roles, becoming extensive cities. Members of royal families and nobility were accompanied by bureaucrats, merchants, warriors, architects and assorted craftsmen – an emerging **middle class**. The hierarchy was controlled by a series of hereditary positions, with a **king** (occasionally a queen) at its head, who also occupied the role of religious leader. At certain times in the calendar kings (and probably other members of the ruling class) communicated with gods and illustrious ancestors by performing ritual **blood-letting** upon themselves, as well as the sacrifice of important captives kept alive for these ceremonial celebrations.

THE MAYA DIET

Maize has always been the basis of the **Maya diet**, in ancient times as much as it is today. It was made into *saka*, a corn-meal gruel, which was eaten with chilli as the first meal of the day. Labourers ate a mixture of corn dough and water, and we know that *tamales* were a popular speciality. The main meal, eaten in the evenings, was similarly maize-based, probably including vegetables, and occasionally meat. As a supplement, deer, peccary, wild turkey, duck, pigeon and quail were all hunted with bows and arrows or blowguns. The Maya also made use of dogs, both for **hunting** and eating. **Fish** were eaten too, as the remains of fish hooks and nets have been found, and those living on the coast probably traded dried fish far inland. As well as food, the forest provided firewood, and cotton was cultivated to be dyed with natural colours and then spun for cloth.

The relationship between the cities and the land, drawn up along feudal lines, was at the heart of Maya life. **Peasant farmers** supported the ruling class by providing labour and food, and in return the elite provided leadership, direction, protection and, above all else, the security of their knowledge of calendrics and supernatural prophecy. This knowledge was thought to be the basis of successful agriculture, and the ruler-priests were relied upon to divine the appropriate time to plant and harvest.

In turn, the cities themselves became organized into a hierarchy, with at times a single city, such as El Mirador, Tikal or Calakmul controlling smaller sites across a vast area. A complex structure of **alliances** and rivalries bound the various sites together in an endless round of competition and conflict, and there were frequent outbursts of **open warfare**. The structure of the alliances can be traced through emblem-glyphs. Only those of the main centres are used in isolation, while the names of smaller sites are used in conjunction with those of their larger patrons.

THE MAYA CALENDAR

For both practical and mystical reasons, the Maya developed a highly sophisticated understanding of arithmetic, calendrics and astronomy, all of which they believed gave them the power to predict events. Great occasions were interpreted on the basis of the **Maya calendar**, and it was this precise understanding of time that gave the ruling elite its authority. The majority of carving, on temples and stelae, records the date at which rulers were born, ascended to power, sacrificed captives and died.

The basis of all Maya **calculation** was the vigesimal counting system, which used multiples of twenty. Just three symbols were used in writing – a shell to denote zero, a dot for one and a bar for five – which you can still see on many stelae. In calculations the Maya used a slightly different notation known as the head-variant system, in which each number from one to twenty was represented by the head of a deity.

When it comes to the Maya **calendar** things start to get more complex. The basic unit of the Maya calendar was the day, or *kin*, followed by the *winal*, a group of twenty *kins* roughly equivalent to our month. In an ideal vigesimal system (as Maya arithmetic was) the next level would be four hundred *kins* – but for marking the passing of a period approximating a year the Maya used the *tun*, comprising eighteen (rather than twenty) *winals*, plus a closing month of five days, the *Uayeb*, a total of 365 days. This so-called "**vague year**", or *haab*, made it a very close approximation of the annual cycle, though of course the Maya elite knew that the solar year was a fraction over 365 days. Beyond this unit, however, the passing of time was ordered in multiples of twenty, with the *katun* being twenty *tuns*.

The 260-day **sacred almanac** was used to calculate the timing of ceremonial events and as a basis for prophecy. Each day (*kin*) was associated with a particular deity that had strong influence over those born on that particular day. This calendar wasn't divided into months but had 260 distinct day names. (This system is still in use among the Cakchiquel in the highlands of Guatemala, who name their children according to its structure and celebrate fiestas according to its dictates.) These first two calendars operated in parallel so that once every 52 years the new day of the solar year coincided with the same day in the 260-day almanac, a powerful meeting that marked the end of one "**calendar round**" and the beginning of the next.

Finally, the Maya had another system for marking the passing of history, which is used on dedicatory monuments. Known as the **long count**, it's based on the "great cycle" of thirteen *baktuns* (a period of 5128 years). The dates in this system simply record the number of days that have elapsed since the start of the current great cycle – it dated from 3114 BC and was due to terminate on December 21, 2012. Because of this, there were worldwide doomsday theories that the world might come to an end in December 2012. But, serious Maya scholars scoffed at that – and explained that it simply means the end of an old cycle, and the beginning of a new one. Since 2012, there have been occasional new predictions on future **end-of-world dates** though these, too, are generally dismissed as simply conspiracy theories.

Astronomy and religion

Alongside their fascination with time, the Maya showed a great interest in **astronomy** and devoted much energy to unravelling its patterns. Several large sites such as Copán, Uaxactún and Chichén Itzá have **observatories** carefully aligned with solar and lunar sequences; in all probability, a building or buildings in each city was dedicated to this role. With their 365-day "vague year", the Maya were just a quarter of a day out in their calculations of the solar year, while at Copán, towards the end of the seventh century AD, Maya astronomers had calculated the lunar cycle at 29.53020 days, just slightly off from our current estimate of 29.53059. In the Dresden Codex their calculations extend to the 405 lunations over a period of 11,960 days, which set out to predict eclipses. They also calculated with astonishing accuracy the movements of Venus and Mars. Venus was important as a link to success in war; there are several stelae that record the appearance of Venus prompting the decision to attack.

Maya **cosmology** is by no means straightforward; at every stage an idea is balanced by its opposite and the universe is made up of many complex layers. To the Maya, the current earth is the third version, the previous two having been destroyed by deluges. This earth is a flat surface, with four corners, each associated with a certain colour; white for north, red for east, yellow for south and black for west, with green at the centre. Above this the sky is supported by four trees, each a different colour and species, which are also depicted as *Bacabs* – gods. At its centre the sky is supported by a *ceiba* tree. Above the sky is a heaven of thirteen layers, each with its own god, and the top layer overseen by an owl. However, it was the underworld, *Xibalba*, "the place of fright", which was of greatest importance, as this was where they passed after death, on the way to the place of rest. Nine layers of "hell" were guarded by "lords of the night", and deep caves were thought to connect with the underworld.

The Maya's incredible array of **gods** each had four manifestations based upon colour and direction, and many had counterparts in the underworld and consorts of the opposite sex. There were also extensive patron deities, each associated with a particular trade or class. Every activity from suicide to sex had its representative in the Maya pantheon.

The combined complexity of the Maya pantheon and calendar gave every day a particular significance, and the ancient Maya were bound up in a demanding **cycle of religious ritual**, upon which success depended. As every event, from planting to childbirth, was associated with a particular divinity, most daily events demanded some kind of religious ritual. For the most important, there were elaborate ceremonies, with the correct day carefully chosen by priests and fasting and abstinence maintained for several days beforehand. Ceremonies were dominated by the expulsion of evil spirits, the burning of incense before idols, an animal or human sacrifice and blood-letting.

In divination rituals, used to foretell the pattern of future events or to account for the cause of past events, the elite used various **drugs** to achieve altered states of consciousness. The most obvious of these was alcohol, made from fermented maize or a combination of honey and the bark of the *balche* tree. Wild tobacco, stronger than the modern domesticated version, was smoked. The Maya also used a range of hallucinogenic mushrooms, most importantly the *xibalbaj obox*, "underworld mushroom", and the *k'aizalah obox*, "lost judgement mushroom".

MAYA TIME – THE UNITS

1 *kin* = 24 hours	20 *pictuns* = 1 *calabtun*, or 57,600,000 days
20 *kins* = 1 *winal*, or 20 days	20 *calabtuns* = 1 *kinchiltun*, or
18 *winals* = 1 *tun*, or 360 days	1,152,000,000 days
20 *tuns* = 1 *katun*, or 7200 days	20 *kinchiltuns* = 1 *alautun*, or
20 *katuns* = 1 *baktun*, or 144,000 days	23,040,000,000 days
20 *baktun* = 1 *pictun*, or 2,880,000 days	

Archeology in Belize

A wealth of new material on the Maya has been unveiled by archeologists in Belize over the last couple of decades. As it emerged from siege by foreign expeditions and looters, the country has now taken control of its own archeological heritage. At least sixteen archeological teams visit Belize annually, some studying the extensive raised-field agriculture and irrigation canals in northern Belize, as well as the oldest known site so far found in the Maya world, at Cuello, near Orange Walk. Even Tikal in Guatemala, once thought to have been the centre of power of the lowland Maya, is now known to have been toppled by Caracol, the largest Maya city in Belize.

The ancient Maya sites of Belize began to be studied in the late nineteenth century, when British amateur archeologists and both British and American **museums** kept up a lively interest in artefacts. Preservation of monuments was not yet "in", and techniques were far from subtle. In some cases dynamite was used, and Belizean artefacts often found their way, unmonitored, into museums and private collections worldwide.

Since 1894 Belize's ancient monuments and antiquities have had loose legislation to protect them, but it was not until 1957 that the Belize Department of Archaeology (now called the **Institute of Archaeology**) was formed to excavate, protect and preserve these remains. Since then, excavation of hundreds of sites has been carried out by universities, museums and other institutions from the US, Canada and, to a lesser

---

FIELD SCHOOLS AND PROJECTS

Many sites in Belize accept paying students (and often non-students): the average two- to four-week stint at a field school costs US$1000–3000. It's fascinating work, but be prepared for sometimes tough conditions. In addition to the projects listed below, it's also worth contacting the **National Institute of Culture and History** (NICH; ⓦ nichbelize.com), which may have information on current archeological digs. Also, it's worth looking at the Archaeological Institute of America's website (ⓦ archaeological.org). Additionally, the websites ⓦ mesoweb.com and ⓦ famsi.org (Foundation for the Advancement of Mesoamerican Studies) have useful links.

Belize Fieldwork Program of Boston University Undertakes research at La Milpa, in the northwest (see p.77) and Xibun, in Cayo. Highly regarded programmes. See ⓦ bu.ed /archaeology.

Belize River Archaeological Settlement Survey (BRASS) Working in the Belize River valley (see p.61) since 1983 and at El Pilar (see p.144) since 1993. Focuses on the El Pilar Archaeological Reserve for Maya Flora and Fauna, emphasizing forest gardens, ceramics, drafting, computers and photography. Contact the MesoAmerican Research Center, University of California, Santa Barbara (ⓦ marc.ucsb.edu).

Blue Creek Archaeological Project of the Maya Research Program (MRP) Conducting excavations at Blue Creek in northwestern Belize for several decades to better understand its role in the region. See ⓦ mayaresearchprogram.org.

Minanha Archaeology Project Social Archaeology Research Program (SARP), Trent University, Canada. Focuses on ancient Maya sociopolitical interaction at Minanha, on the Vaca plateau in Cayo – between Caracol and Naranjo. See ⓦ trentu.ca/anthropology/belize.php.

University of Texas Mesoamerican Archaeological Research Laboratory In partnership with the Programme for Belize Archaeological Project, undertakes research at Río Bravo in northern Belize. Contact Mesoamerican Archaeological Research Laboratory at University of Texas at Austin, ⓦ utexas.edu/cola/orgs/mesolab/contact.php.

extent, Britain, always with permission from the institute. Permits are only issued to those whose proposals conform to the institute's policies and will be of benefit to the country, while the institute also now trains Belizeans to carry out archeological work, and it performs small-scale salvage excavations. The institute is also in charge of all **non-Maya historical and colonial remains**, with immovable man-made structures over one hundred years old and movable man-made items over 150 years old considered ancient monuments and artefacts respectively, under Belizean law. The responsibility of maintaining archeological sites falls to the institute, as does the safekeeping of the vast national collections. To try to stimulate the Belizean public's interest, an educational programme is also carried out, including lectures, slide shows and travelling exhibitions. The **Belize Archaeology Symposium**, held annually in the summer (usually in June or July) offers the chance for all archeological teams to present their latest findings – a fascinating and well-organized event which anyone can attend; check Ⓦnichbelize.com for more contact details and information.

With the wealth of Maya remains, it's extremely unfortunate that **looting** and the black-market sale of antiquities still happens. In Belize, all ancient monuments and antiquities are owned by the state, whether on private or government land or under water – residents are allowed to keep registered collections under licence, but the sale, purchase, import or export of antiquities is illegal. The law is aimed at keeping remains intact so that Belizeans and visitors alike can see the evidence of this splendid heritage. The safekeeping of Maya sites, though, goes beyond the dangers of looting, as evidenced by the devastating damage, by a construction company bulldozer in 2013, of the Nohmul Maya site (see p.76) near Orange Walk. This destruction made headlines across Belize, igniting renewed efforts to protect the country's priceless Maya treasures.

Ancient Maya **maritime trade routes** have been a focus of recent research, with sites on the coast and cayes receiving more attention. In 2011, for example, the Preclassic Marco Gonzalez site (see p.91), on Ambergris Caye, was declared the cayes' first National Park Maya Site, and vigorous excavation is under way.

Furthermore, archeological teams are continually unearthing new finds across the country. In 2016, Xunantunich (see p.147), in western Belize, made headlines with the incredible discovery of one of the largest **royal tombs** ever found in the country. The burial chamber revealed a male corpse, as well as jade, animal bones and ceramic vessels.

THE MAYA UNDERWORLD

Though most evidence of the Maya is above ground, the culture was fascinated by the subterranean, and **caves** held sacred status. They were considered entrances to the **underworld**, called **Xibalba**, the "place of fright", but despite their fearsome nature they also provided privileged access to the dwellings of gods, ancestors and spirits. Extensive **cave systems** form a vast network under much of inland Belize – thanks in large part to the country's porous karst limestone – which have revealed unique findings, including wall paintings, pottery shards and the remains of fires. Because the Maya gods had to be appeased with sacrifices, you'll also see weapons, altars and skeletons, typically left just as archeologists first discovered them.

Perhaps the best cave to visit for its cache of Maya artefacts is **Actun Tunichil Muknal** – or ATM – (see p.126) in Cayo District, involving a short swim and, depending on the water level, a hike through waist-deep water. **Che Chem Ha**, also in Cayo District, is another highlight, with some of the most intact artefacts in the country. In addition to their attraction as Maya sites, caves also invite a slew of adventure activities, heavily promoted by tour organizers. Cave tubing, rappelling and canoeing are some of the more popular activities and run the gamut from relaxing to exhilarating.

Nature and conservation

For its size, Belize has a diverse range of environments: from the coral reefs and atolls of the Caribbean coast, through lowland swamps and lagoons, up the valleys of pristine tropical rivers, to the exposed ridges of the Maya Mountains. Physically, the land increases in elevation as you head south and west; the main rivers rise in the west and flow north and east to the Caribbean.

Away from the coast, which is covered by marine sediments for 10–20km inland, the country can be roughly divided into three **geological regions**: the **northern lowlands**, a continuation of the Yucatán Platform, with Cretaceous limestone overlaid by deposits of alluvial sand; the **Maya Mountains**, where Santa Rosa quartz with granite intrusions rises to high peaks over 3280ft; and **southern Belize**, where more Cretaceous limestone hills with wonderfully developed **karst features** – including caverns, natural arches and sinkholes – give way to foothills and the coastal plain. The **wildlife** is correspondingly varied; undisturbed forests provide a home to both temperate species from the north and tropical species from the south, including indigenous species unique to Belize. In winter, hundreds of native birds are joined by dozens of migrant species from the eastern seaboard of North America. The variety of land and marine ecosystems makes Belize a focus of scientific research.

Belize's impressive network of national parks, nature reserves and wildlife sanctuaries makes up over 42 percent of its land area, a feat made possible by a low population density. It's an amazing accomplishment for a developing country, and with such enlightened strategies to safeguard biodiversity, Belize has gained recognition as the most conservation-conscious country in the Americas. The success of these protected areas is due as much to the efforts of local communities as it is to governmental decisions.

The tropical forest

Belize still has over fifty percent of its **primary forest**, and across most of the country the natural vegetation is technically **tropical moist forest**, classified by average temperatures of 25°C and annual rainfall of 78–157in; the only true **rainforest** lies in a small belt in the extreme southwest. More than four thousand flowering plant species can be found, including seven hundred species of tree (about the same as the whole of the US and Canada) and over two hundred varieties of orchid. Scientists have identified seventy different types of forest: thirteen percent **pine savannah** (known in Belize as "pine ridge", regardless of the elevation); nineteen percent **mangrove and coastal forest** (which includes rare **caye littoral forest**); with the remaining 68 percent **broadleaf forest** and cohune palm – commonly referred to as rainforest.

Diversity characterizes tropical forest, with each species specifically adapted to fit a particular ecological niche. This biological storehouse has yet to be fully explored, though it has already yielded some astonishing discoveries. Steroid hormones, such as cortisone, and diosgenin, the active ingredient in birth control pills, were developed from wild yams found here, while tetrodoxin, derived from a species of Central American frog, is an anaesthetic 160,000 times stronger than cocaine. But despite its size and diversity the forest is surprisingly **fragile**, forming a closed system in which nutrients are continuously recycled and decaying plant matter fuels new growth. The forest floor is a spongy mass of roots, fungi, mosses, bacteria and micro-organisms, in which nutrients are stored, broken down with the assistance of insects and chemical decay, and gradually released to the waiting roots and fresh seedlings. The thick canopy prevents much light from reaching the floor, ensuring that the soil remains damp but warm, a hotbed of chemical activity. The death of a large tree prompts a flurry of growth as seedlings struggle towards the sunlight. But once a number of trees are removed the soil is highly vulnerable; exposed to the harsh tropical sun and direct rainfall, an area of cleared forest becomes prone to flooding and drought. Recently cleared land contains enough nutrients for three or four years of crop growth, but soon afterwards its usefulness declines rapidly and within twenty years can become

CONSERVATION STRATEGY

In 1928 the southern tip of Half Moon Caye was established as a Crown Reserve to protect the rare red-footed booby (*Sula sula*); other **bird sanctuaries** were established in the 1960s and 1970s. The **Forestry Act** of 1960 focused on forest reserves, and was passed primarily to protect the country's timber industry rather than for conservation. In the period since independence, the government has taken numerous measures to increase the area of land and sea under protection, including the **Wildlife Protection Act** of 1981 (amended 1991), which created closed seasons or total protection for endangered species like turtles, dolphins and manatees.

WORLD HERITAGE STATUS

Belize has also ratified and actively implements many **international environmental** agreements. Seven reserves on the Belize Barrier Reef, totalling 55 square miles, were declared World Heritage Sites in 1996: Bacalar Chico National Park, Blue Hole and Half Moon Caye Natural Monuments, South Water Caye, Glover's Reef, Sapodilla Cayes and Laughing Bird Caye. These and other protected areas form the **Belize Barrier Reef Reserve System**, which has the ultimate aim of forming a corridor of reserves from Mexico to Honduras, an aim aided by the Tulum Declaration between all four coastal countries, promoting conservation and sustainable use of the coral reef system.

GOVERNMENT AGENCIES

Three government ministries in Belize shoulder most of the responsibility for conservation legislation, and ensuring compliance. The **Department of the Environment** has overall responsibility for management of the country's natural resources, while the **Fisheries Authority** monitors and enforces fishing regulations, and also manages the country's marine reserves and responsible exploitation of commercially viable species. The **Coastal Zone Management Authority and Institute** is responsible for implementing all policies that affect the use of the coastal zone and for fostering regional collaboration.

Belize's timber reserves (including all mangroves) have always been under the compass of the **Forest Department** (under the Ministry of Natural Resources and the Environment). The department's **Protected Areas Management Division** has responsibility for terrestrial protected areas and the coordination of biodiversity management. Its **Wildlife Management Programme** enforces the Wildlife Protection Act, and conservation officers have been appointed to all the country's forest reserves.

Apart from attracting tourists to Belize and providing them with information, the **Ministry of Tourism** licenses and trains the country's tour guides; you'll find the guides in Belize are highly motivated guardians of the environment. The **National Institute of Culture and History (NICH)** manages all cultural and historical features, including all **archeological sites** (which are also reserves), and has responsibility for developing appropriate tourism packages.

MAKING A PACT

Government agencies have proved extremely successful in coordinating protection of the reserves, almost always with the cooperation of the private sector and a range of local and international NGOs. The dramatic increase in protected land has nonetheless posed the question of financing. The **Protected Areas Conservation Trust (PACT)** was established in 1996 and has since become an international model. The primary source of income is a conservation exit fee of Bz$7.50 per person, payable at all departure points. PACT also receives twenty percent of entrance fees to protected areas and fees from cruise ship passengers; a percentage is also invested in a trust fund as a long-term buffer against the vicissitudes of government funding. For more information visit PACT's excellent website, ⓦpactbelize.org.

completely barren. If the trees are stripped from a large area, soil erosion will silt the rivers and disrupt rainfall patterns.

Belize's forests are home to abundant **birdlife** – 574 species (260 resident) – the most visible of the country's wildlife and a huge draw for visitors. You'll be astonished by the sheer number of birds you can see just by sitting by a cabin in any one of the jungle lodges in Belize. Parrots, such as the **Aztec** and **green parakeets**, are seen every day, and you might catch a glimpse of rare species from the tiny **orange-breasted falcon** to the massive **harpy eagle**, the largest of Belize's raptors. Jewel-like **hummingbirds** feed by dipping their long bills into heliconia flowers, and their names are as fascinating as their colours: the rufous-tailed, the little hermit, the white-bellied emerald and the violet sabrewing, to mention just a few.

Although Belize has sixty species of **snakes**, only nine are venomous and you're unlikely to see any at all. One of the commonest is the **boa constrictor**, which is also the largest, growing up to 4m, and it poses no threat to humans. Others you might see are (venomous) **coral snakes** and (non-venomous) **false coral snakes**; you'd need to be quite skilled to tell them apart. **Frogs and toads** (collectively anurans) are plentiful, and at night in the forest you'll hear a chorus of mating calls. You'll also frequently find the **red-eyed tree frog** – a beautiful, pale green creature about 1in long – in your shower in any rustic cabin. Giant **marine toads**, the largest in the Americas, weigh in at up to 2lb and grow to 8in. These are infamous as the "cane toad", which caused havoc when introduced into Australia; it eats anything it can get into its capacious mouth. Like most frogs and toads it has toxic glands – a characteristic the ancient Maya employed in their ceremonies by licking these glands and interpreting the resultant hallucinations.

One thing you'll realize pretty quickly in Belize is that you're never far from an **insect**. Mostly you'll be trying to avoid or destroy them, particularly mosquitoes and sandflies. But the **butterflies** are beautiful, and you'll see clouds of them feeding at the edges of puddles on trails; the caterpillars are sometimes enormous. The largest and most spectacular are the gorgeous, electric-blue **blue morpho** and the **owl butterfly**, and you can see many more on a visit to one of a number of **butterfly exhibits**. Perhaps the most impressive of the numerous ant species are **army ants**, called the "marchin' army" in Belize, as the whole colony ranges through the forest in a narrow column voraciously hunting for insects. **Leafcutter ants** ("wee-wee ants" in Kriol) have regular trails along which they carry bits of leaves much larger than themselves – which is how they get the name "parasol ants". The leaves themselves aren't food, but they help in the growth of a fungus that the ants do eat. **Spiders** are also very common: take a walk at night with a torch and you'll see the beam reflected back by the eyes of dozens of **wolf spiders**. **Tarantulas**, too, are found everywhere – the fangs may look dangerous but tarantulas won't bite unless they're severely provoked.

The Maya Mountains

The **Maya Mountains** run southwest to northeast across south-central Belize and straddle the border with Guatemala. This wild region, covered in dense forest and riddled with caves and underground rivers, has few permanent residents. The most accessible areas are within the **Mountain Pine Ridge** (see p.130) and the **Cockscomb Basin Wildlife Sanctuary** (see p.193), home to the world's only **jaguar reserve**.

The flora and fauna, though similar to those found in the tropical forests of Guatemala, are often more prolific here as there's much less pressure on the land. Though rarely seen, the **scarlet macaw** is found in large flocks in the southern Maya Mountains and the Cockscomb Basin. All of Belize's cat species are found here, too: **jaguars** ("tigers") range widely over the whole country, but the densest population is found in the lower elevation forests of the west; **pumas** ("red tigers") usually keep to remote ridges; **ocelots** and smaller **margays** (both spotted and called "tiger cat" in Belize, slightly larger than a domestic cat); and **jaguarundis**, the smallest and commonest – you might spot one on a trail since it hunts during the day. Belize's largest land animal, **Baird's tapir** ("mountain cow"), weighing up to 660 pounds, is found near water. Tapirs are endangered but not that rare in Belize, though you're unlikely to see one without a guide.

On the northern flank of the Maya Mountains, the **Mountain Pine Ridge** is a granite massif intruded into sedimentary quartz, resulting in a ring of metamorphic rock. Many of the rivers rising here fall away to the Macal and Belize river valleys, in spectacular waterfalls. On this nutrient-poor soil the **Caribbean pine** is dominant, covering sixty percent of the area; bromeliads and orchids adorn the trunks and branches, and it's a unique habitat with endemic species including frogs and a fish known only by its Latin name; trees are recovering from a severe outbreak of **pine bark beetles**.

Lowland Belize

The forests of Petén, Guatemala, extend into northwestern Belize, where low-lying topography is broken by a series of roughly parallel **limestone escarpments**. The Booth's River and Río Bravo escarpments each have rivers that drain north to the Río Hondo. Here the **Río Bravo Conservation and Management Area** (see p.77) protects a huge area of forest. Further east, the plain is more open; pine savannah is interspersed with slow-flowing rivers and lagoons, wetland habitats that continue to the coast. In the centre, **Crooked Tree Wildlife Sanctuary** (see p.63) covers several freshwater lagoons holding three hundred bird species, including the nesting sites of the rare jabiru stork. The tiny village of Sarteneja is the only settlement between Belize City and Corozal on the coast – holding wading birds, crocodiles (Morelet's and American) and several species of turtle, protected in **Shipstern Nature Reserve** (see p.80). Almost all the mammals of Belize – with the exception of monkeys but including jaguars, ocelots and tapirs – can be found in this mosaic of coastal lagoons, hardwood forest and mangrove swamp. You might also see signs of collared and white-lipped peccaries ("warries"), brocket and white-tailed deer, opossums, weasels, porcupines and armadillos. At the **Community Baboon Sanctuary** in the lower Belize River valley (see p.61), visitors are almost guaranteed to see troops of black howler monkeys ("baboons"), or hear the male's deep-throated roar.

In the south there's only a relatively narrow stretch of lowland between the Maya Mountains and the coast. Along the navigable rivers much of the original forest has been selectively logged for mahogany and is in varying stages of regrowth after hurricane damage; other patches have been replaced by agricultural land and citrus. A boat journey in **Burdon Canal Nature Reserve**, which connects the Belize and Sibun rivers to the Northern and Southern lagoons, and on into **Gales Point** wetland area (see p.65), where manatees congregate, is a wonderfully rich wildlife, mangrove forest and lagoon experience.

Green **iguanas** (along with their similar cousin the spiny-tailed iguana - "wish-willy") are the most prominent of Belize's reptiles; despite protection they're still hunted for their meat and eggs. Rarer, but still fairly frequently seen, the Central American river otter is much larger than its European cousin. Along the New River and in many lagoons you'll see **Morelet's crocodiles**, which can be found in almost any body of water, and are of no danger to humans unless they're very large – at least 9ft long. Previously hunted to the brink of extinction, they've made a remarkable comeback; now frequently spotted in the mangroves of Haulover Creek west of Belize City. Rivers offer great birdwatching, with several species of kingfisher alongside the tri-coloured heron, the boat-billed heron, the great egret and occasionally the 6ft-tall jabiru stork.

Coastline and Barrier Reef

Belize's most exceptional environment is its **Caribbean coastline** and offshore barrier reef, dotted with hundreds of small islands and three atolls. Much of the shoreline is still covered with mangroves, which play an important role in the economy, not merely as nurseries for commercial fish species but also for their stabilization of the shoreline and their ability to absorb the force of hurricanes. Red mangrove dominates, although in due course it consolidates the seabed until it becomes more suitable for less salt-tolerant black and white mangroves. The cutting down of mangroves, particularly on the cayes, exposes the land to the full force of the sea and can mean the end of a small and unstable island.

Just inland from mangrove usually lies salt-tolerant **littoral forest**, many plants characterized by tough, waxy leaves which help conserve water. Species include red and white gumbo limbo, black poisonwood, zericote, sea grape, palmetto and, of course, the coconut palm, though it's not actually native and is now threatened by lethal yellowing disease. The littoral forest supports a high density of migrating birds, thanks to the succession of fruits and seeds, yet it also faces the highest development pressure in Belize due to its slightly higher coastal elevation; **caye littoral forest** is the most endangered habitat in the country.

The basis of the shoreline food chain is nutrient-rich mud, held in place by mangrove, while the roots themselves are home to oysters and sponges. Young stingrays cruise through the shallows adjacent to mangrove roots, accompanied by juvenile snappers, bonefish and small barracudas; you'll see the adult versions on the reef and around the

CONSERVATION ORGANIZATIONS

Numerous nongovernmental **organizations** (NGOs) are active in conservation in Belize, many being members of the **Belize Association of Conservation NGOs** (BACONGO). Co-management agreements between government departments, national NGOs and local organizations play an important role in involving local communities in managing protected areas. The **Belize Audubon Society** (see below) already manages several reserves, and other reserves at the Sapodilla Cayes, Port Honduras, Gales Point and Laughing Bird Caye have co-management agreements in place.

NGOs also undertake scrutiny of government proposals, such as discussions leading to the **Lamanai Room Declaration** (Aug 1997). Signed by thirty NGOs, it sent a strong message to the government that it could not ignore their concerns over proposed developments, including damage to the reef by cruise ships and the sale of logging concessions on Maya lands in Toledo. A proposal by a Mexican company to build a "dolphin park attraction" near San Pedro caused most alarm, dolphins being a protected species in Belize, and in the end the government did not issue the necessary licence.

ORGANIZATIONS WELCOMING VOLUNTEERS AND STUDENTS

Volunteers are often used to help carry out work, from constructing trails and camping facilities to undertaking wildlife surveys. Many other organizations offer study opportunities, particularly in marine biology and conservation.

The Belize Audubon Society (BAS), founded in 1969, is the country's pre-eminent conservation organization and extremely well-respected both in Belize and internationally. While the name might suggest birdwatching as its main focus of activity, BAS is active in all aspects of nature conservation and manages nine of the country's protected areas. It also publishes a range of books, guides and fact sheets. Call in at the office to find out how to get to the various nature reserves. For details write to BAS, 12 Fort St, Belize City, call ☎ 223 5004 or visit ⓦ belizeaudubon.org.

The Belize Foundation for Research and Environmental Education (Bfree) was formed in 1995 by professional biologists to assist the government of Belize in the conservation of the rainforests as well as to coordinate scientific research in the Bladen Nature Reserve and other protected areas in the south. Bfree welcomes interested volunteers. Contact ⓦ bfreebz.org.

The Belize Wildlife Conservation Network (BWCN) works in collaboration with the Belize Forest Department to raise public awareness of Belize's wildlife protection laws and to discourage the acquisition of wild animals. If you're interested in donating or volunteering, contact ⓦ wildlifebelize.com.

cayes. The tallest mangrove forests in Belize are found along the Temash River, in **Sarstoon Temash National Park**, with black mangroves reaching heights of almost 100ft. From a canoe among the mangrove cayes and lagoons you can easily spot the brown pelican, white ibis or roseate spoonbill. American saltwater crocodiles are also here, rarer and larger than the Morelet's crocodile.

The mangrove lagoons are also home to the West Indian manatee. Belize has the largest manatee population in the Caribbean, estimated to be between three hundred and seven hundred, and are protected at **Corozal Bay**, **Gales Point** and **Swallow Caye** wildlife sanctuaries. Manatees can grow up to 13ft in length and seventy stone in weight, but are placid and shy, moving between freshwater lagoons and the open sea. They were once hunted for their meat, but the places where they congregate are now tourist attractions. In shallows offshore, "meadows" of seagrass beds provide nurseries for many fish and invertebrates and pasture for conch, manatees and turtles. The seagrass root system protects beaches from erosion by holding together fragments of sand and coral.

The **Western Caribbean Barrier Reef** is the longest in the western hemisphere, an almost continuous chain of coral that stretches over 350 miles from northern Quintana Roo in Mexico to the far south of Belize. For centuries the reef has been harvested by fishermen, in the past for manatees and turtles; these days spiny lobsters and queen

Green Reef is dedicated to the promotion of sustainable use and conservation of Belize's marine and coastal resources. It's actively involved in implementing management plans for bird sanctuaries on the leeward side of Ambergris Caye. The organization also provides educational programmes for schools in Belize, and accepts volunteers to help with many aspects of its work. Contact ⓦambergriscaye.com/greenreef.

The Manatee and Primate Rehabilitation Centre (see p.81), in Sarteneja, in northern Belize, is run by the nonprofit Wildtracks (ⓦwildtracksbelize.org). The centre engages in a broad range of rehabilitation strategies, including habitat protection, raising public awareness and rehabilitating orphaned, injured or confiscated wildlife. The centre accepts donations and volunteers; for information, check ⓦwildtracksbelize.org.

The Oceanic Society (see p.114) has a field station on Blackbird Caye in the Turneffe Atoll; here they host "volunteer vacations", where you can work alongside researchers and scientists. For information, contact ⓦoceanicsociety.org.

The Programme for Belize (PFB), launched in Britain in 1989, manages over 260,000 acres in the Río Bravo Conservation and Management Area. The programme has bought land to be held in trust for the people of Belize, now managed entirely by Belizeans. For information on visiting the sites in Belize, contact the PFB in Belize City (ⓣ 227 5616, ⓦpfbelize.org).

The Smithsonian Institute operates a marine research station on Carrie Bow Caye, in South Water Caye Marine Reserve. It is primarily a base for marine scientists and supports the institute's Caribbean Coral Reef Ecosystems (CCRE) programme. Contact ⓦccre.si.edu for information.

Southern Environmental Alliance co-manages Laughing Bird Caye National Park and Gladden Spit and Silk Cayes Marine Reserve, off Placencia (see p.203), and provides an environmental education programme. Contact ⓦseabelize.org for volunteer opportunities.

The Toledo Institute for Development and Environment (TIDE) was formed in 1997 to focus resources and attention on the conservation of a network of protected areas in southern Toledo District, linking the Maya Mountains to the Sapodilla Cayes. Visit ⓦtidebelize.org for more information and internship opportunities.

The Wildlife Conservation Society (WCS) works with all the countries involved in the Mesoamerican Biological Corridor to improve management of conservation lands, and to restore degraded habitat for migratory wildlife. Instrumental in establishing marine reserves throughout the barrier reef, it maintains a research station on Middle Caye, Glover's Reef, working closely with the Belize government. Visit ⓦwcsgloversreef.org for volunteer and research opportunities.

The Ya'axché Conservation Trust (YCT), an NGO established in 1997 and based in Toledo District, aims to promote biodiversity and sustainable economic opportunities for the Maya communities in and around the Maya Golden Landscape in Toledo. For information, contact ⓦyaaxche.org.

conch are the main catch, and declining numbers mean they are both now protected during the breeding season.

East of the reef are the **atolls**, roughly oval-shaped reefs rising from the seabed surrounding central lagoons. **Glover's Reef** atoll is considered to be one of the most pristine and important coral reefs in the Caribbean. Whale sharks, the largest fish in the world, are sometimes found here, gathering in large numbers to gorge on snapper eggs at **Gladden Spit**, offshore from Placencia. Beneath the water is a world of astounding colourful beauty, resembling a brilliant underwater forest. Each coral is in fact composed of colonies of individual polyps feeding off plankton. There are basically two types: hard, calcareous, reef-building corals, such as brain and elkhorn (hydrocorals), and soft corals such as sea fans and feather plumes (ococorals). You'll also find garish-pink chalice sponges, appropriately named fire corals, delicate feather-star crinoids and apartment sponges, a tall thin tube with lots of small holes.

Coral habitats are very easily damaged; human interference and increasing toxic runoff and sediment from coastal development adversely affect the already slow growth. "Coral bleaching", a symptom of extensive damage, occurs when the polyp loses some or all of the symbiotic microalgae (zooxanthellae) that live in its cells, usually in response to stress. Bleaching is often caused by above-average sea temperature – such as that which occurred throughout the Caribbean in 1995, during the hottest decade on record. Temperatures continue to be above average, a sign of **global warming**. Recent discovery of oil and its export through Belize's maze of marine protected waters only exacerbates the dilemma.

The reef teems with bright **fish**, including **angel** and **parrot fish**, several species of **stingrays** and **sharks** (the most common the relatively harmless **nurse shark**), **conger** and **moray eels**, **spotted goatfish** and the striped **sergeant-major**. The sea and islands are also home to **grouper**, **barracuda**, **marlin** and the magnificent **sailfish**. Dolphins are frequently seen just offshore, mostly Atlantic **bottle-nosed**, though further out large schools of **spotted dolphins** are sometimes found. Belize's three species of **marine turtles**, the loggerhead, the green and the hawksbill, occur throughout the reef, nesting on isolated beaches. These are infrequently seen, and still hunted for food during a limited open season.

Above the water, the cayes have a wealth of birdlife, providing protection from predators and surrounded by an inexhaustible food supply. At **Half Moon Caye**, right out on the eastern edge of the reef, there's a reserve protecting a breeding colony of four thousand **red-footed boobies**, and you'll also see frigate birds, ospreys and mangrove warblers, among the 98 species there.

Current conservation issues

One of the most vociferous and contentious "conservation or development" debates has focused on the **Chalillo Dam project**, where a hydroelectric dam on the upper Macal River has flooded a beautiful valley that's not only ideal habitat for Baird's tapirs and a threatened subspecies of the scarlet macaw, but also contains unexcavated and undocumented Maya sites. The flooding has damaged legally designated protected areas and may also contravene international conservation conventions to which Belize is a signatory. After years of determined and often bitter opposition by environmentalists and activists, the dam proposal was given the go-ahead in 2004, despite the developers, Fortis, having been shown in court to have erased geological fault lines on a map submitted as part of the Environmental Impact Assessment (EIA). In the 2000s, the dam that was built to save Belizeans money on their energy bills has done anything but: Fortis raised rates yearly. The dam controversy highlights the perpetual problem in Belize of balancing conservation with improving infrastructure.

Today the hottest topic on the conservation agenda is opposition to the meteoric rise in the number of **cruise ships** and their passengers to Belize's shores. The scale of increase in these arrivals is staggering: from just a few hundred passengers per year in the late 1990s to a peak of over 850,000 in 2004. Since then, the yearly cruise ship passenger number has hovered at around 700,000 yearly. Although the government's **Cruise Ship Policy Document** states a recommended upper limit of eight thousand cruise ship visitors per day, this limit is regularly exceeded. Visitor pressure at many archeological sites and certain cayes already exceeds carrying capacity many times over, leading to destructive trampling and environmental degradation. Other current issues include the **de-reservation** of protected areas. In 2016, Norwegian Cruise Line (NCL) opened a custom-built port and resort on Harvest Caye. Though NCL followed ecofriendly and sustainable policies, conservationists continue to be strongly opposed to these kinds of large-scale projects, with great concern for the local reef and wildlife.

The government has also allowed **oil exploration** in several protected areas, such as offshore, in the Belize Barrier Reef, and in Sarstoon-Temash National Park, which encompasses rare and diverse ecosystems and supports indigenous Maya communities. Numerous conservation and tourism organizations have joined forces to resist these and other potentially damaging and unsustainable developments that may hurt Belize's world-renowned record of sound environmental stewardship. To the great relief of conservationists, in 2013 offshore drilling suffered a setback, when Belize's Supreme Court declared offshore drilling contracts previously issued by the government to be null and void. But, according to many conservationists, much stricter laws need to be enacted to ensure a permanent end to drilling.

Further undermining its country's natural splendour, the government continues to sell remote cayes and other lands to other foreign investors and Belizeans returning from overseas. **Mangrove-cutting** by resort developers is technically illegal, though fines are rarely imposed, and construction continues at an unprecedented rate all over the country. The ongoing development of the Placencia Peninsula, including numerous resorts and marinas, threatens the whole area's ecology. Belize also continually catches the eye of eco-conscious celebrities, including actor **Leonardo DiCaprio**, who announced in 2015 that he was going to build an ecotourism resort on Blackadore Caye (see p.100), just west of Ambergris Caye; the resort is expected to be completed in 2018.

Music

For such a tiny country, Belize enjoys an exceptional range of musical styles and traditions. Whether your tastes run to the wind melodies and percussion of the Maya, the up-tempo punta rock of the Garifuna or to calypso, *marimba*, brukdown, soca or steel pan, Belize is sure to have something to suit. For a current list of the best of Belize's recorded music, check Stonetree Records (see box below). The website ⓦbelizemusicworld.com also covers top Belizean artists and musical trends.

Roots and Kriol sounds

Until the demise of the Maya civilization and the arrival of the Spanish, the indigenous **Maya** of Belize played a range of instruments drawn almost entirely from the flute and percussion families. Drums were usually made from hollowed logs covered in deerskin, with rattles, gourd drums and turtle shells providing further rhythmic accompaniment. Trumpets, bells, shells and whistles completed the instrumentation. However, as befits a nation of immigrants, each new group arriving – the Europeans, the Creoles, the mestizos and the Garifuna – brought with them new styles, vigour and variety which today inform and influence popular culture.

Mestizo music combined elements of its two constituent cultures: Maya ceremonial music and new instruments from Spain, such as the classical guitar and violin, and later brass-band music. Mestizo communities (including the Mopan Maya) in the north and west of the country continue to favour **marimba** bands: half-a-dozen men playing two large, multi-keyed wooden xylophones, perhaps supported by a double bass and a drum kit. Up to half-a-dozen bands play regularly in Cayo District: famed healer Elijio Panti presided over the nation's pre-eminent *marimba* group, **Alma Beliceña**, while leading *marimba* bands frequently pop over from Flores in Guatemala, and Mexican **mariachi** bands occasionally make an appearance, too. Nonetheless, traditional mestizo music remains under threat as the youth turn to rock, rap and punta. Traditional artists to look out for include **Pablo Collado**, a Maya-mestizo master flautist/guitarist, and **Florencio Mess**, a harpist maintaining a centuries-old Maya tradition; his *Maya K'ekchi' Strings* is an essential album.

Europeans introduced much of the hardware and software for playing music: "western" musical instruments and sheet music, and, much later, record players, compact discs and massive sound systems. From the mid-nineteenth century onwards, British colonial culture, through church music, military bands and the popular music of the time, was able to exert a dominant influence over what was acceptable music in Belize.

An exciting melange of **West African rhythms** and melodies, as well as drums and stringed instruments, arrived in Belize as a result of the slave trade during the

---

TUNE IN WITH STONETREE RECORDS

Stonetree Records (ⓦstonetreerecords.com) isn't just a Caribbean music label. It has also become the face (and voice) of Belizean music, as producers, promoters, advocates and archivists. Founded in 1995 in Benque Viejo del Carmen, in western Belize, by musician and producer Ivan Duran, Stonetree Records produces a wide range of Belizean music, from Punta to Kriol, all of which you can find on their website. Stonetree also regularly participates in World Music festivals across the globe, like the annual WOMEX (World Music Expo).

ANDY PALACIO

For over two decades **Andy Palacio** influenced, dominated and even helped produce the modern Belizean sound. The country's only truly professional star and music ambassador, his sudden death, due to a heart condition, en route to a show in the US in 2008 shocked and saddened the entire nation. Over the years Palacio succeeded in incorporating a diversity of national and regional styles into a unique popular sound, a consummate performer who established an enviable reputation for producing catchy melodies accompanied by articulate, astute and entertaining lyrics, underpinned by unique **Garifuna rhythms**. Named "UNESCO Artist for Peace" in 2007, it was his pre-eminent final album, *Watina*, firmly based on his Garifuna roots, that catapulted him into the annals of "World Music" stardom, winning him **World Music Album of the Year** as well as the BBC Radio 3 award in January 2008, shortly before he died.

Born in Barranco, he grew up in the rural cosmopolitanism of Garifuna, Maya and mestizo communities, integrating a diversity of linguistic and cultural influences from an early age. As a teenager in the 1970s he experienced first-hand the new Belizean cultural nationalism of the PUP party, which brought the country to independence, introducing a broader ideological dimension to his inevitable cultural affinity with the Garifuna musical tradition. The break came in 1987 when, on an exchange visit to London, he spent a year picking up the latest recording techniques and honing his compositional skills. He returned triumphantly to Belize a year later with enough equipment to open a studio, also bringing with him several London recordings of the songs that would become huge hits back home and transform the music scene.

The biggest song was undoubtedly the 1988 hit **Bikini Panti** – an English-Garifuna, punta rock satire on Belize's burgeoning tourist business – which set a new musical and lyrical standard. But if *Bikini Panti* was the dancefloor killer, it was **Me Goin' Back** that provided the clear ideological expression of the new national sensitivity, as the almost calypsonian lyrics demonstrate:

Now don't buss your brains wonderin what me goin' back to: Rice 'n Beans and a Belikin, Friends FM and a dollar chicken, Pine Ridge and a Swing Bridge, Brukdown, Punta Rock, Sunshine and a cashew wine, Belize Times and Amandala, Maya, Creole and the Garifuna

Palacio's longstanding collaboration with Ivan Duran at Stonetree Records saw three other major releases. *Keimoun* and *Til Da Mawnin* are two great danceable albums displaying a mastery of punta and incorporating Latin and Anglophone Caribbean sounds. *Watina*, recorded with the **Garifuna Collective**, is a more thoughtful and melodic recollection of his origins, featuring master *parranderos* Aurelio and **Paul Nabor**.

---

eighteenth century. However, given that the Baymen purchased slaves from **Jamaica** rather than directly from Africa, it should be remembered that African influences arrived indirectly.

A new, syncretic style, nurtured in the logging camps and combining Western instrumentation with specifically African musical inflections, emerged in the late nineteenth century to create a specifically Belizean musical tradition known as "**brukdown**". Featuring a modern line-up of guitar, banjo, accordion, drums and the jawbone of an ass (rattling a stick up and down the teeth!), brukdown remains a potent reminder of past **Creole** culture. Although the style is slowly fading, as Creole society itself changes, there are a few active practitioners. The style's most prominent figure, the late master accordionist **Wilfred Peters** (who died in 2010), was the founder of the nationally celebrated **Mr. Peters and his Boom and Chime**, and composed countless classics and performed around the world; any of his albums represent a musical journey through Creole culture. Generally, though, brukdown is recreational music best enjoyed in the Creole villages of Burrell Boom, Hattieville, Bermudian Landing and Isabella Bank.

Brad Pattico, an accomplished guitarist and singer-songwriter, similarly does his best to keep the Creole folksong tradition alive – he performed at the 2016 New Orleans Jazz Fest and his recordings can be found in Belizean record stores. Originating from the same cultural roots, and equally conscious of a disappearing musical past, is Brother David Obi, better known as **Bredda David**, the creator of **kungo music**, a mixture of musical styles that includes the traditional Creole music of Belize and the pulsating drum rhythms of Africa. A skilful musician and songwriter, David still plays occasionally in Belize City with his **Tribal Vibes** band; look out for album *Raw*, where rock guitars are overlaid on new-generation Belizean rhythm with lyrical kungo wit.

One of the best-known singers seen to preserve traditional Creole folksong is **Leela Vernon** from Punta Gorda, who plays to highly appreciative audiences at national festivals, often appearing with long-standing pop bands, including **Youth Connection**, **Gilharry 7** and **Santino's Messengers**. Her most famous song, *Who say Creole gat no culture?*, is a national favourite amongst older people and a reminder of pride in Belizean society. Two recordings containing some of these artists are: **Various Artists** *Belize City Boil Up* – a sample of pre-Independence Belize, featuring remastered recordings from the Fifties, Sixties and Seventies, alive with cool jazz, smooth rhythm and blues and even some psychedelic funk – and **Various Artists** *Celebration Belize*, including contributions from Andy Palacio, Mr. Peters, Leela Vernon, Florencio Mess and many others.

More recently, the African elements in Creole music have been expressed through wider **pan-Caribbean** styles like calypso, reggae, soca and rap. **Calypso** enjoyed a brief period of pre-eminence – Belize's most famous calypsonian **Lord Rhaburn** is still occasionally to be seen as a special guest at official functions, increasingly rare performances that shouldn't be missed. In terms of today's popular music, California-based Belizean conscious-reggae outfit **Caribbean Pulse** (ⓦcaribbeanpulse.com) has collaborated with reggae luminaries like Tony Rebel and Damian Marley. Proving that Belizean musicians are breaking boundaries beyond drums and roots is Belize City-born **MKL**, alias Michael Lopez, a New York touring DJ and producer whose sound encompasses soul, jazz, dub and laidback electronics. Back in Belize City, dub poet **Leroy Young the Grandmaster** offers a powerful commentary and new Creole style featuring a wide range of roots rhythms and strings; look out for the album *Just Like That*, released on Stonetree Records. You can also hear Leroy Young on local radio stations such as Positive Vibes FM.

Punta and the Garifuna

If traditional Maya, mestizo and Creole styles retain only a fragile hold on popular musical consciousness, it is the **Garifuna** who have been catapulted to centre-stage over the last two decades with the invention and development of **punta rock**. The key musical developments that led to punta rock were the amplification of several traditional **drum rhythms** originally associated with courtship dances, while keeping faith with other traditional instruments such as the turtle shell – and initially the almost universal aversion to singing in anything but Garifuna. Although many master musicians and cultural nationalists (both from Belize and the other Garifuna communities across Central America) pushed Garifuna culture forward, particular recognition must go to master drummer and drum-maker **Isabel Flores** and the enigmatic singer, guitarist and artist **Pen Cayetano** in Dangriga. Pen pioneered popular Garifuna music, widening the scope of punta with the introduction of electric guitars and helping to spark a new cultural assertiveness that saw dozens of younger musicians take up the challenge. His **Turtle Shell Band** set the standard (*Beginning*, the first-ever punta rock recording in 1982), and within a few years other electric bands – including **Sounds Incorporated**, **Black Coral**, **Jeff Zuniga**, **Mohubub**, **Aziatic** and **Titiman Flores** – consolidated punta's popularity. Titiman's album *Fedu* is a punta rock party album to control the dancefloor from beginning to end. Above all, however, **Andy Palacio** (see box, p.255) developed to become punta rock's most famous star; the seminal compilation *Punta Rockers* (1988) featured recordings by Andy and several other pioneers. Credit should also be given to Dangriga-based **Al Obando** in the development of the punta rock sound. As Belize's pre-eminent sound engineer, Obando produced the hugely popular band the **Punta Rebels** throughout the 1990s and is still relied upon for studio recordings today.

Guardians of more orthodox arrangements, **Lugua and the Larubeya Drummers** marked their debut with the release of *Bumari*, covering the full range of roots Garifuna drumming styles alongside powerful call and response vocals – a telling reminder of the African influence in Garifuna history. Recently there has also been a resurgence of the traditional Garifuna style of **parranda**, performed with acoustic guitars, drums and shakers. This was marked by the international release of the eponymous album, recorded by various *parranderos* living in Belize, Honduras and Guatemala. It is recognized as being one of the best collections to come out of Central America. This movement grows stronger with recent releases – one by Belize-produced Honduran **Aurelio Martínez** (*Garifuna Soul*), demonstrating soulful vocals over a rich blend of Latin, punta and *parranda* rhythms, and another by **The Garifuna Women's Project**, featuring wonderful soulful voices from coastal villages in Belize, Guatemala and Honduras. Another record to look for is **Various Artists** *PARRANDA: Africa in Central America* – three generations of Garifuna incorporating drumming, American blues, Cuban *son* and West African guitar.

Additionally, several up-and-coming Garifuna stars from Dangriga are combining fast infectious punta with reggae dancehall and soca in highly energized performances. This is punta rock for the young generation, relying largely on **sound systems**. Popular punta rock artists include **Super (or Supa) G** – you can tune in to Super G tunes YouTube – his channel is Supa G Belize.

Perhaps the best times to hear and see the full panoply of Belizean musical culture are the various national **events** that regularly punctuate the social calendar (see p.31).

Books

The Belize Audubon Society (see box, pp.250–251) offers a mail-order service for environmental titles, while Cubola Productions is Belize's leading publisher, with a wide range of specialist books; see ⓦcubola.com. Angelus Press in Belize City also offers a mail-order service; see ⓦangeluspress.com. Many books are published only in Belize but are usually available online, at the mega retailers such as ⓦamazon.com and ⓦbarnesandnoble.com.

TRAVEL, LITERATURE, SOCIETY AND ENVIRONMENT

Rosita Arvigo with Nadia Epstein *Sastun: My Apprenticeship with a Maya Healer*. A rare glimpse into the indigenous wisdom of Maya *curandero* Elijio Panti, which ensures the survival of generations of healing knowledge. *Rainforest Remedies: One Hundred Healing Herbs of Belize* was co-authored with Michael Balick of the New York Botanical Garden.

★ **Bruce Barcott** *The Last Flight of the Scarlet Macaw: One Woman's Fight to Save the World's Most Beautiful Bird*. Chronicles the fierce and inspiring crusade by environmentalist Sharon Matola, founder of the Belize Zoo, to save the scarlet macaw.

Les Beletsky *Belize – The Traveller's Wildlife Guide*. A comprehensive single-volume guide to mammals, birds, reptiles, amphibians and marine life, with illustrations.

Zee Edgell *Beka Lamb*. A girl's account of growing up in 1950s Belize alongside the problems of the independence movement. Explores everyday life, matriarchal society and the influence of the Catholic Church. Edgell's *In Times Like These* is an autobiographical account of the intrigues leading up to independence.

Adrian Forsyth and Ken Miyata *Tropical Nature: Life and Death in the Rain Forests of Central and South America*. Tropical nature, in all its wildness and beauty, is celebrated in a series of fascinating essays by two field biologists.

Byron Foster *Heart Drum* and *Spirit Possession in the Garifuna Community of Belize*. Two slim volumes focusing on Garifuna spirituality and the experience of spirit possession, as described by Foster, an anthropologist. Foster's *The Baymen's Legacy: A Portrait of Belize City* is approachable and interesting, while *Warlords and Maize Men – A Guide to the Maya Sites of Belize* is an excellent handbook to fifteen of the country's most accessible archeological sites.

★ **Tim Hagerthy and Mary Gomez Parham (eds)** *If Di Pin Neva Ben: Folktales and Legends of Belize*. A vibrant collection of traditional Belizean folklore, capturing a rich society that fluidly blends its different ethnic cultures. Other Cubola anthologies include *Snapshots of Belize* and *Ping Wing Juk Me*, six short plays which revive the Kriol theatrical tradition.

H. Lee Jones *Birds of Belize*. Comprehensive guide to all 574 species so far recorded in Belize. Highly praised by the experts, this excellent book is written by a resident biologist. It includes 234 range maps and superb colour illustrations by Dana Gardner.

★ **Emory King** *Belize 1798, The Road to Glory*. Rip-roaring historical novel on the Battle of St George's Caye, King's (see p.51) enthusiasm is supported by meticulous research. Also by the author: *Hey Dad, This Is Belize*, a hilarious account of family life; *I Spent It All In Belize*, an anthology of satirical articles on the pomposity of officialdom; and *The Great Story of Belize*, four slim volumes full of larger-than-life characters and presenting a vivid account of Belize's history.

Nancy R. Koerner *Belize Survivor: Darker Side of Paradise*. Gripping novel, based on a true story, of a young countercultural woman who arrives in Belize in the 1970s and discovers untamed nature, wild adventure – and the darker side of human nature.

Carlos Ledson Miller *Belize – A Novel*. Fast-paced historical saga of a Central American father and his two sons – one American and one Belizean. From the eve of Hurricane Hattie in 1961, the reader is transported forty years through colonial unrest to present-day turbulence.

Alan Rabinowitz *Jaguar*. A personal account of studying jaguars for the New York Zoological Society in the 1980s, living with a Maya family at Cockscomb. Rabinowitz was instrumental in the establishment of the Jaguar Reserve in 1984.

John Lloyd Stephens *Incidents of Travel in Central America, Chiapas, and Yucatán*. A classic nineteenth-century traveller, Stephens was American ambassador to Central America: while republics fought it out he was wading through the jungle stumbling across ancient cities. Written with superb Victorian pomposity and great illustrations of Maya sites.

★ **Ronald Wright** *Time Among the Maya*. A vivid, sympathetic and humorous account of travels in the late 1980s from Belize through Guatemala, Chiapas and

Yucatán, meeting the Maya and exploring their obsession with time. Also investigates the violence that occurred throughout the 1980s. Superb historical insights.

Colville Young *Creole Proverbs of Belize*. A wonderful compilation of oral folk-wisdom, written by the distinguished linguist and present governor-general. Sayings and proverbs are written in Kriol and English, and then explained. See also *Pataki Full*, an anthology of Belizean short stories.

HISTORY AND ARCHEOLOGY

O. Nigel Bolland *Colonialism and Resistance in Belize: Essays in Historical Sociology*. The 2003 edition is a comprehensive academic study of Belize, covering colonization, slavery and the progress of Creole culture and nationalism with an emphasis on labour. A compelling and convincing analysis.

Michael Coe *The Maya*. Now in its ninth edition, this clear and comprehensive guide to Maya archeology is the best on offer.

David Drew *The Lost Chronicles of the Maya Kings*. Readable and engaging; an up-to-date account of ancient Maya political history with alliances and rivalries skilfully unravelled, and a revealing analysis of late Classic Maya power struggles.

Joyce Kelly *An Archaeological Guide to Northern Central America*. Practical guide to Maya sites and museums in four countries; an essential companion for travelling the Maya world. Still the most detailed guide available to the Maya sites of Belize, if slightly dated.

Simon Martin and Nikolai Grube *Chronicle of the Maya Kings and Queens*. Highly acclaimed work based on epigraphic studies and re-readings of glyphs. Historical records of key Maya cities like Tikal and Caracol, plus biographies of 152 kings and four queens, and all the key battles.

Heather McKillop *Salt: White Gold of the Ancient Maya*. A groundbreaking work demonstrating that the salt traded throughout the great lowland Maya cities was produced on the coast of Belize, at previously unknown underwater sites.

★**John Montgomery** *Tikal: An Illustrated History of the Ancient Maya Capital*. The most readable book on Tikal, packed with fascinating history and general information, with a chronology of major Maya events. His other books include *A Dictionary of Maya Hieroglyphs*.

★**Megan O'Neil and Mary Ellen Miller** *Maya Art and Architecture*. Explore art and architecture via two hundred detailed illustrations, including maps, reconstructions and photos, in this definitive book by a Yale art historian

★**The Popol Vuh**. The great creation myth poem of the K'iche' (Quiche) Maya of the Guatemalan highlands, written shortly after the conquest and intended to preserve the K'iche' people's knowledge of their history. It's an amazing swirl of fantastic gods and mortals who become gods. The best version is translated by Dennis Tedlock.

Various authors *Readings in Belizean History*. Updated version of a highly acclaimed textbook, with essays by Belizean scholars offering deep insights.

Language

English is the official language of Belize and naturally enough it's spoken everywhere. However, it's really the first language of only a small percentage of Belize's population, since seven main languages are spoken here, including the Mopan, Yucatec and Kekchí Maya dialects. For at least half the population, mainly the mestizos in the north and the west, Spanish is the language spoken at home and in the workplace. The last thirty years have seen a large increase in spoken Spanish due to immigration from neighbouring countries. If you plan to cross the border into Guatemala to visit Tikal, some Spanish will be essential.

The first language of one third of the population – mainly the Creole people – is **Kriol** (the modern favoured spelling, though still often spelt "Creole"), a language partly derived from English and similar to the languages spoken in other parts of the Caribbean colonized by the British. Kriol is the **most widely spoken** language in Belize. English and Kriol are the languages used in public or official situations and for speaking to outsiders. That said, listening to conversations can be confusing, as people switch from, say, English to Kriol to Spanish to Garifuna and back – often in the same sentence.

Many **Garifuna** continue to speak their own tongue as their first language, although the only village where *everyone* does this is Hopkins (see p.187). The **Mennonites** add to the linguistic cocktail with their old form of High German, and the jigsaw puzzle is completed by recent immigrants from Asia speaking Chinese and South Asian languages.

Kriol

Kriol is the *lingua franca* of Belize: whether someone's first language is Maya, Spanish, Garifuna or English, they'll almost always be able to communicate in Kriol. It may sound like English from a distance and as you listen to a few words you'll think that their meaning is clear, but as things proceed you'll soon realize that complete comprehension is out of reach – though those familiar with other English dialects may find understanding easier. It's a beautifully warm, expressive and relaxed language, typically Caribbean, with a vocabulary loosely based on English but with significant differences in pronunciation and a grammatical structure that is distinctly West African in origin. One characteristic is the heavy nasalization of some vowels, for example *waahn* (want) and *frahn* (from).

Written Kriol, which you'll see in some newspaper columns and booklets, is a little easier to come to grips with, though you'll need to study it hard at first. A dictionary is available from some bookstores (Paul Crosbie, editor, *Kriol-Inglish Dikshineri*, 2007), which also explains the grammar, though Kriol will always be much more of a spoken language than a written one.

Only in recent years has Kriol begun to be **recognized** as a distinct language, though there is still much debate as to whether it is just a dialect of English. In **colonial times** Kriol was not accepted as a legitimate language and its use was prohibited in schools, although in practice teachers often lapsed into it. But Kriol always remained the language of the people at home and at work, an integral part of culture and identity. **Independence** brought a growing pride in the language and today a movement is formalizing Kriol, aiming to recognize it as one of Belize's national languages.

For a long time Kriol was solely an **oral language**, but by the 1970s some writers and poets were writing it using ad hoc spelling. In 1980 Sir Colville Young – at that time a school principal and today governor-general of Belize – published his *Creole Proverbs of Belize*, and in 1993 a group of educators and enthusiasts started the **Belize Kriol Project** to work on developing it into a written language. The **National Kriol Council** was formed in 1995 with the aim of promoting the culture and language of the Creole people of Belize. A standardized writing system using a phonemic structure has since been developed and, despite some controversy, is gradually gaining acceptance. Some tips on spoken and written Kriol are available at ⊕belizeanjourneys.com (Kriol section supplied by John Stewart).

USEFUL PHRASES AND PROVERBS

Excuse me, where is the post office?	Eksyooz mi, weh di poas aafis deh?	**How much is a single room?**	How moch wahn singl room kaas?
Where do I catch the bus to Dangriga?	Weh fu kech di bos tu Dangriga?	**I have some dirty laundry for washing.**	Ah gat sohn doti kloaz fu wash.
Do you have any rooms free?	Yu gat eni room fu rent?	**Is there a restaurant near here serving Creole food?**	Weh sel Kriol food kloas tu ya?

PROVERB	LITERAL TRANSLATION	MEANING
Mek di man weh loos taiga tai ahn bak.	Let the man who loosed the tiger tie it back.	Let the man who created a dangerous situation deal with it.
Fish geh kech bai ih own mowt.	A fish gets caught by its own mouth.	Guilt often gives itself away.
Kyaahn kech Hari, kech ih shot.	If you can't catch Harry, catch his shirt.	If you can't get what you want, get the next best thing.

Spanish

The **Spanish** spoken in both Guatemala and Belize has a strong Latin American flavour; if you're used to the intonation of Madrid or Granada then it may be a surprise to hear the soft "s" replaced by a crisp and clear version. If you're new to Spanish it's a lot easier to pick up than the Iberian version.

The rules of **pronunciation** are straightforward and strictly observed. Unless there's an accent, words ending in d, l, r and z are **stressed** on the last syllable, all others on the second last. All **vowels** are pure and short.

A somewhere between the "a" sound of back and that of father.

E as in get.

I as in police.

O as in hot.

U as in rule.

C is soft before "e" and "i", hard otherwise: *cerca* is pronounced serka.

G works the same way, a guttural "h" sound (like the *ch* in loch) before "e" or "i", a hard "g" elsewhere: *gigante* becomes higante.

H always silent.

J the same sound as a guttural "g": *jamón* is pronounced hamon.

LL sounds like an English "y": *tortilla* is pronounced torteeya.

N as in English unless it has a tilde (accent) over it, when it becomes "ny": *mañana* sounds like manyana.

QU is pronounced like an English "k".

R is rolled, RR doubly so.

V sounds more like "b", *vino* becoming beano.

X is slightly softer than in English – sometimes almost "s" – except between vowels in place names where it has an "h" sound – ie Mexico (Meh-hee-ko) or Oaxaca (Wa-ha-ka). Note: in Maya the English letter "x" is pronounced "*sh*", thus *Xunantunich* is Shunan-tun-eech.

Z is the same as a soft "c", so *cerveza* becomes servesa.

Although we've listed a few essential words and phrases, some kind of dictionary or **phrasebook** is a worthwhile investment: the *Rough Guide to Mexican Spanish* is the best practical guide, correct and colloquial, and certainly acceptable for most purposes when travelling in Guatemala and Belize. One of the best small Latin American Spanish dictionaries is the University of Chicago version; the Collins series of pocket grammars and dictionaries is also excellent.

BASICS

please, thank you	por favor, gracias	open, closed	abierto/a, cerrado/a
where…?	¿dónde…?	with, without	con, sin
when…?	¿cuando…?	good, bad	buen(o)/a, mal(o)/a
what…?	¿qué…?	big, small	gran(de), pequeño/a
how much is it?	¿cuánto cuesta?	more, less	más, menos
here, there	aquí, allí	today, tomorrow	hoy, mañana
this, that	esto, eso	yesterday	ayer
now, later	ahora, más tarde		

GREETINGS AND RESPONSES

hello, goodbye	hola, adios	What (did you say)?	¿Mande?
Good morning	Buenos días	My name is…	Me llamo…
Good afternoon/night	Buenas tardes/noches	What's your name?	¿Cómo se llama?
How do you do?	¿Qué tal?	I am English	Soy inglés(a)
See you later	Hasta luego	…American	…americano(a)
Sorry	Lo siento/disculpeme	…Australian	…australiano(a)
Excuse me	Con permiso/perdón	…Canadian	…canadiense(a)
How are you?	¿Cómo está (usted)?	…Irish	…irlandés(a)
Not at all/You're welcome	De nada	…Scottish	…escosés(a)
I (don't) understand	(No) Entiendo	…Welsh	…galés(a)
Do you speak English?	¿Habla (usted) inglés?	…New Zealander	…neozelandés(a)
I (don't) speak Spanish	(No) Hablo español		

NEEDS, ACCOMMODATION AND TRANSPORT

I want…	Quiero…	Can one…?	¿Se puede…?
Do you know…?	¿Sabe…?	…camp (near)	¿…acampar aquí
I'd like…	Quisiera… por favor	here?	(cerca)?
I don't know	No sé	Is there a hotel nearby?	¿Hay un hotel aquí cerca?
There is (is there?)	Hay (?)	How do I get to…?	¿Por dónde se va a…?
(one like that)	(uno así)	Left, right,	Izquierda, derecha,
Do you have…?	¿Tiene…?	straight on	derecho
…the time	…la hora	Where is…?	¿Dónde está…?
…a room	…un cuarto	…the nearest bank	…el banco más cercano
…with two beds	…con dos camas		(ATM is cajero
…with a double bed	…con cama matrimonial		automático)
It's for one person	Es para una persona	…the post office	…el correo
(two people)	(dos personas)	…the toilet	…el baño/sanitario
…for one night	…para una noche	Where does the bus	¿De dónde sale el
(one week)	(una semana)	to…leave from?	camión para…?
It's fine, how	¿Está bien, cuánto es?	What time does it	¿A qué hora sale
much is it?		leave (arrive in)…?	(llega en)…?
It's too expensive	Es demasiado caro	What is there to eat?	¿Qué hay para comer?
Don't you have	¿No tiene algo más	What's that?	¿Qué es eso?
anything cheaper?	barato?	What's this called?	¿Cómo se llama?

DAYS

Monday	Lunes	Friday	Viernes
Tuesday	Martes	Saturday	Sábado
Wednesday	Miércoles	Sunday	Domingo
Thursday	Jueves		

NUMBERS

1	un/uno/una	30	treinta
2	dos	40	cuarenta
3	tres	50	cincuenta
4	cuatro	60	sesenta
5	cinco	70	setenta
6	seis	80	ochenta
7	siete	90	noventa
8	ocho	100	cien(to)
9	nueve	101	ciento uno/una
10	diez	200	doscientos/as
11	once	500	quinientos/as
12	doce	700	setecientos
13	trece	1000	mil
14	catorce	1999	mil novecientos
15	quince		noventa y nueve
16	dieciséis	2000	dos mil
17	diecisiete	first	primero/a
18	dieciocho	second	segundo/a
19	diecinueve	third	tercero/a
20	veinte	fifth	quinto/a
21	veintiuno	tenth	décimo/a

Small print and index

A ROUGH GUIDE TO ROUGH GUIDES

Published in 1982, the first Rough Guide – to Greece – was a student scheme that became a publishing phenomenon. Mark Ellingham, a recent graduate in English from Bristol University, had been travelling in Greece the previous summer and couldn't find the right guidebook. With a small group of friends he wrote his own guide, combining a contemporary, journalistic style with a thoroughly practical approach to travellers' needs.

The immediate success of the book spawned a series that rapidly covered dozens of destinations. And, in addition to impecunious backpackers, Rough Guides soon acquired a much broader readership that relished the guides' wit and inquisitiveness as much as their enthusiastic, critical approach and value-for-money ethos. These days, Rough Guides include recommendations from budget to luxury and cover more than 120 destinations around the globe, from Amsterdam to Zanzibar, all regularly updated by our team of roaming writers.

Browse all our latest guides, read inspirational features and book your trip at **roughguides.com**.

Rough Guide credits

Editors: Greg Dickinson, Melissa Graham
Layout: Jessica Subramanian
Cartography: Ashutosh Bharti, Richard Marchi
Picture editor: Michelle Bhatia
Proofreader: Anita Sach
Managing editor: Edward Aves
Assistant editor: Divya Grace Mathew

Production: Jimmy Lao
Cover photo research: Marta Bescos
Editorial assistant: Aimee White
Senior DTP coordinator: Dan May
Programme manager: Gareth Lowe
Publishing director: Georgina Dee

Publishing information

This seventh edition published October 2017 by
Rough Guides Ltd,
80 Strand, London WC2R 0RL
11, Community Centre, Panchsheel Park,
New Delhi 110017, India
Distributed by Penguin Random House
Penguin Books Ltd, 80 Strand, London WC2R 0RL
Penguin Group (USA), 345 Hudson Street, NY 10014, USA
Penguin Group (Australia), 250 Camberwell Road,
Camberwell, Victoria 3124, Australia
Penguin Group (NZ), 67 Apollo Drive, Mairangi Bay,
Auckland 1310, New Zealand
Penguin Group (South Africa), Block D, Rosebank Office
Park, 181 Jan Smuts Avenue, Parktown North, Gauteng,
South Africa 2193
Rough Guides is represented in Canada by DK Canada, 320
Front Street West, Suite 1400, Toronto, Ontario M5V 3B6
Printed in Singapore
© Rough Guides, 2017
Maps © Rough Guides

272pp includes index
A catalogue record for this book is available from the
British Library
ISBN: 978-0-24128-064-5
The publishers and authors have done their best to
ensure the accuracy and currency of all the information
in **The Rough Guide to Belize**; however, they can accept
no responsibility for any loss, injury, or inconvenience
sustained by any traveller as a result of information or
advice contained in the guide.
1 3 5 7 9 8 6 4 2

MIX
Paper from
responsible sources
FSC® C018179
www.fsc.org

Help us update

We've gone to a lot of effort to ensure that the seventh
edition of **The Rough Guide to Belize** is accurate and up-
to-date. However, things change – places get "discovered",
opening hours are notoriously fickle, restaurants and
rooms raise prices or lower standards. If you feel we've got
it wrong or left something out, we'd like to know, and if
you can remember the address, the price, the hours, the
phone number, so much the better.

Please send your comments with the subject line
"**Rough Guide Belize Update**" to mail@uk.roughguides
.com. We'll credit all contributions and send a copy of the
next edition (or any other Rough Guide if you prefer) for
the very best emails.

ABOUT THE AUTHORS

Todd Obolsky's favourite travel experiences include off-roading in Monument Valley, abseiling into New Zealand's Waitomo Caves, commissioning a traditional sword (in limited Japanese) in Kyoto and sharing the road with a bear cub near Dawson City. He has updated Rough Guides to New York City, New England, Florida, Chicago, the USA and Canada, and wrote and shot images for *The Hedonist's Guide to Miami.*

AnneLise Sorensen writes and wine-tastes her way around the globe, contributing to multiple media outlets and guidebooks, including *New York Magazine*, *Condé Nast*, *DK Top 10 Barcelona*, and Rough Guides to Spain, the USA and Canada. AnneLise also appears regularly as a travel expert on TV and radio, and hosts a video and lecture series, Travel Transforms. Follow her adventures at ⓦannelisesorensen.com and on Twitter (@AnneLiseTravels).

Acknowledgements

Todd Obolsky: Big thanks to Sheila Nale, Lyra Spang and especially Marcus and Theo Stevens (*Parrot Lodge*). Also to Ronald Raymond McDonald, Solveig Hommema and Sarah Hamman, Juan Cho at *Ixcacao*, Renee Brown, Rob Hirons, Christopher Nesbitt at *Maya Mountain*, Brenda Martinez, Lisa Beardsley, Pär at *Reef's End Lodge*, Michelle Hopkins, Claudia Hardegger, Shirley Zapata and Brad Schofield.

AnneLise Sorensen: In Belize, thanks to all who welcomed me in and shared information, tips, stories and lively evenings of chilled Belikin and cashew wine. Thank you to the BTB (Belize Tourism Board) and to the helpful tourism offices around the country. A big thank you to my co-author Todd Obolsky, and to the supremely talented Rough Guides editorial crew, including Greg Dickinson, Edward Aves and Melissa Graham, as well as the top-notch cartographers and the rest of the team. And *gracias* to all my friends, family and *guapo* for their cheery emails and support.

Readers' updates

Thanks to all the readers who have taken the time to write in with comments and suggestions (and apologies if we've inadvertently omitted or misspelt anyone's name):

Gretchen Greer, Joni Miller, Holly Ochs, Lucy Palmer, Sam Palmer, David Patterson

Photo credits

All photos © Rough Guides, except the following:
(Key: t-top; c-centre; b-bottom; l-left; r-right)

1 Getty Images: AWL Images
2 Robert Harding Picture Library: James Strachan
4 Dreamstime.com: Brandon Bourdages
9 Alamy Stock Photo: Roi Brooks (b); imageBROKER (tl); Tips Images (tr)
10 Alamy Stock Photo: Danita Delimont
11 Alamy Stock Photo: Al Argueta (br); Rob Crandall (tr); Kevin Schafer (cr)
12 Corbis: Jane Sweeney / JAI (b)
13 Alamy Stock Photo: Krys Bailey (c); Martin Norris Travel Photography (tr). **Corbis:** Alex Robinson / AWL (tl)
14 Alamy Stock Photo: Al Argueta (b); Frans Lanting Studio (t). **Getty Images:** National Geographic RF / Jad Davenport (cr)
15 Alamy Stock Photo: Al Argueta (b); Joanne Weston (t)
16 Alamy Stock Photo: Natalia Kuzmina (b)
17 Alamy Stock Photo: Brandon Cole Marine Photography (b); Robert Harding Picture Library Limited (t). **Dreamstime.com:** Shelle Russell (cl)
20 Alamy Stock Photo: Nat Spurling
53 Alamy Stock Photo: Christopher Williams (tl). **Corbis:** Michelle Westmorland (tr). **Dreamstime.com:** Lawrence Weslowski Jr (b)

66–67 Alamy Stock Photo: National Geographic Creative
69 Dreamstime.com: Jared Richardson
79 Alamy Stock Photo: Jeff Greenberg (bl); Kevin Schafer (t); Witold Skrypczak (br)
86–87 Alamy Stock Photo: imageBROKER (c)
89 Alamy Stock Photo: Christine Wehrmeier
99 Alamy Stock Photo: Brandon Cole Marine Photography
116–117 Getty Images: Alex Robinson
119 Corbis: Laurent Giraudou (c)
141 Alamy Stock Photo: Danita Delimont (bl)
152–153 Alamy Stock Photo: imageBROKER
155 Alamy Stock Photo: Hemis
167 Alamy Stock Photo: Rob Crandall
172–173 Alamy Stock Photo: imageBROKER
175 Alamy Stock Photo: Zumi
191 Alamy Stock Photo: imageBROKER (tl)
217 Alamy Stock Photo: Steve Taylor ARPS
222 Getty Images: Jane Sweeney

Cover: Kayak on South Water Caye **AWL Images:** Danita Delimont Stock

Index

Maps are marked in grey

Map symbols

The symbols below are used on maps throughout the book

- International boundary
- State/province boundary
- Chapter division
- Major road
- Minor road
- Pedestrian road
- Footpath
- River/coastline
- Airport
- Airstrip
- Transport stop
- Parking
- Petrol station
- Point of interest
- Internet access
- Tourist information
- Post office
- Telephone
- Maya ruin
- Mountain range
- Mountain peak
- Reef
- Ferry route
- Jungle lodge
- Waterfall
- Gorge
- Border crossing
- Cave
- Campsite
- Lighthouse
- Zoo
- Bird sanctuary
- Statue/monument
- Church
- Building
- Stadium
- Cemetery
- Park
- Swamp
- Beach

Listings key

- Accommodation
- Eating
- Drinking and nightlife
- Shopping

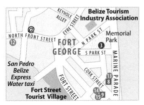

Long bus journey? Phone run out of juice?

TEST YOUR KNOWLEDGE WITH OUR ROUGH GUIDES TRAVEL QUIZ

Denim, the pencil, the stethoscope and the hot-air balloon were all invented in which country?

a. Italy
b. France
c. Germany
d. Switzerland

What is the currency of Vietnam?

a. Dong
b. Yuan
c. Baht
d. Kip

In which city would you find the Majorelle Garden?

a. Marseille
b. Marrakesh
c. Tunis
d. Malaga

What is the busiest airport in the world?

a. London Heathrow
b. Tokyo International
c. Chicago O'Hare
d. Hartsfield-Jackson
   Atlanta International

Which of these countries does not have the equator running through it?

a. Brazil
b. Tanzania
c. Indonesia
d. Colombia

6 **Which country has the most UNESCO World Heritage Sites?**

a. Mexico
b. France
c. Italy
d. India

7 **What is the principal religion of Japan?**

a. Confucianism
b. Buddhism
c. Jainism
d. Shinto

8 **Every July in Sonkajärvi, central Finland, contestants gather for the World Championships of which sport?**

a. Zorbing
b. Wife-carrying
c. Chess-boxing
d. Extreme ironing

9 **What colour are post boxes in Germany?**

a. Red
b. Green
c. Blue
d. Yellow

10 **For three days each April during Songkran festival in Thailand, people take to the streets to throw what at each other?**

a. Water
b. Oranges
c. Tomatoes
d. Underwear